WORLDWIDE FINANCIAL REPORTING

WORLDWIDE FINANCIAL REPORTING

The Development and Future of Accounting Standards

George J. Benston
Michael Bromwich
Robert E. Litan
Alfred Wagenhofer

OXFORD
UNIVERSITY PRESS

2006

OXFORD
UNIVERSITY PRESS

Oxford University Press, Inc., publishes works that further
Oxford University's objective of excellence
in research, scholarship, and education.

Oxford   New York
Auckland   Cape Town   Dar es Salaam   Hong Kong   Karachi
Kuala Lumpur   Madrid   Melbourne   Mexico City   Nairobi
New Delhi   Shanghai   Taipei   Toronto

With offices in
Argentina   Austria   Brazil   Chile   Czech Republic   France   Greece
Guatemala   Hungary   Italy   Japan   Poland   Portugal   Singapore
South Korea   Switzerland   Thailand   Turkey   Ukraine   Vietnam

Copyright © 2006 by Oxford University Press

Published by Oxford University Press, Inc.
198 Madison Avenue, New York, New York 10016

www.oup.com

Oxford is a registered trademark of Oxford University Press

Library of Congress Cataloging-in-Publication Data
Worldwide financial reporting : the development and future of accounting
standards / George J. Benston . . . [et al.].
p.   cm.
Includes bibliographical references and index.
ISBN-13 978-0-19-530583-8
ISBN 0-19-530583-3
1. Accounting—Standards.   2. Financial statements.   I. Benston, George J.
HF5626.W67 2006
657'.02'18—dc22   2005018495

9 8 7 6 5 4 3 2 1

Printed in the United States of America
on acid-free paper

Contents

WORLDWIDE FINANCIAL REPORTING

1

Changes in Equity Markets in the Major Developed Countries and Overview of the Book

Sound financial reporting is one of those things that is taken for granted—until something goes wrong. And in the last several years, much has gone wrong. In the late 1990s, a breakdown in financial reporting contributed to the Asian financial crisis. Investors poured too much money into the region unwisely, in part because the financial reports of private firms were overly optimistic. And investors took their money out of those countries in a hurry, largely because they couldn't trust the official figures for the levels of foreign exchange reserves held by the central banks. Then, in the first part of this decade, poor or rigged financial reports in the United States, and later in Europe, made news headlines and cost investors billions of dollars when once-prominent companies—Enron, WorldCom, Parmalat and others—were revealed to have cooked their books to show profits that really weren't there.[1]

Both sets of events have put a harsh spotlight on the accounting profession, which is supposed to assure investors of the quality of financial reports; some of the financial reporting rules themselves (such as those governing accounting for stock options or financial derivatives); and the way in which standards for reporting and auditing are set throughout the world. Much attention, in particular, has been paid to securing support for a single set of internationally accepted financial reporting standards, those set by the International Accounting Standards Board (IASB). The growing globalization of capital markets is the main argument for a single body of standards, or a single "financial language." As investors increasingly look beyond their borders for places to put their money, they naturally want to be able to compare the performance of companies across countries.

3

While the desire for such "apples-to-apples" comparisons is under-standable, we believe, for reasons spelled out in various parts of this book, that those who want this outcome are likely to be sorely disappointed. Among them are that we doubt that a single set of standards would be a stable outcome, it being more likely the case that the global standards would tend to fragment over time under the weight of accelerating changes in financial instruments and strategies in the private sector. Even if the reporting standard were stable, however, it is even more doubtful that countries would agree to and enforce it with the same degree of vigor as would be applied to a single set of auditing standards. The lack of con-sistency in enforcement of the reporting rules, by itself, would render any attempt to achieve true apples-to-apples comparability across countries virtually impossible to achieve. And even if the national accounting au-thorities could reach and implement such an agreement, reasonable alter-native methods of accounting for the events, assets, and liabilities that are applicable to individual companies make direct comparisons among com-panies, at best, imperfect and often not meaningful.

For these reasons, it is our view that despite the increased globalization of capital markets, companies and investors still will have to look to na-tional bodies to set and enforce financial reporting standards for the fore-seeable future. That is a central reason why we have written this book: to educate investors about the nature and trends in financial reporting in the major industrialized countries and, in particular, those that are home to the largest capital markets in the world. To put the issues into perspective, we precede the chapters on financial reporting in the United States, the United Kingdom, Germany, the European Union, and Japan with analyses of the usefulness of accounting data and standards for investment deci-sions. We conclude by contrasting financial standards in these countries, considering the benefits and costs of a single or multiple standards, rules-based versus principles-based standards, and other contemporary issues.

In the remainder of this introductory chapter, we discuss several thresh-old issues related to financial reporting, beginning with the reasons why investors and countries find equity ownership valuable, and the trends in equity investment around the world that have generated increased interest not only in having a single set of reporting standards worldwide, but also in differences in national reporting rules. We conclude the chapter by outlining the logic of the subsequent chapters of the book.

THE BENEFITS OF EQUITY-STOCK OWNERSHIP DOMESTICALLY AND WORLDWIDE

Equity shares offer individuals and economies considerable benefits. For individuals, they represent investments that can increase substantially in value. Although risky in themselves, put together with other investments equities actually can reduce risk, because their values may increase when other investments lose value.

One of the most important "other investments" is the time and effort individuals put into developing their "human capital"—skills and experience that give individuals the ability to generate income. Many individuals also have a large portion of their wealth invested in personal housing. Investments in equity shares can be useful for diversifying both of these other investments, so that the cash flows people get from their portfolios of human and non-human investments are more predictable and less volatile.

Most people value more predictable and stable cash flows that they can use for consumption and additional investments. (We emphasize "cash flows," because cash and its close equivalents can be used at very low cost to purchase other assets.) Substantial decreases in cash flows are costly, and not only because of the loss of wealth: the shortfall has to be made up with borrowing and/or forced sale of assets, both of which usually are significantly more costly than simply withdrawing money held in a bank or money market account. The same is true of shortfalls made in deferred consumption—of purchases of housing, cars, appliances, vacations and other goods and services, planned education for oneself or one's children, and health maintenance. A shortfall in expected cash flows thus is costly, both monetarily and emotionally.

Increases in cash flows, of course, are highly desired, because they permit individuals to increase their consumption, either currently or in the future. Indeed, this is the driving force behind purchases of lottery tickets, where the expected payout is less than the cost of the ticket. But even unexpected increases in cash flows are somewhat costly. The funds must be invested or otherwise put to use, information must be gathered, and financial advisors may have to be employed who may or may not provide useful information.

Consequently, for all these reasons, most individuals tend to prefer stable and predictable cash flows—which is to say, they are averse to risk. While equity shares can be useful in contributing to rising cash flows, investors must be able to value their shares and determine the extent to which those values might change. This exercise, too, can be costly, particularly if it is difficult for investors to obtain information about how corporations are managed and what returns they might achieve. The less costly it is for investors to get and use this information and the more they believe they can trust its validity, the greater their benefit from owning equity shares. We discuss in detail in the next chapter how and why investors' costs are reduced when they get trustworthy and relevant accounting reports on the financial condition and performance of corporations whose shares they hold or might purchase.

Equity-share investments also greatly benefit economies. The funds companies raise by issuing shares provide entrepreneurs and the managers of established corporations with the resources they require to produce goods and services that enrich a nation and the world. The lower the cost of raising this capital, the more that firms can produce and the lower will be the cost of generating and delivering their goods and services. Meanwhile, the extent to which the cost of capital can be reduced depends substantially on the efficiency with which equities are purchased and sold. Therefore, both consumers and investors benefit from greater efficiency, higher market liquidity, information transparency, and lower costs of trading and holding equity securities.

THE BENEFITS FROM GLOBAL CAPITAL MARKETS

Ownership of equity shares in corporations that do business in countries other than an investor's own country can provide additional diversification beyond that provided by diversifying investments in home-country firms and other investments (in human capital and real estate). The benefits of this additional source of diversification are especially important for people living in small countries, since their jobs, the value of their homes, and the values of home-country equities are likely to be similarly affected by the same events. Furthermore, investments in foreign corporations can potentially yield greater returns if those firms earn higher returns on their investments.

Companies also benefit when they can sell their securities to investors in other countries. These benefits are likely to be the greatest for corporations in countries that have a less well-developed or less-than-competitive banking system or securities markets. Both companies and investors in the source country benefit when capital can flow efficiently to corporations that promise the best risk-adjusted returns.

TRENDS IN DOMESTIC AND GLOBAL EQUITY MARKETS

Before we begin to describe and assess disclosure rules and practices in key countries around the world, readers should know about some broad trends that have affected and likely will continue to affect equities markets:

- The growth in these markets and the increasing trend toward equity ownership in the United States and in the European Union and, to a lesser extent, in many other parts of the developed world.
- Technological changes that are enhancing global equities markets
- Perhaps most important for the purposes of this study, the increasing globalization—or cross-border integration—of capital markets, and specifically the markets for publicly traded equity capital.

The Growth in the Equities Markets

One of the more noticeable changes in the equities markets is the tremendous growth in their size. This is true for all four major countries whose markets and reporting rules we consider in this study.

In the United States, home to the largest capital market in the world, the market value of all publicly traded companies soared from just under $1.6 trillion in 1990 to more than $13 trillion by the end of the decade.[2] Stock prices continued to rise through early 2000, but as of December 2003 had fallen, about 25.4 percent off their peak.[3]

Market trends in the United Kingdom were similar, with equity capitalization among domestic companies rising from £0.45 billion in 1990 to nearly £1.4 billion in 2003; the latter figure was down by 25 percent from its 1999 peak. Companies from outside the United Kingdom, but listed on the London Exchange, are even more significant. Their total equity capitalization stood at £1.1 billion in 1990 and almost £2 billion in 2003 (with their peak, too, in 1999 at £3.5 billion).

Data on equity capitalization for the German domestic equity market are not available before 2000 (largely due to the reorganization of exchanges in that market, coupled with the reunification of East and West Germany in the 1990s). But, as in the United States and the United Kingdom, the data that do exist show a substantial decline in total market capitalization between 2000 and 2003 (after almost certainly having risen prior to 2000), from 1.56 billion Euro in January 2000 to 0.59 billion Euro in April 2003, when it began to rise again.[4]

Even in Japan, where stock prices have fallen sharply since the bubble burst in the later 1980s, the total market capitalization of companies listed on Japanese exchanges rose through much of the 1990s—from 394 trillion yen in 1994 to a peak of 466 trillion yen in 1999—before declining again by some 50 percent by 2002 to 251.0 trillion yen. At this writing (early 2005), Japanese prices have again risen, so the current total is well above the 2002 low.[5]

Market capitalizations of equities generally rose throughout the 1990s in the United States and much of Europe largely because stock prices also generally increased during this period. In turn, share prices rose because of increased demand for stocks, whether through direct ownership or holdings of mutual funds. This is especially true in the United States, where the share of households investing in stock directly or through mutual funds rose from 19 percent in 1983 to 39 percent in 1992 and to 50 percent in 2002.[6]

Stock ownership has also risen in other countries. The pattern in Canada, for example, looks very much like that of the United States. However, stock ownership in Europe and Japan still lags behind the United States significantly. Moreover, the patterns of ownership over time between Europe and Japan differ significantly. For example, in the United Kingdom the percentage of UK shares owned directly by individuals or through mutual funds (unit trusts) was 26 percent in 1990, declining to about 20 percent in 1998 and falling further to 15 percent in 2002. Indirect investments add still more households, but even here, the shares have fallen, from 32 percent in 1990 to 16 percent in 2002.[7] In Germany, the shares of equity held by individuals have fallen from 17 percent in 1994 to 14 percent in 2002.[8]

In Japan, security companies, banks, and insurance companies domi-nate share ownership. But although the fraction of households investing in the stock market is substantially below that of the United States, that fraction has increased somewhat remarkably, given the bursting of the share price bubble over a decade ago. Thus, in 2002, shares held by in-dividuals accounted for some 20 percent of total shares outstanding, al-most double the 11 percent in the mid-1990s.[9]

Technological Changes in Securities Trading

Corporations can sell securities to the public in a variety of ways, de-pending on the legal requirements in their countries. If they want those securities to be traded regularly, they must be accepted for listing on a stock exchange. Stock exchanges impose specific requirements for listing. Examples of these requirements include the publication of detailed pro-spectuses for new issues for which the directors are responsible and that contain past information that must be audited by an independent public accountant (IPA); a minimum percentage of shares that must be publicly held; and rules stating how the corporation is governed. Corporations with publicly traded shares also must conform to the laws of their country that govern securities issues and trading. Companies listed on foreign exchanges are also subject to the law of their home country.

The markets on which equity shares are traded can be classified into three groups, which have evolved over time. The first markets developed when groups of equity holders physically came together to buy and sell securities, either for themselves or for clients. In some markets a single broker specialized in a particular stock or group of stocks and all trades went through that specialist. Other brokers who were members of the exchange (membership of which is limited) offered and bought equity securities through the specialists and sometimes directly (off the floor). This was the situation in the United Kingdom until 1986 and in Japan until 1999; it still is the way the New York Stock Exchange and the Ger-man Stock Exchange operate.

The second type of market developed as technology, in the form of computers and trading screens on which bids and offer prices and numbers of shares are displayed, came into use. Dealers in securities used interlinked computers and programs to trade with each other for the benefit of clients. Membership in these markets, such as the NASDAQ in the United States, is more widespread throughout the world than in the specialist markets. These markets grew largely by attracting newer, technology-based companies.

The third market, currently under development, has grown out of the increasingly widespread use of the Internet; it promises perhaps the most revolutionary change of all. Rather than using computers to complete trades manually, the Internet literally allows the computers themselves to complete trades, automatically matching bids and offers. A variety of these Electronic Communications Networks (ECNs)—such as Instinet and

Archipelago in the United States, Stock Exchange Electronic Trading Service (STS) with the London Stock Exchange, and Xetra with the German and Vienna Stock Exchanges—are taking an increasing share of trades from, or have been incorporated as part of, the already established exchanges.[10] Because ECNs operate with far lower costs than the traditional, manual exchanges (even the second-generation computer-screen exchanges), they have substantially lowered transactions costs to investors [Domowitz and Steil, 2001]. This is a main reason why the New York Stock Exchange acquired Archipelogo and the NASDAQ purchased Instinet in 2005. (Both transactions were still under review by U.S. regulators at the time this chapter was written.)

THE GLOBALIZATION OF FINANCE

The Internet not only has reduced the cost and enhanced the speed of trading, but also, because the Internet itself is global, now allows investors throughout the world to buy and sell securities anywhere around the world. Such trading can take place almost continuously, as securities markets are open somewhere almost all the time. Regulators are uncomfortable with this development, however, and in various countries have attempted to restrict Internet-based cross-border trading. In particular, the U.S. Securities and Exchange Commission (SEC) has ruled that all trades made by a U.S. broker or dealer (all of whom must be registered by the SEC) must conform to U.S. requirements for corporations with securities listed in the United States.

Nonetheless, even without the Internet, financial markets already were well on the way toward becoming "globalized." One way this happened, of course, is the rise over time in gross flows of various kinds of capital—currencies, bank loans, and bond issues—that move across borders (see generally Herring and Litan [1995]). Moreover, many large financial institutions themselves have become increasingly global in their operations, although the acceleration in merger-and-acquisition activity in the financial sector in all major industrialized countries in the 1990s took on a multinational character largely only outside the United States [Group of Ten, 2001]. And last but not least, the accounting profession itself has become global in reach. The "Big Four" accounting firms in the United States (with one of them, KPMG, headquartered in Amsterdam), which are by far the largest in the world, generate about 65 percent of their revenues from locations outside the United States [White, 2001].

Cross-border capital flows certainly are not new; in some ways they were as important, relative to overall economic activity, even before World War I as they are now. But they are fundamentally different in character today, more diversified across industries and relatively more evenly balanced between portfolio investments and direct investment.[11]

The rise of cross-border capital movements has been as much influenced by national policies as by technology. After World War II, nations fixed their exchange rates under the Bretton Woods system, anchored to the dollar, which in turn was pegged to the price of gold (at $35 per ounce). The United States stood ready to convert dollars to gold, while nations throughout the world restricted capital movements to help support the fixed-rate exchange system. This system worked reasonably well for about a quarter of a century—although some nations occasionally changed their exchange rates (almost always through devaluation) when their international payments became too imbalanced—but fixed rates, and with them capital controls, ironically were undermined by the United States, one of the leading architects of Bretton Woods.

In retrospect, fixed rates were doomed when the United States placed a tax on dollar outflows in the 1960s in an effort to support the dollar. Multinational banks, including those headquartered in the United States, responded to the tax by creating dollar-denominated accounts (Eurodollars), leading to rapid growth in dollar-based assets outside the United States. Ultimately, the volume of dollar assets held abroad became so large in relation to the U.S. stock of gold reserves that the U.S. promise under Bretton Woods to exchange its dollars for gold at a fixed price (of $35 per ounce) lacked credibility. In 1971, the United States formally went off the gold standard, and by 1973 fixed exchange rates were officially scrapped. With fixed rates gone, the case for capital controls weakened, and through the 1970s the United States and other developed countries abandoned them. By the 1990s, a number of emerging market economies followed suit (although the loosening of controls over short-term capital inflows, especially debt, has since been widely attacked in the wake of the Asian financial crisis of 1997–98).

In this book, we concentrate primarily on the issuance and trading of equities, and this part of the financial business, too, has expanded beyond national borders in several respects. Figures 1-1 and 1-2[12] depict annual outflows and inflows of portfolio equity or net purchases of securities in either direction as percentages of gross domestic product (GDP) during the 1990s for three of the major countries reviewed in this study: the United States, Germany, and the United Kingdom. For the most part, the charts show an increasing trend toward greater portfolio capital movements, although with significant year-to-year variation.

Gross purchases of equities are much greater in volume. For example, for the United States alone, gross annual purchases by foreigners of U.S. equities in the year 2000 totaled $7 trillion. The comparable figure for gross purchases by U.S. residents of foreign securities in that year was $3.6 trillion. These figures are up by roughly a factor of 10 or more over the last decade [Griever et al., 2001, p. 640].

Another indicator of the growing integration of capital markets, at least among two of the world's major equities markets, is the rising number of cross-listings by companies whose shares are traded on both the New York and London Stock Exchanges, illustrated in Figure 1-3.[13] Companies that cross-list incur the expense of complying with the rules

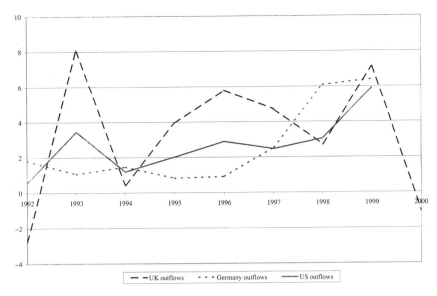

Figure 1-1. Portfolio Equity Outflows as Percent of GDP, 1992–2000. Outflows are the change in Portfolio Equity Assets during the year. *Source:* International Financial Statistics CD-ROM, International Monetary Fund, 2001.

of multiple exchanges, but nonetheless must also believe that benefits, in terms of accessing a wider base of potential investors, more than justify the costs. A substitute for cross-listings, at least for trading in U.S. and European markets, is for a foreign company to trade as a Depository Receipt (DR), a negotiable instrument backed by the shares of the foreign firm, which is typically placed in a trust with a local (U.S. or European) bank. Trading value in American DRs (ADRs) in 2000 exceeded $1 trillion, or about 17 percent of trading in corresponding local markets. In that same year, 115 DR offerings took place in the United States and Europe, a 32 percent increase over 1999 [Claessens et al., 2002]. Though total ADR value has fallen since 2000, the share volume has increased to over $34 billion in 2003, a 14 percent increase over 2002.

A third indication of increasing global markets integration is the increased correlation over time in stock returns across markets. Looking at four core markets (United States, United Kingdom, Germany, and France), Goetzmann, Li, and Rouwenhorst found an increasing trend in correlation in such returns from approximately 0.4 in 1990 to nearly 0.6 in 2000.[14] This is mostly true for markets within developed countries, as the correlation between developed and emerging market country returns, at least through 1998, has been relatively low. However, as the Asian financial crisis demonstrated, volatility in emerging markets at times can certainly infect developed countries' markets [Kaushik and Santicchia, 2000].

Increased cross-border integration, as well as the development of equities markets more broadly, has been highly uneven around the world,

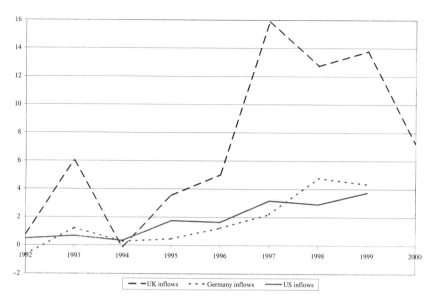

Figure 1-2. Portfolio Equity Inflows as Percent of GDP, 1992–2000. Inflows are the change in Portfolio Equity Liabilities during the year. *Source:* International Financial Statistics CD-ROM, International Monetary Fund, 2001.

however. As of 1998, for example, although emerging market countries accounted for 85 percent of the world's population and 22 percent of its output, their equity markets accounted for less than 9 percent of the world's total market capitalization [Levich, 2001, p. 6]. More broadly, while total capital flows to emerging markets overall rose substantially during the 1990s, reaching almost 30 percent of all equities around the world, they have been concentrated in a relative handful of countries, primarily in Southeast Asia and a few countries in Latin America [see generally World Bank Policy Research Report, 1997]. If attention is paid just to long-term capital flows, or foreign direct investment (FDI), the picture is especially distorted: among all FDI sent to developing countries, the share of FDI going to countries defined by the World Bank to be "low income" fell from 13 percent in 1990 to just 7 percent in 2000 [World Bank, 2001A, p. 39]. Moreover, while FDI flows to developing countries as a whole marched steadily upward during the 1990s, they were interrupted by the Asian crisis and by the end of the decade accounted for roughly the same share of global FDI—20 percent—as they did at the beginning of the 1990s [World Bank, 2001B].

In any event, measures of cross-border integration based solely on the volumes of flows can be misleading. As integrated as they have become, financial markets still remain less integrated across national borders than within countries. One easy measure of this proposition is to compare portfolio compositions of domestic residents or institutions. If equities of foreign and domestic securities were viewed as substitutes, one would

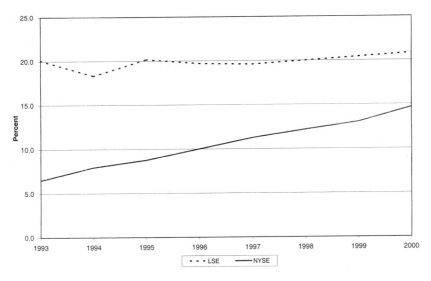

Figure 1-3. International Companies Listed on NYSE and LSE as Proportion of Total Listings, 1993 through 2000. http://www.londonstockexchange.com/market/historic.asp, http://www.nyse.com/pdfs/nonussum010813.pdf, http://www.nyse.com/pdfs/10_HISTORICAL.pdf.

expect equity portfolios to be divided among domestic and foreign stocks in proportion to the relative share valuations of domestic country markets as a share of the worldwide market. Yet the data reveal otherwise. Although the allocations have been increasing modestly over time, investors in the United States, Europe, and Japan devote 10 percent or less of their portfolios to foreign stocks, far below the shares one would expect if investors considered foreign and domestic stocks to be perfect substitutes.[15]

Several factors are most likely to account for this "home country bias" on the part of investors: language barriers, currency exchange risk, higher transactions costs on foreign stock purchases, uncertainty about and the costs of filing tax returns that include foreign-sourced dividends and capital gains, and risk aversion on the part of investors to putting their money into companies with which they are not familiar. The latter impediment is noteworthy even inside countries: U.S. investment managers display distinct regional preferences in picking stocks [Coval and Moskowitz, 1999]. Another key factor limiting international diversification of equity portfolios, of course, is the disparity in information about companies in different countries, to which the differences in the quality of corporate disclosure in various countries contribute. We discuss this in greater detail below and in subsequent chapters.

We also still do not live in an age where investors in any country may buy stocks from other countries in their own local currencies during their own normal business hours. The major impediment to that happening now is the settlement and clearance system, which currently works for trades only in the currency of the markets in which stocks are listed and traded. That is why the DR was developed: to allow American investors to buy shares of foreign stock in U.S. markets in U.S. dollars. Equities markets will become truly global and DRs unnecessary when the settlement and clearing systems allow investors to pick and choose the time and currency in which they want to execute their trades of stocks from any country. Of course, when that day arrives—or, most likely, well before it—regulators will have to confront and surmount a series of cross-border policy challenges, including the applicability of insider trading laws, stockholder rights, margin rules, tax compliance, and reporting of trades in different markets [Blume, 2002].

Given all that has happened in the world economy in recent years, from the Mexican and Asian financial crises in the 1990s to the global economic downturn in 2000–01, accentuated by the demonstrations against globalization each time some international body, such as the International Monetary Fund, World Bank, or Group of Seven meets, it is useful to ask whether more cross-border trading and listing of stocks across national borders is necessarily a good thing. The weight of the evidence, which is positive, is clearest for foreign direct investment, which transfers not only resources but also skills and technology to recipient countries.[16] But there is also a strong case to be made for encouraging further two-way movement of portfolio equity, or stocks that typically are held for shorter periods than FDI, which is inherently longer term. Inward portfolio equity helps to add liquidity to local or regional equities markets, and thus enhances the ability of local firms to go public when they are ready. Institutional investors, in particular, can help improve local corporate governance by providing the same kind of monitoring functions of the companies they invest in as they do in developed markets. Outward equity flows, meanwhile, allow local investors to diversify their portfolios and, thus, lower their risks and/or enhance their returns from saving. Further cross-border integration of financial markets, equity markets in particular, therefore remains in the economic interest of all countries and their citizens throughout the world.

IMPLICATIONS FOR INFORMATION DISCLOSURE

The forces rocking the equities markets around the world have several important implications for corporate disclosure. As equities play a greater role in individual and institutional saving, reliable and timely disclosure of relevant and reliable information becomes increasingly important. This is less true, however, to the extent that individuals invest in markets through index funds. In these cases, timely information is unnecessary, except to the extent that its disclosure is required for listing and other regulatory purposes. However, reliable information still is desirable, particularly when reliability is based on audits by IPAs that act to prevent or mitigate misuse of corporate resources, because corporate officers and insiders fear disclosure of their misdeeds.

Meanwhile, although technical developments in equities markets have lowered the cost to individuals and institutions of trading equities and bonds in stock exchanges in many countries, this change has not been greeted with equanimity by the regulatory authorities. From their point of view, globalization diminishes their power to regulate securities dealings by residents of their countries. Worldwide stock trading also has brought to public and regulatory attention the diversity of rules and practices that govern the preparation and presentation of financial data and other information that are useful to investors.

Does this mean, therefore, that the world must move toward common disclosure and enforcement standards? Certainly not, if one looks to the exchanges as being the arbiters of the rules. As long as there are major national exchanges, it is only natural to expect that the exchanges will compete for business on both price and regulatory dimensions. For this reason alone, any proposals (discussed later in this book) that might give greater authority over disclosure matters to exchanges cannot be expected to produce harmonized disclosure standards. To the contrary, we would expect competition in standards and/or disclosure to be the order of the day if responsibilities in this area were eventually given to the exchanges.

Perhaps surprising to some, we hold the same view with respect to disclosure regulation by national or international bodies. For reasons discussed at the outset of this chapter and later in this book, we do not believe that harmonized rules—which the authorities currently feel committed to—are either desirable (because they are likely to lag behind market developments by substantial margins) or are a stable outcome (because national bodies are likely to depart from international norms in the meantime).

OVERVIEW OF THE REST OF THE BOOK

But all of this is to come. In the next chapter, we begin our analysis explaining why and to what extent financial accounting statements are useful and necessary for most investors (those who do not invest through index funds). We argue that the current move to fair value accounting by some standard-setters is not desirable because the resulting numbers are not trustworthy if there are no active markets, and they cannot be audited by IPAs. Financial reports are useful only to the extent they are governed by some standards. Chapter 3 explains the roles and usefulness of both accounting and auditing standards and discusses who would be best equipped to set these standards.

Chapters 4 through 8 then discuss corporate disclosure regimes in the major industrialized countries, beginning with a brief look at their history and then their present regulatory regimes. We review financial disclosure required by listed and unlisted companies, accounting standards, investor protection, corporate governance, auditing, and enforcement. Based on these reviews, we discuss shortcomings and current issues in these countries. We begin our country analyses with the United States (Chapter 4) and proceed through the major European capital markets (the United Kingdom in Chapter 5, Germany in Chapter 6). We then consider the ever-increasing influence of the European Union for financial disclosure (Chapter 7) and conclude with a discussion of disclosure in Japan (Chapter 8). Overall, we find that all countries we review have adapted their disclosure regimes over time to deal with pressures from the globalization of capital markets, but also in response to accounting scandals. Particularly, the European Union, Germany, and Japan have introduced regimes that seem to correspond to those of the United States and the United Kingdom.

Chapter 9 compares and assesses these different regimes. We find evidence that diversity in financial disclosure regimes continues to exist, even though the reviewed countries have been following a more common approach recently. This observation leads to our pessimistic view of current efforts to institutionalize a global accounting standard. In Chapter 10 we develop further the important current issues of global versus competitive accounting standards and argue for constrained competition in standards. We also discuss the effect of the Internet on access to financial information and problems of enforcement of accounting and auditing standards. We conclude in Chapter 11 by discussing the validity of current accounting theories, while highlighting some important issues in corporate disclosure that remain to be resolved.

2

Why and How Audited Financial Accounting Statements Are Useful

Financial information about corporations—or, indeed, about enterprises generally—is useful to many different types of people associated with those organizations. These people include investors, creditors, customers, suppliers, managers and other employees, regulators, and government officials. Because their requirements differ and because preparers of financial statements generally have incentives to serve them all to some degree, the numbers presented in financial statements necessarily are of limited, but often of substantial, value to any one group of users. Although we concentrate in this study on the needs of investors in publicly traded corporations (as do many standard setters when they explicitly give priority to informed investors), it is important to recognize that the rules governing the data presented in the statements are meant to serve the requirements of other users as well. These rules are referred to as generally accepted accounting principles (GAAP), which are coupled with generally accepted auditing standards (GAAS). When the standards are referred to without qualification (GAAP rather than, for example, U.K. GAAP), we mean them to be generic concepts. We also recognize that financial disclosure is part of the greater picture of corporate governance mechanisms of corporations.

Investors, whether present or prospective, generally benefit from learning about how their investments have been and might be used by the managers of their companies. One source of such information is financial reports that managers render to their boards of directors and shareholders. These statements are the principal formal means by which managers convey how they have managed the enterprise's resources over a period, usually no longer than a year, and the resultant financial condition of the enterprise at the end of a period, as determined by their accounting records. Prospective investors realize that once they have committed their funds to a corporation by purchasing new shares directly or from an existing shareholder, they usually have little control over how the corporation is managed. Non-controlling shareholders, in particular, have reason for concern. Consequently, they usually are interested in how those over whom they have no control have used corporate resources, and the extent to which these controlling persons (including senior managers) have conflicts of interest that might result in costs being imposed on the non-controlling shareholders. Financial reports also help to motivate managers to operate their corporations in the interest of shareholders. Reporting in these areas is called the "stewardship" function of accounting.

In addition to a report of stewardship, investors would want data that help them determine the present and possible future economic value of their investments. If the corporation's shares are actively traded in a share market, shareholders can obtain unbiased estimates of the economic value of their investments from share prices. But these prices are based, in part, on the information provided in financial reports. If this information were not relevant and reliable, its receipt would not change the value given to shares or provide investors with insights that they want. Hence, prospective investors might have to incur costs to obtain information elsewhere or discount the amount they were willing to pay for the shares, using the information currently available to them. This would make the shares worth less to them. Thus, present shareholders, including those who can exercise some control over the corporation, also benefit from their managers providing potential investors with financial reports that the investors find trustworthy.

Creditors must determine the likelihood that they will be repaid if they advance funds to the enterprise. They also are well advised to monitor how the funds are being used, that the conditions imposed by loan covenants have been satisfied, and the extent to which the borrowers' ability to repay debt as promised has changed. Suppliers to the corporation want to be paid for their goods, a likelihood about which financial statements can provide useful information. Customers who purchase products that require replacement or servicing must determine whether the vendor is likely to continue in business. Thus, suppliers' and customers' interests are similar to those of creditors: they want assurance that their contractual relationships with enterprises will be fulfilled as promised. Consequently, they tend to be concerned only with the possibilities that the enterprise will not be able to repay its debts or honor its obligations. Because this ability is affected primarily by the enterprise's present and possible future losses rather than by increases in economic value, creditors and suppliers generally favor conservative accounting rules, or those where all expected losses are recorded and gains are delayed until they are almost certain. They also usually want statements of cash flows, and current asset market or (in situations of financial distress) current liquidation values.

Employees often find financial information useful for determining the extent to which their employer has prospered and the possibility that they might lose their jobs, or get a promotion or pay raise. Managers' and other employees' bonuses and other rewards often are partially based on the financial performance of their firms, as measured by financial accounting data reported in financial statements. Thus, their concerns are similar to those of investors, except that the bulk of their wealth (human and financial capital, particularly for senior managers) tends to be tied to their company. Unlike investors, they rarely can hold a portfolio of investments that is sufficiently diversified to offset potential losses with gains, except for very wealthy top managers. They also may have been compensated with share options that could become worthless (or considerably less valuable) if their corporation's share prices decline. Therefore, they are concerned with the impact of accounting figures on the share's price performance in the market. For these reasons, employees and senior managers tend to worry about the possibilities that their firm might appear to have performed badly, resulting in the loss of their positions and investments in company share and retirement plans. Furthermore, those senior managers whose bonuses, job security, and prospects are based on financial accounting data, rather than on share prices, have reason to want financial-accounting reports to present numbers that benefit them. For example, they would like the statements to show that they have done at least as well as predicted by share analysts and report net earnings that are sufficient for them to earn bonuses.

The *taxing authorities* of some governments (e.g., Germany and Japan) base tax liabilities on financial statement data. In some other countries (e.g., the United Kingdom and the United States), the tax authorities refer to these data to assess the validity of the numbers reported in tax returns, because both are based on the taxpayer's accounting records. They recognize that company (as well as other) taxpayers would prefer to pay as little in taxes as possible, often to the extent of deliberately understating the amounts on which taxes are based. Consequently, the authorities are concerned about the validity of the numbers presented in financial statements.

Antitrust authorities and competition authorities generally often make their decisions on market performance analyses based on rates of return and market shares constructed from data presented in financial reports. Regulatory authorities (such as the SEC in the United States and the Financial Services Authority in the United Kingdom) are charged with assuring investors that stock markets are "fair" and that the financial reports they receive are unbiased and, if possible, include information that is useful for them or their agents to aid in determining the value and performance of publicly traded equity and debt investments. Public policy towards corporations, especially industry regulation, often is based on the profits or losses corporations report in their financial statements. Government and its agencies have a wide range of interests in this reporting of enterprises' activities; for example, accounts also serve as the basis for national income and similar statistics. The general public is affected by enterprises in a wide variety of ways, and accounting statements may help provide relevant information.

Thus, although different users of financial statements want somewhat different information for often very different reasons, we believe that they have one interest in common: they want numbers that they can trust.

THE USEFULNESS OF AUDITED FINANCIAL ACCOUNTING DATA TO NON-CONTROLLING INVESTORS

Our primary concern is with the usefulness of audited financial accounting data to non-controlling investors in publicly traded corporations. By virtue of their positions, controlling shareholders usually can obtain whatever information they demand; hence, we are not concerned with them, other than how they may affect information supplied to others. Creditors, suppliers, customers, and employees often can request any information that they might find useful, depending on their importance to the corporation, or they can decline to deal with the corporation or seek to charge enough for their products or services to compensate them for the lack of information.[1] (As we note earlier, corporations have strong incentives to provide information that those who deal with them would find useful.)

Non-controlling shareholders have a strong interest in the trustworthiness of financial numbers for at least three reasons: (1) stewardship (motivating, evaluating, and rewarding corporate officers and reducing the cost of potential conflicts of interests, misappropriation of resources, and fraud by those in control); (2) increasing share value for all investors; and (3) maximizing the value of their own shares. Financial figures will be trustworthy, in turn, only when they are based on accounting standards that provide figures that faithfully represent what they purport to represent and that can be independently verified.[2] As we discuss in more detail later, ensuring that figures are reliable is the principal purpose of audits by independent public accountants (IPAs), such as Certified Public Accountants (U.S. and Japan), Chartered Accountants (UK), or Wirtschaftsprüfer (Germany). By their attestations of the validity of the numbers presented, IPAs indicate and provide surety that they have examined the corporate records in a manner that is expected to be sufficient to uncover material misstatements and omissions and that they have conducted an audit that conforms to GAAS.

As for the stewardship function, it is sufficient for the numbers presented to be trustworthy and the audits be designed to uncover and the financial statements to reveal misuse of corporate resources, misstatement of income and expenses, and understatement of liabilities. These numbers should reveal the extent to which managers and controlling shareholders have misappropriated corporate resources and (of greatest importance) thereby give the managers and controlling shareholders a strong incentive to forbear misuse of corporate resources. Incomplete and inadequate reporting of income, expenses, and liabilities often is not discovered without unrestricted access to corporate books of account. Only an audit, therefore, can verify this information. (GAAS make this process more efficient, as we discuss in the following chapter.) Trustworthy reports of the acquisition, presence, and disposition—if not the value—of costs and revenues and of assets and liabilities is necessary for managerial performance measurement and for decision-making.

However, for the purpose of evaluating managers' performance and for investment decisions, it would be desirable if financial statements also could report the value to investors of their corporation's resources at the beginning and end of an accounting period. Net income or loss for the period, then, would be the difference between the beginning-of-year and end-of-year values, adjusted for distributions to and additional investments from shareholders. For these purposes, economic market values for assets and liabilities, rather than historical costs, would be most relevant. Indeed, this is an important motivation for those urging the use of "fair values." This seemingly innocuous but important term is defined by the Financial Accounting Standards Board (FASB) in FAS 140, paragraph 68: "The fair value of an asset (or liability) is the amount at which that asset (or liability) could be bought (or incurred) or sold (or settled) in a current transaction between willing parties, that is, other than in a forced or liquidation sale." Fair values are supposed to serve as a proxy for economic market values in place of historical costs in the accounting standards adopted by the FASB and the International Accounting Standards Board (IASB).

The use of fair values in accounting, though, can and often does require numbers that may not be—indeed, often are *not*—trustworthy. Many fair values, perforce, have to be based on estimates rather than market values. Unfortunately, as we demonstrate next, a financial report based on fair values rarely can be achieved consistent with the requirement that the numbers also be trustworthy—reliable and verifiable.

It often is said that there may be a trade-off between trustworthiness and relevance, but relevant information will be weighted in decision-making to the degree that it is reliable; that is, the degree of belief attached to decision-relevant accounting items will be attenuated by the degree of reliability associated with those items.

Trustworthiness is a stronger objective than reliability, in that financial figures are trustworthy only where they are verified according to well-accepted accounting standards. As paragraph 44 of the FASB's "Statement of Financial Accounting Concepts No. 2: Qualitative Characteristics of Accounting Information" recognizes: "almost everyone agrees that criteria for formally recognizing elements in financial statements call for a minimum level or threshold of reliability of measurement that should be higher than is usually considered necessary for disclosing information outside financial statements."

We are aware that the trustworthiness criteria might mean that some potentially useful information might have to be conveyed outside the financial statements, a topic we address in Chapter 11. We emphasize, though, that the lack of trust may render otherwise useful accounting items valueless. Indeed, trustworthy numbers often are more useful and relevant than fair values that are not based on prices determined from arm's-length market transactions because these are more subject to managerial manipulation than is historical cost. This is particularly the case where fair values are based on managerial estimates. Investors and others who want to estimate the economic market value (other than by simply looking at the market price of its shares) of the enterprise must and can look to other sources of information.

GAAP-based audited results do contain estimates, but these can be regarded as trustworthy insofar as they are based on verifiable empirical evidence. For example, bad-debts provisions follow accepted professional rules for deriving estimates from previous experience. Depreciation is based on standard procedures that incorporate generally accepted professional valuation where allowed, such as specific property valuations taken from active markets. We do not conclude, though, that fair values could not or should not be used, only that they should be used only when they are trustworthy. Indeed, performance measurements and investment decisions require a substantial amount of information that goes beyond trustworthy financial accounting numbers, including current and expected changes in market conditions, competitors' products and performance, the potential value of new products and processes, prospective changes in foreign exchange rates and domestic inflation rates, government policies, employee and customer relations, and the quality of management. Financial accounting numbers presented in audited reports do not provide direct information on these often vital issues and many others. Nevertheless, the numbers that are presented can be particularly useful for investors' decisions because they are trustworthy and relevant, not because they are the sole or even the most important source of information.

INFORMATION REQUIREMENTS AND THE INHERENT LIMITATIONS OF FINANCIAL ACCOUNTING

Concerns about the usefulness of financial statements for investment decisions have increasingly dominated discussions about financial accounting as investments in publicly traded corporate equities and bonds have increased. Financial accounting data are useful but of limited value for this purpose. The inherent limitations must be understood and accepted, or the substantial benefit to investors and others of obtaining trustworthy accounting data might be lost.

Information Required for Investment Decisions

The limits of financial accounting data can easily be demonstrated by considering the information that investors and traders must take into account in order to make well-considered investment decisions. As the following list should indicate, the kinds of data investors should call for are uncertain and subjective, and thus unlikely to meet any trustworthiness test.

For investors, a corporate share is an asset, and the value of an asset generally is the present value of expected future cash flows. This calculation requires estimates of both the amounts and timing of the cash flows the asset (the corporation) will generate and the probabilities that these will be as predicted. The cash flows are affected by the expected demand for the corporation's products, which requires analysis of the market conditions (the competitive environment, government regulation, and consumer tastes and preferences) in which it operates, at present and in the future. The amounts that the corporation must expend to obtain, enhance, and distribute its products and services must be estimated. Financing and administration costs (among others) also affect expected cash flows. Expected changes in the purchasing power of the monetary unit (inflation and deflation) and in relative prices and exchange rates with other currencies must be taken into account. The present value of the expected cash flows requires determination of a relevant discount rate, one that measures the opportunity cost of investment in the asset compared to alternatives (including consumption) over the time periods of the expected cash flows. The expected cash flows and discount rate necessarily are uncertain. Hence, the cash flows must be converted to certainty equivalents by calculating their expected values at each point in time, or by adjusting the discount rate with a "risk premium." The risk premium is affected by the investor's preference for or aversion to risk and his or her other investments and time preferences.

Financial accounting data cannot possibly provide investors with all the information they require (which we outlined just above) for investment decisions. Rather, accounting data are designed primarily to provide a record of individual assets and liabilities and a measure of changes in shareholders' claims as a result of the operations of the enterprise. Although investors might want these numbers to reflect economic values (which require estimates of the present value of future cash flows), financial accounting data are of limited use for this purpose.

THE INHERENT PROBLEMS IN MEASURING ECONOMIC VALUES

One problem in determining economic values stems from the cost and difficulty—often the impossibility—of measuring the value of assets to an enterprise ("value-in-use") and to investors whose decision criteria differ from that of the enterprise. Value-in-use is the present value of the net cash flows expected from the use of an asset (including its disposal) by the enterprise in combination with other assets and liabilities. The net cash flows from individual assets (or even groups of assets) are difficult to estimate, even subjectively.

Moreover, when assets are used jointly or in common to produce output, their individual present values cannot be determined, because the sum of their marginal contributions to the value of the product necessarily exceeds the actual total amount. For example, consider a manufacturing process where three machines are used sequentially to produce a part that is sold for $100. The present value of machine 1 equals the cash inflow from sale of the part less the cash outflow from the materials, labor, and so forth used to produce the part, say $40, or a net of $60. The net cash flows from using machines 2 and 3 are also $60, because each is necessary to produce the part. Obviously, the net cash flow generated from producing the part from all three machines is not $180, but $60. Hence, the economic values of the machines individually cannot be obtained from a present value calculation, but (perhaps) from the machine's replacement value (assuming that it would be replaced if it were irreparably damaged).

Furthermore, the cash flow estimates are likely to change over time as other enterprise operations, market conditions, and general and specific prices change. Although formal or informal estimates of the present values of assets must be made before they are purchased, these estimates need only indicate that the present value of net cash flows exceeds the cost of the asset or the present value of net cash flows from alternative assets. Furthermore, this analysis (called "capital budgeting") often is costly to implement. Consequently, a formal analysis usually is made sporadically; repeating it for each periodic balance sheet would be very costly. Fixed assets, such as buildings, equipment, and land used for operations, even where there are good markets, provide prime examples of these problems. Even more difficult to estimate are the values of intangible assets produced by a company.

In addition, the value of an enterprise to an investor is almost always greater than the sum of the values of its assets less the sum of its liabilities. That is one of the principal reasons that companies exist. Their owners obtain rents (positive externalities) from the combination of assets and liabilities that represent the company, which increase expected net cash flows above the amounts these assets and liabilities separately or in other combinations would have generated. (If the whole were not worth more than the sum of the parts, the company should be liquidated, in which event the value-in-use would be the net disposal value.)[3] An extreme example of this situation is closed-end mutual funds. Most of these funds hold securities that are regularly traded in public markets. Nevertheless, these funds often are quoted at prices that are greater or smaller than the sums of the market prices of their individual assets. The premiums and discounts reflect investors' assessment of the funds' managers, cost structure, and other variables. Thus, for almost all corporations, even if investors and IPAs were willing to accept as trustworthy the managers' economic valuations of assets and liabilities, the amount shown as "shareholders' equity" would not equal the economic value of the enterprise.

However, valid proxies for the economic values (value-in-use) of some individual assets and liabilities can be obtained from market prices. Where the exchange value of assets can be determined from market prices or can be reliably approximated and verified and, consequently, are trustworthy, the numbers clearly would be more relevant to investors than historical costs, particularly when prices have changed substantially. Market prices represent valid proxies for economic value under three conditions. One is that the value-in-exchange of an asset is greater than its value from further usage, in which event the value-in-exchange less the cost of disposal equals the value-in-use, because the best opportunity is to dispose of the asset. The second is when the company is a going concern that expects to purchase similar assets (e.g., inventory), in which event the market price of equivalent services (plus the cost of acquisition) is the value of its existing comparable assets, because this is the maximum amount the company would be willing to pay for these assets. The third is when the assets have value to the enterprise as temporary or short-maturity investments. In this event, market or possibly fair value is the asset's value-in-use. This is the situation for securities and other financial instruments that are regularly quoted and for which transactions costs can be estimated reliably.[4] Even then, financial instruments might generate synergies within the firm—for example, by improving its risk position and credit rating, which makes their value-in-use greater than their market or fair value. Some financial securities, though, such as specialized (nonstandard) derivatives, do not have market prices and must be valued with an analytical model. In many cases, the values are sensitive to the assumptions required for the model, often resulting in a wide range of "reasonable" values.[5]

With the notable exception of long-term fixed-interest-bearing obligations and inventories, other current assets and liabilities have traditionally been reported at their approximate economic values. Accounts receivable is a close approximation when reduced by an allowance for doubtful accounts that is not understated to deceive regulators or investors or inflated to reduce income taxes with higher bad debt expenses. Although fixed-interest-bearing notes and bonds receivable and payable could reliably be revalued at current applicable interest rates, this adjustment is made inconsistently under most standards, including U.S. GAAP and International Financial Reporting Standards (IFRS), and applies only to financial assets. The international Joint Working Group of Standard Setters (JWG) draft standard on Financial Instruments 2000, though, if adopted, would have liabilities reported at fair values.

Inventories, which often represent a substantial proportion of many companies' current assets, could be valued at their opportunity costs. Purchased inventory that the company expects to replace could be valued at replacement cost, including the cost of transportation and stocking. Manufactured inventory could be valued at the variable cost of manufacture when the company is not manufacturing at capacity, provided that these cost figures can be validated. If the production were at capacity, the inventory would be valued at the selling price less the variable costs required to effect the sale (net sales value). At present, GAAP in all countries use historical cost for inventories, with various assumptions about which goods were used and which remain in inventory (e.g., first-in, first-out; last-in, first-out; or an average), because historical cost does not recognize the as yet unrealized holding gains on inventory. (We note that this is inconsistent with fair-value accounting for financial assets and liabilities.)

Property, plant, and equipment generally cannot be readily or reliably valued. Some of these assets or similar assets might be traded in efficient markets, especially property from which purchase prices might be obtained. Appraisals by presumably independent experts could be used to estimate fair values for specific assets not actually traded at a given time on existing efficient markets. Such appraisals would be generally based on the market prices of assets actually traded in the market during the financial year or, in some cases, replacement costs, which are often equated to open market value. IFRS and U.K. GAAP permit this revaluation. Present-value estimates also could be used when the expected cash flows and the appropriate risk-adjusted discount rate can be estimated reliably. However, as we discussed earlier, the numbers used for these estimates may be subject to manipulation and substantial error, although some standard setters believe that this is unlikely with professionally provided estimates based on active markets.[6] In any event, these numbers are unlikely to provide a close measure of value-in-use.[7] Should it later appear that the numbers actually were not trustworthy, the IPA is likely to get sued and/or lose reputation value.

Accounting for mergers and acquisitions under present U.S. GAAP and IFRS provides a good illustration of the use and misuse of fair-value estimates. The total value of an acquired enterprise must be recorded at its fair value to the acquiring corporation, as measured by the market value of its shares given in exchange. Then, fair-value estimates must be determined for the individual assets and liabilities acquired, with the difference between the sum of these values and the amount exchanged for the acquired firm recorded as "goodwill." Many of these individual fair values must be based on estimates because actual market prices are not available. The revalued assets and liabilities of the acquired firm are added to the assets and liabilities of the acquiring firm, which remain recorded at historical costs less depreciation and amortization. Thus, the sum is a mix of old and more up-to-date values, some of which may not be trustworthy. Indeed, a similar situation arises with purchases of almost any asset. Under U.S. GAAP, existing (already purchased) assets cannot be revalued to reflect subsequent increases in fair values. Note, however, that GAAP generally require that decreases in the values of assets must be recorded. This is the "conservative" bias in accounting, which we discuss further in the next chapter. This problem also arises with IFRS but is moderated by allowing the revaluation of property, plant, and equipment. Once this exercise is complete, goodwill should be reexamined to determine the extent to which its economic value has decreased (been impaired).

Finally, most enterprises have very important assets that are not traded and were not purchased but that generate net cash flows that are very difficult to estimate. Many intangible assets fall into this category. For example, the willingness of employees to work harder and more effectively to advance their specific company is a valuable asset. Patents, trademarks, and processes developed by a company often have economic value greatly in excess of the amounts expended to develop them. Good relationships with suppliers and customers are valuable. However, it rarely is possible to determine trustworthy or even reasonably reliable values for these assets.

THE LIKELY MANIPULATION BY MANAGERS OF REPORTED ECONOMIC VALUES

The economic values of many very important assets and liabilities can be obtained only with estimates of net cash flows and discount rates that are not only difficult and costly to estimate but also very difficult or impossible for IPAs to verify or accept as reliable. Managers who want to make it appear as if they had done well in a particular accounting period can readily increase their estimates of cash inflows, decrease their estimates of cash outflows, or decrease the applicable discount rate (as long as net present value is positive). They can easily work backward toward the numbers they want, constructing a rationale for the estimates they make that IPAs would find difficult or impossible to refute. If the cash flows they estimated turn out to be incorrect (as they inevitably will, even if the managers sought only to make unbiased estimates), the managers can argue that conditions have changed (as they inevitably do). They can argue further that they could not reasonably have predicted the changes or that they did correctly forecast a range of outcomes with associated probabilities, but that the outcome was not equal to the mean—the "expected" amount. The lack of trustworthiness led the German legislature to prohibit fair-value measurement as early as the 19th-century *Gründerzeit* after many instances of fraud and speculation. IPAs who lend their reputations to managers who present such estimates of economic values by attesting to their statements are in danger of losing those reputations if it turns out that the values were substantially misstated in light of subsequent events.

Both the FASB and the IASB have put considerable effort into providing extensive guidance on the determination of fair values to restrict managerial discretion.[8] Both have developed a fair-value hierarchy that prefers measurement of fair values by reference to market prices of the same item or similar items and use other valuation techniques only if no such market prices exist. The standard setters also increasingly require the disclosure of assumptions underlying the estimation of fair values. However, there is still much leeway in estimating future cash flows that the extensive guidance cannot address.

TIMELINESS

The preparation of financial statements is not instantaneous. Audits of the numbers presented in the statements take even more time, even if substantial resources are devoted to the audit. Investors in publicly traded shares can benefit from obtaining or interpreting information sufficiently quickly or effectively so as to purchase or sell the shares at less or more than their values when revised in light of this information. They are unlikely to wait until the corporations have produced audited financial statements. Consequently, for publicly traded corporations in particular, much that is presented in financial statements does not reflect timely information that is useful for immediate investment decisions. This assessment may change with new information technology. Of course, auditing procedures would have to change accordingly so as to continue to ensure the quality of such information. And even if the procedures were technologically feasible, they would have to be cost-effective to be adopted.

To summarize, some individual assets and liabilities can be reliably valued at economic values. These generally are limited to assets and liabilities traded in efficient markets, although some countries and regions, notably the United Kingdom, Australia, and the European Union, allow revaluations based on professional appraisals of classes of property that are regularly traded in active markets. When these numbers can be verified and accepted by IPAs, they could be reported in financial statements and used to calculate a number for income that investors would find useful.[9] However, some elements of many important classes of assets, particularly specialized plant, equipment, and intangible assets, generally cannot be measured reliably. Unreliable numbers are of doubtful value for investment purposes, even if opportunistic managers and controlling shareholders did not manipulate such numbers to the detriment of non-controlling shareholders and other users of financial statements. Furthermore, by the time the financial statements are audited and available to investors, many of the numbers that are shown are stale. Investors are better served by realizing that they must obtain useful numbers for decision-making from other sources rather than being lulled into believing that financial statements can provide them with all the data they require. However, we also believe that financial statements should include supplementary numbers that investors might find useful, as long as the extent to which these numbers can be relied on is made clear. We discuss these supplementary disclosures in Chapter 11.

THE USEFULNESS OF FINANCIAL STATEMENTS TO INVESTORS, CONSIDERING THE LIMITATIONS OF REPORTING ECONOMIC VALUES

Although financial statements that report the *economic* position of an enterprise at the end of an accounting period and changes in that position over the previous period cannot be reliably produced by managers, financial statements nevertheless have great value to investors in addition to the modest amount of new information they contain.[10] One benefit is that, as currently produced, balance sheets include trustworthy economic values for some usually important assets and liabilities, numbers that IPAs have examined and verified as having been based on actual costs or on prices determined from arm's-length transactions. These numbers (some of which are presented in footnotes) include cash and marketable securities, accounts and notes receivable; current liabilities; and interest-bearing assets and liabilities when interest rates have not changed. Other numbers at least report the physical presence, if not the present economic values, of inventories, and interest-bearing obligations when interest rates have changed. Appraisal values for land, property, and equipment, where these come from active markets, may be included in statements based on U.K. GAAP and IFRS. GAAP generally could be changed to have inventories and interest-bearing assets and liabilities reliably stated at economic (present or fair) values. However, even then, in volatile markets, numbers reported as of the balance sheet date may not reflect current prices.

Second, even where the reported numbers do not reflect economic values, at least investors can be assured that the numbers are not designed to be misleading. Moreover, as we discuss in more detail in the next chapter, numbers produced in accordance with GAAP allow investors to determine efficiently what they reflect. For example, GAAP should not permit managers to increase the value of buildings or decrease the amount of depreciation so as to give investors the impression that their investments increased in value when trustworthy valuations cannot be made. Revenue should not be recorded unless the corporation has substantially completed all it must do to be entitled to future cash inflows. Indeed, even though the income statement is not (and, as we discussed above, cannot be) a report of the change in shareholders' wealth embodied in the corporation over a period, net of dividends and new investments, it provides investors with a generally useful indicator of periodic changes in wealth.

A third benefit is trustworthy documentation and confirmation of prior announcements of a company's financial condition and earnings by the company's managers. As we have already noted, by the time audited financial statements are published, market participants usually have learned and acted on much of the information about the corporation's financial condition and changes over the period. This information often comes from corporate announcements of earnings per share, write-offs of discontinued facilities, and changes in earnings prospects as the result of contracts, employee layoffs, and management changes. Much of this information is also reported in the financial statements, often with more detail and with more precise information. Because the statements are attested to by IPAs, investors and creditors can be assured that the announcements that reflect or affect the numbers in the statements are unlikely to be fabrications. That assurance improves the efficiency of share transactions, meaning that the cost of information is lower and that share prices very quickly reflect changes in the economic value of corporate shares. Both of these impacts reduce the corporation's cost of capital. In addition, we again emphasize the importance of audits for uncovering misappropriation of resources by insiders and misreporting (particularly of income, expense, and liabilities); this information rarely can be revealed without an audit.

A fourth benefit, the usefulness of the numbers presented for analyses of trends, follows from the other benefits. As long as analysts and investors have assurance that the numbers presented are consistently produced, they can use these data to identify trends and changes—such as growing or shrinking sales and profit margins, inventories, capital investments, and income and expense ratios to sales and assets—that help them evaluate and predict company performance.

A fifth benefit is that accounting data do provide one useful measure of economic performance, namely the traditional accounting definition of net income from operations. Deliberate departure from the standards governing the calculation of net income has been the greatest problem for public financial accounting. This may be one reason why accounting standard setters in the United States, the United Kingdom, and the IASB have been moving away from the traditional "revenue/expense" model, replacing it with the "asset/liability" model. We have already suggested that to the extent this movement requires statements of "fair values," it is a mistake, largely because fair values can be readily manipulated by management. Furthermore, accounting statements that contain a mix of historical and re-estimated fair-value numbers cannot provide a meaningful measure of the economic value of a company at any point in time. For theses reasons, we believe that the traditional revenue/expense accounting model, which emphasizes the income statement rather than the balance sheet, provides investors with a more useful indicator of company performance.

THE TRADITIONAL ACCOUNTING MEASUREMENT OF NET INCOME

To determine net income, it is necessary to properly recognize both gross income and expense. Revenue recognition, in turn, has two essential features: proper timing and reliable measurement.[11] Revenue may be recorded when a corporation has essentially fulfilled its obligations to the purchaser, in whole or in part. When the transaction is complete, title to the product should have passed to the purchaser. When the product is delivered contractually over more than one accounting period, the proportion of revenue called for in the contract that is completed in a period should be reported as revenue in that period. This point of recognition often is termed the "critical event."

For example, although the conversion of materials, labor, and overhead into finished goods available for sale usually increases their value above the sum of the resources expended, revenue is not recognized because the critical event is the sale to a customer. But when there is a firm contract that essentially transfers title to the goods when they are manufactured, their completed manufacture is the critical event. In contrast, a consignment would not be treated as producing revenue to a company, because the

critical event is sale of the consigned goods by the recipient and its acceptance of an obligation to pay the company. A similar situation is a sale
that is financed by the seller, either directly with a loan or indirectly with a
guarantee of a loan made to the buyer by a third-party lender (e.g., a bank)
where the prospect that the buyer will pay for the goods as promised is
unclear. The critical event occurs when payment is received from the buyer
or the buyer's repayment of the loan and release of the seller's obligation.
Revenue should be recognized as the payments are made, not when the
product was transferred. (Alternatively, the account or note receivable
could be reduced to the amount of expected repayment.)

These "rules" for revenue recognition are generally well established
and have recently been made more explicit under most GAAP, although
they often are violated when managements seek to manipulate and mis-
state net income. We note, however, that since 2002, the FASB has been
working jointly with the IASB on a redefinition of revenue recognition
rules based on a strict asset/liability approach. Critical events that lead
to entries in the books would have to be based on whether the firm has
been given a right or has incurred an obligation due to the transaction in
question.

Reliable measurement is necessary to determine the value of assets
received or liabilities extinguished in exchange for the goods and services,
and hence the amount of revenue earned. The amount of revenue earned
should be determined by the value of the asset received. Where the market values of assets received in exchange cannot be reliably measured,
revenue should not be recorded until reliably measured values can be
determined. For example, if a company receives in exchange a product
of the purchasing company, the revenue amount should be no greater
than the amount that the product received could be sold for in an arm's-
length transaction. Thus, an Internet company that "sold" time on its
website in exchange for time on another Internet company's website
should record as revenue no more than the amount for which it could sell
the time received. If either or both of the companies have surplus time that
they cannot sell in arm's-length transactions for cash or other assets that
can be reliably valued, the "sale" has no value and no revenue should be
recorded.

Another, often encountered example is a tied sale, where a company
sells its product for a reliably measured asset, such as cash or a receivable,
but agrees to purchase the buyer's product, perhaps at an inflated price.
In this and other situations, the issue is whether the asset purchased is
valued at an arm's-length-determined price. If the price paid is greater
than the arm's-length price, the difference actually is a discount of the
sales price, which should be recorded as a reduction of revenue.

This would not be the case, however, in another fairly common situation that often involves commodities, where companies inflate their sales
with largely offsetting sales and purchases to each other. For example,
Company S sells electricity contracts to Company B for a reliably specified

amount, but in exchange informally agrees to buy the same or very similar amount of Company B's electricity contracts for almost the same price. These may be "sham" sales, but they are very difficult to distinguish from legitimate sales that may have been undertaken to diversify risk. Unless IPAs can determine that such sales really are shams, they have no alternative except to attest that the companies' financial statements accord with GAAP. Financial statement users should recognize this and other basic limitations of auditing and financial accounting. They also often can discover and adjust for such situations by examining whether increases in revenue are associated with decreases in gross margins.

It also is important for managers to distinguish between revenue earned from the operations of the enterprise and income derived from the sale and revaluation of assets and liabilities. Many financial statement users (particularly investors) base their calculations of a company's prospects on its past performance, as reflected by its revenue and net income from its continuing operations. In the past, accountants sought to limit the income statement to these numbers, with non-operating and extraordinary revenue and expenses recorded directly to shareholders' equity in the balance sheet (then called "earned surplus"). However, experience revealed that managers tended to exclude the effect of many unfavorable events from the income statement. Consequently, the U.S. accounting profession adopted the "clean surplus" approach, under which almost all income and expenses are reported in the income statement. Hence, it is important that revenue (or sales) and the associated expenses include only the results of the ordinary operations of an enterprise.

A very important task for the IPA, then, is to determine that the requirements for recognizing and classifying revenue have, in fact, been met. An important part of this determination is the GAAP requirement that the financial records must be presented in a manner consistent with earlier reports, unless otherwise noted and explained. Thus, a consistently applied recognition rule would tend to prevent managers from recording, say, a substantial increase in revenue from one previously specified source in a particular period to cover up losses or a substantial revenue decline from a different previously specified source.

The second key step in arriving at a proper measure of net income is matching the expenses incurred (whether beneficially or not) to obtain the revenue recognized. These are the costs of acquiring the revenue less their remaining economic value at the end of the accounting period. This "matching concept" has served accounting very well over a long time. Some expenses, such as the cost of resold merchandise and salespersons' commissions, can readily be matched with revenue. Many expenses, though, are incurred before or after the associated revenue is recognized. In general, accruals are designed to deal with this situation. Expenditures for tangible assets that will generate revenue in future periods, such as buildings and equipment, are "capitalized" and charged against revenue (e.g., through depreciation expense) over the period of their estimated useful economic lives. Expenses incurred to generate currently reported revenue that will not be paid for until future periods, such as the cost of warranties and pension benefits, are charged against that revenue while creating liability for the future expected expenditure. The charge should be for the present value of the liability, preferably discounted at a rate no higher than the yield on the company's debt. Expenses that are predominantly time-related, such as administrative and property expenses, generally are charged against revenue in the period in which they are incurred. The rationale is that the resources created, such as goodwill and other intangibles, rarely can be reliably measured and, if they were recorded as assets, would be untrustworthy and subject to manipulation by managers.

Similar reasoning, though, has not been applied to manufactured inventory, perhaps because it is a tangible rather than an intangible asset. Operating overhead expenses that are fixed (do not vary with inventory produced) are allocated to inventory using arbitrary but not readily manipulated procedures (e.g., direct labor per dollar or hour). These fixed amounts, though, ought to be charged to the period in which they were incurred, based on the assumption that the opportunity value of the inventory in the process of manufacture or finished goods is the cost to replace it, or variable costs incurred. Indeed, German GAAP grant firms an option to value products at variable cost and allocate fixed costs to periods. Where the inventory cannot be replaced at variable cost because the plant is operating at capacity, the asset value of the inventory should instead be the lower of the estimated replacement cost or net realizable value.

As suggested by E. Edwards and P. W. Bell [1961], assets and liabilities that can be valued reliably as of the end of the accounting period should be recorded and the difference between those values and the recorded values should be reported as income (or expense) from holding gains (or losses). The most important element is trustworthiness. In general, this means that the amounts are those that are or, if based on accepted independent valuations, would be based on prices determined from arm's-length market transactions.

Finally, there is a traditional "conservative" bias in accounting that urges delay in the recognition of income and acceleration of the recognition of expense when there is substantial uncertainty about both the timing and the amounts involved. For example, if a construction firm has undertaken a contract spanning several years, where the amount it will eventually gain cannot be determined until the contract is completed, revenue is not reported until it is clear that it has been earned and will be (or has been) received. Alternatively, if the percentage of the completion of the contract can be reliably determined (perhaps by expert engineers), revenue may be reported in proportion to the amount that was earned. (This percentage-of-completion rule is under scrutiny by the IASB and the FASB, as it follows the matching concept and does not conform to the asset/liability approach, which we consider in Chapter 11.) Expenses incurred to earn that revenue will be similarly delayed or matched to the reported revenue, although if they exceed the expected revenue, they will be reported as expenses (reductions in equity) in the current period.

Accountants necessarily must estimate some items of revenue and expense. For example, the amount of revenue that will be earned on a project and employees' pensions that will not be paid until some future time can only be estimated. The estimated revenue, though, will rarely be reported until there is reliable evidence of its amount and that it has, indeed, been earned and will be received. The estimated expense, though, will be reported currently.

One reason for the conservative bias is to act as an offset to managers' optimistic propensity and to incentives for inflating revenue and understating expenses (particularly in bad times), a factor in many recent scandals (as described in Chapter 4). Another reason reflects the view that individuals are upset when they learn that events are worse than they believe they were led to expect, but usually are happy when events are better than expected. Hence, it is better to delay the good news until it is likely to occur and recognize the bad news earlier rather than later. However, excessive conservatism, wherein assets are written down arbitrarily and revenue is deliberately understated, is not acceptable, as it results in an upward bias to reported net income in a future period.

MANAGERIAL DISCRETION IN REPORTING NET INCOME CANNOT BE ELIMINATED

The traditional accounting measure of net income (with or without the change suggested that would incorporate trustworthy current values of inventories and other assets and liabilities) necessarily must be derived, to some extent, from assumptions and judgments, which give managers some ability to affect reported net income. For example, the amount of depreciation of plant, equipment, and other fixed assets is determined by assumptions about the useful economic life of those assets and the rate at which their cost is written off as expenses. The relevant measure would be the reduction (or possibly increase) in the value-in-use of depreciating assets. However, these measurements generally are unreliable and would be subject to deliberate misrepresentation. Accountants, therefore, have used predetermined procedures, such as straight-line or accelerated allocations of the historical cost of fixed assets, to determine periodic depreciation expenses.

The treatment of depreciation illustrates the tradeoff between relevance and reliability. As long as financial statement users understand that, at best, these numbers only approximate the cost to equity holders of holding and using depreciable assets, they can make adjustments to the reported net income numbers, including, at the extreme, ignoring depreciation as a meaningful measure of economic user cost.

Liabilities that must be estimated also give managers an opportunity to affect reported net income. For example, a company's liability for warranties and employee retirement benefits require assumptions about expected future cash flows and discount rates. The amounts that are charged as current-period expenses can vary considerably, depending on those assumptions.

Managers can also time transactions and take advantage of alternative accrual procedures to alter revenue recognition and expense incurrence. For example, they can delay or speed up revenue recognition between accounting periods by specifying when title passes to a purchaser. Period expenses that are not inventoried as part of manufactured goods, such as advertising, research and development, and maintenance, can be reduced or delayed, or incurred earlier than need be so as to affect the amount charged against revenue in an accounting period. IPAs may not object to these actions, because they represent the effect of actual events. Newly appointed CEOs might decide that the values of substantial assets are impaired and write them off (a procedure known as the "big bath"), thereby reducing future expenses. IPAs can and should examine the rationale for such write-offs for conformity with the matching concept and the reflection of economic values.

However, the ability of opportunistic managers to manipulate reported net income with timing and accrual assumptions is limited by three factors. One is the self-correcting nature of accruals. Earlier revenue recognition that overstates net income in a period results in understated net income, usually in the next period. Because direct charges of "extraordinary" events to retained earnings that bypass the income statement are not self-correcting, they rarely are (or should be) accepted by IPAs. The second is managers' decisions to advance or delay the acquisition, purchase, and use of resources. Unfortunately for shareholders, this form of manipulation is more than cosmetic; it can be detrimental to economic performance (although this impact should be mitigated by the fact that lower sales and higher expenses reduce reported income). Third, GAAP does not allow IPAs to accept numbers that are inconsistently determined from period to period. Hence, although managers can, say, initially reduce depreciation expense by assuming a longer economic life for a fixed asset, in the future the depreciation expense must be greater.

Howard Schllit [2002] has identified seven ways that managers have manipulated accounting data. Three involve misreporting revenue: recording revenue too soon or of questionable quality, recording bogus revenue, and boosting income with one-time gains. Three involve violations of the matching concept: shifting current revenue to a later period, shifting current expenses to a later or earlier period, and shifting future expenses to the current period as a special charge. The seventh is failing to record or improperly reducing liabilities. He shows how analysts can detect these "shenanigans" and offers his proprietary computer-based service for detecting these practices.

Thus, users of financial statements should be aware of possible managerial manipulations of financial accounting data that IPAs accept because they conform to GAAP rules and could accurately reflect the operations of a company, or because those IPAs are not competent or have been (perhaps unknowingly) suborned. Users then can evaluate and interpret the reported data.

To summarize, net income should be the amount that can be reliably reported as having increased the claim of equity holders over the net assets of their corporation, although some of the numbers are derived from estimates and judgments. The balance sheet will partially reflect the economic market values of individual assets and liabilities, as of the balance sheet date. To some extent, managers can manipulate the numbers presented in the income statement. That is the best that accounting can do, and, when the numbers reported are trustworthy, that is very valuable to investors and other users of financial statements.

THE VALUE OF AN IPA AUDIT AND ATTESTATION

IPAs audit and attest that the financial statements present a "true and fair" view of the financial condition of the companies whose records they review. This is a valuable service because users otherwise would have reason to be skeptical of the numbers that are reported. Managers who have not performed well, particularly those whose bonuses are based on the numbers reported, might manipulate or even falsify those numbers. Indeed, managers have a variety of reasons for not wishing to publish "bad news," and existing shareholders in their companies may have similar wishes. Successful managers who have satisfied their bonus targets might restrict information and defer the release of "good news" until a later period. In their shareholders' interests (and possibly their own), the managers similarly might misrepresent their enterprise's financial condition and performance to creditors and other users, including rivals. As a consequence, users of financial statements are likely to discount the past performance, financial strength, and prospects of the enterprise relative to that disclosed in the financial statements.

Audits also provide value in detecting errors in the financial statements that are not the result of manipulation by managers but are "noise" (due, for example, to an inadequate internal control system). Correcting this problem makes the numbers more accurate and hence more informative.

Alternatively or concurrently, users might find it worthwhile to spend resources on conducting "due diligence" investigations and obtaining additional information on their own behalf to verify or supplement the numbers reported. Or interested parties such as prospective investors or creditors may forebear from advancing funds if the cost of uncertainty and/ or search and the cost of due diligence exceed the expected benefit from committing resources to the enterprise. The enterprise's owners (shareholders) bear the cost of compensating actions by financial statement users and their unwillingness to invest or extend credit. The reason is that costs borne by potential investors and creditors reduce the expected returns on their funds. Enterprises that impose higher costs on investors, therefore, must promise higher returns as compensation. Shareholders can reduce the costs to users of financial statements, and hence benefit themselves, if they can convince the users that the information conveyed in financial statements is trustworthy (provided it is relevant). As we have already noted, this assurance can be and usually is conveyed when IPAs attest that the statements (in the words of the U.S. standard form) "present fairly, in all material respects, the financial position of X Company as of December 31, 20XX, and the results of its operations and its cash flows for the year then ended in conformity with generally accepted accounting principles."

In most countries, IPAs usually are hired by the boards of directors (often in practice by the senior managers), whose accounting records they audit and whose financial statements they evaluate for conformance with GAAP. In the United States, the U.S. Sarbanes-Oxley Act of 2002 vests the power and responsibility to hire, monitor, and fire IPAs in the board of directors' audit committees (all members of which must be independent of management) of publicly traded corporations. In Germany, the supervisory board or the audit committee within the supervisory board initially appoints the auditor. In the United Kingdom, the audit committee recommends the auditor to the board of directors, and shareholders vote for or against this nominee at the annual general meeting. Although shareholders can vote to reject the directors' choice of auditor, they almost never do. Thus, in many instances, IPAs really are hired by the managers whose reports they audit, or by corporate directors who often are in effect appointed and controlled by those managers.

For this reason, why should users of financial statements believe IPAs' attestations, considering that those users themselves rarely engage IPAs? This question is especially relevant in the light of recent high-profile audit failures. The answer is that IPAs back their attestations with the value of their reputations and professional licenses (which is to say, their current and future income), their financial wealth, and their professional expertise. If there were ever any doubts about the importance of these incentives before Enron failed, there cannot be now: one of the world's largest IPAs, Arthur Andersen, essentially was forced out of business by its shoddy audits of the company. That failure, in turn, has sent a shudder throughout the accounting profession around the world. The Enron debacle and the later failure of WorldCom, also audited by Arthur Andersen, led to the passage of the Sarbanes-Oxley Act of 2002, which created a new regulatory body in the United States to oversee auditors and to punish them for their misdeeds. The new body, the Public Company Accounting Oversight Board, essentially replaced regulation of auditors by the Securities and Exchange Commission (SEC), the states, and the auditors' own professional society, the American Institute of Certified Public Accountants.

The United States has an additional safeguard to ensure that auditors do their jobs. Individuals who relied on financial statements that were attested to by IPAs to their detriment may and often do sue them. Shareholders of corporations registered with the SEC do not even have to show that they relied on or even saw the financial statements; they only must show that the financial statements were materially misleading and that the attesting IPAs were grossly negligent.

Other countries do not grant shareholders such broad rights. The United Kingdom, for example, allows shareholders to sue IPAs for negligence—failure to exercise reasonable care and skill—but they also must show that they relied on the work of the auditor and this reliance resulted in a measurable loss.[12] In Germany, it is mainly the client firm itself that can sue IPAs for negligence, although recently German courts have allowed shareholder suits, as in the United Kingdom. Japan has the toughest rules. Though it allows class-action shareholder lawsuits, such actions are, in practice, very difficult to mount.

Considering the number of audits conducted and financial statements attested to by IPAs, they rarely have been sued, even in the United States. This record might be explained by the difficulty of bringing lawsuits in countries where such actions are costly to pursue, rather than evidence of the quality of IPAs' work. For example, plaintiffs in the United Kingdom who lose their actions usually have to pay the defendant's costs, which reduces the expected benefit to aggrieved financial statement users from suing. This is not the case in the United States, where aggrieved investors can file class actions to recover damages from IPAs. If Arthur Andersen had not been convicted for the criminal offense of obstruction of justice after the Enron failure, it more than likely would have met the same fate as a result of the class-action lawsuits that were or would have been lodged against the firm.

The demise of Arthur Andersen, coupled with the additional regulatory scrutiny of IPAs, almost certainly has induced all IPAs auditing public companies in the United States to be more conservative, and thus more likely to "over-audit" than "under-audit."[13] Because there are costs associated with all audits and these costs increase as auditing becomes intensive, it is not clear that the post-Enron/Sarbanes-Oxley outcome in the United States is optimal. It is not likely to be clear for some time—if ever.

3

Auditing and Accounting Standards: Their Roles and Usefulness to Independent Public Accountants and Investors

Financial statements were audited and attested to by independent public accountants (IPAs) long before the rules governing their application were codified into auditing and accounting standards. Considering our claims in Chapter 2 that the managers and owners of enterprises benefit from presenting financial statements recognized to be trustworthy to potential investors, creditors, and others, and that IPAs have strong incentives to attest competently and truthfully that the enterprises' statements are trustworthy, one might ask why codified and enforced auditing and accounting standards are necessary. We begin by answering that question and then proceed to examine a series of issues relating to the roles of auditing and accounting standards.

THE USEFULNESS OF GAAS AND GAAP FOR IPAs

Codified standards (GAAS and GAAP) help to protect IPAs from three potentially costly problems.[1] First, financial-statement users who lost funds from an investment in or dealings with companies may believe or allege that IPAs conducted incompetent or dishonest audits or allowed their clients to present misleading numbers. With codified standards, IPAs can defend themselves by showing that they followed professionally and, in some countries, governmentally accepted procedural and disclosure rules.

Second, a client might demand that an IPA attest to a number that is potentially misleading because it is inconsistent with a generally accepted definition, and threaten to use the services of another IPA if the IPA does not agree. For example, the CFO of a company might insist that it is unnecessarily costly for the IPA to physically verify inventory. Or the CEO might want to report contingent sales as current-period sales because the goods were "as good as sold" and this treatment better reflects the economic situation of the company. The CFO may also quote opinions of the company's internal accountants or "authoritative" commentators that this is the best treatment. Rather than having to say that the CFO may be biased or misinformed, or that the CEO was overoptimistic, or that the managers wanted to mislead financial statement users, the IPA can point to the codified audit inventory requirement and accounting definition of sales and say that although the CFO and CEO might have good arguments, the IPA is not allowed to violate the GAAS or GAAP rule. The IPA can then point out that *all* IPAs must follow the standards and thereby show such clients that their threats to employ other compliant but reputable IPAs would be ineffective.

Third, "rogue" IPAs might impose costs on other IPAs by trading on the general reputations of IPAs to attest to statements without having conducted proper audits. Or some IPAs might agree to a client's insistence on presenting unusual and potentially misleading numbers in exchange for larger fees or to avoid losing the client's business. If all IPAs must follow GAAS and GAAP, rogue IPAs cannot argue that they just interpreted auditing or accounting rules differently than other IPAs. Rather, they risk losing their certificates and having few viable defenses in lawsuits that charge them with malfeasance.

WHY AUDITING AND ACCOUNTING STANDARDS ARE USEFUL FOR OTHER PARTIES

GAAS and GAAP enable users of financial statements to conserve resources required to validate and evaluate the statements and the bases used to record and report transactions and revaluations. Because these users expect IPAs to audit financial statements in accordance with a known set of standards—GAAS—they can readily discern the extent to which the reported numbers represent what they purport to represent. Of course, some financial statement users might not be conversant with or understand the requirements and content of GAAS and GAAP. However, they can (and should) rely on professional advisors or analysts who have this knowledge. In fact, investors in securities traded in efficient markets can usually rely on the securities' prices as unbiased reflections of the information contained in audited financial statements. Thus, because GAAS requires auditors to verify assets and liabilities using specified procedures, professional analysts and other users have reason to trust the amounts presented for those assets, at least to the extent that a GAAS audit is likely to uncover substantial fraud and misrepresentation. Of course, auditors cannot always detect frauds. Indeed, public expectations for fraud detection may be too high, because it is both economically inefficient and virtually physically impossible to detect all frauds.

Furthermore, some countries' GAAS rules specify that IPAs should have examined and tested a client's system of internal controls and that the IPAs should disclose in their report material problems that were not corrected. Consequently, users of the statements do not have to be concerned about this important aspect of the trustworthiness of financial statements.[2] However, in Japan, auditors are not required to attest to the management's report on internal control.

GAAP similarly make reading and analyzing financial statements more efficient. Knowledgeable users can rely on the definitions having fixed meanings. For example, "current assets" are cash or assets that are expected to be converted into cash or used instead of cash within a year or the accounting cycle, whichever is longer. Under most countries' GAAP, "revenue" means "the actual or expected cash inflow that result from an entity's central operations" [Wiley [US] GAAP, 2002, p. 67]. Cash inflow is "expected" when the entity has substantially completed all it must do to be entitled to future cash flows (or to retain cash already transferred). Revenues generally are measured by the values of the assets exchanged (or liabilities incurred) [ibid., pp. 67–68].

SETTING THE STANDARDS

Accounting standards today are set not by professional accounting organizations as they once were, but instead by more widely representative organizations, such as the Financial Accounting Standards Board (FASB) in the United States and the International Accounting Standards Board (IASB). This has come about for several reasons. The private sector bodies were perceived to act too slowly, in large part because individuals on loan from IPA firms staffed them. The bodies were also seen to be too parochial, with the implication or direct charge that they tended to protect the interests of IPA firms rather than investors and were subservient to the wishes of management, their "real" clients. Private professional bodies also lack political authority and often did not have the power or will to enforce their standards.[3]

In contrast, standard setting by organizations, such as the FASB and the IASB, has been justified on several grounds. One favorable factor is that these bodies include interested parties other than IPAs, which many believe enhances political power and thus forestalls governments from interfering with the standards process. A related advantage is their ability to avoid or deter parochial interests. For example, the standard setters have been charged with reducing managerial discretion to choose among alternative accounting procedures. This charge probably would be more difficult to fulfill with a profession-only standard setter, members of which would have a tendency to represent the individual and conflicting interests of clients.

Another presumed benefit is that these organizations have greater financial support, which has enabled them to hire full-time professional

staffs, overseen by full-time directors. A fully staffed and funded organization should produce more cohesive, effective, and timely responses to
general and emerging issues. Nonetheless, securing financial support remains a problem even for some of these entities. For example, the IASB
relies on voluntary contributions for some 90 percent of its financial needs.

In subsequent chapters we discuss how, nonetheless, governments increasingly have become involved in setting accounting and auditing
standards. Of course, governments have been so involved for some time.
Both the United Kingdom and Germany required publication of financial
statements and audits in the 19th century. The United States did not have
such a requirement until 1934, vesting authority for accounting standards
in the Securities and Exchange Commission (SEC), which in turn has delegated that responsibility to a private body (currently the FASB and formerly the American Institute of Certified Public Accountants [AICPA]). But
in response to the accounting scandals of the past several years, auditors
are now regulated and the standards under which they operate are now set
by a quasi-official government body, the Public Company Accounting
Oversight Board (PCAOB) in the United States and a similar independent
body in the United Kingdom.

Regulation is one thing; government standard setting is quite another.
The basic drawback of having governments set accounting or auditing
standards is that the standards are then likely to be as much the product
of political pressure as they are of professional judgment. To be sure,
private-sector standards bodies, such as the FASB in the United States
and its counterparts in other countries, are also subject to such pressures.
Zeff [2002] describes several instances of governmental or interest-group
interference. The Australian parliament voided a standard that would
permit acquisition at book value. The American Bankers' Association was
successful in getting the FASB to retreat from requiring all debt securities
to be reported at market value. And extensive lobbying of the U.S. Congress by high-tech firms through much of the 1990s dissuaded the FASB
from requiring the expensing of stock options (which the FASB now has
finally required). But unlike private-sector bodies that at least are outside
direct government purview, government agencies almost necessarily are
subject to political pressure because they are a product of the political
system. Once a government agency is involved in setting rules, it is fair
game for citizens to try to change those rules in their favor.

There are clear examples where this has occurred. For example, in the
United States, some oil and gas producers were successful in persuad-
ing the SEC to overrule the action by the FASB in SFAS 19 that required all producers to use successful-efforts rather than full-costing
accounting. Following hearings before the SEC, the FASB rescinded
SFAS 19 and replaced it with SFAS 25, which suggested, but did not
require, successful-efforts accounting. Japan provides an additional example: during that country's banking problems in the 1990s, the Japanese
government relaxed a number of accounting standards associated with

"bad" loans to allow firms to give a better picture of their affairs in a poor economic environment, thereby allowing the issue of accounting reports that were misleading but nonetheless complied with audit requirements.

Government bureaucracy can also lead to increasingly costly and detailed rules that may make financial statements less—rather than more—informative to investors and more costly to shareholders. Government agencies generally are faced with an asymmetric set of punishments and rewards. If they fail to protect the public or are perceived as having been derelict in their responsibilities, they often face severe criticism. On the other hand, they rarely get credit for preventing problems (which usually are not recognized if they do not occur). Nor do they receive credit for allowing new entrants into the fields they regulate, because firms that are kept from entering rarely complain and consumers do not miss what they never experience. In addition, government agencies tend to serve their existing constituencies (which rarely want more competition) to which the agencies look for budgetary and other support, which exacerbates this situation.

Furthermore, government agencies usually do not face competition themselves; hence, they have fewer incentives to become more efficient and to reduce the costs they impose on those they regulate. As a result, they tend to continue requirements that offer investors no or few benefits, particularly those that were imposed in response to a perceived problem that no longer exists.

Most importantly, government agencies tend to multiply and codify rules of practice as they attempt to respond to each individual situation brought to their attention by the press, auditors, and registrants. Worse yet, the rules adopted tend to be those that relate to the specific scandal; consequently, they may not have much relevance for future shortcomings while imposing costs on investors.[4] Rather than rely on the judgment of IPAs to determine that corporate financial statements adhere to the substance rather than just to the letter of GAAP, government agencies tend to prefer and promulgate sets of specific rules. This specificity often is a reaction to a situation where that judgment appears to have been exercised incorrectly. To show legislators and the public that it has dealt with the situation, regulators adopt rules to reduce the scope of IPAs' judgment. An unintended consequence is that corporate managers can argue, often successfully, that their auditors should not object to a potentially misleading practice because it is permitted by a provision of the codified GAAP.

In fact, there are drawbacks or costs associated with giving standard setting to any body outside of the professions. Stakeholders other than IPAs and their clients are likely to demand more data than are optimal for shareholders, because the shareholders bear all the costs but do not get all the benefits. These stakeholders' demands are likely to be looked on favorably or even extended by an independent, professionally managed and staffed standard-setting organization.

Any standard setter, private or government, also is likely to proliferate rules; after all, that is its job. But there are reasons for this tendency.

Standard setters are subject to constant requests from company managers and IPAs for clarification, which leads to more rules or at least interpretations of rules already promulgated. In the United States, where IPAs have been subject to litigation, IPAs want bright lines and specific rules that they believe can help shelter them from liability.

Left to its own devices, therefore, the market would demand that companies disclose information about themselves under the guidance of accounting and auditing standards set *by at least some organization*. This is not the conventional wisdom, of course. In the conventional view, it took bold government action after the stock market crash of 1929 to create the SEC and to give that body authority to set accounting standards—authority it eventually delegated to private bodies, first to the accounting profession itself (through the AICPA), and then to the FASB in 1974.

But the fact is that, despite difficulties, GAAS and GAAP were well developed *without government intervention*, at least in commercially advanced countries [Benston, 1969]. As we discuss in the next chapter, in the United States the accounting profession reached general agreement about generally accepted auditing and accounting procedures before establishment of the SEC, and the New York Stock Exchange (NYSE) adopted these standards. In the United Kingdom, France, Germany, and other countries, private-sector standard setting has occurred within a legal framework that has included general accounting disclosure and audit requirements. Prior to the existence of formal standard setting, as public interest in investing increased, stock markets adopted financial reporting standards that must be followed by companies they accepted for listing—evidence of a different sort that markets can and will demand disclosure, even without governmental mandates [Benston, 1975].

Indeed, for many years in the United Kingdom, the Companies Acts and other legislation have required just a minimum level of financial disclosure by all companies and generally required valuation at historical cost. The Acts require only audits and specify that an auditor must be a member of a recognized body of accountants and must be independent. Those bodies laid down audit guidelines and later produced GAAS, which is now set by an independent body outside the profession (see Chapter 5). The London Stock Exchange also has imposed audit and disclosure requirements based on U.K. GAAS and GAAP.[5]

In Germany, the stock exchanges acted by requiring corporations listed in particular market segments to disclose financial statements in accordance with International Financial Reporting Standards (IFRS) or U.S. GAAP, and large corporations successfully lobbied the government to give them the option to prepare such financial statements in lieu of financial statements under German GAAP years before the European Union (EU) adopted IFRS set by the IASB. This led to a partial replacement of government-established GAAP by privately developed GAAP due to the need to enhance the ability of users to understand and compare financial reports of listed corporations with their international peers.

Some parties have benefited, however, from government-mandated disclosure standards. For example, there is some reason to believe that established corporations and investment banks benefit because they are or become familiar with existing rules. The larger of these companies also benefit from economies of scale in adopting their records to meet standards that require complex data processing. The costs for new and foreign corporations to meet these standards limit their entry into the market for resources. This may be one reason that the SEC has insisted that foreign companies that want to have their securities traded directly in the United States reconcile their financial statements with U.S. GAAP.

However they are developed, whether privately or under the auspices of governments, the existence of nationally developed GAAP does not mean that investors necessarily are unable to compare financial reports from companies headquartered in different countries. If the different national standards are substantially similar in their objectives (as they are for U.S. GAAP and IFRS, for instance) and the differences are clear and can be substantially reconciled at low cost, the existence of alternatives can be beneficial if corporations can choose among the standards. The benefits result from the development and empirical testing of procedures that are, indeed, reasonable alternatives. For example, U.S. GAAP do not permit internally produced identifiable intangible assets (e.g., patents and trademarks) to be recorded as assets, while IFRS requires recognition of development costs if certain conditions are met and even allows revaluations of recognized intangibles, although under restrictive circumstances. Experience with revaluations can provide evidence about the reliability of numbers produced and attested under those circumstances.

On the other hand, when the individual GAAP requirements are very detailed and specific, reconciliation could be costly. Any gain from a similarity of standards may be obtained at the cost of freezing innovations in standard setting. We analyze those difficulties and costs of reconciling U.S. GAAP and IFRS in Chapter 9 and analyze the larger issue of benefits and costs of a single or multiple global financial-accounting standards in Chapter 10.

PRINCIPLES-BASED VERSUS RULES-BASED ACCOUNTING STANDARDS

Accounting standards in the United States are characterized as "rules-based." The standard independent auditor's report states: "the financial statements present fairly, in all material respects, the financial position of X Company as of Date, and the results of its operations and its cash flows for the year then ended in conformity with generally accepted accounting principles." Thus, if the enumerated and codified accounting principles have been followed as specified, presumably the IPA firm has done its job. Furthermore, considering the propensity of attorneys to sue IPAs on behalf of aggrieved investors, specific rules have been seen as a shield behind which IPAs can take cover.

However, the rules-based U.S. accounting standards have been blamed for allowing and even encouraging opportunistic managers to structure transactions to produce misleading financial statements that their IPAs would have to or could attest did "fairly present the financial condition of the corporation in accordance with generally accepted accounting principles." In particular, with respect to Enron, the audit firm Arthur Andersen was charged with designing financial instruments that met the technical requirements of GAAP while violating the intent. Public disclosure of Enron's procedures has given rise to a renewed debate over whether accounting standards should be based on rules or principles.

Proponents of the "principles-based" approach (which we favor) point out that it is not possible for the accounting authorities to write rules that can cover all situations. The attempt often results in very long statements that are difficult to read, to say nothing of applying their provisions. The best example is FAS 133 (as amended by FAS 138 and FAS 149) on financial instruments, which is presented in 449 pages (FASB, 2003, Volume II); the comparable IAS 39 has 289 pages (including illustrative examples and implementation guidance; IASB 2004 bound volume), plus there are four amendments of the FAS outstanding (as of July 2004).

A less extreme example is accounting for leases, wherein a distinction is made between finance (capital) leases (which give rise to an asset and a liability) and an operating lease, which is not included in a balance sheet. IAS 17 (22 pages) defines a finance lease (all others are operating leases) as "a lease that transfers substantially all the risk of rewards incident to ownership of an asset" (IAS 17.3). A lease is a finance lease when its term is for the "major part" of an asset's economic life or the present value of the minimum lease payments is "substantially all" of the fair value of the leased asset. FAS 13 (48 pages) specifies that the lease term must be at least 75 percent of the estimated economic life of the property or that the present value of the minimum lease payments must be at least 90 percent of fair value of the property less any related investment tax credit realized by the lessor. Under the broader, more principles-based IAS, accountants might account for the same leases differently, depending on how they interpret "a major part" and "substantially all." Under the more specific FAS, a manager who wants to have lease recorded as operating rather than financing can structure it with a term that is 74.5 percent of the estimated economic life or that violates some other prescribed attribute. Thus, both approaches might result in differences or be abused.

The United Kingdom has followed a principles-based approach continuously. As we discuss in Chapter 5, chartered accountants are given professional responsibility for determining that accounting statements show a true-and-fair view. Until 2000, all extant U.K. accounting standards took up "only" 900 pages. More recent standards have become bulky and more detailed, reflecting both the more complex items being considered and the standard setters' desire to harmonize with U.S. GAAP and IFRS (which follows the U.S. rules-based approach).

We favor a principles-based approach with a "true-and-fair override" for several reasons. One is that it would return to IPAs both the opportunity and responsibility to use their professional judgments as to whether the financial reports of a company they audited actually fairly represent its financial condition, operations, and cash flow. This should serve to reduce the propensity of professionally staffed accounting standard-setting organizations from proliferating excessively detailed standards. Another factor in favor of principles is that it should increase the IPAs' power over their clients, who could no longer claim that the IPAs must attest that company statements are "fair" because they conform to the letter of GAAP. We recognize, though, that giving IPAs the authority to apply their professional judgment requires oversight to ensure that those IPAs who fail to act professionally (because of a lack of probity, skill, or willingness to refuse or withdraw from an engagement when necessary) are effectively disciplined. In Chapter 10 we propose some structural procedures that should achieve this goal.

OTHER FORMS OF GOVERNMENT INVOLVEMENT

In addition to the forms of government involvement previously mentioned are attempts to prevent IPAs from acting in ways that discourage competition with their profession, which can impose unnecessary costs on firms and their shareholders. This has been a problem in some countries. In Germany, for example, the (public) *Wirtschaftsprüferkammer*, with compulsory membership of auditors, has had rigorous admission clauses, such as university degree and now 4 years (before 1995, 5 years) of practice in accounting firms, and then a wide-ranging final examination. This has had the effect of restricting entry into the profession to persons who are almost 30 years of age. Entry to the accounting profession in Japan is similarly restricted, and the pass rate for the government-controlled examinations is very low.

However, although in the United Kingdom there have been a number of investigations of the possible anticompetitive behavior by the accounting profession, evidence of such behavior has not been found. In the United States, prior to the creation of the SEC in 1933 there were no government-imposed requirements that enterprises use the services of IPAs. Nevertheless, stock exchanges required IPA audits, and many financial institutions expected their larger borrowers to present IPA-audited financial statements. At present, only corporations that are subject to the U.S. Securities Acts must obtain IPA attestations. As we describe in Chapter 2, financial statement users who want such attestations will impose costs on enterprises that do not provide them, such as higher interest on debt and lower prices paid for equities.

Prior to active government involvement, however, auditing and accounting standards do not appear to have been established by the accounting profession as a means of restricting competition. In countries such as the United Kingdom and Germany, which had early government-mandated financial disclosure, any professionally qualified IPA could fulfill the requirements. The rules imposed by the SEC in the United States were more complicated, which served to restrict audits by smaller IPA firms. Over time, as the rules became more complex, it became increasingly difficult for smaller firms to compete. The FASB expanded the corpus of GAAP in the United States, as did other standard setters in other jurisdictions, although to a somewhat lesser extent. In part for this reason, various mergers reduced the number of top-tier accounting firms from eight to five. The demise of Arthur Andersen now leaves just four such firms, a situation that may lead to higher costs for audited firms and investors (beyond the costs associated with more intensive auditing in the post–Sarbanes-Oxley environment) as a result of less competition, both in terms of pricing and ideas as to how auditing can be conducted efficiently and how financial information can be presented effectively.

The United States is not the only country that has largely abandoned self-regulation by professional bodies in the wake of various accounting scandals. In 2002, the United Kingdom established an independent body similar to the PCAOB. The European Union also has proposed rules for enhanced disciplinary systems for auditors. These include a quality-assurance system of statutory audits that most member states have already implemented and public oversight and regulatory arrangements. The disciplinary measures include the possibility of revoking the approval of the statutory auditor. Furthermore, where fraud is involved, governments can and do criminally prosecute those involved. At this writing, a number of former Enron executives have been convicted for such offenses. European governments also have the ability to bring criminal prosecutions. We discuss the extent to which these measures are necessary and effective in subsequent chapters.

4

Corporate Financial Reporting and Regulation in the United States

We review in this chapter the history of rules governing financial disclosure by corporations in the United States. We begin with an overview of state regulation, which preexisted federal legislation enacted in the 1930s and which still exists. We then turn to the federal regulatory regime.

STATE REGULATION

Before the Securities Act of 1933 and the Securities Exchange Act of 1934 were enacted, only individual states regulated the issuance of securities. Securities trading was not specifically regulated but fell under state laws governing contracts and transactions generally. Legislation governing the issuance of securities was first passed by Kansas in 1911, followed by 22 additional states (primarily southern and western) in the next 2 years.[1] This legislation was motivated by the "populist" sentiment in these states, where eastern bankers and speculators were distrusted by largely rural populations. Indeed the title for these statutes—"blue-sky laws"— originates from the description of securities promoters as people who "would sell building lots in the great blue sky."

The first blue-sky laws required registration of securities that would be offered for sale to state residents and gave a state administrator the power to determine whether or not a security should be sold initially to state residents. After World War I most of the eastern states also passed laws that regulated the sale of securities, although these laws generally were not as restrictive as the earlier blue-sky laws. Today, all states except Connecticut have laws that require registration for stock issues offered exclusively to state residents. All but a few states (most notably New York) require registration whether or not the securities are subject to the federal Securities Act of 1933.

These state laws cover one or more categories: (a) regulation of brokers, dealers, and investment advisers; (b) fraud statutes; and (c) registration of securities. Most states' laws address two or three of these objectives. The first two categories are broadly similar to the provisions of the U.K. Prevention of Fraud (Investments) Act 1958.

The provisions for registration of securities may be further categorized into "merit" regulation and "disclosure" requirements. Merit regulation is used in some form and to some degree by most states, empowering an administrator to deny permission for a security to be offered to state residents if the administrator believes that the potential purchasers might be defrauded or might otherwise lose their investments. Section 306a of the Uniform Securities Act, for example, which has been adopted in whole or part by a majority of states, enables a state administrator to issue a stop order or not accept a registration statement if the administrator finds that the offering would constitute a fraud on the purchaser; the underwriting and selling discounts are unreasonable; promoters' profits or participation are unreasonable; or amounts or kinds of options are unreasonable. In other states, administrators can deny registration if they find that the issuer is in any way dishonest, the issuers' affairs are in unsound condition, or the activities of the issuer are not based on sound business principles. Some states require their administrators to find that the securities offered for sale are "fair, just and equitable" and "not working (constituting) a fraud."[2] Other states require some form of disclosure of financial information, underwriter's fees and commissions, and so forth, but do not judge the merits of the securities issued.

The principal stock exchanges—the New York and American—also imposed disclosure requirements on listed corporations. While the extent of disclosure was not as great as that which evolved under the Securities and Exchange Commission (SEC), the items given were, for the most part, quite extensive. For example, an examination of data published by New York Stock Exchange (NYSE)-listed companies in *Moody's Manuals* revealed that, in 1926, all provided balance sheets and income statements, 82 percent of which were audited by certified public accountants [Benston, 1969B, p. 519]. All the balance sheets separated current from noncurrent assets and liabilities. On the income statements, all reported net income, 55 percent revealed sales, 45 percent the cost of goods sold, and 71 percent depreciation. By 1933 (before passage of the Securities Exchange Act of 1934 appeared to be politically possible), these percentages had risen to 62 percent for sales, 53 percent for cost of goods sold, and 93 percent for depreciation. Fully 94 percent of the companies indicated audits by CPAs. Given that the NYSE accounted for 70 percent of security transactions on all exchanges and that the American Stock Exchange (and possibly the others) had disclosure rules similar to those in force at the

NYSE, it is fair to conclude that disclosure in the United States, on the whole, did not await legislative action. Periodic disclosure requirements were not applied to over-the-counter companies until after 1964.

What about regulation of accountants? The United States imported independent professional accounting and auditing from the United Kingdom. Indeed, the important U.S. accounting firms began as branches of U.K. firms. Prior to the 20th century, the principal users of financial statements were creditors and controlling owners of enterprises who were concerned about how the managers of those enterprises had used the resources entrusted to them (the stewardship function). Financial statements were (and still are) seen as managerial reports that are audited and attested to by independent public accountants (IPAs). As general public ownership of corporations increased and stocks increasingly were traded on organized exchanges (particularly following World War I), financial statements that presented numbers that could be useful for decisions on what stocks to buy or sell—past net income that might foretell future earnings—were demanded.

In 1917, the American Institute of Accountants (AIA, predecessor to the American Institute of Certified Public Accountants [AICPA]) endorsed an influential memorandum entitled "Approved Methods for the Preparation of Balance Sheet Statements."[3] In 1929, this memorandum, rewritten and entitled "Verification of Financial Statements," was approved by the Council of the Institute and endorsed by the Federal Reserve Board. In 1930, the NYSE began a cooperative venture (headed by George O. May) with the AIA to formalize acceptable accounting and auditing policies and practices. In 1932, the Committee outlined five "principles" on which audited statements should be based [American Institute of Accountants, 1932–1934].[4] The "principles" were adopted by AICPA. In 1933, the NYSE required that newly listed companies send annual audited financial statements to their shareholders, a practice already followed by almost all listed companies.

FEDERAL REGULATION

Despite the disclosure initiatives of state governments and the stock exchanges and the absence of compelling (or even much) evidence that inadequate disclosure had been a problem, the trauma of the 1929 stock market crash and the later (unrelated) depression that began about October 1930 led to strong demands for the federal government to become involved in regulating securities markets and disclosure by corporations whose shares were traded on public markets. There was also significant support in Congress at the time for federal merit regulation. Notably, a number of bills were introduced in Congress that would have established a federal blue-sky law and commission. Nonetheless, President Roosevelt rejected merit regulation of securities issuance and trading and instead introduced a disclosure statute. In his message to Congress, he described the philosophy of the Securities Act of 1933, the first piece of securities legislation Congress ultimately adopted, as follows:

> There is, however, an obligation upon us to insist that every issue of new securities sold in interstate commerce shall be accompanied by full publicity and information, and that no essentially important element attending the issue shall be concealed from the buying public. This proposal adds to the ancient rule of *caveat emptor* the further doctrine "let the seller also beware." It puts the burden of telling the whole truth on the seller. It should give impetus to honest dealing in securities and thereby bring back public confidence.

The 1933 Act sought to protect investors by requiring that prospectuses be filed that included specified financial data audited by independent public accountants. The following year, Congress enacted the Securities Exchange Act of 1934, which required *periodic* financial statement disclosure of corporations for the first time (while also requiring the registration of stock exchanges and securities dealers and brokers).

The SEC has used its authority under these acts to specify reporting requirements for publicly traded corporations. Originally, this "Regulation S-X" applied only to corporations whose stock was traded on registered exchanges or who had registered securities under the Securities Act of 1933 and had over $2 million in assets. Unlike the United Kingdom, but similar to Germany, not all publicly traded equity securities are listed on a stock exchange. A large portion of the stock in publicly held corporations is traded on the over-the-counter market, which is highly decentralized. Securities of local corporations may be traded only in their areas, while a large number of better-known over-the-counter securities are traded regionally or nationally. However, in 1964 Congress amended the Securities Exchange Act of 1934 to apply to all corporations (where stock is not owned entirely by residents of a single state) that had (at that time) over $1 million in assets and a single class of equity securities held by over 750 holders.

Both securities acts, therefore, now essentially apply to all but small or intrastate-owned corporations. But, unlike the accounting regime in the European Union, the large number of small, privately owned companies with limited liability are not required to make their accounting reports public.

In retrospect, it is interesting to consider why Congress got into the act of regulating corporate disclosure, despite evidence that the states and the exchanges had already addressed the issue. Furthermore, almost no evidence was presented in the U.S. Senate Stock Exchange Practices (Pecora) Hearings showing that inadequate and/or misleading disclosure was associated with subsequent losses to investors. One reason may be the agitation throughout the 1920s by such writers as William Z. Ripley [1927], who accused publicly owned corporations of giving the public dishonest and deceptive financial reports. Stephen A. Zeff reports that a 1926 article by Ripley resulted in widespread consternation, marked by a decline in the stock market and one of President Coolidge's rare reported utterances

("The stock market suffered a decline when premature news of the article leaked") [Zeff, 1972, pp. 119–120]. However, most of the examples of non-disclosure and misleading accounting given by Ripley in his book [1927, especially Chapter VI] are from the early 1900s.

Overstatement of assets or capitalization (also called "watered stock") was an often-criticized practice. Henry Clews [1908, p. 250] claimed that "on average, the railroads of the country were capitalized at probably 50 percent in excess of their cost." He particularly noted [ibid., pp. 205–206] that the J.P. Morgan syndicate increased the recorded value of the assets of the companies they combined to form U.S. Steel, from which they took $62,500,000 in fees.[5] Indeed, there appears to have been a considerable amount of litigation about the "true" value of property exchanged by promoters for stock. A thorough review of the U.S. court records to about 1929 by David L. Dodd [1930] listed almost 300 cases that were in some way related to watered stock. Most of these cases dealt with non-fraudulent differences of opinion about the value of property. But Dodd stated [ibid., p. 21], "The present state of American law with regard to the rights of a stockholder is such that it is exceedingly difficult for him to prove compensation for the loss which he suffers because his stock was watered."

Because of the 1930s' Great Depression and the 1929 stock market crash, the U.S. Senate held hearings in 1933 and 1934 on the allegations made by Ripley and others. Yet a survey of the 17 volumes of the 1934 hearings that preceded the imposition of periodic disclosure requirements revealed only two instances of alleged dishonest and deceptive reporting [Benston, 1969A, pp. 52–53]. Nevertheless, allegations were made and widely publicized by the press that the hearings had revealed a series of dishonest or at least questionable practices that mislead investors, which (it was alleged) caused or at least exacerbated the collapse of the securities markets.

For example, in his book *Wall Street Under Oath* [1939, p. 251], Ferdinand Pecora (a brilliant New York prosecutor who conducted the hearings for the Senate committee) gave the example of the Guardian Group of banks. Its stock sold at around $250 to $300 a share in 1929, but within the year the price dropped to $75 to $80. Pecora said that the directors tried to shore up the market by paying dividends and issuing glowing earnings reports, but "[t]he beautiful annual financial statements which had aroused so much enthusiasm and congratulations among their banking colleagues did not arrest the debacle." Pecora did not analyze, however, the extent to which unanticipated losses and declining business conditions might have caused the decline in the Guardian Group's stock price.

OVERVIEW OF THE PUBLIC SECURITIES MARKETS TODAY

Corporations that publicly issue securities may list them on one of several markets. The stock exchanges, where trades are made through securities brokers, include the NYSE, the oldest and most prestigious market; the American Stock Exchange (AMEX), which lists smaller corporations; and five specialized or regional exchanges (the Boston, National [formerly Cincinnati], and Philadelphia Stock Exchanges and the International Securities and Pacific Exchanges). NYSE dominates the exchanges, with 99 percent of the value and 73 percent of the number of the approximately 3,000 stocks listed on exchanges in 2001. About an equal number of corporations are listed on NASDAQ, where stocks are traded by and through dealers rather than brokers. In 2001, 84 percent of trading volume went through NYSE. Volume on NASDAQ, though, in recent years has exceeded the volume on the NYSE. In recent years, however, trading over the new electronic communications networks (ECNs)—which match trades directly by computer without human intervention—has increased substantially. As of 2001, nine ECNs were registered with the SEC. The growth of ECNs has been fueled, in large measure, by low trading costs.

Under the Securities Exchange Act of 1934, exchanges must be registered with the SEC, which must approve the rules adopted by the exchanges. The SEC also registers brokers and securities dealers and investment advisors. However, much of the securities industry is self-regulated. The SEC has delegated to the exchanges and the National Association of Securities Dealers (NASD) day-to-day oversight of trading.

Equity investments by households are made directly and indirectly through mutual funds and pension funds. As of Dec. 31, 2001, U.S. residents and companies held a bit more than $15 billion in corporate equities, of which $1.2 billion (8.0 percent) was in foreign equities.[6] Households held 41.6 percent of total equities directly or in bank personal trusts (representing only 2.1 percentage points of the 41.6), 20.6 percent in pension funds, and 18.8 percent through mutual funds. The balance of stocks is held by insurance companies (6.8 percent), the foreign sector (10.1 percent), and other investors (2.2 percent).

The relative holdings of equities have changed substantially over the past half-century. In 1950, households held 90.2 percent of the equities. The percentages dropped to 78.5 percent in 1970 and 56.4 percent in 1990. Pension funds' holdings grew from 0.8 percent in 1950 to 9.2 percent in 1970 and to 24.4 percent in 1990. Mutual funds also increased substantially, from 2.0 percent of the total in 1950 to 5.2 percent in 1970 and 7.0 percent in 1990. Since 1990, mutual fund holdings have accelerated, increasing by 11.8 percent, primarily as a consequence of shifts from direct to indirect equity holding by households. Thus, a substantial proportion of equities in the United States are purchased and sold by professionals employed by mutual funds and pensions. However, ownership by households still is large, slightly exceeding the amount held by institutions that invest for them.

SEC RULES GOVERNING FINANCIAL DISCLOSURE OF PUBLIC CORPORATIONS

The U.S. securities acts differ from the contemporary U.K. Companies Acts (on which they were based) primarily in the creation of a commission to administer the statutes actively. Unlike the Companies Acts, which required disclosure of specific items and additional disclosure as required to give a "true and fair view," the U.S. statutes specify that the financial statements shall be "in such detail and in such form as the Commission [SEC] shall prescribe." In this important regard, the U.S. securities acts are based on the state "blue-sky" laws, with the important difference that the federal acts require only disclosure rather than prior approval of securities that might be offered to the public. However, from its inception, the SEC has imposed requirements that go well beyond disclosure.

First, corporations with securities listed on registered exchanges (after 1964, all but small, closely held or totally intrastate-owned corporations) must report directly to the SEC.[7] The Securities Act of 1933 requires that registration statements be filed with the SEC and that most of the data be contained in a prospectus be given to potential purchasers of securities in advance of a solicitation. The Securities Exchange Act of 1934 requires that annual and other reports (e.g., 10-K, 10-Q, 8-K) be filed with the SEC, where the public may inspect them. (Since 1996 these statements have been available over the Internet through the SEC's EDGAR system.) However, the SEC is not just a repository for prospectuses and periodic reports. It serves as an enforcement agency with respect to the laws. It undertakes investigations, administrative proceedings, civil cases, and injunction actions. Cases that require criminal prosecution are referred to the Department of Justice.

Second, the SEC controls the information that is provided to investors. It requires corporations to send annual reports, including financial statements, to stockholders in advance of meetings. SEC Rule 14a-3 (as amended) states that a company must note and explain any material differences between the statements presented to shareholders and those filed with the SEC. Although the SEC does not specify the form of the reports made by management to security holders, Rule 14a-3 effectively puts the contents of the statements under its control.

The SEC's control over the contents of financial statements could be almost absolute. Sections 19a of the 1933 Act and 13b of the 1934 Act give the SEC the power to prescribe

> the items or details to be shown in the balance sheet and the earnings statements, and the methods to be followed in the preparation of reports, in the appraisal or valuation of assets and liabilities, in the determination of depreciation and depletion, in the differentiation of recurring and nonrecurring income, in the differentiation of investment and operating income. And in the preparation, where the Commission deems it necessary or desirable, of separate and/or consolidated balance sheets or income accounts . . .

For the most part, the SEC has not used this power extensively, but has rather followed the generally accepted practices followed by the accounting profession. Although disclosure rather than approval is supposed to be the philosophy of the securities acts, the SEC has taken the position that:

where financial statements filed...are prepared in accordance with accounting principles for which there is no substantial authoritative support, such financial statements will be presumed to be misleading or inaccurate *despite disclosures* contained in the certificate of the accountant or in foot notes to the statements provided the matter involved are material. [SEC Accounting Series Release No. 4, 1938, emphasis added.]

"Substantial authoritative support" has been defined, operationally, to be those procedures adopted by the public accounting profession.[8] In part because of earlier criticism of accounting practices that allegedly permitted corporations to overstate assets, and in part because the agency has wanted to avoid criticism that might follow if, ex post, registered corporations were allowed to overstate assets or net income, until the 1990s the SEC encouraged and enforced the conservative bias generally followed by public accountants. Most prominently, the SEC was a very strong force in banishing the practice of writing up assets above their original cost [Defliese, 1958, p. 71]. Furthermore, as Louis H. Rappaport noted [1963, p. 53], "there was a period . . . when the SEC was conducting something in the nature of a campaign to eliminate goodwill from all balance sheets filed with it." The SEC also did not allow registrants to give investors estimates of future earnings [Rappaport, p. 73], statements of assets at fair market value [Barr and Koch, 1959, pp. 181–182], and appraisals of almost any sort [Defliese, 1958, p. 71]. These earlier actions are instructive, considering the current movement by the SEC (and the accounting standards authorities in the United States and the European Union) toward requiring corporations to include market values in their balance sheet and reflect changes in those values in their income statements.

In 1940 the SEC adopted Regulation S-X, which contains the rules governing accounting disclosure that must be followed in statements filed with the Commission. The regulation does not specify the statements that must be filed—these are given in the instructions to the required forms (e.g., S-1 for the registration of securities under the 1933 Act and 10-K for annual reports required under the 1934 Act). But Regulation S-X governs the form and content of those statements. These are very detailed and include the generally accepted accounting principles adopted by the AICPA and its standard-setting committees and (at present) the Statements of Financial Accounting Standards adopted by the Financial Accounting Standards Board (FASB). Regulation S-X also specifies the qualifications and the reports required of accountants.

More recently, the SEC has tended to emphasize market-based data. In 1976, it imposed a requirement for registered corporations to report the replacement value of fixed assets (ASR 190). The requirement was rescinded in 1978 when the SEC recognized that the data were costly to estimate, of limited reliability, and of no apparent value to investors. In 1978 the FASB adopted FAS 33 to replace replacement accounting with supplemental reporting of price-level–adjusted financial statements that might reflect the changes in the purchasing power of the dollar. This requirement was removed in 1982 when the numbers reported were seen to be of limited value to investors. The SEC ruled against the FASB's 1977 decision (in FAS 19) to require oil and gas producers to adopt the successful-efforts method, whereby the cost of discovering and developing unsuccessful (dry) wells is written off as a current expense rather than capitalized and written off against the production from successful wells (full-cost allocation). Instead, in 1978 the SEC proposed that oil and gas producers include the present value of discovered product (reserve recognition accounting [RRA]) in their financial reports on an experimental 3-year basis. But, as in the case of replacement cost accounting, the cost of applying this method was very high, the results were very unreliable, and the requirement for RRA was not extended. In November 1982, the FASB issued FAS 69, which required disclosure (but not inclusion) of much of the information that had been required for RRA.

Despite its negative experience with firms reporting the present values of oil and gas and its earlier (1930s) experience with overstated estimates of asset values, the SEC has supported the increasing emphasis of the FASB to require companies to include the market values of financial assets in financial statements. At the same time, though, the agency has continued some its previous conservative policies, such as requiring companies that have substantial "up-front" customer-development expenses to expense rather than capitalize (defer) these costs and write them off against future revenue that is expected to be generated from these investments.

THE ROLE OF THE AICPA

Until FASB was created in 1973, the AICPA, as the principal non-government authoritative body, had considerable power to prescribe accounting disclosure and measurement. Although the AICPA did codify general standards before 1933, it seems clear that the considerable increase in its post-SEC activity was due to the creation of the SEC and its chief accountant's policy that it was preferable for the AICPA to promulgate its own accounting rules and principles.

The AICPA's Committee on Accounting Procedure (CAP), created in 1936 and enlarged in 1938, issued 51 Accounting Research Bulletins (ARBs) until it was disbanded in 1959. The ARBs suggested rather than demanded specific practices and, on occasion, allowed that several alternative methods were acceptable. However, the AICPA's ARBs generally had the force of the SEC behind them. Also, the SEC could veto or change an opinion. One example of this is the CAP's failure, because of SEC opposition, to issue an ARB in 1950 that accepted upward revaluation of assets in a quasi-reorganization, despite its unanimous approval by the Committee [Zeff, 1972, pp. 156–157].

In 1959 the Accounting Principles Board (APB) was established because of dissatisfaction with the "progress" of the CAP, particularly by the SEC. Unlike its predecessor, the APB commissioned research projects that were

supposed to lead to pronouncements. However, less than half the pronouncements were preceded by published studies. Before its replacement
in 1973 by the FASB, the APB issued 43 ARBs and four statements. The
major opinions covered topics such as investment credit, funds statements, leases, reporting the results of operations, income tax allocation,
convertible debt, earnings per share, business combinations, intangible
assets, investments in common stock, accounting changes, and interest on
receivables and payables. These opinions were not always universally
accepted. For example, Opinion No. 2, on investment credit accounting,
was rejected by some of the eight major accounting firms and the SEC and
was partially rescinded by Opinion No. 4. ARB No. 43 codified the preceding revised and non-rescinded ARBs.

In the main, the thrust of the APBs was to eliminate or at least reduce
alternative accounting methods for what appeared to be the same transaction. This approach was dictated, in large measure, by the criticism the
profession received from the financial press, lawsuits against CPA firms,
and pressure from Manuel Cohen, then the SEC chairman. To bolster support for APB opinions, in 1964 the AICPA membership adopted Rule 203 of
the restated Code of Professional Ethics. It requires that a "member shall not
express an opinion that financial statements are presented in conformity
with generally accepted accounting principles if such statements contain any
departure from an Opinion of the Accounting Principles Board which has
a material effect on the statements taken as a whole." An exception is allowed if the member believes that the statements would otherwise be
misleading, in which event the departure and its effects must be disclosed,
but the onus is on the accountant to justify the deviation from the opinions.

Nevertheless, the criticism continued, directed largely at the accounting
practices of conglomerates and other firms that grew by mergers and acquisitions, and of land development and real estate companies. In addition,
the number of lawsuits filed against accountants, with accompanying news
stories, increased. The AICPA and the SEC also were criticized for having
accounting rules established by volunteer CPAs who continued their associations with their firms and their firms' clients. In 1971, the AICPA
appointed two committees to study how financial principles should be
established. One of these, the Wheat Committee, issued its report in 1972.
It recommended that the APB be abolished and replaced with an independent and well-funded and staffed organization, the Financial Accounting Standards Board (FASB). The Study Group on Objectives of
Financial Statements (the Trueblood Committee) issued its report in 1973,
which became the basis for the FASB's *Statement of Financial Accounting
Concepts No. 1*.

STANDARD SETTING BY THE FASB

The FASB was established in 1973 with a large budget and staff (now
including about 40 professionals), a well-paid seven-member board who

must have severed all prior connections with their firms or institutions, and the determination to reduce the area of choice among alternative accounting practices. The SEC accepts its pronouncements as authoritative [Accounting Series Release 150, December 1973]. The Board is appointed by the 16 trustees of the Financial Accounting Foundation, 11 of whom represent the AICPA and eight other organizations (American Accounting Association; Association for Investment Management and Research; Financial Executives International [FEI]; Government Finance Officers Association; Institute of Management Accountants; National Association of State Auditors, Comptrollers and Treasurers; and Securities Industry Association), and five of whom serve as at-large members and are selected by the Board of Trustees.

The FASB issues Statements of Financial Accounting Standards (FAS) that CPAs must follow in accordance with Rule 203 and that the SEC has adopted as generally accepted accounting principles (GAAP). The FASB also issues Interpretations that modify or extend the contents of previous issued FAS. These also are considered to be part of the mandatory first layer of GAAP. Through October 2004, the FASB has issued 150 FAS, 33 of which were superseded or rescinded, leaving 117 outstanding, and 46 Interpretations, 14 of which were superseded or rescinded, leaving 32 outstanding.

In July 1984 the FASB created the Emerging Issues Task Force (EITF). It has 13 voting members, including senior technical partners of major national CPA firms and representatives of financial-statement-user organizations (e.g., the FEI) and the active participation of the SEC's chief accountant. The EITF meets every 8 weeks. If its positions are ratified by the FASB at a public meeting, they become part of GAAP. Through December 2002 it issued 447 Issue Pronouncements and 105 Discussion Memoranda. The FAS and EITF pronouncements are elaborated on in question-and-answer (Q&A) form by implementation guides. Through December 2002, 16 have been issued, many of which have hundreds of Q&As. In addition, Technical Bulletins, prepared by the FASB staff, provide guidance on accounting and reporting problems; 50 were issued between 1979 and 2002. They are part of the last layer of GAAP, which contains strongly recommended rules.

The large number of FASB and AICPA statements and interpretations reflects the U.S. rules-based approach to accounting standards. An indication of the extent of these rules governing accounting disclosure is the 1,043 pages of the *Wiley GAAP 2002: Interpretation and Application of Generally Accounting Principles*, plus a 37-page "disclosure checklist" [Delaney et al., 2001].

Presumably, the FASB's FAS and interpretations are supposed to be based on their Statements of Accounting Concepts. In fact, several standards are inconsistent with them.[9] As described by FASB member John M. Foster and FASB Senior Project Manager L. Todd Johnson [2001, p. 2] these concepts are supposed to (a) provide a framework that "narrows the range of alternatives to be considered by eliminating some that are inconsistent with it" and (b) "guide the development of accounting standards that are intended to facilitate the provision of evenhanded, or neutral, financial and related information." Foster and Johnson [ibid.] explain further:

> Moreover, without a framework, rational debate cannot occur because positions about the appropriate accounting treatment for a given transaction can neither be defended nor refuted—the appropriate treatment is simply "in the eye of the beholder." That was the case with the AICPA's committee on Accounting Procedure which preceded the Accounting Principles Board (APB), and it largely was true of the APB as well.

The framework provided by the Statements of Financial Accounting Concepts (SFAC) tends to reject the periodic matching of costs and revenues, as delineated by Paton and Littleton (1940).[10] This "matching concept," which has dominated accounting practice, emphasizes reporting of periodic income "as a test-reading by which the gauge the effect of the efforts expended" [Paton and Littleton, 1940, p. 7]. Assets are seen "as balances of unamortized costs" [ibid., p. 11]. Similar to Paton and Littleton, SFAC No. 1, "Objectives of Financial Reporting by Business Enterprises," states that financial statements should enable current and future investors, creditors, and other users to make investment and credit decisions. Paton and Littleton, though, emphasize the income statement to the exclusion of the balance sheet (they do not mention the statement of funds flows), while Concept No. 1 emphasizes that the enterprise's economic resources and obligations should be reported.

"Qualitative Characteristics of Accounting Information" (SFAC No. 2) concludes that the choice between alternative accounting methods should be based on which method provides information that is most useful to decision makers, net of the costs of provision. "Usefulness" is a function of relevance (the information makes a difference in a decision) and reliability (the faithfulness with which it represents what it purports to represent) and other related features (e.g., understandability, predictive value, timeliness, verifiability, representational faithfulness, neutrality, comparability, and materiality).

"Recognition and Measurement in Financial Statements of Business Enterprises" (SFAC No. 5) provides guidance on what information should be recognized and incorporated into financial statements and when it should be reported. The most important change from the matching concept that characterized previous practice is the addition of "comprehensive income." This differs from traditional income by including such items as unrealized holding gains and losses (net of income taxes) on financial assets designated as "available for sale," unrealized gains and losses resulting from translating foreign currency financial statements of consolidated majority-owned subsidiaries into U.S. dollar amounts, and unrealized losses resulting from recognition of pension obligations under FAS No. 87.

"The Elements of Financial Statements" (SFAC No. 6) defines the 10 elements of financial statements that are used to measure the performance and position of enterprises: assets, liabilities, equity, investments by owners, distribution to owners, comprehensive income, revenues, expenses, gains, and losses. "Using Cash Flow Information and Present Value in Accounting Measurements" (SFAC No. 7) is less substantive than the other concept statements and deals with the use of present-value estimates in accounting measurement to estimate fair values when (and only when) market prices are not available. In Chapter 2 we demonstrated that fair values obtained in this way are too subjective for use in financial accounting reports.

AUDITING STANDARDS OF THE AICPA

Financial reports that are attested to by CPAs must be prepared in conformity with generally accepted auditing standards (GAAS). Ten GAAS were developed and adopted by the AICPA in 1947. These statements fall into three broad areas. *General standards* define the personal qualities required of the auditor, including training and proficiency, independence, and the exercise of professional care. *Standards of fieldwork* deal with planning and supervision, internal control, and sufficiency and competency of audit evidence. *Standards of reporting* deal with the application of GAAS to GAAP, particularly the adequacy of financial statement disclosures and the expression of opinions in audit reports. GAAS requires auditors to assess and deal with audit risks. Emphasis is placed on understanding and testing the audited enterprise's internal controls to assess the extent to which material misstatements and frauds will have been prevented or detected.

The AICPA's Auditing Standards Board (ASB) has issued 101 Statements of Auditing Standards (through April 2003). Previously issued Statements of Auditing Procedures (SAPs) (Nos. 1 through 54) that were of continuing interest to the profession were codified in 1972 by the AICPA's Auditing Standards Executive Committee (now the Auditing Standards Board) in Statement of Auditing Standards (SAS) No. 1, "Codification of Auditing Standards and Procedures." In addition, the ASB issues specialized audit guides for a number of industries.

The AICPA established an SEC Practice Section (SECPS) in 1977. Before its functions were superseded by the Public Company Accounting Oversight Board (PCAOB), which was established by the Sarbanes-Oxley Act of 2002, AICPA-member firms that audit corporations reporting to the SEC had to be SECPS members, which required that they have established professional standards and had the technical capability to meet SECPS membership requirements.[11] SECPS members had to undergo peer reviews of their accounting and auditing practice every 3 years. The SECPS Peer Review Committee established standards that governed these reviews, oversaw the program, received peer review reports, and determined the appropriateness of firms' actions in response to those reports. It could then order additional reviews. In January 2004 the AICPA created the Center for Public Company Audit Firms to replace SEPCS. Its membership is voluntary and open to all CPA firms. The AICPA announced that it "will develop technical and educational guidance, serve as a forum for member firms to express their view of technical and regulatory matters and administer a peer review program for member firms that will focus on the audits of nonpublic companies."[12]

The Public Oversight Board (POB) was created in 1977 by the AICPA as an independent private sector body charged with overseeing and reporting on the programs of the SECPS. In 2001 it was given authority to oversee the Auditing Standards Board as well. But as a result of the Enron Corporation's failure and the accompanying accounting-disclosure scandal, its members resigned on March 21, 2002, and the PCAOB replaced it. During its tenure, the POB conducted reviews of member firms' operations at least every 3 years. Member firms had to report alleged audit failures involving SEC clients arising from litigation or regulatory investigations to the Quality Control Inquiry Committee (QCIC), which consisted of 12 representatives of member firms, most of whom were retired. The QCIC conducted in-depth inquiries. If it believed that the firm might be guilty of a serious infraction or had not corrected an important problem, the QCIC could order a special review. According to its last report, since its inception in 1988 through June 30, 1999, the QCIC ordered 72 special firm reviews, determined that firms took appropriate corrective action in 133 instances, asked appropriate AICPA technical bodies to consider the need for 49 changes in professional standards or the issuance of 23 Practice Alerts, and referred 46 individuals to the AICPA Professional Ethics Division [Panel on Audit Effectiveness, 2000, p. 196].

The AICPA also has a Professional Issues Task Force (PITF), which is charged with issuing Practice Alerts on potential audit concerns. Formerly, these were referred to it by the QCIC, as well as other sources.[13] It includes members from several AICPA committees.

THE PUBLIC COMPANY ACCOUNTING OVERSIGHT BOARD (PCAOB AND AUDIT STANDARDS)

Established under the Sarbanes-Oxley Act of 2002, the PCAOB has five "financially literate" members who are appointed for 5-year terms. Two members must be or have been CPAs and the remaining three must not have ever been CPAs. The chair may be a CPA but may not have been in practice for at least 5 years. Board members receive salaries of $484,000 annually, with the chair receiving $595,000. The PCAOB funds itself from fees paid by issuers of securities in proportion to their market capitalization.

The PCAOB, which reports to the SEC, has been given substantial powers over IPAs and public companies. It registers public accounting firms, inspects them annually if they audit more than 100 "issues" or at least every

3 years, and conducts investigations and disciplinary proceedings. It then may impose appropriate sanctions against both firms and individual IPAs. It also has authority to establish standards related to auditing, quality control, ethics, independence, and other standards related to the preparation audit reports.

The Sarbanes-Oxley Act of 2002 specifies that registered public accounting firms must maintain records for 7 years, a second partner must review and approve audits, and the lead audit or coordinating partner and reviewing partner must rotate off the audit every 5 years. The audit client may not employ a CEO, controller, CFO, or chief accounting officer who was employed by its external auditor during the 1-year period following the audit. It now is unlawful for a registered public accounting firm to provide specified non-audit services to an audit client. These include financial systems design and implementation, appraisal or valuation services, fairness opinions, actuarial services, internal audit outsourcing services, management function or human resources, securities and banking services, and legal services. Tax service, though, may still be provided to audit clients. In addition, public accounting firms are not prohibited from offering non-audit services to the audit clients of other firms.

INVESTOR PROTECTION AND CORPORATE GOVERNANCE

Before passage of the federal securities laws, corporate governance was (and still is) a function of state laws and securities exchanges.[14] State laws, under which corporate charters are granted, define the roles of directors, officers, and shareholders. Unlike the situation in some other countries (notably Germany), employees and other stakeholders have no legal corporate-governance role. Shareholders may vote for directors and on major corporate changes, such as a merger or dissolution, sue the directors and officers if they breach their duty of care (a situation that is difficult to demonstrate, except where there is blatant fraud), or sell their shares. Under state law, officers have subordinate roles with duties defined by the board of directors (although, in practice, they often control the boards). In general, state courts, especially those in Delaware, which dominates the issuance of corporate charters, tend not to interfere with corporate decisions. State laws, though, give stockholders the right to vote on such issues as the election of directors, filling of vacancies, and amendments to the bylaws and articles of incorporation. Stockholders also must vote on some major structural issues, such as mergers and liquidation and sale of substantially all of the assets.

The listing requirements of the stock exchanges additionally affect corporate governance. By the 20th century, the NYSE required corporations to issue annual financial statements and, in 1923, quarterly statements. A one-share, one-vote requirement was included in 1926, and in 1932 independent audits were required. A requirement for a minimum quorum was added in 1953, for shareholder approval of stock issuances greater than 20 percent of outstanding issues in 1955 (which exceeds the state law requirement),[15] and for two directors to be independent in 1956. A requirement that audit committees include only independent directors was adopted initially in 1977 and again in 1998. In 2003 the NYSE and NASDAQ adopted a requirement that board of directors' audit, compensation, and nominating committees include a majority of independent directors and for directors to meet without the presence of company managers. Shareholders also may disapprove equity compensation plans adopted by the directors.

Federal statutes dealing with corporate governance were included in the 1930s securities acts. These laws enhance state statutes in that they provide for greater disclosure with proxy materials, which give shareholders information on which to base decisions that are required under state law. More directly, the Securities Act of 1933 requires preparation and delivery of a prospectus to potential investors in publicly held companies and specifies the disclosures that must be made in the prospectus for public offerings of securities.[16] A publicly held company (Form S-1) prospectus includes descriptive, specifically required information about the company issuing the securities, the securities being offered, and the method of their distribution. Regulation S-X additionally requires disclosure of specified additional information on the face of the statements or in footnotes thereto. It also specifies very precise thresholds for the separate disclosure of certain items, such as intangible assets that exceed 5 percent of total assets. In addition, separate financial statements of significant companies acquired or to be acquired must be presented.

The Securities Exchange Act of 1934 requires publication of annual and quarterly financial statements and specifies the material that must be included in proxy statements that are sent to shareholders prior to annual meetings. The act also makes illegal various forms of market manipulation, particularly securities trading by insiders and associated persons ("tippees") based on non-public information.

The Sarbanes-Oxley Act of 2002 substantially extended federal regulation of corporate governance. Only independent directors may serve on audit committees, and the committees now have the authority to hire, independently monitor, meet with, and dismiss auditors. The CEO and CFO must state their responsibility for and assessment of internal controls and certify that they have reviewed the annual (10-K) report, that it does not contain any untrue statement of material fact or omit to state a material fact necessary to make the statements not misleading, that the statements fairly represent the financial condition and results of operations and cash flows of the registrant, and that all deficiencies in internal controls and frauds involving management were disclosed to the audit committee. Sanctions that might be imposed for noncompliance or a misstatement are not as yet known. Presumably, the attesting auditor will not sign and the SEC will reject filings without these declarations. The SEC could recommend prosecution by the Department of Justice of corporate officers who made false statements, and private attorneys could seek damages for their clients based on false statements. Apparently, though, a corporate officer could claim that he or she relied on assurance from the company's accountants and external auditors that the requirements were met.

The board of directors, meanwhile, is supposed to represent the stockholders. It has the power and responsibility to hire, monitor, reward, and dismiss the managers of the corporation, particularly the CEO. The board members, though, often owe their positions and the rewards of their office to the CEO, as CEOs tend to dominate their boards and control who is appointed and retained as a board member. This was particularly the situation when boards of directors included "insiders"—senior officers of the corporation, legal counsel, and family members. "In the 1960s, most had a majority of inside directors. Today, almost all have a majority (usually a large majority) of outside directors, most have a majority (often a large majority) of independent directors, and an increasing number have only one or two inside directors" [Bhagat and Black, 2001, p. 232]. Indeed, "until around 1970, insiders numerically dominated boards of directors...By 1980, the proportion of inside directors...had dropped to 43% [from 54%] and the proportion of independent directors had risen to 31% [from 20%]...By 1983, inside directors had fallen to 34% and independent directors had grown to 54%" [ibid., p. 238].

In their study of 934 of the largest U.S. corporations, Bhagat and Black found that in 1991 70 percent of those firms had majority-independent boards and only 6 percent had majority-inside boards. The median firm had 11 board members: seven independent directors, one an affiliated outsider, and three insiders (typically including the CEO and CFO). By 1997 the number of insider directors had dropped to two. Using these data, Bhagat and Black examined and largely rejected the hypothesis that corporations with more independent boards (measured by the fraction of independent directors minus the fraction of inside directors) outperform other corporations, where "performance" is measured by the ratio of the market-to-book value of assets (measured as the sum of the market value of common stock and book values of preferred stock and debt divided by the book value of total assets—Tobin's Q), operating income to sales or assets, sales to assets, and sales to employees. Accounting for CEO, board, and outside block (5 percent or more) ownership, board size, firm size, and industry performance, the investigators found no significant consistent association between firm performance and the proportion of independent board members (or board size, or CEO, outside director, or block ownership). Indeed, according to one measure (Tobin's Q), there was a statistically significant *negative* association with the proportion of independent board members. Further, they found that firms that performed poorly tended to increase the proportion of independent directors, but their subsequent performance did not improve. Bhagat and Black also cited and discussed earlier and less extensive studies, the findings of which were consistent with their results. Thus, the "conventional wisdom" that shareholders benefit from more independent boards is not empirically supported by one of the most thorough studies of this issue.

We are not aware of any empirical studies that examine the benefits or costs to investors of corporations having an independent chair of the board, probably because relatively few corporations have followed this practice. A March 2004 (and February 2003) study of corporations in the S&P 500 found that 77 (79) percent of the CEOs chaired their own boards, 15 (13) percent of the chairs were former CEOs of the corporation, and 3 (1) percent were executives other than the CEO. Thus, only 5 (6) percent of the chairs were independent, and half of these appeared to be only nominally independent [The Corporate Library at www.thecorporatelibrary.com].

Nevertheless, in the light of "corporate scandals of the recent past," the Conference Board's (an influential private group of leading corporations) Commission on Public Trust and Private Enterprise recommends that corporations separate the roles of CEO and board chair [Conference Board, 2003, p. 6]. The Commission recommends three alternative approaches [ibid., pp. 8–9] to "provide the appropriate balance between the board and CEO functions": (a) The roles of chair and CEO would be performed by two separate individuals; (b) the same separation of chair and CEO, but the chair is not an independent director (e.g., founder or major stockholder), in which event an independent director would be designated as the lead director; and (c) the same person can serve as chair and CEO, in which event an independent director would be designated as presiding director, who would have some of the chair's function. The Commission prefers the first approach—separation—and recommends that corporations that do not adopt it should explain their reasons.

Although there has been no strong move among corporations to separate the roles of chair and CEO, boards of directors have increasingly appointed one of their members to be the lead director. The February 2003 study found that only 6 percent of the S&P 500 corporations had appointed a lead director; a year later, 32 percent had established this position.

Other stakeholders, such as employees, creditors, and customers, are not protected as are shareholders by U.S. state or federal securities laws; rather, they are protected by general statutes dealing with fraud and misrepresentation. They also can and usually do protect themselves by establishing contractual relationships, insisting on financial statements audited by IPAs that are acknowledged as having been prepared for their use as well as for shareholders, and by the desire of ongoing concerns to deal honestly and fairly with employees and customers rather than lose out to competitors.

CURRENT ISSUES RELATED TO FINANCIAL DISCLOSURE AND ACCOUNTING STANDARDS

The financial scandals of the past several years have led IPAs, their clients, standard setters, and policymakers to consider and debate a host of issues relating to financial disclosure and accounting standards. We believe that this debate should be informed by available studies, which, it turns out, shed light on many of the issues. In the sections below, we review some of the key findings from these studies and what they imply for each of the issues.

The Scope of Auditor Practices

Despite the considerable cost to investors and the public condemnation of auditors of fraud by corporate managers that is not detected in audits, auditors have maintained that a usual GAAS audit is not a forensic engagement, wherein the auditor is asked to examine the records and other documents in sufficient detail to establish whether or not and to what extent there was a crime. Such examinations usually are costly. In part, this insistence is based on avoiding legal liability for frauds, which often is very costly. In part, a cost-benefit analysis (if it could be specified) probably would conclude that the expected cost of an undetected fraud is less than the cost of additional auditing. As the Panel on Audit Effectiveness [2000, p. 76, ¶3.6] put it, "a GAAS audit provides only reasonable, but not absolute, assurance that material misstatements will be detected." Consequently, Statement of Auditing Standard (SAS) No. 47, *Audit Risk and Materiality in Conducting an Audit*, sought to limit the auditor's responsibility to detecting frauds that might result in a "material misstatement" of the numbers presented in financial statements. SAS No. 82, *Consideration of Fraud in a Financial Statement Audit*, amended SAS No. 47 to include a requirement that the auditor specifically assess the risk of theft and management misappropriation of assets and the effectiveness of internal controls that would prevent or detect fraud.

Nevertheless, the Panel on Audit Effectiveness, which was appointed in 1998 by the chairman of the SEC and the Public Oversight Board (POB) to "thoroughly examine the current audit model," concluded [ibid., p. 15, ¶2.26]:

> A major objective of auditing standards should be to help audits serve not only to detect material fraud but also, by being perceived as rigorous, to deter fraud from occurring in the first place. Toward that end, the Panel recommends that auditing standards require auditors to possess a far deeper understanding of the entity's business processes, risks and controls, and that substantive tests with the principal objective of detecting material financial statement fraud be designed and performed on all audits.

Summarizing its findings, the Panel stated [ibid., p. 86, ¶3.46]:

> The risk assessment and response process called for by SAS No. 82 falls short in effectively deterring fraud or significantly increasing the likelihood that the auditor will detect material fraud, largely because it fails to direct auditing procedures specifically toward fraud detection.

Earnings manipulation is another matter. GAAP do not (and, as we discussed in Chapter 3, inherently cannot) prevent management from exercising discretion in choosing among alternative accounting procedures (e.g., depreciation methods, inventory valuation, and deferral of expenses) or business activities (e.g., the timing of maintenance, research and development, and advertising) that will affect the net income reported in a particular accounting period. Consequently, auditors cannot prevent some degree of earnings management. However, as the Panel on Audit Effectiveness [ibid., p. 78, ¶3.16] pointed out: "Earnings management also may involve intentionally recognizing or measuring transactions and other events and circumstances in the wrong accounting period or recording fictitious transactions—both of which constitute fraud." Indeed, such manipulations characterize many of the frauds perpetrated upon auditors and, thence, upon investors.

The Panel commissioned Professor Thomas Weirich of Central Michigan University to conduct a study of SEC Accounting and Auditing Enforcement Releases (AAERs, which specify briefly serious misstatements and frauds in materials submitted to the SEC) issued between July 1997 and December 1999 involving the Big 5 audit firms. Professor Weirich delineated 38 different matters. In 12 of these situations, "the auditors discovered the fraudulent activities, reported them to the audit committee and resigned or required restatements, or both" [Weirich, 2000, p. 224, ¶7]. Weirich reported [ibid., p. 225, ¶9]:

> Most of the misstatements involved relatively routine transactions and accounts rather than complex judgmental areas and more esoteric transactions and accounts, such as derivatives or other complex financial instruments, restructuring reserves, business combinations or in-process research and development charges.

Beasley et al. [1999] and the SEC [2003] conducted research similar to Weirich's. Beasley et al. examined 204 randomly selected AAERs among the approximately 300 issued from 1987 through 1997. As directed by Section 704 of the Sarbanes-Oxley Act of 2002, the SEC [2003] reviewed 227 enforcement investigations of "fraud and other improper conduct." The study identified 380 "bad" practices, since many investigations involved more than one practice. Table 4-1 outlines the findings of these and other studies. The research found that most of the problems involved improper revenue recognition, followed by overstated assets and understated expenses. Among the small corporations that dominated Beasley et al.'s study, misappropriated assets were of some importance. Senior management was implicated in most of the problems. The external auditor was charged with misconduct in about a quarter of the cases, although the largest firms (the Big Five at that time) were implicated in just a few. Weirich [2000], for example, reported: "In most of the 38 cases, one or more members of the top management were involved in or aware of the activities that resulted in materially misstated financial statements" [ibid., p. 228, ¶17]. These managers, he noted, "often were very concerned about concealing them from the auditors and ensuring that the numbers

Table 4-1 Studies of Financial Statement Fraud, Misstatements, and Restatements

	SEC AAERs and Enforcement Investigations			Restatements of Financial Statements		
	Weirich [2000]	Beasley et al. [1999]	SEC [2003]	FEI [2000]	Palmrose & Scholz [2002]	GAO [2002]
Data studied	Big Five CPA firms	All AAERs involving fraud, etc.		Various data bases		Lexis-Nexis
Period of data	7/97–12/99	1987–97	1997–02	1977–00	1995–99	1/97–6/02
Number of observations	96 involving 38 matters	204 randomly selected	227 involving 380 practices	224	492	845
Proportion where problems were encountered (not mutually exclusive)						
Improper revenue recognition and overstatement of accounts receivable	68%	50%	33%	38%	37%	38%
Overstated assets	26%	50%				
Understated expenses and liabilities or improper expense recognition	58%	18%	27%	28%		16%
Misappropriated assets		12%	11%			9%
Inadequate disclosures in MD&A						
Improper accounting for business combinations			6%		10%	5%
Failure to disclose related-party trans.			5%			3%
Loan loss				9%		
In-process research and development (IPR&D)				6%	19%	4%
Parties charged or implicated:						
CEO		78%				
CFO		43%				
Senior management			69%		8%	
External auditor		27%	25%		7%	
External auditor at major CPA firm		5%				

and the relationships among them would 'look right' to the auditors when they performed their analytical procedures" [ibid., p. 227, ¶15].

Restatements of financial statements have also been the subject of at least three large-scale research reports by the FEI [2001], Palmrose and Scholz [2002], and the General Accounting Office (GAO) of the U.S. Congress [2002]. All three studies examined various databases with keyword searches for reports of restated financial statements due to irregularities or errors, whether reported voluntarily or forced by a corporation's auditors. As shown in Table 4-1, similar to the studies of SEC enforcement actions, improper revenue recognition was the predominant reason for the restatements, followed by understated expenses.

The "restatement" studies also are interesting because they report information on the number of restatements produced over time and thus provide some evidence on the extent to which restatements really present a problem. The FEI study found 224 restatements between 1977 and 1989 (17 per year on average), 392 from 1990 through 1997 (49 per year), and 464 between 1998 and 2000 (155 per year). The peak was 207 in 1999, primarily because of 57 restatements that resulted from SEC objections to software companies' accounting for in-process research and development (IPR&D). This substantial increase after 1997 appears to be due to three factors. One is the concern by then SEC chairman Arthur Levitt [1998] about accounting manipulations and IPR&D accounting.[17] Second, the SEC directed registrants to make adjustments (such as errors that previously were considered as immaterial) to prior-period statements by restating the affected financial statements rather than by reporting them prospectively in future statements. Third, companies conceded and made small restatements to avoid having their registration statements held up by the SEC. Thus, the substantial increase in the number of restatements in recent years appears due more to change in the SEC's practices than to deterioration of corporate accounting practices.

Palmrose and Scholz [2002] identified 492 companies that announced restatement over the 5-year period from 1995 through 1999. The number increased each year: 44, 48, 90, 106, and 204. The GAO [2003] included all material restatements due to an accounting irregularity made by publicly traded corporations, "regardless of its impact on the restating company's financials" [ibid., p. 76]. The study found 845 such restatements, and the number increased each year, from 83 in 1997, to 195 in 2001, and 110 in the first 6 months of 2002. Over this period, the percentage of publicly traded corporations that restated their financial statements increased substantially, from 0.89 percent in 1997 to 2.95 percent in 2002, in part because the number of corporations listed on the exchanges decreased from 9,275 to 7,446.

The studies also measured the impact of the restatements on the restating corporations' stock prices. The FEI [2000] measured 3-day losses in the restating corporations' market values when restatements were announced.

The losses were relatively small before 1998—an average of $0.9 billion a year. But in 1998, 1999, and 2000, these annual losses were $17, $24, and $31 billion, respectively, mostly due to the top 10 firms making restatements. In total, the losses for all the corporations making restatements were less than 0.2 percent of their total market value. The GAO measured a 3-day loss of 10 percent of capitalization (adjusted for changes in the market) of 689 corporations surrounding restatement announcements, or a total of $95.6 billion.[18] This loss, though, represented 0.11 percent of the total market capitalization of listed corporations.

Thus, the several studies yield similar findings. The number of restatements has increased but still is quite small in relation to the approximately 12,000 corporations that reported to the SEC. Until recently, smaller companies tended to restate their financial statements. The most pervasive reason for restatement is misstatement of revenue. A substantial minority of companies that restate financial statements and a smaller number of their auditors are sued. Losses to investors who hold diversified portfolios that possibly result from misstatements that are corrected are small overall, although the losses can be substantial (particularly recently) for investments in those companies.

However, the revelation of serious accounting irregularities and apparent frauds at large, very-well-known corporations, particularly the Enron Corporation, had a greater impact on U.S. accounting practices and regulation than their numbers would indicate. Enron's failure in 2001 was preceded and followed by substantial restatements of the financial statements of other such corporations. For example, in 1998 the Sunbeam Corp. reduced its 1997 reported earnings by 65 percent, and Waste Management restated its pre-tax net earnings by $3.54 billion.[19] Enron's failure was followed by substantial misstatements of reported net income by such well-known corporations as IBM, Xerox, Merck, PeopleSoft, Adelphia, Global Crossing, Qwest, Tyco, Rite Aid, HealthSouth, and WorldCom. Indeed, WorldCom, which admitted to overstating net income by $4 billion, displaced Enron as the largest U.S. bankruptcy.

Enron's failure also resulted in the failure of one of the (then) Big Five audit firms, Arthur Andersen. This analysis provides substantial support for our previous conclusion that fair-value accounting that is not based on trustworthy numbers is very dangerous for both investors and auditors.

Auditors' Independence and Their Provision of Non-Audit Services to Audit Clients

Auditors in the United States may not serve as officers or directors of clients, nor may they have any direct or indirect interests in public audit clients. However, there has been almost continuous concern by the SEC and others that the provision of non-audit, management advisory services (MAS) to clients might impose actual or perceived conflicts of interest on auditors that could result in their performing inadequate audits or in permitting clients to manipulate net income. The Panel on Audit Effectiveness [2000, Appendix D] reviewed the history of this concern. The Panel reported that in 1966 a committee of the AICPA studied the issue and "found no evidence that non-audit services impair independence, but found that some users believe that such services created an *appearance* of lack of independence" [ibid., pp. 203–204, emphasis in original]. A 1974 study by the independent Cohen Commission raised similar concerns but reported no instances of actual conflicts that impaired audits.

The U.S. Senate then examined the issue. An extensive staff report, *The Accounting Establishment*, published in 1977, generally concluded that audit firms' provision of management information services created a conflict of interest. However, a review of that report [Benston, 1979/1980] revealed that, in fact, no evidence of such conflicts was presented. Nevertheless, the AICPA reacted to the Senate report by forming the SECPS, introducing peer reviews, establishing the POB, and restricting audit firms from providing some ancillary services to clients (e.g., psychological testing, public opinion polls, and executive recruitment). SECPS members were required to report the amount and nature of MAS provided to their clients' audit committees. The POB studied the issue again in 1979 and concluded: "From the voluminous record before the Board, it is apparent that documented evidence of MAS abuses or impairment of independence through the use of MAS is virtually nonexistent."[20]

Since 1978, the SEC has required disclosure of MAS fees in the annual proxy statements of public corporations. These data reveal that MAS have grown considerably over time. In 1990, 71 percent of the revenue from SEC audit clients of the Big Five audit firms was derived from accounting and auditing; in 1999 this percentage declined to 48 percent. Consulting grew from 12 percent to 32 percent over this period, with tax service revenue increasing from 17 percent to 20 percent. However, in 1999, 75 percent of these clients received no consulting services from their auditors (80 percent in 1990) [Panel on Audit Effectiveness, 2000, p. 112].

Nonetheless, in response to Congressional and SEC concerns about the *possibility* that MAS *might* impair the conduct or perception of the validity of audits, the AICPA issued a series of ethics rulings that delineated the services offered by audit firms that might impair their independence (Interpretations 101-3, 101-13, 101-14, 102-2, 102-6). In 1999, the Independence Standards Board (ISB) adopted Standard No. 1, which requires auditors to disclose annually, in writing, all relationships between them and the audit client that may reasonably be thought to bear on independence.

The Panel on Audit Effectiveness [2000, Chapter 5] considered the issue at some length. It conducted its own analysis of audit practices and concluded: "The Panel is not aware of any instances of non-audit services having caused or contributed to an audit failure or the actual loss of auditor independence." Nevertheless, some members of the Panel "believe that, with very limited exceptions, audit firms and their affiliates should be excluded by rule from marketing and furnishing management services to their audit clients that do not directly advance the interest of investors in objective and reliable financial reports on the stewardship of management" [ibid., p. 118, ¶5.32]. The Panel then presented 18 reasons why such a rule should be enacted [ibid., pp. 119–126, ¶5.39]. Other members of the Panel "believe that audit firms can provide both audit and non-audit services to the same public audit client and maintain independence, objectivity, and integrity. Nothing in the long history of the profession's providing non-audit services has indicated otherwise" [ibid., p. 127, ¶5.40]. This conclusion was supported by 19 reasons why MAS not only do not impair auditors' independence, but also enhance the effectiveness of audits [ibid., pp. 127–132, ¶5.41-5.59].

Following a public hearing and after receiving hundreds of comments, the SEC issued an amendment of its Auditors' Independence Rule 201(b), effective February 2001.[21] The lengthy discussion accompanying the release emphasizes the importance of the *appearance* of independence. This led the SEC to rule that CPAs may not provide the following nine kinds of MAS to their SEC-audit clients: (a) bookkeeping or other services related to the audit client's accounting records or financial statements; (b) financial information systems design and implementation; (c) appraisal or valuation services and fairness opinions; (d) actuarial services; (e) internal audit services; (f) management function, such as acting as a director or officer or performing decision making, supervisory, or ongoing monitoring; (g) human resources, such as searching for executives, engaging in psychological testing, acting as a negotiator on the audit client's behalf, and recommending hires; (h) broker-dealer services; and (i) legal services.

The circumstances associated with the failure of the Enron Corporation in 2001 appeared to have validated the SEC's action when it was revealed that Enron's independent public accountant, Arthur Andersen, received non-audit consulting fees of $29 million and audit fees of $27 million for year 2000 and did not object to financial statements that were shown to be grossly misleading. The press, regulators, and legislators assumed that there was a causal relationship,[22] and Section 201 of the Sarbanes-Oxley Act of 2002 made it unlawful for a registered public accounting firm to provide the nine non-audit services listed above contemporaneously with the audit.

Failures in the Enforcement of Auditing Standards

The SEC is the primary enforcement vehicle for ensuring that corporations with publicly traded securities comply with GAAS (and GAAP). (The Public Company Accounting Oversight Board, which since 2002 has direct jurisdiction over auditing and auditors, reports to the SEC.) The agency may refuse and often does not accept financial statements filed with it unless they conform to U.S. GAAP and the SEC's rulings and interpretations. The SEC also established rules governing auditors' independence. The agency can and sometimes has undertaken investigations and recommended criminal and criminal actions to the Department of Justice. It also may censure auditors and audit firms by refusing them permission to attest to financial statements that corporations must submit to the SEC.

Despite these regulatory powers, the SEC has rarely used its authority to discipline IPAs. The GAO [2002] analyzed 150 AASRs issued from January 2001 through February 2002. They found that 39 CPAs were suspended or denied the privilege of appearing or practicing before the SEC, 23 for 3 years or less [ibid., p. 53]. In addition, one large (then non-Big Five) accounting firm was permanently barred, one Big Five firm and one other firm were given cease-and-desist orders, and one Big Five firm was censured. The GAO [ibid., Appendix V, pp. 113–234] also presented 16 "case studies" that detail the reasons for, effects of, and actions taken by the SEC as a consequence of these corporations restating their financial reports.[23] Ten of these cases involved important and substantial violations of GAAP (e.g., liabilities not reported, improper recognition of income, expensing costs that should have been capitalized, falsification of expenses, and rampant self-dealing by management). The SEC took action against the auditors in only three of these cases.

In Sunbeam, the auditor, Phillip Harlow, was charged with having his firm (Arthur Andersen) sign unqualified statements, even though he knew about the misstatements. Harlow "consented to the entry of the [SEC's] order [charging him with engaging in improper professional conduct] without admitting or denying the findings therein [and] the Commission withdrew and dismissed its complaint in district court" [SEC Litigation Release No. 17952, January 27, 2003]. In Waste Management, the firm (Arthur Andersen) issued unqualified statements, even though its auditors had identified and quantified the improper accounting practices. Arthur Andersen was fined $7 million. Two of the three auditors were fined $50,000 and $40,000 and barred from practice before the SEC for 5 years; the other was barred for 1 year. The GAO stated that they continued to be active partners of Arthur Andersen. In Enron, Arthur Andersen was charged with destroying documents in advance of an SEC investigation, and in a jury trial it was found guilty only of a related offense of an Andersen attorney obstructing justice by asking that an e-mail be altered to exclude her name. No mention was made of Andersen's partner-in-charge of the audit, David Duncan, who destroyed the documents. When the Supreme Court reversed Arthur Andersen's conviction, Duncan withdrew his having plead guilty to obstruction of justice, without objection by the Department of Justice. The GAO did not indicate any actions taken by the SEC against the audit firms or the CPAs who conducted the audits of the seven other corporations where there were serious errors, misclassifications, and omissions that substantially overstated reported net income and assets and understated liabilities.

The AICPA also can discipline auditors. It could have refused them membership in the SECPS (before it was disbanded in 2003), which would effectively have barred them from attesting to financial statements filed with the SEC, and, hence, to corporations with publicly traded securities.

Members of SECPS were subjected to periodic peer reviews of their audit practices. The findings of these reviews could have caused them to change practices or, if the charges were upheld, have excluded them from auditing companies with publicly traded securities. However, the AICPA has rarely censured its members. One reason is it does not have the resources to investigate professional misconduct and would be subject to lawsuits if it acted without due process and without demonstrating good cause. Indeed, the *Washington Post* found that over a decade the AICPA took disciplinary action against fewer than 20 percent of accountants who had already been sanctioned by the SEC [Hilzenrath, 2001].

State boards of accounting, which grant CPAs their licenses, can and do revoke those licenses, but such actions are taken almost only against CPAs who are charged with and admit to failure to fulfill important obligations to clients, who have been found guilty of fiduciary or criminal offenses, or who do not maintain their required continuing professional education.[24]

Perhaps of greatest importance is IPAs' concern for the costs imposed by private litigation. Before enactment of the Securities Act of 1933, the legal rule of "privity" constrained investors from suing independent auditors because their contract was with the corporations that engaged them. Section 11 of the Act not only removes that impediment, but also removes the common law requirement for investors to show that they relied on financial statements that were materially misstated as the result of grossly negligent or fraudulent acts by the auditors. Now, investors only have to demonstrate that the financial statements contain a material omission or misstatement. In their defense, auditors must prove "due diligence," namely that after reasonable investigation they had reason to believe and did believe that the financial statements included in a prospectus were "true." The auditors' responsibility continues to the time the statements become effective (declared by the SEC to be available for public use), even though this is after completion of the audit and preparation of the report.

SEC Rule 10b-5 extends to periodic financial statements the auditors' liability for making any untrue statement or omission of a material fact. Furthermore, class action suits, under Rule 23 of the Federal Rules of Civil Procedure, on behalf of a very large number of investors, can and often are used by attorneys to mount cases against auditors. This substantially increases the auditors' potential liability.

Finally, because firms of auditors almost always are the only party after a bankruptcy to have the resources to pay an adverse judgment, they tend to be sued. And, unlike the situation in the United Kingdom and other European countries, under U.S. law, if the plaintiffs are unsuccessful, they are not liable for the legal costs of the defendants, but if the plaintiffs win their lawsuit, they are awarded costs as well as damages.

Two more recently enacted laws might appear to limit external independent auditors' concerns about private litigation. The Private Securities Litigation Reform Act of 1995 (PSLRA) generally made it more difficult for class action plaintiffs to sue CPA firms for accounting abuses, and the

Securities Litigation Uniform Standards Act of 1998 (SLASA) abolished state court class actions alleging securities fraud. However, the PSLRA did not exempt external independent auditors from liability; all it did was to cut back their joint-and-several liability for accounting misdeeds when there are several defendants before the court.[25] The PSLRA also raised pleading standards and restricted the extension of the anti-racketeering (RICO) statute that calls for a trebling of damages. The rationales for these reforms were (a) to prevent plaintiffs from digging into the deepest pockets among a group of defendants, regardless of the degree of culpability of individual defendants, and (b) to discourage plaintiffs from bringing extortionist lawsuits against CPAs in the hope of a settlement. The SLASA abolished only state court class actions alleging securities fraud; federal class actions can still be brought against accountants. Significantly, the legal changes have not kept plaintiffs from suing the audit firms associated with corporations that restated their financial statements.

Perhaps the most important asset of audit firms that is at risk in the event of an audit failure or material misstatement in a financial report is their reputations. As we discussed in Chapter 3, IPAs' principal products are their expertise and integrity. Should they be found guilty of being parties to misleading investors, that asset will be damaged; they sometimes get punished severely. Consequently, IPAs have strong incentives to avoid situations that would subject them to lawsuits. We believe that both the large number of audits performed annually by CPA firms and the potential monetary benefits to plaintiffs' attorneys of bringing lawsuits against the firms explains why so few lawsuits have been successfully mounted against CPAs in the United States.

Benston [2003A] pointed to an important limitation of the effectiveness of governmental and private litigation for reducing the incentives of IPAs to overlook or even participate with their clients' desire to present misleading or even fraudulent financial statements rather than risk losing revenue from the client. Although audit firms have strong incentives to refuse attestations that might result in damage to their reputations, individual partners-in-charge of the audits might benefit substantially from taking such risks. Their compensation usually is based on the audit fees they generate. Loss of a partner's major client is likely to be very costly to that partner. Although the firms have strong incentives to monitor the behavior of their partners, the individual partners probably realize that if their firms are cited by the SEC or sued by private litigants, their firms will defend rather than discipline them. Should the firms fire or otherwise punish a partner for having supervised and approved an incompetent or inadequate audit or agreed too readily to a client's demands, the firm would be admitting its collective guilt to regulators and present or potential plaintiffs. Furthermore, unlike the situation in European countries, the audit letter published with clients' financial statements is signed only with the firm name. Thus, the names of the auditor in charge and the confirming partner are not revealed.

Principles-Based Versus Rule-Based Accounting
Standards—Again

Enron's failure and the revelation that its financial statements greatly understated liabilities and overstated assets, net income, and cash flow from operations have led U.S. authorities to question whether the essentially rules-based GAAP promulgated by the FASB and SEC should be replaced by principles-based standards. Enron's accountants were particularly adept at following the letter of GAAP in order to produce financial statements that violated the intent of GAAP. Arthur Andersen, Enron's external auditors, not only accepted Enron's financial-engineering approach to GAAP, but also helped them design such procedures (for substantial fees), as did several investment banking organizations (see the extensive detailed reports of Neal Batson, Examiner in Bankruptcy, Enron Corporation).

In October 2002 the FASB issued a paper addressing these issues entitled *Proposal: Principles-Based Approach to U.S. Standard Setting.* The Proposal's introduction [FASB, 2002, pp. 2–3] explains: "in the Board's view, much of the detail and complexity in accounting standards has been demand-driven, resulting from (1) exceptions to the principles in the standards and (2) the amount of interpretive and implementation guidance provided by the FASB and others for applying the standards." According to the FASB, the exceptions result from the Board's having to make compromises with presumably powerful interest groups that prevented it from implementing its fair-value asset/liability-based principles. The Proposal makes particular mention of FAS 133, *Accounting for Derivative Instruments and Hedging Activities,* whose complexities resulted from the Board being forced to make such exceptions. The objective of comparability has required the Board to issue interpretive and implementation guidance, or rules that seek to provide a single answer to every question. Indeed, the proposal [ibid., p. 9] states that one cost of a principles-based approach is that it "could lead to situations in which professional judgments, made in good faith, result in different interpretations for similar transactions and events, raising concerns about comparability."

The Proposal suggests, however, that the benefits of a principles-based approach may be greater than the costs. These benefits include "standards [that] should be easier to understand and implement . . . [and] more clearly convey the economic substance of the transactions and events covered by the standards" [ibid., pp. 9–10]. In addition, a principles-based approach could facilitate convergence of U.S. GAAP and IFRS. On balance, the Board believes that "the benefits of adopting that [principle-based] approach would outweigh its costs" [ibid., p. 10].

The FASB's Proposal is merely a prelude to a "request for comments." The Proposal asks six questions, none of which outline what might be principles on which the standards would based, although from the example given it seems clear that the standard the FASB would implement is the asset/liability fair-value approach rather than the revenue/expense approach. The 135 responses that the FASB received are posted on the Board's website (though none since February 2004).

As required by the Sarbanes-Oxley Act, the SEC [2003A] published a Report that considers whether the United States should adopt a principles-based accounting system. We discuss this Report in Benston et al. [2005] and review it briefly here. The SEC rejects a "principles-only" standard, in part because it would provide insufficient guidance to preparers and auditors [ibid., p. 23] and result in "a loss of comparability because of management and auditor discretion in the application of the principles" [ibid., p. 13]. Rather than "principles-only," the Report proposes "objectives-oriented" standards.[26]

In many ways the Report is a disappointment, especially considering its length and authorship. The concept of "objectives-orientated standards" is not explicitly defined, other than that it should reflect the economic substance of transactions and be consistent with and derived from a coherent conceptual framework, from which there are few exceptions. That framework is defined as the asset/liability, balance sheet approach. The Report would have the standard setter identify the assets and liabilities that are created, eliminated, or changed by a transaction or event, such that it is not too narrow or too broad. This concept is illustrated with the FASB's standard for business combinations, SFAS 141 [p. 27]:

> A business combination occurs when an entity acquires net assets that constitute a business or acquires equity interests in one or more other entities and obtains control over that entity or entities.

The Report indicates that this is straightforward: there must be control for there to be consolidation; hence, equity-method investments do not have to be explicitly excluded. But it does not consider a common situation where the acquirer has 49 percent of the equity, which obviates consolidation, but almost always is indicative of control. As a more extreme example, Enron determined and Andersen concurred that it did not control an entity where it had a majority of the voting stock, but the minority shareholders (whose returns were, in effect, guaranteed by Enron) could elect half the directors, although they never did. Nor is it necessarily clear what "constitutes" a business. Again, Enron determined and Andersen concurred that the acquisition of two different assets (an airplane lease and a security) from a single seller constituted a "business." Nor does the Report consider that the purchase method results in adding together the estimated market values of the acquired assets and liabilities with the historical book values of the acquirer's assets and liabilities. What does the sum of these numbers mean in terms of representational faithfulness?

The issue of principles-based versus rules-based accounting standards for the United States is not yet resolved and may not be for some time, if ever. On the surface, official opinion appears to be in favor of principles-based accounting standards, but not with much enthusiasm. There seems to be a great reluctance, both by the authorities and by CPA firms, to live with standards that offer only general guidance and that would permit a wider range of interpretations. In part, this reluctance is based on fear of lawsuits, given that the U.S. legal system often makes weak suits potentially profitable to plaintiffs' attorneys. Aside from the cost of lawsuits, we believe that the reluctance to abandon rules is well placed, at least in the U.S. context, as long as the FASB and SEC favor the asset/liability approach and fair-value measurements when these are not based on trustworthy numbers-based approach. As we discussed in Chapter 2, there is good reason to fear that opportunistic managers will take advantage of the uncertainties of fair-value estimates that are not derived from market values to inflate reported income.

The solution, we suggest, is principles-based accounting standards, but those only if these standards are based on the traditional revenue/expense income-statement model (see Chapter 2). We explore this proposal in greater depth in Chapter 11.

CONVERGENCE WITH INTERNATIONAL ACCOUNTING
STANDARDS BOARD (IASB) STANDARDS

In 2005, stock-market-listed corporations in all European Union countries will have to prepare their financial statements in accordance with the International Financial Reporting Standards (IFSR) promulgated by the IASB. (We discuss this development and the standards in some detail in succeeding chapters, particularly Chapter 7.) Until recently, the SEC has essentially taken the position that U.S. GAAP is superior to all other versions. In effect, corporations that would issue securities in the United States and have their securities listed on U.S. stock exchanges (and, hence, be subject to the SEC's authority) were told: "the U.S. way or no way." Although foreign corporations may prepare their financial statements in accordance with GAAP accepted in their own countries, they must reconcile on Form 20-F their net income and stockholders' equity with the amounts that would be computed under U.S. GAAP. Thus, foreign corporations had to comply with U.S. GAAP and SEC Regulation S-X.

The Enron and other accounting "scandals" apparently shook the SEC's and the FASB's confidence that U.S. GAAP offered the only standard that would protect investors in the United States. The increasing acceptance of IFRS also probably played an important role in weakening this rather arrogant position. In October 2002 the FASB and the IASB agreed to a *Memorandum of Understanding* "formalizing their commitment to the convergence of U.S. and international accounting standards." As part of the project, the FASB has published detailed comparisons of these standards [FASB, 1999]. (We outline the major differences between U.S. and IASB GAAP in the Appendix to Chapter 9.) The project actually includes only minor issues that are not part of major standard-setting projects. Specifically, in December 2003 the FASB proposed adopting the IFRS position by amending its statements on asset exchanges, the reflection of idle capacity in inventory valuation, classification of certain liabilities, changes in accounting policies, and the earnings per share calculation.

Nonetheless, the FASB has qualified its position: "because of the volume of differences and the complex nature of some issues, the FASB anticipates that many differences between U.S. and international standards will persist well beyond 2005 [when] all EU-listed public companies are being required by the European Union to prepare their consolidated financial statements using IASB Standards." Major European companies listed in the United States still hope that the major differences will be eliminated, at least by 2007, the latest time when EU companies with shares listed outside the EU must provide consolidated financial reports using IFRS. However, the number of differences has recently risen again with the promulgation of new IFRS. It is unclear if U.S. GAAP and IFRS will converge substantially in the future—and we are not convinced that this is even desirable (see Chapter 10, where we argue for a constrained competition among standards). What is desirable in such a scenario, though, is that the United States would be more open to accepting IFRS financial statements as a listing requirement for foreign firms without reconciliation to U.S. GAAP.

APPENDIX: FINANCIAL DISCLOSURE BY AND AUDITS OF NON-PUBLIC COMPANIES

Only companies subject to the Securities Act of 1933 and the Securities and Exchange Act of 1934 are subject to the SEC's audit and reporting requirements. New securities issues need not be registered with the SEC if they (a) are entirely intrastate, (b) do not involve a public offering, or (c) meet "safe harbor" conditions. The intrastate exemption requires that the issuer be incorporated in and does business principally within a state, the securities are offered and sold only to bona-fide residents of the state and the proceeds used within the state, and there can be no immediate resales of the security across state lines. A nonpublic or private issuance must be limited to sophisticated and knowledgeable investors with resources sufficient to make it unlikely that the securities would be resold.

Because the criteria are vague, the SEC created the third "safe harbor" exemption. Its Regulation D specifies three exemptions. Rule 504 allows issues of up to $1 million to any number of investors, and Rule 505 allows issues up to $5 million to no more than 35 investors plus an unlimited number of "accredited investors" (e.g., wealthy people or eligible financial institutions). Rule 506 allows for private placement to up to 35 purchasers and an unlimited number of "accredited investors." State "blue-sky" laws (discussed earlier) also apply to securities issues.

Periodic reporting and audits are not required for companies not subject to the Securities Exchange Act of 1934, nor need these companies obtain an attestation by an IPA. However, IPAs may not state that the statements they sign are prepared in accordance with GAAP based on a GAAS audit, unless such is the case. If they do, their state-issued licenses could be revoked. If they were members of the AICPA, they would also be violating that organization's Code of Ethics. Users of financial statements may, but often do not, require IPA attestations to financial statements. The tax authorities do not require IPA-audited and -prepared tax filings. Thus, the financial records of a very large number of companies and small non-publicly traded corporations need not be audited and their financial statements need not be prepared in accordance with GAAS and GAAP.

5

Corporate Financial Reporting and Regulation in the United Kingdom

This chapter reviews the regulation of financial markets and investor protection, the required accounting disclosures of both listed and non-listed firms, the role of corporate governance as it affects investors and other stakeholders, and prevailing enforcement mechanisms in the United Kingdom.[1] It incorporates some of the most important reactions in the United Kingdom to the recent U.S. corporate collapses and related accounting scandals during 2001–02.

U.K. FINANCIAL SYSTEM

The financial system in the United Kingdom has always been strongly market-oriented, similar to the United States in many ways. This contrasts with countries where financial intermediaries often have a close relationship with their corporate customers, such as France and Germany. The difference in funding is reflected in the ratio that total national banking assets bears to total equity capitalization in different nations. For example, in 1993, a time of relatively stable markets, countries with market-oriented financial systems had ratios of 0.64 for the United States and 1.85 for the United Kingdom, whereas more banking-oriented countries, France and Germany, had a ratio of approximately 4.15 [Allen and Gale, 2000, Table 3.1, p. 47].

The United Kingdom has a strong primary equity market for initial public offers and very active secondary markets for trading existing shares. The United Kingdom has in common with most other commercially developed countries a strong reliance on retained earnings for financing. The prices generated by these markets are important for accounting, because accounting items are more likely to be seen as value relevant to investors if they are correlated with such prices.

The London Stock Exchange (LSE) is the third largest equity market in the world (after New York and Tokyo), with around 1,500 corporations listed (November 2004[2]), including some 400 non-U.K. corporations. The LSE also provides the Alternative Investment Market, with over 900 listings, which trades young companies not ready for full LSE listing. The London International Financial Futures and Options Exchange (LIFFE) provides a market for options in quoted shares.

All these markets use electronic information systems and order books. The over-the-counter market, which is not organized by the LSE, allows trading in shares with a lesser track record. The International Equity Market also has been recently established, hosting trades of shares issued in other countries. Recently, an increasing number of electronic trading systems (ETS) have developed, which provide competition to established markets based on lower costs and greater flexibility [Board et al., 2001].

A major characteristic of the U.K. equity market is the importance of institutional investors, such as pension funds and insurance companies. These institutions hold some 55 percent of UK equity, spread about equally between insurance and pension funds [Buckle and Thompson, 1998, p. 47]. (In contrast, U.S. pension funds hold 21 percent and insurance companies 7 percent of equities.) The importance of pension funds is unique to the United Kingdom, reflecting substantially the relative low state pensions compared with other commercially developed countries. It has been the tradition that these institutions restrict their operations to securities trading, including bonds, and do not actively intervene in the management of the companies in which they have ownership interests.

There is also a rich set of bond markets. Both government bonds (Gilts) and corporate bonds are traded on the LSE. The corporate bond market is relatively small compared with countries where the financial system has traditionally depended much more on banks and other commercially developed markets, because in the United Kingdom debt tends to be raised by banks. The retail banking system is highly concentrated, a national characteristic shared with many other financial systems except the United States, which, until 1994, required banks to operate branches only within a state and which restricted bank holding companies from operating nationwide.

HISTORY OF THE PRESENT REGULATORY STRUCTURE

The U.K. financial system has a long and generally distinguished history, especially with regard to innovation. It is also a history of learning from financial crises. The Bank of England was founded in 1694 and the LSE in 1802, though there were markets for stocks prior to this. Banks also developed early. By the beginning of the 20th century national networks existed, although they did not generally provide long-term loans to firms. Companies were generally given limited liability in 1855, and further inhibitions on company formation were removed in 1856.

Market development was strongly encouraged by the need to provide capital for the railway industry in the United Kingdom and abroad. Thus, the strong market orientation of the U.K. financial system, where financial markets were major suppliers of long-term funds, emerged very early in the development of the system.

Developments in accounting lagged relative to these market developments, even though a number of professional accounting institutions were formed in the mid- to late 19th century. (A charter was granted to Edinburgh accountants in 1853, and the Institute of Accountants formed in London was granted a charter in 1880.) Published accounts of a variety of types, usually including a balance sheet but not necessarily an income statement (profit and loss account), were presented in this period but were not required except for a short period before 1856. The content of financial reports at this time was generally not regulated. Indeed, the regular and systematic provision for depreciation was subject to much controversy.

Generally, both the financial system and accounting were free from major regulation. The various institutions, such as the LSE and the accounting institutes, were set up by statute or the equivalent. Regulation was left to these institutions as self-regulating organizations, except where major crises led to additional legislation. Banks were supervised by the Bank of England, but generally informally via authoritative guidance. The major external instrument used to question conduct and to enforce performance was litigation by firms and individuals. The courts tended to take the view that commercial problems were best adjudicated by relying upon the most compelling expert opinion.

This general regime for financial markets survived up to what was called the Big Bang in 1986, which restructured the financial markets in a major way. Brokerage commissions became fully negotiable, while additional regulation was introduced to protect investors. Trading using a computerized system was introduced. The ultimate aim was to improve the international competitiveness of the financial markets in the United Kingdom and allow them to play their part in the dynamic changing global finance market, with its many new financial products and organizations.

THE REGULATORY REGIME FROM 1986 TO THE PRESENT

This revised market regulatory regime dates from the Big Bang in 1986, when regulation was formally placed on a self-regulation basis and considerably extended, especially in the area of investor protection. Authority for overall regulation of securities markets and market participants was given by statute to a Securities and Investment Board, which licensed three second-tier bodies, responsible respectively for the regulation of securities and future markets, retail investment business, and investment management. Individual regulators also were established for most other financial sectors. This resulted in a substantially fragmented system, an outcome most likely due to an unwillingness of policymakers to make radical changes in the preexisting system. But that new regime could not cope with a rapidly developing financial environment and did not prevent the scandals associated with the misleading sales of personal pensions in the late 1980s and early 1990s. Ultimately, the United Kingdom did embrace more radical change in 1997, introducing a comprehensive financial regulator—the Financial Services Authority (FSA)—that ultimately was given oversight over the safety and soundness and other practices of the entire financial industry. (We discuss the FSA in more detail shortly.)

EVOLUTION OF ACCOUNTING "REGULATION"

Prior to 1970, the United Kingdom had no mandatory regulation of accounting reports other than a rather minimal law, which, however, did require consolidated accounts well before other countries. Accounting practices were quite varied, with a large number of different treatments both generally and for the same items. These practices included a variety of "window-dressing" approaches and reserve accounting. Following a substantial number of major accounting scandals in the 1960s, including the collapse of a major firm (Rolls Razor) just after publishing "clean accounts" and the use of different valuations that gave firms quite different valuations in takeovers (AEI/GEC and Leasco/Pergamon), a private sector Accounting Standards Steering Committee was formed in 1969 by the Institute of Chartered Accountants in England and Wales, reflecting the government's wish that the accounting profession better regulate itself.

The combined accountancy bodies of the United Kingdom and Ireland formed the Accounting Standards Committee (ASC) in 1976. This body, with membership of some 20, mainly senior auditors, had no formal authority in the commercial community, nor did the government formally back it. The ASC promulgated standards, which each of the six professional accountancy bodies could accept or reject. The only formal means the ASC had for enforcing its standards was the threat of disciplinary procedures by the relevant accountancy body to those directors who were accountants. The majority of directors thus faced no penalty. Without explicit authority or strong enforcement powers, the ASC did well to get some quite controversial standards accepted, including those on leasing and on foreign currency transactions, although the latter included accounting treatments that might not have been included without commercial pressure. However, the ASC could not obtain acceptance for its several inflation-accounting proposals in the late 1970s and early 1980s. It gradually came to be felt in the commercial community and in the accountancy profession that there was a need to base accounting standards on an explicit conceptual framework, and that the ASC was unable to cope with increased "creative" accounting and with the complexity of modern accounting issues.

The incorporation of the European Community's accounting directives into U.K. law in the 1980s introduced detailed codified accounting reports into accounting, where certain items had to be disclosed in one of a number of standard formats with substantial extra disclosures. These directives were promulgated after a long period of discussion and bargaining in the European Community. They are a blend of substantially different accounting practices in several countries. They incorporate the U.K. "true and fair" view where the giving of such a view is the ultimate legal objective of accounting reports. Specific rules are to be followed unless exceptionally these do not give a true and fair view, in which case the rules may be overridden with the auditor's concurrence and full disclosure. The directives also incorporate the continental practice of highly structured accounts. The directives, however, have been interpreted differently in the law of different countries. (See also Chapter 7 on the European Union [EU].)

THE PRESENT REGULATORY STRUCTURE OF FINANCIAL INSTITUTIONS

The creation of the FSA in 1997 shifted regulation of banks and eventually all financial institutions from the Bank of England to a newly structured FSA. The former retains responsibility, however, for the operation of monetary policy and for ensuring the financial stability of the economy.[3]

The FSA is independent of the government and of the financial markets. It is a single statutory regulator for financial services with the broadest regulatory portfolio in the world, combining prudential regulation and business and market conduct regulation across the full range of financial services. Although other countries have a similar single regulator, the FSA is the first one in a major international financial market.

The Financial Services and Markets Act, 2000, fully implemented in 2001, provides full powers to the FSA.[4] Initially its responsibilities were limited to bank supervision, overseeing the regulation of investment business, supervision of insurance companies, and being the competent authority for listing on the LSE. The 2000 Act gave the FSA additional regulatory responsibilities, including supervision and regulation of building societies (which provide home loans), investment management, retail investment, and the securities and derivatives businesses.[5]

The FSA is not designed to be a detailed regulator for all areas of the financial markets; rather, in some areas it registers self-regulatory bodies, establishes their rules of behavior, and monitors their conduct. Thus, the LSE sets its own detailed rules within the more general regulations of the FSA, though listing rules are laid down and enforced by the FSA [Board et al., 2001]. The FSA also authorizes individuals to carry out investment business and ensures compliance by visiting and inspecting firms regularly. This approach is in line with the government's general policy on regulation, which is to encourage competition rather than to enforce in detail. Strong, proactive, and independent competition authorities are supposed to attack all forms of anticompetitive activities with penalties that bite heavily.[6]

The FSA has substantial powers in order to pursue its functions. It has the power to recognize investment exchanges and clearinghouses. The major recognized exchanges include the LSE, the LIFFE, and the London Securities and Derivatives Exchange (OMLX). Clearinghouses run settlement systems for the London Metal Exchange and the International Petroleum Exchange and are responsible to the FSA. The FSA also regulates the over-the-counter market. It authorizes firms and persons to participate in the investment market and vets senior employees in most financial sectors that trade in the United Kingdom. It also has strong powers for ensuring the prudential management of institutions across the financial markets, which require it to achieve a close understanding of the individual institutions. The powers to enforce its various roles are very substantial and include strong intervention, the withdrawing of authorization for trading, and the ability to levy very high fines.

There are two other aspects of the U.K. financial system outside the purview of the FSA that are important. The first is the LSE's Panel on Takeovers and Mergers, which establishes voluntary rules for the information required by the LSE during a takeover or a situation that may suggest a takeover, thereby ensuring transparency and supplementing the less-stringent statute law. Second are strong legal prohibitions on the use of confidential inside information, similar to those in place in the United States. By law, price-sensitive information cannot be given to an unconnected person other than for the operational purposes of the subject firm. It is now illegal to publish any such information other than to the market as a whole, similar to SEC Regulation FD in the United States. This has called into question meetings by corporate executives with investment analysts and even private calls to them.

CURRENT ACCOUNTING REGULATION

As has been the tradition in the United Kingdom, financial regulators in the past and the FSA currently have had no direct role in determining the contents of accounting reports, except for detailed regulation of prospectuses. The FSA can, of course, specify accounting reports for any set of entities coming under its control, although this has not been done in the past and the FSA has not used this power. Indeed, FSA literature infrequently mentions accounting or accounting standards. Although the LSE listing agreement requires additional financial information, these rules are dealt with in a general way by accounting standard setters.

A major objective of the FSA is to ensure transparency in markets. This involves not only the transparency of market trades, but also transparency concerning corporations in which the public invests. The FSA therefore

encourages corporations generally to increase disclosure, to avoid accounting that may mislead investors, and to follow best practice. The
FSA's interest in the contents of financial statements is also derived from
its supervisory responsibilities. These rest on the various measures of
adequate performance, such as capital adequacy and liquidity measures
that are based on accounting figures.[7]

More generally, the quality of accounting and auditing standards is
a key component for giving full information to investors for decision-
making.[8] A high quality of standards should result in reported numbers
that are as transparent as possible and relevant to investment decisions
and are internationally acceptable and, ideally, internationally comparable. These accounting qualities are directly related to the FSA's goals of
protecting the investor and the provision of fair, efficient, and transparent
markets, and they put considerable weight on the apparatus for setting
accounting and auditing standards and, especially, their enforcement.
They also require the independent verification of financial statements by
professional and external auditors, fully trained to an agreed high international standard.

Thus, we expect that agencies like the FSA will expand their demands
on accounting to encompass valuations that are believed to have greater
decision relevance, favoring the use of market values and fair values
where these can be determined objectively. We also expect accountants to
apply methods that provide some guidance as to the value of intangible
(soft) assets and to improve relevant accounting aspects for what have
been called "new economy" firms, such as information technology companies and web companies. But a question naturally arises: how far can
auditors be expected to lend credibility to such information, and to what
degree? Similarly, it can be expected that the statements like the Operating and Financial Review (OFR) in the United Kingdom (equivalent to
the Management Analysis and Discussion statement in the United States)
will become more important and will contain more forward-looking information, as suggested in value reporting [Eccles et al., 2000], and more
of their content will be mandatory, as confirmed by changes made to the
OFR in the United Kingdom in 2004 (to be discussed later).[9] A second
question therefore surfaces: to what extent can auditors be expected to
provide validity to such statements?

The structure sketched above was not affected by the changes implemented in the face of collapses in companies such as Enron and WorldCom,
except that the listing rules are being reconsidered.

FINANCIAL DISCLOSURE BY CORPORATIONS WITH
STOCK LISTED ON SECURITIES MARKETS

The accounting architecture in the United Kingdom is formed by statute
law (including EU directives enacted into U.K. law), the common law,
accounting standards established by the Accounting Standards Board

(ASB) (see later) and, from 2005, those of the International Accounting Standards Board (IASB) for the consolidated accounts of listed companies, the advice of other authorities, and generally accepted practice. All these requirements have applied generally to all limited liability companies, not just to listed companies (as is the situation in the United States).

Statute Law

Until the 1980s, the legislation concerning financial reports was fairly general, requiring a balance sheet at the end of the year, a profit and loss account (income statement) for the year, and a directors' report for the year, but it did, unusually at the time, require consolidated accounts and probably was stricter on secret reserves than in continental European countries. The directors' report, which was to be encompassed in the OFR that was to be mandatory for listed companies from 2005 (reversed by the government in 2005; see later), is a narrative discussion of the business; it generally includes little information. Auditors have to indicate whether the report is inconsistent with the financial statements.

The law requires certain conventional disclosures. It also says that that historical cost is the basic valuation principle, but alternative valuation rules may be used. Dividends can be paid only out of realized income, which is not defined. There are no other payout rules, as distinct from other countries, including some in Europe.

Generally, the law left accounting details to the profession. Importantly, the overriding requirement was that the financial statements give a true and fair view of the company's state of affairs at the end of the year and that the profit or loss declared was also true and fair. Ideally, this gave directors the ability to report substance over form and to override accounting requirements that would distort the economic picture of the corporation. The requirement to report a true and fair view was viewed as much stronger than and different from the U.S. requirement to "present fairly in conformity with generally accepted accounting principles." The true and fair concept was fairly alien to continental Europe, where following usually statutory accounting rules has been required. The relatively nonrestrictive approach changed in the 1980s with introduction of accounting directives of the then European Community (EC; now the EU), which sought to harmonize EC accounting practices into national laws. This resulted in U.K. accounting moving nearer the approaches of continental Europe, but still a long way from the detailed codes laid down by some EU governments.

The Fourth Directive (enacted in the Companies Act 1981, amended by the 1985 Act), in particular, required firms to adopt one of a number of possible formats for accounting statements. These involved much more detailed disclosure, including some expenses, than was usual in the United Kingdom and required conformance with mandatory accounting principles and valuation rules for accounting items, which ruled out some practices common in the United Kingdom.[10] The Seventh Directive, enacted into U.K. law in 1989, dealt with consolidated accounts and followed U.K. practice. It did, however, introduce into U.K. accounting the possibility of exempting small and medium-sized companies from some accounting requirements.

Generally, the transition to a more European approach to accounting in the United Kingdom went well. The directives allowed considerable flexibility and avoided a number of difficult accounting issues. This allowed different emphases and interpretations to be placed on the directives in different countries, thereby easing acceptance but weakening harmonization. A similar approach would ease the acceptance of international accounting standards by firms and countries that wished to maintain their favored treatments, but actually would work against the objective of having international accounting standards in the first place. The directives did incorporate the concept of a true and fair view and allowed it to be used by individual firms to override accounting legal requirements in certain circumstances. This override has also (perhaps illegitimately, as any override is meant to be available to only individual corporations) been used in the United Kingdom to write into some accounting standards elements that conflict with the Companies Acts.

The Company Law Review Steering Group (hereafter the Company Law Review Group [CLRG]) was set up by the government in 1998 to recommend changes to company law. It issued its final report in 2001 [dti, 2001]. The government has acted on most of its suggestions to be implemented in 2005 [Stationery Office, 2002]. Listed companies will have to put their accounting documents on their website within months of their fiscal year-end, though the details of this requirement have not yet been enacted.

A major recommendation in the accounting area was to require an OFR as part of the annual report that would evaluate the directors' performance and present the expected changes in the business, including trends and strategic direction. Other items to be discussed in the OFR included corporate risk and social and environmental impacts. This recommendation was accepted enthusiastically by the government and enacted quickly to take effect in 2005. However, the requirement for a mandatory OFR was withdrawn in late 2005. A further discussion of the OFR is contained in Chapter 11, where we discuss the usefulness to investors of the disclosure of supplementary information outside the financial statements.

That the U.K. was requiring companies to report additional information outside the financial statements complicates the twin challenges of making accounting statements comparable internationally and ensuring that investors have decision-relevant information. Many would think it is difficult to rely on the good-faith judgment of managers as suggested by the CLRG and would expect more rigorous auditing requirements, albeit of a different character to those for financial statements. Some type of safe harbor provision would seem necessary, as would standards for major items of information. A major problem not considered by the CLRG is ensuring comparability across such reports without inhibiting their development.

Statute law and common law (derived from judgments in specific cases before the courts) still form the fundamental foundations for considering accounting and commercial issues, as any resolution has to be consistent with the statutory law and previously adjudicated cases, where not overridden by the law. Indeed, it has been argued that the possibility of litigation is a significant spur to the practice of high-quality accounting in a country [Ball, 2001]. But in reality, litigation has not acted as a major force in the United Kingdom. Litigation is expensive and class actions are not yet allowed. Furthermore, the findings are too case-oriented to be used to enforce generally good-quality accounting. Courts tend to look only at the issues before them, few accounting cases have yet been heard, and most court actions do not bind the general decisions of other courts. Generally, commercial cases tend to be settled out of court, although a small number of cases where auditors have been sued for negligence have gone to the highest appeal court.

There seems to be growing interest in the United Kingdom, however, in accounting litigation. Generally, awarded damages have become larger, more experience has been gained in class actions (in other areas), and lawyers have recently been allowed to work on a contingency fee basis in some areas.

Accounting Standards

The Accounting Standards Board (ASB) replaced the ASC in 1990. The ASB is independent and organized on much more professional lines (a much smaller number of members, two of whom are full-time, who are paid and are provided with better technical support). It has an infrastructure for standard setting broadly similar to the U.S. Financial Accounting Standards Board (FASB) and that now adopted by the IASB. Its umbrella body is the Financial Reporting Council (FRC), with wide representation from the financial community; accountants make up only half of its membership. The FRC provides guidance to the ASB and ensures that it is properly funded. The Financial Reporting Review Panel (FRRP), a body reporting to the FRC, investigates accounting reports that may not show a true and fair view and can apply to the courts for the restatement of deficient accounts. An Urgent Issues Task Force, organized by the ASB, issues guidance about reasonable interpretations of the Companies Acts and current accounting standards. The ASB views this guidance as contributing to generally accepted practice.

The Companies legislation has been revised to recognize accounting standards and some aspects of standard setting. The 1989 Companies Act contained the first legislative reference to accounting standards. It required companies to state whether these had been followed in preparing accounts.

A problem that remains is whether the courts will treat adherence to accounting standards as necessary to showing a true and fair view. In the United States, although some courts do not take this line, it is generally the case that firms that comply with prevailing generally accepted accounting principles (GAAP) are immune from liability. In the United Kingdom, both the profession and the ASB believe that following standards is necessary for showing a true and fair view, though this interpretation has not yet been explicitly considered before an authoritative court.[11] Nonetheless, any doubts about the authority of accounting standards will be rendered moot, at least for listed companies, when in 2005, along with the rest of the EU, they must use International Financial Reporting Standards (IFRS) issued by the IASB for their consolidated statements.

The Statement of Principles

After some 10 years of work and extensive consultation, the ASB published its Statement of Principles in 1999. The Statement describes the underlying reasoning of the Board. It is broadly in line with most conceptual frameworks and is very similar to that issued by the (then) International Accounting Standards Committee (IASC, the predecessor of the IASB). In common with most other similar statements, it gives primacy to informed investors as users of accounting statements and puts the emphasis on investor decision-making rather than performance measurement. Again, in common with other similar statements, it takes a strong balance sheet approach. Income is conceptually determined by comparing opening and closing balance sheets for a period. Assets and liabilities are defined relative to the future economic benefits flowing from past transactions or events. Assets have to be in the control of the entity.

This approach represents a considerable move away from conventional U.K. accounting, which emphasized a profit and loss account generated by matching costs and revenues over time and measured assets as balances of expenditures not yet recovered (see Chapter 2). In line with the emphasis on decision-making, the Statement of Principles is not transaction-oriented, and it reduces the explicit roles of prudence and of realization in the accounting framework.

The Statement highlights a problem with the decision-making approach to accounting, however. Decisions are about the future, and useful information helps to assess the amounts and timing of future cash flows and any associated risk. Past information can help but cannot be used on its own to generate forecasts. Incorporating forecasts into accounting statements means that they cannot be validated using traditional auditing procedures. They can be given elements of credibility by assessing whether the forecasts make sense relative to the entity's past, and whether the forecasts are based on reasonable assumptions that have been tested against generally accepted procedures. Forecasts also can be tested to see that they include all the relevant variables and are generated using state-of-the-art technology or other models. It is an open question, however, how much users of financial statements actually value these forecasts.

Guidelines of the Institute of Chartered Accountants in England and Wales

Over the years, the Institute of Chartered Accountants in England and Wales (later all the professional bodies) has issued non-mandatory guidelines on accounting issues, called technical releases, which provide interpretations to fill gaps in the law and accounting standards. For example, technical releases have been issued on what constitutes realizable profits and the materiality of accounting items.

Other noteworthy inputs to what becomes generally accepted practice are publications on accounting issues by the large accountancy firms. A number of these firms also issue detailed manuals on U.K. GAAP,[12] which provide some opinions on controversial issues.[13] Relatively few researchers study individual accounting standards or write commentaries on standards (as they do in other countries, notably Germany).

International Influences on U.K. Accounting

The major current international influence on U.K. accounting is that of the EU. As discussed in Chapter 7, until recently the EU's accounting directives attempted to harmonize accounting rules across EU countries. In 2000, the EU adopted an alternative strategy when the Commission proposed that all listed companies in the EU must by 2005 prepare their consolidated accounts on the basis of IFRS. Additionally, companies could use IFRS for their individual accounts with the permission of their national government. The United Kingdom has allowed this as a one-off choice from 2005.

The EU's new rule has not generated as much debate in the United Kingdom as other accounting controversies. The ASB has been seeking convergence with IFRS, as there are considerable differences between some ASB and IASB standards [Cairns and Nobes, 2000]. This is true of even recent ASB standards (e.g., on retirement benefits and financial instruments), even though most recent complex draft standards have been developed in conjunction with the IASB and standard setters from a number of countries. It is not entirely clear what the role of the ASB will be when IASB standards are permitted generally in the United Kingdom. At the very least, the ASB will oversee implementation of IFRS in the United Kingdom, deal with any problems that arise, and establish standards for individual entity reports that continue to follow U.K. accounting standards.

More important, both for accounting harmonization and for the development of accounting thought, is whether the United Kingdom would continue to influence the IASB, and accounting more generally, if the ASB were disbanded or its resources reduced. A similar question arises with other national standard setters. The ASB played an important role on the former IASC and has had considerable influence on the IASB. All U.K. standards indicate how they differ from the relevant IFRS and, often, any differences from the standards promulgated by FASB. The ASB also maintains close relationships with other standard setters.

FINANCIAL DISCLOSURE BY SMALL AND MEDIUM SIZED COMPANIES

U.K. accounting does not distinguish between listed and non-listed companies in terms of their required accounting disclosure, except that the LSE listing agreement imposes some additional requirements concerning the publication of interim and preliminary reports and the disclosure of specific items in these reports. Generally, accounting requirements in the past have not varied with company size, although non-quoted companies do not have to follow certain corporate governance requirements.[14] This approach, however, changed because of the EU's accounting harmonization policy, which makes this distinction and allows smaller companies certain disclosure relief (although the EU generally requires all limited liability companies to satisfy its accounting requirements). The Companies Act 1981 therefore allowed small and medium-sized limited liability companies to file modified accounting reports with Companies House, but a full set of accounts still had to be provided to shareholders. In 1985, some exemptions were granted to small companies with regard to shareholder accounts, which still had to give a true and fair view and therefore had to follow accounting standards. These exemptions include not requiring consolidation. Other laws deal with partnerships.

Given these statutory requirements on small and medium-sized companies, there has been an ongoing debate as the degree (if any) that such companies should be exempted from the requirements of accounting standards. The first *Financial Reporting Standard for Smaller Entities* was issued by the ASB in 1997 and has been updated as required. The "smaller entity standard" consolidates all the requirements from all standards that are deemed relevant to smaller companies. It is optional, in that a smaller firm can decide whether or not to comply with all accounting standards. The IASB has begun to look at issuing a similar standard.

The definition of smaller companies is provided in the Companies Act 1985, which classified such companies according to their turnover (sales) and number of employees. These numbers will be regularly updated to the EU maximum. The 1985 Act and the Reporting Standard together make the accounting requirements on small companies substantially less onerous. However, they do not change the general structure of the accounts the companies must provide. There are relatively few statutory exemptions for medium-sized companies, and generally these are based on the size criteria.

INVESTOR PROTECTION GENERALLY

A major objective of securities legislation is to protect those trading in securities. Prospectuses for new issues are required and highly regulated by the FSA, going beyond the requirements of the relevant EU directives and the U.K. law. Most of the duties and powers to ensure fair and equal treatment of investors, transparency in financial statements generally, and fair selling by qualified firms and individuals are vested in the FSA, where not otherwise directed by statutes. Investors also are protected by company law requirements that call for annual general meetings and the right to vote on major decisions, such as takeovers. A very extensive framework for investor protection exists based on the assumption that investors are highly likely to be exploited without stringent regulation. Nevertheless, there are still strong views that protection is insufficient, especially with regard to retail sales and management's ability to manage earnings.

CORPORATE GOVERNANCE

It is important to consider in some detail the rules of corporate governance in the United Kingdom that affect financial reporting. For example, a properly operating audit committee made up of external (non-executive) directors should enhance investors' confidence in the company's financial reports and create an expectation that serious audit problems will be considered without top management interference. When corporations are properly governed, there are "ex ante" incentives for management to report financial results accurately. Regulation of accounting, in contrast, is an ex post way of preventing accounting irregularities.

Corporate governance is covered by the common law, the LSE Listing Agreement, and some FSA requirements. As a broad generalization, rules relating to corporate governance have been tightened since the 1980s and 1990s, when there were major scandals (e.g., Maxwell scandal, where one man was able to make decisions without any regard to shareholders, pensioners, or the workforce) and also in reaction to the governance problems that have surfaced in the United States.[15]

The right to direct and control a company is vested in a single unitary board of directors in the United Kingdom, subject to general control by shareholders at the annual general meeting (AGM). Shareholders have "general control" over the approval of the appointment of the company's auditors, the election of both executive and non-executive directors, and approval of a dividend (if any) recommended by the directors. The constitutions (charters) of companies may also reserve various decisions for the shareholders and the AGM, such as merger proposals and major dispositions of assets.

Technically, unhappy shareholders can request that an item be discussed at the AGM or call for an extraordinary meeting, if they can obtain the required percentage of shareholders to support them in this request. However, usually the directors of diffusely owned companies have sufficient proxy votes to control the business of the AGM. Shareholders may sue the company for breaches of the company's constitution and other agreements. They may in some cases sue the directors individually or severally. However, such lawsuits are rare because they are costly to pursue, and perhaps especially because of the "English rule" covering attorneys' fees: the losing party must cover the costs of the winner. In the United Kingdom class actions also are not allowed, which diminishes incentives for plaintiffs to sue. In essence, dissatisfied shareholders really have only option: they can sell their shares.

Although institutional shareholders have more voting power, they generally have avoided public conflict. Their privately expressed views, though, have been important in a number of cases. A 2001 report to the U.K. Treasury urged institutional shareholders to be more active [Myners, 2001]. Both the Company Law Review and the government have considered how more intervention could be achieved without harming corporate performance. At this writing, the matter remains under government review.

U.K. law directs corporate boards to run their companies in the best interests of shareholders, to present accounts, and to maintain proper accounting records. The law also put restrictions on loans to directors and requires directors to disclose any "material" transactions they may have with their companies (although there have been difficulties making this requirement fully operational) and to disclose their compensation, including gains from exercising share options and amounts received under long-term incentive schemes and pension contributions paid (the obligations are less strong on non-quoted companies). In light of recent concerns in the United States and the United Kingdom about "excessive" executive salaries, the British government added new requirements in 1999 and 2002 requiring companies to provide additional information in their financial reports on directors' compensation. Regulations issued in 2002 also require that the remuneration report be approved as a whole by the shareholders at the AGM and that corporate policy on directors' contracts and any payments for loss of office be discussed.

Like the United States, the United Kingdom imposes joint-and-several liability on directors for a large range of responsibilities under both the civil and criminal law. Legislation requires that directors conduct their activities in a professional manner, and allows for the possibility that they can be charged with negligence in the discharge of their duties. The Company Law Review has suggested that directors' duties should be defined more widely to include an obligation that they comply with the company's constitution, act loyally to promote the purposes of the company, and advance shareholders' interests. Although directors should take into account the wider effects of their decisions, the overriding concern with the shareholders' interest would remain unchanged. This approach recognizes that there is no obvious way of enforcing directors' "duties" to the wider community, which the government accepts and is codifying into a statute [Stationery Office, 2002].

Corporate Governance Codes

A major effort to improve corporate governance has been made in a series of codes for disclosures outside the financial statements for listed companies, which gain some force by being appended to the LSE Listing Agreement.[16] These codes have been consolidated into what is called the Combined Code. The Code places seemingly, but as yet untested by the evidence, common-sense requirements on directors, such as that non-executives should form the majority of the board and exclusively form the remuneration and audit committees, and that the board should have a sound internal control system. The Code requires that these matters be reported upon in the annual financial statements. Auditors are required to state whether the company has complied with the major provisions of the Code. Quoted companies are required to state how they have applied the principles of the Combined Code and whether or not they have complied with the specified principles of the Code with details of any noncompliance ("comply or explain"). An infrequent but important departure is a failure to split the roles of the chairman and chief executive. Companies have generally complied with the Code, although when they do not, they sometimes do not give (as is required) reasons for the departure.

In the accounting area, directors have to explain their responsibility to prepare accounting reports and provide a fair assessment of their behavior in all public reports of any price-sensitive information and report that the firm is a going concern. The auditors must explain their responsibilities.

There is no doubt that the Codes have substantially changed corporate governance of large companies, but generally this improvement has not spread to smaller companies.

As part of the government's review of the report of Company Law Review and in the context of the problems caused by Enron and other companies, in 2002 the government set up the Higgs Review to consider the role and effectiveness of non-executive directors, and the Smith Review to consider the role and effectiveness of the audit committee.[17] Many of the recommendations of these reviews were incorporated into a revised Combined Code in 2003 [Financial Reporting Council, 2003]. Generally, the Higgs Review confirmed and made more rigorous the existing requirements of the Combined Code. The Review gives detailed guidance on the meaning of independence from the company—independent in character and judgment and without any relationships with the firm. Thus, for example, a former employee cannot be regarded as independent within 5 years of severing any connection with the company. The independent non-executive directors should meet on their own at least once a year. There should be a senior independent director.

That corporate governance is an area of continuing conflict is evident from the managerial criticisms of some other Higgs recommendations. The first of these contested recommendations, which were not included in the Combined Code, is that the senior independent director should have separate meetings with major shareholders. It was felt this would dilute and cause confusion concerning the position of the chairman. The second is that current CEOs should not take over as chairman of the board of directors, in order to restrict the power of and help ensure the independence of the chairman. The revised Combined Code does allow an outgoing CEO to serve as chairman, providing that the reasons are given to the shareholders. Higgs recommends that non-executive directors should not be paid with stock options, but can be remunerated with company shares. The Combined Code allows remuneration with stock options, subject to ensuring that this does not imperil the non-executive directors' independence.

The Smith Report's recommendations on audit committees were incorporated into the revised Combined Code. These include the stipulation that the audit committee shall have at least three members, at least one of whom should have relevant and recent financial experience. Additionally, the audit committee should monitor and review the company's internal audit function and the external auditor's independence and make recommendations to the board concerning the appointment of external auditors. If the board rejects such recommendations, an explanation shall be given in the annual report. This is less strong than the U.S. equivalent, which gives the audit committee appointment power. Finally, the audit committee must have a policy concerning the supply of non-audit services by the company's auditor.

Effects on Other Stakeholders

Commentators who take a wider societal view regard the Companies Acts as blatantly omitting concern for other stakeholders in the corporation. The Companies Acts do refer to a duty to have regard for the interest of employees. The government has said, following the Company Law Review, that directors' duties should include, where appropriate, considering other stakeholders, community and environmental impacts, and business reputation and should report on these matters. Other stakeholders have some rights by other legislation (e.g., employees have rights in health and safety legislation and in employment legislation). In contrast to other countries, such as Germany, generally the relationship of other stakeholders with the company is restricted to the terms of their contracts. Some large companies voluntarily issue very good social and environment reports with a degree of audit assurance.

One weakness in the corporate governance code is the reliance on firms to "comply or explain" (they often do not). This approach thus relies on the good judgment of managers to pursue shareholders' interests.

However, some matters, such as the remuneration of corporate officers, nominations to the board of directors, and, especially, the responsibilities and membership of the audit committee, are so important that they may need to be enforced rather than left to a "comply or explain" regime. In contrast, U.S. practice is to regulate these matters specifically. The support given in the United Kingdom to dissatisfied non-executive directors is weak. Board minutes must simply note disagreements, if requested. Dissenting directors also have a right to give a statement to the shareholders if they resign.

The overwhelming weakness of corporate governance in general is that little attempt has been made theoretically or practically to show that such requirements will have an impact on corporate behavior. For example, will the prior satisfaction of any independence requirements ensure that non-executive directors are not "captured" by powerful executive groups? Similarly, where requirements are brought in to remedy specific past abuses, generally little effort has been made to show that these remedies will cure the abuses that gave rise to their instigation.

AUDITING AND THE ATTESTATION OF FINANCIAL REPORTS

In the United Kingdom, the responsibility for preparing proper accounts lies with the directors of a company, as does the responsibility for their contents. In the past, the financial statements of all public limited liability companies were subject to a full audit. The government has now exempted smaller companies from audit. Auditors' responsibilities are governed by statute law, the auditing regulator (now the FRC, and its subsidiaries), the Listing Rules of the LSE, and professional practice. Auditors have a duty of care only to existing shareholders, and then only with respect to their rights in the company; that is, unlike the United States, there is no general duty to those who use the accounting reports for decision-making.

The auditors must state whether, in their opinion, the financial statements give a true and fair view and must agree to any use by the directors of the true and fair override (which allows the presentation of accounts that do not follow specific GAAP rules if these rules would otherwise provide misleading disclosure). A very limited override will be available after the adoption of IFRS in 2005 for quoted companies. The IASB and the EU currently think such a provision is unnecessary with the use of IFRS, and in any case expect the use of the override to be exceptional. The auditors also must state that the accounts are properly prepared, in accordance with the Companies Act, and whether the company has kept proper accounting records and has provided all necessary information and explanations to the auditor. The auditors also must ensure that other information presented in the annual report, such as the OFR, is consistent with the financial statements. Listed companies must also report on compliance with the Combined Code. Auditors are not required to express an opinion on corporate governance or internal controls, though the profession has issued guidelines concerning the assurance of internal controls.

The Companies Act also prescribes that only members of professional accountancy bodies who have completed a training period in auditing can act as auditors.[18] The Audit Practices Board (now reformed, see below) was a self-regulatory body funded by the profession that issued auditing standards and guidance and regulated auditors. There are disciplinary structures within the profession to consider alleged misconduct of audits. A peer review process for large audit firms that audit listed companies has been operated by the profession.

The profession has agreed to the rotation of the lead auditor on an audit after 5 years. The Institute of Chartered Accountants in England and Wales has also agreed to a 2-year "cooling off" period before clients can employ auditors, which is enforced by disciplinary powers over its members.

Building on the existing self-regulating framework and a new structure for audit regulation set up by the profession in 2000, the government introduced an independent and complex structure for auditing regulation, the FRC. This followed reviews of the regulatory regime by a government working party set up by the Secretary of State for Trade and Industry, published in 2003, and by a coordinating group on audit and accounting issues appointed by the Secretary of State for Trade and Industry. The government considered the previous structure to be too slow in getting started, too complex, and not fully independent. The FRC is now the umbrella body for the regulation of the profession. The regulation and review of auditing also has been transferred from the professional accounting bodies to the FRC. It has incorporated three subsidiaries that are associated with audits.

First, the existing Audit Practices Board, which sets audit standards, is charged with setting standards of audit independence, objectivity, and integrity.[19] The Board takes over responsibility for monitoring the audit of listed companies, major charities, and pension funds. Second, the Professional Oversight Board generally oversees the regulatory responsibility of the profession and has regulatory responsibility for recognizing the professional supervisory bodies and the qualifications required to be an auditor. The Board's primary function, though, is to provide oversight of the audit regime. The Audit Inspection Unit reports to it. Third, an Investigation and Discipline Board is responsible for public interest cases. It remains to be seen whether the new body will hand down strong penalties, including exclusion from the auditing profession. The earlier professional disciplinary boards were accused of being "soft" in their penalties and using very time-consuming procedures. Less important cases will continue to be handled by the profession, which will continue to have responsibility for the training, qualification, and monitoring of the behavior of members, and ensuring members' compliance with auditing standards.

Generally, the costs of these new arrangements will be broadly shared between the government, business, and professional bodies. There has been no change in the disciplinary penalties that can be used and no legal powers to obtain evidence. The formal arrangements for all this are still being made.[20]

ENFORCEMENT MECHANISMS

The enforcement regime for the regulatory system is highly complex and of a variety of types and draws on a variety of authority sources. Generally, each act within statute law provides penalties for breaches. The company law includes a number of technical offenses, such as failure to file accounts on time, which carry minor criminal penalties or automatic penalties. Major offenses of a criminal nature, such as fraud, carry severe penalties. However, only a few such cases have been brought, most likely because of their complexity. Nonetheless, the threat of criminal prosecution provides incentives for parties to comply with the law.

The relevant government minister has power to apply to the courts to remedy deficient accounts (a power also delegated to the FRRP), and costs may be recovered from individual directors rather than from the company. Shareholders and others may sue a company for breaches of duties to them. Such cases, though, are infrequent as they may be very complex, and therefore of high risk and very costly. As a practical matter, shareholder cases can be brought only where large numbers of affected persons are willing to support any action, in their individual capacities and not as a class (since class actions are not allowed). Equitable Life, a mutual assurance company, provides an example (though one focusing on contractual responsibility) where shareholders did mount legal action. Ultimately, the highest court in the United Kingdom (the House of Lords) agreed in July 2000 with members (shareholders) of the company with guaranteed annuities that directors acting unilaterally could not unilaterally vary the terms of their contracts.

The FSA has a very strong set of penalties that it can use. It can deny authorization to individuals and organizations that do not meet its qualifications after inspection or investigation. It can apply for injunctions to stop unauthorized activities and in some cases prosecute those involved in such activities and request financial restitution. The FSA can also issue private warnings, publicly censure ("shaming and naming"), levy severe financial penalties, and order compensation to ill-treated consumers.

In contrast, accounting standards setters (the ASB) have no enforcement power, except to apply to the courts, via the FRRP (a sister body of the ASB), for rewriting financial statements that are deficient in terms of giving a true and fair view. Auditors should signal material breaches of standards. Until recently the FRRP only reacted to potential deficient financial statements brought to their attention. So far the ASB seems to have had no major problems with enforcement, but regulators in the United Kingdom generally have less ability to enforce accounting standards than their counterparts in some other countries. It is not clear why nonetheless the ASB has been generally regarded to be effective. One possible explanation is that companies and auditors prefer this type of self-regulation relative to regulation by government or an SEC-type body. Another possibility is that the ASB engages in a very careful due process and detailed consultation process. The ASB also has been able to demonstrate that its conceptual framework supports many of its existing and draft standards. But one thing is clear: the ASB has not been captured by preparers or auditors, since some of its standards and work programs are seen as very controversial by the financial community. To what extent the IASB will enjoy the same respect in the future remains to be seen, however.

There are no tools available to enforce the Combined Code of corporate governance other than that companies must declare instances where they have not followed the code and auditors must review aspects of a company's compliance statement.

SHORTCOMINGS OF THE PRESENT REGULATORY REGIME

It is difficult to judge the success of the current regulatory structure in the United Kingdom because almost every part of it has either been revised recently or is under study for reform. There is as yet little empirical evidence to bring to bear on this question. Following the accounting scandals related to the bankruptcy of several well-known U.S. corporations, the government mainly built on reforms already under way and avoided introducing specific rules based on the U.S. situation. Many of the changes are relatively general, and their effects will depend on the approach taken to them by the corporate community. Overall, the new arrangements for the regulation of financial markets by the FSA are comprehensive, allow for detailed regulation, and encompass almost the complete span of financial markets. The FSA is highly accountable for its own behavior.

However, there are problems arising from a time when the FSA did not have the full responsibilities described earlier. The mis-selling of pensions and other long-term saving products has attracted much attention from the FSA. A major review of these practices is in progress, and misled investors were and continue to be substantially compensated for their losses. Another controversy arose over the FSA's involvement (or lack of fully effective involvement) in the Equitable Life situation discussed earlier.

Other concerns that have been expressed are that the FSA may seek to regulate in a too detailed way, and that its various divisions may additionally act too independently, to the detriment of the overall regulatory regime. That the FSA is the independent regulator for the whole set of financial services may cause confusion for regulators in other countries. There are concerns that there is no competing authority to provide the

FSA with an incentive to be efficient. It has also been questioned whether the FSA has sufficient intelligence and practical background to see trouble looming. This may be especially true of cross-border investment and listings.

It has been argued that there are insufficient avenues for individuals or groups of individuals in the United Kingdom to seek remedies through litigation. Shareholders can use the courts to obtain their rights as equity holders in a company, and the rights of minority shareholders are protected to a degree. These rights generally stem from contract law, and in many cases negligence would need to be proven. Investors have few rights with respect to companies in which they are not shareholders, even if they rely on information provided by such companies. This suggests that litigation cannot be relied upon to act as a major market-based regulatory control, as it is claimed to do in the United States.

Studies of accounting statements and studies of specific standards suggest that noncompliance with accounting standards by some important companies can always be found.[21] Financial directors and interested parties generally mount strong campaigns against some proposed standards. More generally, there is a view that accounting standards are becoming too complex and that only skilled professionals can understand accounting reports based on them. There is also a strong feeling that the ASB and IASB are seeking to take accounting reports down an "economic-based" path that rejects elements of traditional accounting that have served well in the past.

The United Kingdom probably has one of the strongest formal architectures in terms of depth and span of any corporate governance system in the world. This structure is all geared toward inhibiting top management from taking advantage of their positions or with rendering their actions transparent. An alternative approach would be to give them incentives to pursue shareholders' interests by, for example, requiring individual directors to have a significant holding in the shares of companies of which they are directors, with a large proportion locked in over a substantial period of time. There are considerable concerns that existing corporate governance tools do not give small shareholders sufficient powers. A current example is unhappiness with the perceived very high compensation packages received by directors and, especially, golden parachutes paid to departing directors, chairmen, and CEOs of apparently poorly run companies. This has led to the questioning of the role of the remuneration committee, a central pillar of the governance codes, because it is made up of non-executive directors who often are or have been in very senior positions in other companies. It is argued that such senior executives have an incentive to bolster managerial remuneration in their own interests.

Although there are many corporate governance requirements, generally their enforcement is weak. Statute law is infrequently enforced, usually long after the event, and only when there have been major scandals. It is too early to assess the objectives and ability of the FSA in this area, but

its predecessor bodies seemed not overly zealous. More aggressive enforcement in the retail investment area is likely in the future, but this
will depend on whether the FSA has sufficient resources to successfully
scan the environment for problem cases. Some enforcement can be expected where companies are directly supervised by the FSA. This will
depend on the expertise of the staff of the FSA, their ability to interpret early
and vague signals, and limitations on the resources made available to
them.[22]

At least two major problems face the FSA, and these will also plague
attempts to harmonize accounting standards across any type of group
of organizations. First, financial market firms from the EU trading in
the United Kingdom are bound by the requirements of their home-market
regulator, not the FSA. Second, companies may react to what they see
as overly onerous regulations by threatening to relocate to more favorable domains, although there is little evidence of this happening so far.
Nonetheless, the possibility that it may occur may cause the FSA to
moderate its regulatory regime, given the government's wish to encourage firms to enter the U.K. market.

The current enforcement arrangements with accounting standards have
worked well, in the sense that companies generally agree to rewrite their
accounts. The possibility of criticism of deficient accounts by the FRRP
should influence companies and improve auditor independence [Fearnely
et al., 1998, pp. 27–54]. The penalty of publicly "naming and shaming"
companies may be sufficient to deter others, although in the past the Panel
has not monitored company behavior generally. The Panel has now
agreed to be more proactive and will now study 300 to 400 accounting
statements a year, and the FSA will draw its attention to the accounting
statements of companies that it identifies as being at risk. The enforcement
powers relative to accounting standards may be sufficient in the current
environment but may be insufficient in an environment where standards
of increasing complexity are not originated by "home" standard setters,
because, among other reasons, the influence of companies on the IASB
may be diluted and the standard-setting procedure will be seen as less
open. Moreover, there may be objections that the international standards
do not allow for the domestic context and, therefore, resort should frequently be made to any very limited EU true and fair override that may
exist.

Detailed compliance with the corporate governance code is voluntary. It
is difficult to imagine that a quoted company failing to follow the code will
be de-listed. Stringent enforcement would end up in the courts and would
be very expensive and time-consuming. Enforcement problems would
plague even a minimal attempt to harmonize corporate governance across
countries, as there are very different approaches to enforcement. For a
further discussion, see Chapter 11.

There are three major problems with audits in the United Kingdom,
most of which are shared by a number of other countries. These problems

also impinge on suggestions to use auditors in some way to ensure the quality and comparability of accounting reports internationally.

The first problem is the "expectations gap," which arises when users of accounting reports believe that clean audit reports protect them from corporate failure and from fraud. The second concern relates to auditor independence. This issue has been "resolved" in some large accounting firms by separating clear consultancy and non-financial accounting activities from auditing, but the audit arms of firms still undertake activities that could be regarded as consulting and are allowed to take on a wider range of activities than in the United States.

The third problem relates to auditor liability. Currently, large audit firms are subject to lawsuits for any corporate failure with which they can be associated, as they are often the only party perceived to have substantial resources and insurance. Although many cases have been brought, most have been settled out of court. Such settlements inhibit any review of auditor conduct by the courts.

The government has recently allowed limited liability audit partnerships to be formed. This provides one vehicle for helping to overcome the problems of individual auditor liability, although auditors still can lose the entire monetary and human investment they have made in their firms. The government in 2004 decided against capping auditors' legal liability but suggested that it might in future allow auditors to contract with their clients to limit their liability, with the contract being legally binding on third parties, as suggested by the CLRG . Many would prefer an approach that limits the liability on auditors to an amount proportional to their share of the overall fault in a situation. However, the CLRG rejected this approach.

Acknowledgments We would like to thank PricewaterhouseCoopers, David Gwilliam, and especially David Cairns for very helpful comments.

6

Corporate Financial Reporting and Regulation in Germany

Germany has a very different regulatory tradition than the other countries we cover in this book, except for aspects of the Japanese system, and it is therefore useful to contrast it with them. Despite different traditions, many of the same kind of economic events—economic crises and collapses of major firms—were the cause for the introduction of increasingly comprehensive disclosure regulation. After a brief review of the relevant history, we describe in detail the current state of financial disclosure for listed and for non-listed companies, the legislative and regulatory environment, investor protection, corporate governance, auditing, and enforcement. There are currently several legislative efforts under way that significantly affect the current environment. Finally, we discuss shortcomings of this situation, proposed remedies, and current issues.

A BRIEF HISTORICAL GUIDE

Governmental regulation of accounting in the then various states in the German territory began in the late 18th century. Before that, there were only few requirements for maintaining corporate financial records, and these related to providing evidence in judicial proceedings.[1] The first accounting regulation dates from the Prussian Civil Code enacted in 1794. This Code drew heavily on the French "Ordonnance de Commerce," or Code Savary of 1673,[2] which had a long-term influence on accounting practice. The Code included some basic rules on inventory valuation and required a balance sheet in case of bankruptcy.

Annual balance sheets were first developed in Germany in the early 19th century. They were used to state wealth over "interim" periods of an enterprise's total life and, by comparing balance sheets over time, to measure changes in wealth—or profit or loss—during each period.[3]

Over the 19th century, several German states developed company laws that included a few accounting rules. The Prussian Stock Corporation Law of 1843 introduced a charter (concession) system and state supervision for stock corporations, which was seen as a counterweight to the granting of limited liability. The law also required stock companies to publish balance sheets. Stock corporations were later required to establish legal reserves out of retained earnings; legal reserves are still part of current company law. In the course of the political unification of Germany (German countries at the time included Austria, Prussia, and many small states), the General German Commercial Code of 1861 was reformed. This Code included rules for drawing up inventories and balance sheets, and valuation rules; moreover, it required companies to state in their statutes the principles they used to measure and distribute income. The Code was applicable to every businessman (*Kaufmann*), except for stock corporations, because they were already subject to state supervision, which was deemed sufficient.

After the war between Prussia and Austria in 1866 that led to the establishment of the German empire (as a combination of Prussia with several small states), the next legal reforms were undertaken as part of a broader effort of economic liberalization. The Stock Corporations Act (*Aktiengesetz*) of 1870 abolished the concession system for stock corporations and replaced it with corporate governance requirements and a mandatory, but still restricted, disclosure regime. This liberalization led to an enormous increase in the popularity of stock corporations, from only 200 stock corporations before the Act to more than 800 within 3 years after the Act became effective.

The major objective of financial statements, though, was the protection of creditors rather than of shareholders and other stakeholders. Disclosure of a balance sheet and an income statement was required, although no formats were prescribed. The Act obliged stock corporations to install a board of managing directors and a supervisory board, and to hold general meetings. The audit function was the responsibility of the supervisory board, not of independent professional auditors. However, an external audit was required if requested by holders of at least 10 percent of outstanding stock.

In 1874, two German states, Saxony and Bremen, were the first to introduce laws that made financial accounts the basis for taxation. This tax conformity rule, also known as the authoritativeness principle (*Maßgeblichkeitsprinzip*), has since been a key characteristic of German financial statements.

Few recognition principles and valuation methods were codified. One was that assets were to be measured at the value attributable to them at the balance sheet date. This was interpreted as a "current" value. In a time of growth and investment (*Gründerzeit*) around 1870, speculation and fraud increased substantially. Corporate failures and liquidations were common, which led to a major economic crisis and, finally, to a stock exchange crash in 1873. The crisis was precipitated by a relatively minor event, a cholera outbreak that led to the economic failure of the World Exhibition in Vienna. Given already slowing growth, these events led to a mistrust of stocks.

A common fraudulent practice was to overstate assets (above current value) and, based on the inflated net assets and income, to pay out dividends to shareholders to the disadvantage of creditors. The negative effects of this practice were reinforced by the lack of owners' capital, as stock corporations were permitted to start operations with only 10 percent of nominal capital paid in. Not surprisingly, some corporations were founded only for speculative and possibly fraudulent reasons. As a response, the Stock Corporations Act was amended in 1884 after extensive and contentious discussion. The principle of historical-cost valuation for fixed assets was adopted, which limited the overvaluation of assets. The amendment also introduced the requirement to publish a balance sheet and an income statement.

Another typical fraudulent practice was to overvalue the assets contributed when corporations were formed. Creditors advanced money or debt to the corporation based on an apparently sound equity structure, which actually was nonexistent. This type of fraud was hindered by the introduction of a compulsory audit by independent professional auditors of the initial balance. A statutory audit of annual statements was established only in 1931, but by around 1900 some 60 percent of stock corporations had voluntary audits.[4]

In 1897, a new Commercial Code for the first time referred to the "principles of proper bookkeeping" (*Grundsätze ordnungsmäßiger Buchführung*), which were meant to be the best accounting practices followed by careful businesspeople. The Code included only few basic accounting rules and referred to the principles of proper bookkeeping for details. The guiding idea was to keep the law flexible so that new developments could be easily embraced without the need for amendments. However, it resulted in different practices among companies. Over the next decades, this flexible legislative approach was undermined as more and more detailed rules were enacted, driven by individual abuses or even tax considerations, without too much care for logical consistency. Despite this practice, several accounting problems, such as leasing, foreign exchange translation, and hedge accounting, are still not mentioned by current law and have to be deduced from general principles.

The Stock Exchange Act and the Stock Exchange Listing Act, first enacted in 1896, introduced the requirement for disclosure of a prospectus and additional information. Although these requirements were not very detailed, over time these laws were amended to include ever more rigorous provisions.

The Great Depression of the 1930s led to the breakdown of Germany's second largest insurance group and some major banks, and later to the bankruptcy of many other companies. The breakdown revealed fraudulent accounting by some banks that were hit by the downturn. The German head of state reacted by issuing Stock Corporations Emergency Decrees in 1931, which introduced additional rules for financial statements and, more significantly, required stock corporations' annual statements to be audited. This requirement initiated the establishment of recognized professional auditors. The major amendment of the Stock Corporation Act of 1937 was based on these Decrees and made some of them more explicit.

By the beginning of the 20th century, banks and insurance companies were subjected to state supervision and to regulations governing financial disclosure. The regulations were amended and stiffened in both the 1920s and 1950s.

In 1937, the Stock Corporations Act was amended by rather detailed rules prescribing recognition, measurement, disclosure, and external auditing. Like earlier regulation, the 1937 Act still focused on creditor protection. The rules essentially provided strict upper bounds, but no lower bounds, for the valuation of assets, which, together with prudent rules to set up provisions, left corporations much discretion to build up secret reserves. In 1965, the Stock Corporations Act was amended to reduce this discretion somewhat by restricting arbitrary downward asset valuations and the arbitrary setup of provisions for future liabilities. But shareholder protection still was not a major concern. For example, the executive board was allowed to withhold net income totally from distribution to shareholders. This rule was designed to serve creditor protection, but management used it often as a low-cost and less transparent means for internal financing of the company.

The amended Stock Corporation Act also required corporations with subsidiaries to prepare consolidated financial statements. Previously, the rules applied only to financial statements of individual corporations (subsidiaries were recognized as investments). In 1969, the Disclosure Act (*Publizitätsgesetz*) extended the requirement to prepare and disclose individual and consolidated statements to very large (measured by total assets, sales, and net income) enterprises of "any legal form." The broader language "any legal form" was added largely to prevent companies from avoiding consolidation by structuring groups as private partnerships rather than a corporation as the parent company. The fact that the private partnership's shares could not be listed on the stock market was unimportant, because partnerships generally did not want or need to raise equity.

Finally, in the 1980s the harmonization endeavors of the European Union (EU) required a great legal reform, which affected virtually all German laws dealing with financial reporting. The major directives relevant for accounting and auditing—the Fourth, Seventh, and Eighth—were essentially enacted into German law in 1985. This required many small adjustments but also some fundamental revisions of preexisting law, particularly in the method by which consolidated statements were prepared.[5]

While the directives were restricted to limited liability companies, Germany decided to amend financial reporting for all enterprises. In a similar effort, capital market laws were revised to comply with the relevant European directives in the late 1980s and early 1990s.

THE CURRENT REGULATORY REGIME

The current system of regulating corporate disclosure in Germany is best understood against the backdrop of the German financial system. Broadly speaking, this system usually has been described as a relationship-based or insider system rather than an arm's-length or outsider system.[6] Moreover, German finance has long been a bank-dominated system, where companies rely on financing from retained earnings and bank loans.

For a long time, German companies maintained a close relationship with a single bank, the *Hausbank*, which provided long-term debt financing. Until the past decade or so, few German companies issued equity as a means of financing their activities. For example, in the 1980s and early 1990s, there were fewer than 20 initial public offerings (IPOs) in Germany per year. This number steadily mounted, however, during the rest of the 1990s, to 175 in 1999 and 142 in 2000, though annual IPOs fell back to the 20s in 2001 and 2002, after the "tech bubble" in U.S. and European stock markets had burst. Even so, where German companies do raise equity, they typically accomplish this through private placements by major current shareholders rather than public offerings.

As a result, ownership of German companies tends to be highly concentrated. The high degree of ownership concentration is reflected in the nature of the German capital market, where bonds are much more important than equities.[7] Bonds represent some 75 percent of financing volume and some 60 percent of trading volume. Banks play an important role both in issuing and in trading bonds.[8]

German accounting and financial disclosure is geared to the insider financial system. Capital market demands for information were not (until recently) a major driver to enhance transparency. Few small private investors invested money in the equities markets. Banks and other financial intermediaries could get most of the information they needed to make informed investment decisions either through lending covenants or through having a trusted person, such as a bank manager or a lawyer, serve on the supervisory board. Moreover, the same large banks dominated the capital markets.

Given Germany's particular financial structure, the total market capitalization of listed enterprises relative to Germany's gross domestic product is relatively low. In 2001 it amounted to 58 percent, rising from some 25 percent 10 years before, but still low compared to the average of the Euro countries with 71 percent, the United Kingdom with 152 percent, and the United States with 136 percent.[9] Even allowing for the possible understatement of equity positions, there are several possible reasons why Germany's reliance on equity is unusually low.

One possible factor is an insufficient supply of money for investment in capital markets. In many countries, pension funds are a major investor; in Germany, pension benefits granted by companies are usually not funded, but companies recognize pension provisions. Private investment in stock increased in the late 1990s because of the bubble in the stock markets, which was used by many young growth companies to raise money on the capital market. After the bubble burst, most of these investors fled the market and invested their money elsewhere. Another related reason for the relatively low market capitalization is traditionally low shareholder protection, which we discuss later.

The federal government regulates the framework under which German states act with respect to capital markets. The federal Stock Exchange Act requires national government approval for establishing a state stock exchange. It includes the legal framework for the organization of stock exchanges, such as the composition of the board and management, supervision by local state authorities, the trading system, dealers, and admission to listing. The Ministry of Finance sets more detailed rules with decrees, which, in practice, have the same mandatory power as laws. An example is the Stock Exchange Admission Regulation, which outlines the details of how these legal requirements are translated into practice. Subject to the federal framework, individual states have the legal authority to oversee and control institutional financial markets.

The most important German stock exchange is the *Deutsche Börse*, which operates the exchange in Frankfurt and seven regional exchanges in other cities. It has a high percentage of foreign listings and trades. From its origin in 1585 until recently, it was owned by its major "customers" (namely, large banks and brokers) and by the regional exchanges. It went public in early 2001, and its shares are now widely held by banks, brokers, and institutional and private investors. The largest single shareholder is the Deutsche Bank, with some 10 percent ownership.

FINANCIAL DISCLOSURE OF LISTED CORPORATIONS

Financial reporting and disclosure is regulated by company law, which is part of German commercial law. German laws are national transpositions of European legislation, which provides minimum requirements and member state options. The process of setting rules in Germany follows the formal due process for enacting laws. The Ministry of Justice prepares draft legislation, considering the input of major political lobbies, including, among others, business associations, unions, the banking community, and auditors, all of which have a say in the process. These groups influence the political process, typically by private communications but also via public statements.

Accounting standard setting and interpretation have been considered a domain of lawyers. This led to a legal rather than a professional approach to accounting. Law provides many detailed rules on financial disclosure and is relatively inflexible with respect to emerging issues. It includes few guidelines on how to apply and interpret these rules for specific settings. Any interpretation draws from the general structure of how to apply a legal rule, mainly on the basis of deductive reasoning about what the rule implies, and the presumed intention of the legislature.

Courts can authoritatively interpret the laws. They have rendered few judgments on financial accounting issues but many on income tax issues. Tax laws relate closely to financial statements via the "authoritativeness" principle (explained below), and thus these court decisions are relevant for financial accounting as well. In particular, the high Federal Fiscal Court (*Bundesfinanzhof*) issues judgments that have a bearing on the interpretation of financial accounting rules. The court decisions established many detailed rules for recognition and measurement.

Professional associations are another source for the application and interpretation of legal rules. The *Institut der Wirtschaftsprüfer* (IDW), the German Institute of Public Accountants, has been particularly active in issuing opinions and recommendations on accounting and reporting rules. These recommendations have no legal standing but nevertheless are highly influential in practice, since they implicitly bind auditors who are expected to justify departure from the IDW's guidance in case of disputes.

Then there are commentaries on the laws. These voluminous books collect articles authored by many experts from both academia and practice and describe the application of the law in great detail. These commentaries can be regarded as a private opinion market whose value depends on the academic and professional reputation of authors and editors.[10] Needless to say, their value to enterprises also depends on whether they include well-argued interpretations that support the companies' positions.

Following many other countries, particularly the Anglo-American countries, a 1998 law allowed the establishment of a private standard setter.[11] This was a remarkable turnabout, as the establishment of a similar institution was discussed in the 1980s but not enacted mainly because industry argued against it. But this time, driven by desires to raise external equity capital and the demands of capital market investors, industry changed its view and supported a private standard setter.

A few months after the law was enacted, the German Accounting Standards Committee (GASC) was founded as a private standard-setting association and acknowledged as such by the Ministry of Justice.[12] The GASC established the German Accounting Standards Board (GASB) as a standard setter with seven (part-time) independent members. The Board's organizational structure closely resembles that of the U.S. standard setter, the Financial Accounting Foundation (FAF) with the Financial Accounting Standards Board (FASB). The law gives the GASB the following tasks: (a) development of standards for the application of principles for consolidated accounts, (b) consultation with the Ministry of Justice on legislative projects with respect to accounting, and (c) representation of Germany in international standard-setting bodies. The GASC even has an Accounting Interpretations Committee (AIC), which until recently has been inactive; it issued its first interpretation (which considers presentation issues under IFRS) in July 2005.

The GASB has no power to set legal rules. Its standards, the *Deutsche Rechnungslegungsstandards* (DRS) or German Accounting Standards, must comply with existing law, a requirement that confines it to interpreting or refining the legal rules and that limits the Board's chance of developing accounting innovations. However, the GASB can and does issue recommendations to the legislature for changing rules for consolidated and individual statements. From a legal point of view, the standards are recommendations; they become influential in practice as they obtain the status of generally accepted accounting principles through their recognition by the Ministry of Justice, which is implicit in the publication in the government's "Federal Gazette" after a standard is passed.

The limited role of the GASB is a result of necessary compliance with national law, which states that financial accounting is regulated by law and not by a private organization. Thus, the GASB's position in the German legislative system remains controversial, because many question its legitimacy to set standards in the stakeholder-oriented environment underlying much of the company laws in Germany.[13] A particular concern is the composition of the GASB, because it does not represent all stakeholders. Currently, the Board is essentially made up of auditors and preparers.

Most of the GASB's work has been to develop standards for financial reporting by groups that choose to report under German GAAP. This task has become important, as in the late 1990s the government started regulating only basic requirements, leaving concrete specifications to the GASB's standards. Examples of this approach include cash flow statements, segment and risk reporting, and interim reports; law obliges listed corporations to prepare and disclose these reports but is silent on their form and content. International Financial Reporting Standards (IFRS) and U.S. GAAP have heavily influenced the resulting standards, both in the issues they deal with and in the solutions they provide. In some ways, the GASB seemed to want to find a way to combine the rules in the respective IFRS and U.S. GAAP standards that would lead to disclosure requirements even stiffer than those in either IFRS or U.S. GAAP. But some observers have criticized application of the German standards to companies that deliberately choose not to report under the international standards. The GASB has responded to these concerns by making sure that few of its standards extend beyond those already adopted by other standard-setting bodies. It came up with few innovations. A notable example is a standard on risk reporting that has no international precedent.

Also controversial is the development by the GASB of standards that reduce the number of options provided by the law, in part to increase conformity with internationally accepted accounting principles. This work raises the question of the relationship between the law and the standards; it is unclear what would happen if a company used an accounting method that is explicitly allowed by law but not by a GASB standard. For example, Standard DRS 4, dealing with acquisitions in the consolidated statements, requires companies to recognize and amortize goodwill from acquisitions, thus implying that the popular direct charge-off of goodwill against retained earnings is not proper accounting. In this case, matters became even fuzzier when the law was revised after the standard was published but did not eliminate the direct-charge-against-equity option. In practice, some 30 percent of listed companies that reported under German GAAP in 2000–2002 still elected this reporting option [Gebhardt and Heilmann, 2004].

Currently, few companies report in their consolidated statements whether they followed the DRS, and the auditor is not required to make such a statement. The limited role of the GASB in German accounting standard setting is reflected in the low coverage of the DRS in financial accounting textbooks relative to that of the legal requirements and even IFRS and U.S. GAAP. With the requirement for listed corporations to prepare IFRS financial statements as of 2005, the GASB's role becomes even less influential. Its limited role was one reason that the majority of the GASB members and many GASC board members were replaced in 2003 after more or less voluntary resignations.

Meanwhile, listed corporations must publish both individual and consolidated financial statements. The objectives of individual statements are to provide a true and fair statement of the company's financial position to its stakeholders and to serve as a basis for determining several legal requirements, most importantly the distribution of dividends and the assessment of income tax. The sole objective of consolidated statements is to inform stakeholders. They have no legal consequences, as there are no legal rules referring to them in establishing rights or obligations, such as distribution of profit[14] and tax assessment. This is evidence of their low esteem in the traditional institutional accounting framework in Germany. Before an amendment of the law in 2002, consolidated statements did not even require approval by the supervisory board and the annual general meeting (AGM). The reason is that the requirement to draw up consolidated statements was introduced only in 1965, when company law was already settled.

Individual statements measure "realized" profit with the view that this profit is available for distribution after approval of the statements at the AGM. Distributable profit is net income of the period, adjusted by changes in retained earnings, profit or loss for future dividends carried forward from the prior year, plus a few accounting book gains that are blocked from distribution (e.g., from deferred tax assets). Capital and legal reserves can be used only to cover a loss. Even though these rules are designed to protect creditors, debt overload as a condition for bankruptcy is not measured using the balance sheet amounts of assets and liabilities, because it is widely acknowledged that these figures do not purport to be their "real" values in case of bankruptcy. Accordingly, specific measurement rules apply in bankruptcies.

A key characteristic of German financial accounting is the tax conformity rule (or authoritativeness principle), which states that the single entity statement serves as a basis for assessing income taxes. As long as there is no specific tax accounting rule, the principles of proper bookkeeping and even the resulting values of assets and liabilities carry over to measure taxable income. Before 2001, German tax laws provided a deduction of dividends paid out against corporate taxable income; dividends then were subject to individual income tax at the normal personal tax rate. The tax system was structurally changed in 2001. Dividends are now subject to corporate tax similar to undistributed income, but at a lower tax rate than before, and the individual income tax has been cut to about half. The total tax burden on (wealthier) shareholders for dividend income is approximately the same as it was before the change.

The authoritativeness principle, invented in the 19th century mainly with the aim of facilitating clerical accounting work, was later increasingly seen as an informal barrier against attempts by tax authorities to change accounting rules solely for the purpose of generating more tax revenue. For example, conservatism as a basic principle carries over to tax measurement, thus (temporarily) reducing a firm's tax burden. The tax authorities, however, have found ways to partly overcome this barrier. For tax purposes they have enacted restrictions on the recognition of certain expense provisions, so that only actual expenditures reduce tax— thus prohibiting some accruals. Nevertheless, financial and tax statements are largely identical for the majority of companies in Germany.

A key aspect of authoritativeness principle—actually the "reverse authoritativeness principle"—is that in order to achieve a particular taxable income by (tax) earnings management, companies must use the same method in the financial statements as they do for tax purposes. An unwitting downside of this principle is that "tax management" now influences the preparation of financial statements, which may make them less useful to both outsiders and insiders alike. On the other hand, the principle also gives companies an incentive to not overstate income.[15] Given the contrasting effects, it is not surprising that the use of the authoritativeness principle has become more controversial, especially with the mandated use of IFRS for all EU-listed corporations.

German enterprises recognize the limited usefulness of financial accounting for management decisions and performance measurements that result from the authoritativeness principle. Academia and practice developed cost accounting systems that are based on costs and revenues derived from financial accounting data using an elaborate set of adjustments, such as adopting longer useful lives of depreciable assets and recognizing certain intangibles, using fair values or replacement values, and reducing of provisions. However, with the increasing adoption of IFRS, companies find these adjustments less useful and have started to use them more sparingly. Indeed, some large companies have even abandoned their use.

In addition to the financial statements and the notes, corporations must disclose a management report (*Lagebericht*), which contains a description of the business situation and trends and nonfinancial information, including risks. Management must comment on events after the balance sheet date, anticipated future developments that are likely to affect the corporation, and research and development. While the law is relatively unspecific about the contents of the management report, DRS standards and an IDW opinion contain principles governing and detailed lists of what corporations should report. Surveys and rating competitions carried out by business magazines indicate that the information content of management reports varies greatly. While disclosure-friendly corporations use the report as an instrument to give much background information on corporate and segment strategies, investments, research and development, human resources, and social reports, other management reports contain little useful information. An amendment of the law in 2004 extends the required disclosures to include a discussion of management goals, strategies, business chances, and risks including the underlying assumptions. It also requires large companies to report nonfinancial performance indicators, including environmental and social aspects. The management report is audited for consistency with the financial statements and published together with them. German corporations that prepare their consolidated statements according to IFRS or U.S. GAAP must also prepare a management report under German GAAP, because neither IFRS nor U.S. GAAP require a comparable report (although the U.S. Securities and Exchange Commission [SEC] does mandate a management discussion and analysis).

More disclosure requirements are included in securities laws. Listed corporations must prepare semiannual financial reports. These need not be audited. However, corporations listed in the prime standard market segment of the Frankfurt Stock Exchange are required by their listing contracts to prepare and disclose quarterly reports. A GASB standard extends this requirement to all listed corporations.

Another law requires continuous reporting by listed corporations, called *ad hoc* disclosure—that is, disclosing without delay to the capital market any information that is not yet publicly known, if it is likely to be price-sensitive. Before publication, the supervisory state office and the stock exchange have to be informed. The corporation may apply for exemption from disclosure, if damage to its interests is likely.[16] This seldom happens, however. On the contrary, many corporations started overusing this instrument to flood the market with information, often of a more public relations type of information rather than price-sensitive information.[17]

THE ROLE OF INTERNATIONAL ACCOUNTING STANDARDS

Large German corporations historically refused to list their shares on the New York Stock Exchange (NYSE) because they would have to prepare financial information in accordance with U.S. GAAP. Daimler-Benz (now

DaimlerChrysler) broke with this pattern by listing on the NYSE in 1993 and, hence, published a U.S. GAAP reconciliation, as it was required to do by the SEC.[18] Many other German corporations have followed Daimler's example by publishing consolidated statements in compliance with IFRS and U.S. GAAP, essentially because they felt this would benefit their investor relations activities abroad. The German stock market picked up the signal and soon began to require consolidated statements prepared under IFRS or U.S. GAAP in the listing rules for specific market segments, such as the (then) *Neuer Markt*.[19]

But German companies have also realized that it is costly to produce two different consolidated statements and, even more troubling, that they can create confusion among users. For example, if a company reports a net gain under one standard and a net loss under the other, it is difficult for investors to know whether or not the company was successful in that period, or whether management should earn a bonus. For this reason, companies that reported under either IFRS or U.S. GAAP lobbied the government to provide relief from the requirement to publish consolidated statements under German GAAP.

In 1998, the government enacted a law with the descriptive name Law to Facilitate Raising Capital (*Kapitalaufnahmeerleichterungsgesetz*) that exempted listed corporations from preparing their consolidated statements under German GAAP if they publish consolidated statements according to internationally accepted accounting principles. These principles were interpreted as being either IFRS or U.S. GAAP. The consolidated statements were subject to the same auditing and enforcement strictures imposed on German GAAP. Individual financial statements were unaffected by this law, as they still must follow German GAAP. Hence, capital and dividend payout restrictions and corporate tax assessment continue to be based on income calculated under German GAAP.

The law placed some necessary conditions for entitlement to the exemption. The most important one was that the statements must accord with the accounting directives.[20] Others require that the statements have information content that is similar to that presented in statements under German GAAP, and they had to explain any differences between German GAAP and the international standards. The company's auditor had to confirm that these conditions are satisfied.

These aspects of German law governing financial reporting and disclosure had been controversial from the beginning. Some lawyers argue that they contradict the German constitution because the legislature gives up its right (or duty) to set financial reporting standards and, rather, leaves it to some foreign private body. Nonetheless, listed corporations increasingly opted to report under international standards.

The legal exemption was available only until the end of 2004, which indicates that it was considered an interim solution from the beginning. The time limitation was a kind of self-commitment by the German government to modernize financial reporting regulation so as to put the

German system in a position to compete successfully with international standards. It has turned out that the 2004 end-date was just right because in 2002, the EU issued a regulation requiring listed corporations to use IFRS for their consolidated statements by 2005. While this move is generally welcomed in Germany, there have been critical voices, mainly among academics, who are concerned about the high potential for earnings management that certain IFRS provide. For example, as we also argue in this book, the move of the IASB to increasingly use fair value measurements that are not based on existing markets has been criticized.

EU member states can extend the 2005 deadline to 2007 for corporations with shares listed in a non-member state and use U.S. GAAP for purposes of listing requirements (an exemption lobbied hard for by Germany) and for corporations with only listed debt securities. Member states also have the option to allow or require other companies to adopt IFRS in their consolidated statements, and to allow or require companies to prepare their individual statements under IFRS.

There has been much debate about how Germany should use these options, if at all. In October 2004, the government enacted a new law (*Bilanzrechtsreformgesetz*) that addresses the implementation of international accounting standards. It extends the EU requirement for listed corporations to prepare IFRS consolidated statements to corporations that apply for a listing on a stock exchange (capital market-oriented corporations). All companies that prepare consolidated statements are given an option to use German GAAP or IFRS (not U.S. GAAP anymore). The law also grants to listed corporations for which the IAS Regulation applies the option to extend the deadline for using IFRS to 2007.

The decision whether to allow or even require individual statements to be prepared under IFRS generated much discussion within Germany. One view is that individual statements should continue to be prepared under German GAAP. A key argument supporting this view is that German GAAP have proved successful in the view of many, and that any change would require enormous legal work to adjust laws that refer to accounting constructs and numbers.[21] Against this, a requirement to prepare IFRS individual statements would bring the financial accounting of all companies into line with that of listed companies' consolidated statements and with best international practice. However, IFRS have been developed mainly for capital markets, while the accounting objectives for the statements of other companies also provide a basis for distribution of profits and tax measurement. Current IFRS do not address small and medium-sized companies, although the IASB is considering developing financial reporting standards for companies that do not have public accountability. Providing an option would resolve these concerns, as enterprises could choose according to their own cost–benefit tradeoff. However, such an option would require many changes in the legal setting, including new dividend distribution and tax assessment rules, because of the concept of equality that legal consequences must not depend on a company's choice of the financial reporting standards.

This latter argument was decisive for the amendment of the law that now includes a compromise solution. Each company must prepare individual statements under German GAAP. If it (voluntarily) prepares individual statements under IFRS in addition to German GAAP, it is allowed to satisfy any publication requirements (which exist for large limited liability companies) by submitting only the IFRS statements. Of course, the unpublished German GAAP individual statements will be available for shareholders and courts, among others. The existence of two sets of individual financial statements for a company using IFRS in both consolidated and individual financial statements with different uses is costly and may be confusing to investors and other users.

FINANCIAL DISCLOSURE BY NON-LISTED COMPANIES

The regulatory structure of financial disclosure of companies of any legal form is the same as for listed corporations. Financial reporting and disclosure are regulated by commercial law; capital market legislation does not apply.

Most accounting rules do not differentiate between listed and non-listed corporations, though the amount of disclosure varies.[22] Non-listed companies need not prepare cash flow statements and must disclose only limited segment reports. They must prepare their statements under German GAAP; the option to prepare consolidated statements under IFRS or U.S. GAAP introduced in 1998 was available only for listed companies.[23]

The criteria used to differentiate between non-listed enterprises are the size[24] and legal form of the enterprise. The most extensive disclosures apply to large corporations and other limited liability companies, as well as very large enterprises independent of their legal form. A lower degree of disclosure applies to medium-sized and small companies with limited liability, and there are no public disclosure requirements for partnerships (except for those that are very large). Partnerships are granted several options to create "silent reserves," or "reasonable" write-downs over and above a necessary impairment loss. Partnerships also need not reverse an impairment loss from prior years if the reason for the impairment has disappeared.

INVESTOR PROTECTION

Investor protection in a wide sense is the major aim of German capital market laws, in particular the Stock Exchange Act, the Stock Trading Act, and the Act on the Prospectus for Securities Offered for Sale. These laws provide measures to ensure fair and equal treatment of investors by including rules for the issuance of equity capital, for regular trading, and for disclosure of corporations' information that is deemed relevant to investors.

Before offering stock to the public for the first time, corporations are required by law to publish a prospectus that describes in detail the corporation and the shares to be listed, including the financial situation of the corporation, management, strategy, and forecasts. The contents of the prospectus are regulated by a decree issued by the Ministry of Justice, a legislative instrument that is one tier below a federal law but is equally binding in practice.

The Securities Trading Act includes rules of conduct for investment services companies, including banks and financial services companies that trade on behalf of third parties and conduct commission and agency business. These institutions are required to provide sufficient information to investors concerning the risks and costs of investing in stock, and they are obliged to install comprehensive organizational features to provide and ensure the integrity of professional services and avoid conflicts of interest. The Federal Financial Supervisory Authority (*Bundesanstalt für Finanzdienstleistungsaufsicht*, BaFin), a state enforcement body discussed below, issues guidelines detailing the requirements. Efforts to ensure full transparency are made by the banks and an expert commission at the Ministry of Finance.

Investor protection by means of a high degree of transparency is provided by requirements to disclose information in annual statements and interim reports and by continuous disclosure. In addition to these publicly available disclosures, investors have the right to ask specific questions to the board at the AGM, but the board, at its own discretion, may decide not to provide answers if they may harm the corporation or the group.

With respect to investors' rights in takeovers, mergers, and other major changes in ownership or economic restructuring of the corporation, the German government has relied on voluntary regulation. In the late 1970s, an expert commission within the Finance Ministry developed principles for takeovers, which were largely ignored by industry. In 1995, a voluntary takeover code was implemented which, relative to the general acceptance of similar codes (such as those in the United Kingdom), was accepted by some 75 percent of the listed corporations. Finally, in 2002, a new takeover law came into effect that regulates offers to buy out minority shareholders, information release, transparency, and minority rights in general.

The German government has striven to improve corporate governance by extending transparency and providing measures to ensure equal and fair treatment of investors. Recently, the government enacted a series of legal rules to achieve this goal, so that many corporate governance principles are now incorporated in the law. For example, there are strict insider trading rules, and listed corporations are required to report directors' dealings and concentrations (above 5 percent) of voting rights to the Federal Financial Supervisory Authority, which makes them publicly available. In 2002, a new takeover law was enacted, which defines stronger minority shareholder rights and replaces the former voluntary code.

Despite these measures, investor protection in Germany is generally considered to be low. A key reason is that there are cross-shareholdings by corporations, and large banks and insurers own significant shares of many public corporations that give them formal and informal power over many listed corporations. These cross-holdings, sometimes dubbed *Deutschland AG*, and the involvement of banks in credit financing and share trading give the impression that there are capital participants who are much better informed than others. In recent years, though, the size of cross-holdings has become smaller.

Another reason for the relatively low degree of investor protection is that while capital markets law is aimed at investor protection, financial accounting rules are oriented more toward creditor than shareholder protection. This emphasis is evidenced, for example, by the importance of conservatism in the recognition and measurement rules and restrictions of dividend payouts.[25] Thus, it can be difficult for investors to demand the payout of dividends, which are usually seen as a means of making capital allocation more efficient. Share repurchases are another means of paying out capital. As of 1998, earlier restrictions of stock repurchases have been liberalized so that a corporation now can repurchase in total up to 10 percent of its subscribed capital. Many large corporations made use of this facility to influence share prices, provide for employee stock options, or make equity repayments to investors, which are normally tax-exempt.

CORPORATE GOVERNANCE

Stock corporations are required by law to install a two-tiered board system with an executive board (*Vorstand*) and a supervisory board (*Aufsichtsrat*).[26] According to the Stock Corporations Act (*Aktiengesetz*), the executive board manages the corporation with due consideration of the interests of shareholders, employees, and the public, which indicates a stakeholder orientation. The executive board is responsible for all operational decisions required to run the corporation, including the preparation of the accounts and corporate disclosures. Neither the supervisory board nor the AGM can exercise influence or control operational decisions or instruct management to carry out specific orders.

The AGM is the regular meeting of the stockholders in which they receive information about the corporation and approve decisions, including the distribution of dividends and the appointment of the auditor (proposed by the supervisory board). Other decisions made at the AGM are the appointment of the shareholder representatives to the supervisory board and changes in corporate bylaws. Minority rights, such as challenging management decisions or requesting special audits, require minimum shareholdings with thresholds depending on the importance of the respective right. Traditionally, banks commonly exercised voting rights of stock they hold in security accounts for private investors in the AGM at their own discretion. As of 1998, the banks' discretion was restricted by law, so that their de facto voting power has now been much reduced.

The supervisory board is composed of outside directors and oversees the executive board's activities. The balance between executive and supervisory boards is subject to codetermination regulated in several laws. The roots of codetermination date back into the 19th century and are attributed to various principles, such as equality of capital and labor as production factors, democratic rules, and control of power. In large companies only half of the members of the supervisory board are appointed by the shareholders at the AGM, while the other half is appointed by the employees of the company.[27] The chairman usually is elected from among the shareholders' representatives on the board, and he or she has a double vote to break ties; in the coal, iron, and steel industry, the supervisory board elects an additional neutral member to avoid deadlock situations. Recently, codetermination in the supervisory board has become subject to public discussion. It is an almost unique rule within Europe, holds only for the business located in Germany, may hinder effective supervision, and often collides with international corporate governance requirements. One alternative discussed is the establishment of a separate consultation council that takes care of the information and participation rights of employees.[28]

Bank representatives still play a big role in the governance of German corporations. One study shows that 70 percent of the large listed corporations had at least one bank representative on the supervisory board, and in 42 percent of the corporations, bank representatives constituted more than a quarter of the board members representing capital contributors.[29]

The supervisory board appoints the members of the executive board and approves strategic and other major decisions as defined in the bylaws, such as investment decisions above a certain threshold amount, but it cannot control operational decisions by the executive board. In practice, the supervisory board was often considered just a formal board that approved without much discussion almost everything the executive board suggested. In part this was due to the membership of the supervisory board, which generally consists of some combination of retired executives, executives of other corporations who similarly have company executives on their board, or persons with limited specific knowledge. In recent years, the supervisory board has become more active, mainly due to public concerns about corporate governance and an increase in personal liability its members face in case of a major business failure.

A task of the supervisory board is to examine and approve the individual financial statements and to appoint and contract with the auditor. The board's examination of the individual and consolidated financial statements involves a comprehensive review based on the long-form auditor reports. The auditor must attend the meeting of the board at which the financial statements are discussed in case further information is requested. The supervisory board assesses the compliance of the financial statements with federal law and the corporation's bylaws and determines whether the accounting principles actually applied are appropriate. It reports in written form the results of this examination at the AGM. There is no legal requirement to set up special committees of the supervisory board, such as an audit committee. The two-tiered governance system ensures the separation of supervision and management in any case.[30]

Following the EU's failure to agree on a common corporate governance structure before 2000, two committees formed in Germany, mainly from business, industry, and academia, developed codes or principles of corporate governance.[31] These initiatives moved away from direct regulation of corporate governance to a more private form of regulation. Both codes encouraged corporations to voluntarily adopt the codes and disclose compliance with them in their annual reports. There was no suggestion for a compliance audit or any means of enforcement. A survey study among the DAX 100 corporations in early 2001 found that few had adopted (any) corporate governance principles, and even fewer adhered to the codes they reported as having adopted.[32]

Parallel to these private initiatives, the government established the Government Panel on Corporate Governance to suggest legal measures to improve the competitive position of German corporations and the German financial market, while enhancing investor protection. In 2001, the Panel's final report made detailed proposals for modernizing corporate law with respect to the management and control of corporations.

One of the Panel's notable recommendations was that the government set up a commission to develop a (unified) code of corporate governance. In response, the Government Commission issued the German Corporate Governance Code in early 2002, with a provision for annual review. It includes two sets of rules, recommendations that corporations should "comply or explain" the reasons for noncompliance, and other suggestions that do not need an explanation of noncompliance. Initially, a report on compliance with the code was voluntary. However, soon afterward, the 2002 law on transparency and disclosure (*Transparenz- und Publizitätsgesetz*) introduced a legal requirement for listed corporations to publish a statement on compliance (or noncompliance with explanation) every year.[33]

The rules of the code are broadly in line with the requirements of international capital markets, adjusted for German legal and institutional peculiarities. Some rules have been controversial, such as that on disclosure of management compensation. The general tendency has been to avoid disclosure of too many details about the compensation system and individual directors' compensation. The 2003 version of the Code required such disclosures as a "comply or explain" rule. More recently, a new law requires detailed individual directors' compensation disclosures, although with an opting-out clause that states that the AGM may decide to not require such disclosures; such a decision is due for reconfirmation within 5 years.

As noted earlier, creditor protection has been a major objective of financial reporting regulation in Germany, mainly affected by capital maintenance and conservatism principles and by disclosure rules. Bank-ruptcy laws regulate the rights of creditors in case of insolvency, particu-larly acknowledging their rights if they hold secured loans. Reorganization procedures are relatively restricted. There are no legal rules that would grant creditors influence over the governance structure of corporations. In practice, though, large creditors, and in particular banks, are often re-presented on the supervisory board, through which they receive superior private information.

Employees have the right to participate in strategic and certain other important decisions via their representation on the supervisory board (co-determination). However, they cannot intervene in operative management decisions, as this is not within the supervisory board's powers.

AUDITING OF FINANCIAL REPORTS

Annual financial statements and the management reports of listed corpo-rations, including both individual and consolidated statements, are subject to statutory auditing by independent public accountants (*Wirtschaftsprüfer*). The statutory auditor is nominated by the supervisory board and ap-pointed after approval at the AGM. Several legal requirements to qualify for appointment to an audit should ensure the professional qualification and independence of the auditor. Among them are that the auditor must not hold shares of the auditee, must not have provided work in relation to the preparation of the financial statements, and must not have earned more than 30 percent of total revenue from the auditee (audit and con-sulting fees) over each of the past 5 years. The recent amendment of the law (*Bilanzrechtsreformgesetz* 2004) requires an internal rotation of the lead auditor within the audit firm; external rotation requirements have been discussed but have not been adopted. The amendment increases the scope of services prohibited to the statutory auditor. It follows the principle that a "self-audit" should be avoided; in effect, this excludes consulting ser-vices such as bookkeeping, preparation of financial statements, internal audits, management and financial services, and actuarial and valuation services that relate to the audited financial statements. These rules are inspired by discussions in the EU and the U.S. Sarbanes-Oxley Act, al-though they are less strict than the requirements imposed by that Act, which excludes such consulting services even if they are unrelated to the audited statements. This observation is true also for a new require-ment to disclose audit fees: the German law requires only disclosure of total fees and an indication of whether the fee for other services exceeds the audit fee.

Commercial law defines the purpose and scope of the audit. The audit should be of sufficient scope to reveal misstatements or offenses against the law and, if applicable, corporate bylaws. The auditing procedures are invariant to whether the corporation reports under German GAAP or under IFRS (and, earlier, under U.S. GAAP). The audit also examines whether the company has installed an effective internal control system. Since the management report contains much descriptive and qualitative information, the audit examines the report's consistency with the financial statements and with other information that becomes available to the auditor. The result of the audit is a long-form report addressed to the supervisory board, which consists of a (sometimes lengthy) description of the items in the financial statements, the scope and methods employed in the audit, and the audit opinion. The opinion explicitly states whether the financial statements and the management report comply with legal requirements and the corporation's bylaws, and whether risks are accurately reported. A particular wording consisting only of three sentences (that the financial statements comply with legal requirements, that they provide a true and fair view, and that the management report is in accordance with the financial statements) was required until 1998. Now the law requires a description of the scope of the audit and the procedures, and the audit result. Most opinion formulations follow a recommendation issued by the IDW that is essentially consistent with the International Standards on Auditing (ISA). The audit opinion must be disclosed to the public; in contrast, the long-form audit report is neither published nor disclosed to the shareholders at the AGM or to any other parties.[34]

The German auditing profession is governed by law, which regulates formal qualifications for and general principles of auditing. Auditors are allowed to form limited liability partnerships or companies. The public *Wirtschaftsprüferkammer*, the Chamber of Auditors, which was created only in 1971 by law, sets and monitors auditing requirements and admissions and accreditation of auditors. Every auditor must be a member.[35] In contrast, the IDW, established in 1932, is a private body with voluntary membership. It issues standards or opinions on how audits should be carried out. These standards are not formally imposed, because a private body issues them; nevertheless, their practical impact is significant. Both bodies operate disciplinary schemes for alleged misconduct.[36] There is no competition between the *Wirtschaftsprüferkammer* and the IDW, as they work closely together. Both are members of the IFAC and, as such, are obliged by virtue of the IFAC charter to promote the use and application of IFAC standards, in particular the ISA. The national auditing standards cover most issues included in the ISA, but they were originally structured differently from the ISA and were less detailed. From 1998 on the IDW started to revise the standards so that they are consistent and compatible with the ISA, and that they state any differences that might exist. Currently, many standards are in the process of revision.

Beginning in 2001, an amendment of the law governing the auditing profession introduced a requirement for peer reviews for audit firms. This was triggered by the failure of a large German construction corporation, although it also followed a recommendation by the European Commission from 2000. Auditors are subject to a peer review by the end of 2005, and then every 3 years. Participation in the peer review is a requirement to serve as a statutory auditor. The peer review process is coordinated by the *Wirtschaftsprüferkammer* and is overseen by an independent public oversight board, the *Qualitätskontrollbeirat*, none of whose five members is an auditor. The public oversight board is responsible for overseeing the appropriate functioning of the quality control system and for its further improvement.[37]

ENFORCEMENT MECHANISMS

Enforcement of financial disclosure is complex and highly regulated in Germany but has at the same time not been very effective. It basically starts at the level of members of the executive board and the supervisory board. If a board member presents the financial situation of the corporation in the annual financial statements or management report in an inaccurate or misleading way, he or she can be punished by imprisonment of up to 3 years or a fine. This extends to providing false information to the auditor. Violations are prosecuted by public officials. In practice, though, such prosecutions are of little relevance, because it has proven difficult to collect sufficient information to support a case being brought. The principal cases have been major bankruptcy cases or frauds in connection with investments, loans, or subsidies. In these situations, usually the company management is actively pursuing the case and provides inside information on it. Fines can be imposed by the Commercial Registration Court for not following the rules governing preparation or disclosure of financial information. The court currently acts only upon third-party notice from shareholders, creditors, or other parties with vested interests. This is about to change to allow the court to act on its own initiative. While these sanctions are an important deterrent, particularly for small corporations, they do not practically affect listed corporations, which are subject to more effective enforcement provided under securities markets laws. Currently, there is an "enforcement gap" in the sense that the sanctions generally do not apply to breaches of DRS or internationally accepted accounting standards (IFRS, U.S. GAAP) that a corporation can use to prepare consolidated statements.

The current capital market enforcement system was established by the Securities Trading Act in 1994 and is characterized by a three-layered structure, starting with offices of stock exchanges, the exchange supervisory authorities of individual states, and the then Federal Securities Supervisory Office (*Bundesaufsichtsamt für den Wertpapierhandel*, BAWe) as an independent federal authority. In May 2002, this body was integrated into the newly established Federal Financial Supervisory Authority (*Bundesanstalt für Finanzdienstleistungsaufsicht*, BaFin), which integrates securities supervision with the supervision of banking and insurance, which were formerly supervised by separate authorities. The Federal Financial Supervisory Authority is a separate legal institution governed by public law and closely related to the federal Ministry of Finance.

These bodies monitor and investigate listed corporations' compliance with the legal requirements of market transparency, continuous reporting, insider trading, ownership, and takeover processes. Additional monitoring systems are administered by banks that are involved in securities transactions. Noncompliance is usually penalized with administrative fines. However, insider trading violations are subject to criminal prosecution.

The effectiveness of these penalties for noncompliance depends in part on the ability of the Federal Financial Supervisory Authority to monitor or keep under surveillance corporations' compliance with disclosure rules. In 2002, the Authority reported 69 new investigations of the suspicion of insider trading, and 33 cases were forwarded to official prosecution. In the same year, 1 case ended with imprisonment, 2 cases ended with fines against insiders, and another 13 cases were dropped after a penalty was paid.[38] The fines inflicted were usually much lower than the upper limit possible. The stock exchanges also impose fines and may publicize this punishment. They can also revoke the listing admission if the corporation does not comply with listing requirements. So far, no instance of a revocation has been observed.

It is remarkable that this monitoring system covers financial disclosure only in prospectuses and continuous reporting requirements. The governmental bodies and the stock exchange offices check only formal requirements, such as whether disclosure is made in time and includes all required statements, but make no attempt to perform a material investigation into the contents of disclosure. If they note an obvious mistake they can request more information from the corporation. This essentially means that the content of financial disclosures is what the statutory auditor says.[39]

This situation is about to change. In October 2004, the German government enacted a new law on the enforcement of financial statements (*Bilanzkontrollgesetz*) to strengthen enforcement. Following public discussion and recommendations by the Government Panel on Corporate Governance and the IDW, the government set up a two-step enforcement system, combining elements of the U.K. model of a private agency, the Financial Reporting Review Panel, and of the U.S. model of a government agency, the SEC. The new law allows for the establishment of a private financial reporting review body and states general rules of composition and procedure that this body would have to follow to ensure acknowledgment by the Ministry of Justice. Such a private body has already been established in a structure that is reminiscent of that of the GASC. Its founding members are the major representation bodies of preparers and users. It finances and supervises the *Deutsche Prüfstelle für Rechnungslegung* (DPR; Financial Reporting Enforcement Panel), which is the operative review body. The enforcement became operative in mid-2005.

In the first step of enforcement, the review body examines individual and group financial statements of listed corporations for breaches of legal rules. It can act retroactively upon notice of alleged breaches and upon demand of the Federal Financial Supervisory Authority, and proactively as indicated by inferences from sampling. A condition for action is that there is public interest in such a review. The aim is to reach a unanimous resolution with the corporation of any breaches of accounting regulation. The Federal Financial Supervisory Authority supervises the reviews. If the corporation is a financial institution or insurance company, the Authority can directly undertake a review as part of its supervisory responsibility. If a corporation is not cooperative and does not provide information in the course of a review, in the second step the Federal Financial Supervisory Authority takes over the case. The Authority has strong intervention powers and can require corporations to correct any errors. It also publishes the result of the review. Moreover, it can apply to the courts for prosecution of involved persons.

The costs of the review body and the enforcement by the Federal Financial Supervisory Authority are financed by a charge to all listed corporations. Costs of individual enforcement actions by the Authority are recovered from the corporation examined (and not from individual directors). The first step in the enforcement system is an attempt to outsource from the public domain as much of the enforcement as is acceptable under the German legal structure; any enforcement action, though, remains within the Federal Financial Supervisory Authority, which is a public body. It is too early to evaluate the effectiveness of this enforcement mechanism, in particular how effective the first step in the procedure will be.

Currently, litigation by shareholders is rarely directed against individual managers but is brought against the company as such as a derivative action. If shareholders succeed, in practice they pay part of the damages awarded to them and the legal fees (both of which are funded by the company's shareholders' equity). Litigation against management and supervisory boards based on a case of misleading or missing financial disclosure has been almost nonexistent in Germany. This is because there are few legal provisions that would give a basis for such litigation. One is corporation law, which requires members of the executive or supervisory boards to act with due care and diligence. If they do not, damages can be claimed by shareholders and, in case of default, by creditors. However, such behavior and the causal relationship of mismanagement or fraud with damage are difficult to prove in court. Moreover, German law restricts the personal liability of responsible board members. In Germany, class action suits are not allowed; neither are contingent legal fees. Thus, in general, the cost of litigation to shareholders is high and the outcome highly uncertain, so that it is not surprising that few cases are brought. However, in 2005 the government published a law (*Kapitalanleger-Musterverfahrensgesetz*) that aims to facilitate legal action from a minority of shareholders against management; it also includes a business judgment rule to avoid the abuse of this instrument.

Penalties, as well as litigation similar to that against members of the management or supervisory board, can be inflicted on auditors who issue a false report, namely one that hides substantial events or includes a false audit opinion. Auditors' legal liability complements the general liability rule for contracts. Auditors are also liable to compensate the corporation for damage caused by noncompliance with legal rules. Liability is joint and several. If noncompliance is not intentional but negligent, liability is limited to €4 million for listed corporations' statutory audits, an amount that has been increased substantially since 1998. Auditors are required to hold insurance coverage for such a liability. Moreover, auditors can be penalized for unprofessional behavior with admonition, fines, and disbarment. While these sanctions are severe, they have been imposed only rarely.

Commercial law does not include a rule concerning auditor liability other than to the corporation that engaged the auditor. Notably, shareholders and creditors are excluded. With reference to civil law, liability may only arise among contractual parties and only for intentional noncompliance, which is probably rare and, if it occurs, is difficult to prove. Neither the courts nor the legislature have yet agreed on a system for third-party liability, and few such cases have been filed in the courts. Thus, the legal situation is confusing and risky for enforcing rights. The situation is different for the audit of prospectuses, where third-party liability exists even for negligence. Other services delivered by the auditor are subject to common contract law, and there is no limited liability constraint.

ASSESSMENT OF THE PRESENT REGULATORY REGIME

German disclosure regulation rests on two different systems of law, commercial and capital markets. Commercial law regulates financial reporting and disclosure for all business enterprises, and capital markets law regulates the disclosures by listed corporations. From a regulatory perspective, the legal systems are the responsibility of different ministries (justice and finance, respectively), which implies a need for coordination that has sometimes been difficult to achieve.

As part of commercial law, the material accounting rules do not differentiate between listed and non-listed companies. To be sure, there is also good reason to regulate financial accounting for all companies similarly. It prevents disparate developments of financial reporting, and it improves comparability across companies within Germany. Listed companies are subjected to higher disclosure standards (but not recognition and measurement rules) to meet the demand for corporate information in capital markets.

We note, though, that the objectives of financial reporting are different for private and listed companies. Financial reporting is not specifically oriented toward the needs of capital markets, but more toward stakeholders in general—summarized perhaps best by the term "general purpose financial statements." Creditor protection shows up in conservative recognition and measurement, and in capital and dividend payout restrictions, which, however, formally apply solely to the individual statements of the legal entity. Moreover, tax assessment is based on individual financial statements. Consolidated statements follow the same rules. Hence, they suffer from the same bias toward creditor protection and toward tax considerations, although to a lesser extent and not necessarily. Consolidated statements are not well integrated in commercial law because there are no legal consequences tied to them. In commercial law, groups are not legal subjects and cannot sign contracts; hence, the consolidated statements depict a fictitious "company." They serve "merely" as additional information to stakeholders beyond that which they can infer from individual statements. The capital market law also does not regulate consolidated statements, which is in contrast to countries such as the United States.

Financial disclosure is highly regulated by law. Legal rules are often inflexible and slow in reacting to emerging issues or popular earnings management strategies,[40] although commentary literature seeks to provide guidance about how to deal with emerging issues. Legislation has been trailing the economic forces for more internationalization of accounting; generally, policymakers have reacted to perceived international demands and to lobbying by large corporations in a not-very-systematic way. For example, the option for listed corporations to select among German GAAP, IFRS, and U.S. GAAP for their consolidated statements was introduced and enacted without much reflection on the future regulation of accounting in Germany. It led to highly diverse accounting practices that Ordelheide [1998] described as "anarchic tendencies in the process of internationalization."[41] The introduction of a private standard setting body, the GASB, appears to be a reaction to the fact that observers abroad wondered where the "German standard setter" was. There are heavy restrictions imposed on the GASB's tasks. Its standards received critical reviews, and there is an ongoing discussion over whether it is really needed and, if so, what its tasks should be. This occurred both before and after the EU's decision to require IFRS consolidated statements for listed corporations.

The GASB has shown a low profile on the international accounting standard-setting scene, particularly compared with standard setters from other countries such as Canada and Australia. In 2003, with the replacement of many members of the executive board of the GASC and of the GASB, a reorientation has taken place with regard to the future work of the GASB; it now pursues building an international profile and reducing national standard setting.

The regulatory approach is currently in a state of flux. The German constitution and legal system are significant barriers for the involvement of private sector standard setting. In some areas of financial disclosure, Germany started to regulate by law only main principles, leaving the determination of details to a commission or a standard setter, such as the GASB. This is very much in line with the current EU approach that shifts power from the European Parliament to the Commission and to committees, perhaps to overcome the slow regulatory process (see Chapter 7). Major examples are reporting requirements specified by the GASB and corporate governance standards that are promulgated by the Government Commission for the Corporate Governance Code. In the area of takeover rules, however, the government replaced voluntary compliance with a strict regulation by law.

There are deficiencies in the enforcement of the rules governing annual financial reports, as well as interim reports. While the 2004 law on the enforcement of financial statements establishes an enforcement mechanism for listed corporations, there is still a lack of enforcement for all other companies that publish financial reports. To some extent, this is a budgetary issue, considering the large number of companies obliged by law to provide financial statements. Thus, quality assurance of financial disclosures in the annual financial statements lies in the hands of external auditors.[42] Other financial disclosures, such as interim reports, need not be audited or reviewed. Qualifications for an auditor who performs a statutory audit are not different whether these are prepared under German GAAP or international accounting standards. Finally, litigation does not substitute for the lack of enforcement. Court decisions are rare because there is only a small chance of succeeding against a company, and the costs of bringing a lawsuit almost always exceed the expected benefits to the plaintiff.

CURRENT ISSUES

As we have discussed, Germany has in the past few years initiated a large number of changes to its present financial reporting regime. They are an attempt to improve corporate transparency and investor protection and cover a broad range of issues, including the governance structure of corporations, accounting standards, disclosure, auditing, enforcement, and liability.

An ongoing issue that has not been fully resolved is how to implement the options of allowing or requiring IFRSs in the EU's IAS Regulation. The way Germany chose to use the options, there will continue to coexist consolidated financial statements prepared under IFRS and under German GAAP. While previously only listed corporations could choose among the standards, now unlisted corporations are able to select their consolidated reporting, too. This option provides for a constrained market setting among these two sets of accounting standards.[43] The choice does not extend to the individual financial statements, where German GAAP statements are still required. Under the premise that IFRS statements are more informative than German GAAP statements, the law allows companies to publicize individual IFRS financial statements instead of the German GAAP statements. However, this option requires simultaneous preparation of financial statements under two standards, which is costly and ultimately does not avoid confusion to many users, as the German GAAP statements are still the basis for dividends and other legal consequences.

A potential remedy is a quiet convergence of German GAAP to IFRS. Indeed, the EU paves the way for such a strategy. For example, it granted an option to the member states to allow or require measurement of certain categories of financial instruments at fair value. The motivation was to avoid conflict with IAS 39 on financial instruments. Germany still hesitates to make use of such options. The law for implementation of international accounting standards and for quality assurance of audits (*Bilanzrechtsreformgesetz* 2004) does not allow fair value measurements but refers to the option to use IFRS in consolidated statements that include such rules. However, the material accompanying the law announces a potential inclusion in a future amendment of the law that aims at adapting German GAAP to international developments. The current tendency seems to be to extend disclosures rather than change accounting policies. Another indicator of convergence is that the interpretation of German GAAP rules increasingly considers the respective IFRS and other countries' GAAP.

Apart from accounting rules, a major deficiency we identified above is the ineffectiveness of enforcement by means of litigation by shareholders. The Government Panel offered several proposals to improve investor protection measures. Some of them were taken up by the government in a 2005 law that facilitates legal action against management. However, class (or representative) action suits and contingent lawyer fees are not included in this initiative because many of their implications are considered undesirable.

More open issues remain. Some of them are less controversial, like improving electronic access to certain disclosures. Some are more controversial, such as the proposal to require quarterly reports. Others are curiosities of the present law, such as the provision that the supervisory board of a holding firm has no legal right to view the financial documents of subsidiaries, despite their duty to examine the consolidated statements. The discussion does not exclude even difficult political issues, such as codetermination in the supervisory board, because these could be negative factors in the competition for business location within the EU.

In summary, we believe the ground for the developments in financial disclosure was prepared by a shift of large German corporations away from the traditional insider-oriented financing to one that makes more use of equity markets. This shift is associated with the new information demands: instead of the commercial-law–based system, a new transparency- and investor-oriented system became important. Many measures taken by the legislature are motivated by an attempt to improve the quality, transparency, and decision usefulness of financial disclosures. Most measures follow closely models developed in Anglo-American countries, some of them decades ago. Germany trails the developments in those countries that have a long history of active capital markets and does not attempt to develop unique measures focused on the German institutional setting.

The EU is in a similar position and is active in amending financial markets regulation, including financial disclosure, with a view to compete better for international capital. As an EU member, Germany must implement any EU legislation, and in many instances it is necessary to wait and see what the EU decides to do—although Germany has a strong position in the EU and would be able to influence the outcome of any discussions. Competition between national capital markets seems to drive convergence, even if this means overreacting to certain events, independent of the net benefit in the institutional setting in a particular country. In the meantime, there is no consensus within the German financial community that all of the current developments worldwide are (net) improvements.

7

Corporate Financial Reporting and Regulation in the European Union

In this chapter, we examine the efforts undertaken by the EU[1] to harmonize the financial disclosure of companies headquartered in the EU member states. The EU is a supranational regulator that exercises its powers only with the consent of all or a large majority of the member states. The previous chapters on corporate financial reporting in the United Kingdom and in Germany discuss two member states that have highly diverse accounting traditions and regulatory structures. For many market participants, it seems hard to believe that the United Kingdom and German financial statements have a common ground in the EU accounting laws. The experience in these two member states highlight the difficulties of achieving harmonization or, even more demanding, standardization of financial disclosure in the EU.

Examining the EU is particularly relevant to the objectives of this book, since developments in the EU provide a real-world illustration of the ups and downs of harmonizing financial disclosure across a set of countries that have agreed to synchronize their economies to a great extent. Harmonization has not become easier following the integration of 10 more states in May 2004.

Starting at the end of the 1990s, the European Union (EU) entered a new epoch of regulating financial disclosure. The current approach has been changed, and massive activities are under way to clear the way for a shift in paradigm as of 2005.

Financial markets in the EU exhibit a great variety of individual national capital markets. The third largest equity market in the world, the London Stock Exchange, is located in the EU; other big players are the Frankfurt

Stock Exchange and Euronext, the merger in 2000 of the stock exchanges of Paris, Brussels, and Amsterdam. Each EU member state has traditionally at least one stock exchange, implying a fragmented capital market. By the end of 2000, a total of 8,699 corporations were listed in the EU, a number that increased by some 16 percent over 1999. In comparison, at the end of 2000 there were 7,194 listed corporations in the United States, a decline of some 4 percent against the year before, and 2,096 in Japan, an increase of 8 percent.[2] New equity capital raised in EU financial markets also is increasing. While company financing was largely debt-driven, equity financing grew in importance. In 2000 €386 billion (4.3 percent of market capitalization) was raised in the EU market, whereas corporations in the U.S. market raised €390 billion (2.4 percent of market capitalization). The introduction of the Euro in 11 member states has further stimulated European equity markets, mainly by removing exchange risk and by increasing transparency, comparability, and cross-border liquidity.

DEVELOPMENT OF THE PRESENT ACCOUNTING AND DISCLOSURE REGULATORY REGIME

The fundamental objectives of the EU, laid out in the Treaty of Rome in 1957, include the freedom of establishment for firms and the free movement of capital, which requires a common environment under which enterprises conduct their business. Accounting legislation is part of the company law harmonization program, which aimed to give equivalent protection to all third parties who have dealings with companies throughout the EU. This explains why accounting legislation is embedded in company law, why accounting is the business of lawyers in many member states, and why there are links between financial accounting and taxation.

Unlike many individual states, the EU does not have a long history of financial disclosure regimes. Until recently, there were no major changes in the regime; rather, development progressed gradually.

The EU legislation governing financial disclosure for companies provides a framework and a set of minimum requirements that member states should implement. Similar to the legislation in many other fields, financial markets and disclosure have normally been regulated by directives. After adoption, which is the result of a usually lengthy process that involves the European Commission, the European Parliament, and the Council of Ministers of the member states, a directive commits member states to incorporate the provisions in the directive into national law within a certain period, usually 2 years. Another legislative instrument is a regulation that is directly effective without requiring the transposition into national law. While it had not been generally used to regulate financial disclosure, this instrument gained popularity recently when important regulatory actions were enacted by regulations, notably the requirement in 2002 that listed corporations use International Financial Reporting Standards (IFRS) in their consolidated statements.

The most influential acts in the EU are the Fourth (Company Law) Directive of 1978, which deals with the accounts of limited liability companies, and the Seventh Directive of 1983, which contains rules for consolidated statements. Subsequently, there have been other directives with rules for banks and insurance companies, for small and medium-sized companies, and for auditing.

The objective of the EU's disclosure regulation is to harmonize financial disclosure across the member states. Harmonization does not require that the *same* rules be applied in all member states—this would be full standardization—but that the prevailing rules are compatible with those in other member states. The harmonization of financial disclosure is achieved by agreeing to the same basic principles and to a number of minimum requirements, and by determining a set of accounting rules, often including optional rules. The goal is to reduce the number of differences in accounting standards of the member states. However, many individual rules found in the directives are compromises to the approaches found in different member states. In fact, the Fourth Directive includes some 60 and the Seventh Directive some 50 options.[3] They represent various accounting methods followed in large member states, such as for valuation bases (cost or fair value) and accounting for goodwill. The directives are silent on special accounting issues, such as leasing, construction contracts, and foreign currency translation. Even in the area of the disclosure layout, which is a major element regulated by the directives,[4] there are various forms for the presentation of the balance sheet and the income statement. There is no requirement to draw up a cash flow statement, and segment reporting requires only the breakdown of sales with respect to business and geographical segments, with an exception if the company fears an adverse response from a competitor.[5] Therefore, the enacted accounting rules in the member states may continue to be quite different and accounting practice even more so. Even if the rules were the same, their application often varies because the rules are interpreted in the context of national regulatory environments.

Under the requirements of the Fourth Directive, the European Commission established the Contact Committee, a group comprising member state representatives and other interested parties, including the accounting profession, to facilitate the harmonized application of the accounting directives. The direct impact of the Contact Committee was low.

Directives addressing financial disclosure are embedded in company law rather than capital markets law, and the scope of the directives includes all limited liability companies, covering over 2 million small and medium-sized companies. Consideration of the needs and peculiarities of these companies puts the focus on capital maintenance and creditor protection rather than on investor-oriented disclosures, which are more important for listed companies. This focus may explain why the legal form of the company, and in particular limited liability, is the focus for regulatory action rather than capital market listing. The major goal is the protection of creditors, less so the protection of shareholders, employees, and other stakeholders. There is also a premise in many EU member states that rigorous accounting and disclosure requirements act as a counterweight to the advantage of limited liability.[6]

It is interesting to note that the early discussion of the accounting directives pondered whether the harmonization effort should be directed exclusively toward listed corporations. That this was not done is considered by some as a major strategic mistake, hampering full harmonization.[7] No attempt was made to develop rigorous accounting rules for listed corporations in the capital-markets–oriented directives, perhaps for fear that different accounting standards would develop for listed and non-listed companies. This was seen as particularly undesirable, as accounting serves as a basis for comprehensive legal rights and duties in many member states. Different accounting standards, therefore, would create unequal treatment before the law. Nevertheless, as we discuss below, current changes in EU law do differentiate more than ever between listed (or, more generally, public interest) companies and others. Although the arguments have not changed, their emphasis has shifted.

THE TURN TO INTERNATIONAL ACCOUNTING STANDARDS

In the late 1980s the European Commission, together with some member states, tried hard to achieve mutual recognition by the United States of financial statements prepared in accordance with the directives for listing of EU corporations in U.S. securities markets. The U.S. Securities and Exchange Commission (SEC) did not (and still does not) accept them without reconciliation with U.S. generally accepted accounting principles (GAAP).

After these efforts were unsuccessful, the Commission turned toward participation in the work of the (then) International Accounting Standards Committee (IASC) rather than working on the revision of the directives. To facilitate this participation, the European Commission established the Accounting Advisory Forum (AAF) in 1990 to advise the Commission on a technical level in the area of accounting legislation. Its members came from standard-setting bodies of the member states and from European organizations representing industry, unions, stock exchanges, and analysts, among others. The AAF produced statements on several accounting issues but did not gain much practical relevance because the statements remained vague and inconclusive.[8]

The EU's main argument in its negotiation with the SEC was that large multinational corporations domiciled in the EU were reluctant to accept the reconciliation requirements of the SEC and consequently decided not to list on a U.S. stock exchange. Only a few European corporations were listed in the United States, often from the United Kingdom. The New York Stock Exchange (NYSE) pushed for further growth of listings by appealing to large European corporations. As we discussed in the previous chapter, Daimler-Benz broke the ice with its listing on the NYSE in 1993, and it received support by the SEC in that it was able to negotiate a favorable and unique treatment of several accounting issues under U.S. GAAP. The move by Daimler-Benz undermined the bargaining position of the EU with respect to achieve acceptance without reconciliation.[9] In 1994, several other large European corporations followed suit and began to prepare their consolidated financial statements under U.S. GAAP or IFRS. This further weakened the European Commission's position vis-à-vis the SEC. The cross-listing of European companies on the NYSE increased over time (from 26 in 1990 to 146 in 2001) but is still low.[10]

In July 1995, after several years of preparation and discussion, the IASC achieved an agreement with the International Organization of Securities Commissions (IOSCO) that included a "core standards work program." After its completion IOSCO would consider endorsing it for cross-border capital raising and listing purposes. This agreement, combined with the pressure exerted by global players, led the European Commission to change its strategy fundamentally. In a December 1995 document, "New Strategy Vis-à-vis International Harmonisation," it acknowledged the achievements of the IASC in setting international accounting standards[11] and confirmed the EU's intention to actively support the IASC and contribute to its further efforts instead of developing its own rigorous accounting standards. In fact, the EU has been influential in some of the more recent IFRS. For instance, it lobbied successfully for the inclusion of a fair presentation override that, in extremely rare circumstances, requires departure from an IFRS rule to achieve a fair presentation,[12] and for layouts adopted for the balance sheet and income statement that are far more flexible than, but do not conflict with, the directives.

The new strategy also affected the interpretation of the EU directives. In the late 1980s, the European Commission saw many differences between IFRS and the directives. By 1996 the Contact Committee published several papers comparing the directives with the relevant IFRS and found that substantial conflicts were rare, even considering that many IFRS had become much tighter, which would seem to create even more conflicts. Of course, its interpretation of the directives was politically motivated and deliberately aimed at reducing potential conflicts.[13] In fact, the argument was often made that the directives do not literally state a requirement differently. In cases in which conflicts were not resolvable by interpretation, the EU began amending the directives.

For example, in 2001 the new IAS 39 (Financial Instruments: Recognition and Measurement), which requires fair value measurement of (many) financial instruments, eventually became operative. Since the Fourth Directive prescribed historical-cost measurement, this would have generated a major conflict between the directives and IAS 39. Shortly afterward, the directives were amended in 2001 to give member states the option of allowing or requiring fair value accounting for certain types of financial instruments, to avoid conflict with IAS 39. Notice that this amendment need not affect any member state's accounting rules, because the state could decide whether to use the option or not. Introducing additional options, though, could end up generating even more accounting diversity across the EU.

In addition, the European Commission encouraged member states to offer at least the global players domiciled in their countries the option to prepare consolidated financial statements under IFRS. In fact, about half of the member states allowed the use of IFRS but usually also U.S. GAAP for consolidated statements under the restriction that the statements are in accordance with the directives. Since the European Commission pushed for virtually no differences between IFRS and the directives, this restriction is a mild one for IFRS but appears to have more bite for U.S. GAAP (at least formally). The EU consciously targeted its approach to meet the needs of the global players in the EU, particularly their desire to report under internationally accepted financial disclosure standards at no cost disadvantage to the companies.

SHAREHOLDER PROTECTION

The accounting directives include few measures to protect shareholders because of the presumption they could protect themselves via their direct access to company information and their decision rights. This is true only for controlling shareholders, however, and less so for minority shareholders and those with shares in large companies with widely dispersed ownership.

Roughly at the same time as the accounting directives were developed, the EU began to harmonize capital-markets laws in member states to ensure minimum standards for listings on regulated markets and to facilitate (limited) competition among European capital markets. The Commission's White Paper in 1985 set forth an approach to ensure that the national rules meet certain minimum standards and to require their mutual recognition across other member states so as not to give a country a competitive advantage. Mutual recognition was a political goal, since it required the acceptance of financial disclosures not fully comparable among the states.

The relevant directives include conditions for admission to listing, such as the public offer prospectus, interim reporting, publication of major share holdings, and immediate disclosure of market relevant information.[14] The directives also include the general obligation of member states to mutually recognize prospectuses and financial statements.[15] However, the EU has been less successful in creating a common takeover system. Work on a takeover directive commenced in 1974; after many attempts a final draft was declined by the European Parliament in July 2001; and in December 2003 the European Parliament eventually accepted a compromise that was reached between the Parliament and the European Council against the proposal of the Commission. Symptomatic of many such legislative processes, the compromise consists of options and opt-outs in the core rules.

Other means taken by the EU to achieve its goal of integrating capital markets within the EU include the deregulation of capital markets and liberalization of cross-border transactions. In particular, new forms of financing were admitted for trading; taxes and other transaction costs were reduced or abolished; and specific approval procedures on trading instruments that had been imposed by some governments were abolished. With the increasing global pressures for market efficiency, these developments facilitated national changes in the rules governing securities markets, the first being the London Stock Exchange, which in 1986 reorganized admittance requirements, liberalized transaction commissions, and introduced a screen-based quotation system (SEAQ).

The capital-markets–related directives do not include material financial accounting and reporting rules. Instead they rely on the accounting directives, which, as mentioned above, form part of company law and apply to all limited liability companies. These had a different focus than IFRS (but also than U.K. standards), which is a reason that the EU initially held a negative view of IFRS and relied on the principle of mutual recognition of financial reports for listing across the EU instead.

AUDITING

The original accounting directives contain the general requirement that individual (entity) and consolidated financial statements must be audited. While the auditing requirement encompasses all limited liability companies, member states may (and most do) relieve small companies[16] from an audit of their individual statements, presumably because the costs of an audit would exceed its value. Most small companies are managed by the owner(s) and have no dispersed ownership. Since all limited liability companies must publish financial information, the exemption of small companies from an auditing requirement has the consequence that these firms publish non-audited financial statements.

The accounting directives do not include rules for the statutory audit and the auditor but rely on national laws. The demand for harmonizing auditing was met to some extent by a separate directive, the Eighth Directive, which sets minimum standards for the qualification, independence, and professional integrity of auditors. It does not change the fact that the member states remain the major regulatory force. Individual states authorize auditors in their state and require qualification under the law of the state.[17] A main reason for this situation is that there are differences in national educational programs and in legal environments that would make it difficult to legislate a single EU qualification. However, the importance of national authorization can act as a barrier to the internationalization of audit firms, because the majority of management must be persons approved in the respective state. Even auditors approved in another EU member state may need additional approval.

Auditor appointment, dismissal, and liability currently are not regulated at the EU level. These issues formed part of the materials that should have entered the Fifth Directive. Its objective was to provide a framework for many corporate governance issues in public limited companies, but it failed to be adopted. The most recent draft is from 1991, which already indicates that some of the issues, particularly codetermination, have been highly controversial and are unlikely to be resolved in the near future.

ENFORCEMENT

There does not yet exist any EU legislation regarding the enforcement of accounting and disclosure rules. Enforcement is left to the member states, which are to provide sanctions for failure to follow the national standards for financial disclosure. A few general provisions for sanctions are included in the company law directives. They, however, do not form a sufficient basis for the harmonization of enforcement in the member states.

SHORTCOMINGS OF THE OLD REGULATORY REGIME

The member states that belong to the EU are individual countries with diverse national historical and economic backgrounds, cultures, legislation, and pride. Therefore, the constitution of the EU delegates only limited regulatory power to the European Commission and the European Parliament. EU regulatory action is not always welcomed by governments of member states, as it tends to reduce their power to conduct their affairs in a way that is most useful to their potentially idiosyncratic and perhaps short-term political interests. The EU constitution thus provides many procedural steps to ensure that the opinions and, often, national provisions in policymaking of each member state are reflected. In many cases, decisions require a unanimous vote of all member states, which gives much power to individual national interests, whatever their relative country population or size of territory or national income. Such a regulatory regime works well as long as there are not many decisions to address or the matters that are up for decision do not have much impact on the states. The higher the degree of integration becomes, the more important are the decisions to be made, and the less efficient is such a regime.

Accounting was perceived as an important element in achieving a common European economic market. Nonetheless, there has not been a broad consensus on financial reporting issues. As a result, the development of accounting legislation has been very slow and sometimes ineffective. To arrive at a legislative act on the EU level, the Commission or some states usually make a proposal to regulate an issue; a group is set up that considers the issue in detail; and then there is negotiation among the member states. Often, member states wish to protect the status quo of their national legislation or to individually improve the effects on their country. In some cases, negotiations may be affected by trade-offs on totally unrelated issues, in the sense that a country succeeds with a desirable rule in accounting by giving in on, say, a rule governing agricultural subsidies that is desired by another country. Of course, there are conflicts among member states, and the situation is not ameliorated by the fact that the EU consists of both large, economically powerful and smaller, less powerful member states. Thus, it is more difficult for the European Commission than it would be for a national government to develop and introduce new legislation. Moreover, the European Parliament often amends or changes proposed legislation, and one sometimes gets the impression that this activity serves purely as a justification of its very existence. There are also interventions by the European Council. In cases where no consensus could be reached during negotiations, the directives introduce options. One might say, the more controversial such issues, the higher is the number of options in the directive or the more ambiguous the text.

In addition, the agenda for harmonization has been very selective. Not unexpectedly, the EU tried to harmonize areas that promised to be the more successful. As mentioned earlier, corporate governance issues that should be part of the proposed Fifth Directive, including the codetermination of workers on boards, were not resolved. A recent exception is the establishment of a new legal form for cross-border undertakings, the Societas Europaea (SE), which is a public limited liability company. It was introduced by a regulation in 2001 after decades of extended discussion among countries that tried to save their own national institutions. But even here national peculiarities prevail. For example, financial reporting is governed by the standards applicable for public companies in the member state in which the head office is located.

The directives bind only the member states; they are not directly applicable to individual companies. Business is governed by national legislation, which adopts the contents of the directives in national law.[18] Consequently, there has not been an immediate need to interpret rules in the directives.[19] Member states have considerable flexibility in transpositioning (the process of enacting into national law) directives and generally use it to keep as much of their previous legislation as possible. While the official text of directives is adopted in the languages of the member states, a translation can have a slightly different interpretation in different national contexts (such as the meaning of "realized" in the sense of either realizable or finally realized). The language translation had even been part of negotiation in critical issues.

The development of the first accounting directive regulating individual accounts is illustrative of the regulatory process. Work on what later became the Fourth Directive began in 1965, at a time when the EU comprised only six member states. The first draft of this directive, published in 1971, was prepared under strong German influence and drew heavily from the German stock corporation law. Shortly afterward, three more countries, including the United Kingdom, became members of the EU. The United Kingdom, however, was not prepared to accept rules that were essentially based on the German accounting framework, which stands in stark contrast to the U.K. framework. Due to the shift of powers in the EU resulting from the United Kingdom's integration, the draft directive was revised heavily to incorporate many provisions of the U.K. accounting framework.[20] Eventually, the Fourth Directive was adopted in 1978, 13 years after the initial discussions.

Member states were required to transpose the Fourth Directive into national laws by mid-1980. No member state met this deadline. Actual implementation by member states occurred between 1981 and 1991, roughly 25 years after the Fourth Directive's first conception. The European Commission can take enforcement actions against member states. Usually, noncomplying member states, after some informal persuasion, are referred to the European Court of Justice. This disciplinary approach is not very effective, since it takes a long time and its results are uncertain. For example, the Commission took Italy to the European Court in 1986 for not having implemented the Fourth Directive. Italy nevertheless failed to implement the Directive until 1991. Germany was taken before the European Court for not having provided sufficient enforcement power over small limited liability companies that failed to publish abridged statements, as required in the Fourth Directive. This case was decided in 1998 against Germany, but the outcome seems to have had little effect on actual practice. The development of the second major accounting directive, the Seventh Directive on consolidated accounts, was similar.

The European Commission, well aware of the slow and inflexible regulatory process, undertook several initiatives to remedy the problems. It proposed a "comitology" procedure for amending accounting standards, which would delegate decision-making on well-defined, usually technical, issues to the Commission, which again would delegate it to an expert committee. An attempt in 1976 to give constrained decision-making authority to the Contact Committee failed because member states and the European Parliament did not accept delegating legislative power to such a committee.

With regard to disclosure regulation, the EU tried to influence practice in the member states with recommendations. For example, in 2001 it issued a recommendation on the recognition, measurement, and disclosure of environmental issues in annual reports.[21] Member states should promote and ensure that companies account for and report on environmental issues. To our knowledge, this recommendation has not had much impact on practice. Member states fear that these issues are politically motivated and should not affect financial statements, which already include sufficient standards for how to account for environmental issues. Another recommendation concerns quality assurance of audits (which we discuss below).

PERSISTING DIVERSITY

The directives addressing financial disclosure generated several major achievements in harmonization, many of which are taken for granted these days. For example, they achieved some convergence in the objectives of financial reporting and auditing in general. Consolidated financial statements were introduced in several member states that had not previously required them, and the consolidation methods of those states that already required consolidated statements converged. The directives also reached a compromise between the different legal approaches found in the member states, most notably the legalistic approach (as in Germany) and the case law approach (as in the United Kingdom).[22] In many ways, the sheer number of companies that are subject to the directives created an enormous effort in many countries. Nevertheless, most countries found it difficult to reconcile the requirements of the directives with their national approaches. Some countries used financial statements mostly to measure and restrict dividend payouts or for tax purposes, whereas others used them mainly to provide information to capital markets. They often discovered ways around the directives. For example, the United Kingdom dispensed with the depreciation of investment property, and Germany with the true and fair view override.

A comparison of the detailed rules governing financial disclosure across European countries shows that diversity persists.[23] Diversity can exist because countries enact different rules; however, even if they have the same rules, the accounting methods chosen in practice can differ. A simulation by Simmonds and Azières [1989, p. 36] of a hypothetical company's reported income under different countries' accounting standards in 1989 shows that reported net income ranged from some 20 to 200 million ECU (European Currency Unit, a predecessor to the Euro), with the average around 130 to 150 million ECU. Only recently has the globalization of capital markets changed member states' minds so that they now generally support the EU's advancement of the single capital market within Europe. National legal systems of various kinds prevail, however, and are a barrier to the EU's objective of creating an integrated financial market. Also, the financial systems across European countries have not converged but have exhibited a high degree of inflexibility over the years.[24] The reasons include the complementarities of many elements that make up the financial systems and the difficulties of changing the overall system by considering changes in but a few elements at a time.

The national accounting standard-setting bodies and processes vary substantially across the EU.[25] Some countries have legally accepted standard setters, others just organizations that issue opinions and recommendations. Some half of the member states have standard setters that are public committees, whereas the others have private organizations. Funding of private organizations comes mainly from the accounting profession, while public committees typically rely on government funds. We were unable to find a pattern of commonalities among the countries that follow either a more public or private regulatory approach. The approaches also do not appear to follow the legal origin (common or code law)[26] or any typical classification schemes for accounting systems,[27] nor the size of the country or capital market. The composition of the organizations varies. Some include mostly accountancy professionals, while others include preparers from companies, stock exchange representatives, academics, investors, financial analysts, and regulators. The legal status of the standards ranges from mandatory rules to recommendations. The scope of standard setting ranges from listed corporations and consolidated statements to all companies and all statements, from certain industries to the public sector.

Quality assurance of financial disclosure is another area that exhibits diversity.[28] Corporate governance differs widely, ranging from the single board system to the two-tiered system with separate executive and supervisory boards. The responsibilities with respect to financial disclosures also vary. However, most member states developed corporate governance codes that differ in many respects but are highly convergent on the major issues.[29]

Harmonization in auditing was modest because auditor admission requirements, qualification, appointment, and legal liability follow national legislation, for which the Eighth Directive sets only basic principles.[30] Although not addressed by the EU legislation, auditing standards are much more homogenous in the member states. According to a study by the Fédération des Experts Comptables Européens (FEE), a private association of European professional bodies of accountants, the national auditing standards in EU member states are substantially in line with the International Standards on Auditing (ISA).[31]

Diversity is apparent in the enforcement systems. There were approximately 40 enforcement organizations in the then 15 EU member states.[32] Some are set up by the stock exchanges, others are part of stock exchange regulatory bodies or government departments, and others are private bodies. A substantial number of countries do not have an oversight system that goes beyond simple formal checks. In some countries, enforcement is limited to listed corporations; in others it extends to all publicly disclosed financial reports. Some oversight bodies work on a proactive basis, whereas others react to any third-party complaints. While all countries have some form of sanctions, they range from civil to criminal procedures, and the consequences differ widely. Because enforcement is considered a national task, it has not been subject to standardization at the EU level. National cultural differences also frustrate attempts to standardize corporate governance and investor protection. Consequently, existing legislation is highly country-specific.

CURRENT ISSUES

This section discusses the current issues and initiatives in the EU with respect to financial disclosure. Many of the following themes are still at the stage of proposals or, if enacted, have only recently become effective. Therefore, their impact on the practice in the EU is difficult to assess.

The Financial Services Action Plan

Forced by the ever-increasing globalization of capital markets and the introduction of the Euro, the European Commission accelerated the regulatory process for financial markets. With the view of completing the internal market for financial services by 2005, the Commission set forth the Risk Capital Action Plan in 1998, which suggests measures to promote private equity investments. A year later it issued the Financial Services Action Plan, which incorporated the financial accounting measures that were originally contained in the Risk Capital Action Plan. With these Plans, the EU moved away from the traditional distinction between company law and capital market laws with respect to financial disclosure and focused on all corporations with securities listed on a regulated capital market in the EU. The effect on other companies has not yet become clear.

The Financial Services Action Plan aims at creating an integrated financial market and, indeed, at "transforming Europe into the world's most competitive marketplace."[33] It includes three strategic objectives: (a) the creation of a single EU wholesale market, (b) open and secure retail markets, and (c) state-of-the-art prudential rules and supervision. To achieve these objectives, several important changes in the current EU regulatory environment were proposed, including facilitating access to equity markets to raise capital and trade securities, a higher degree of transparency of corporations, internationalization of financial disclosure, and improved supervisory structures. Overall, the Financial Services Action Plan includes an ambitious work program of 42 original measures, which should be affected by changes in the institutional and regulatory environment and by new or amended directives on securities market issues.

The EU set up the Committee of Wise Men on the Regulation of Securities Markets in 2000 to make recommendations on how best to proceed with the implementation of the ambitious goals set by the Plan. The Committee's final report (Lamfalussy Report) was released in early 2001 and was endorsed by both the European Council and the European Parliament. Not surprisingly, the Report identifies the EU regulatory process as a key impediment to effective regulation of financial markets and proposes a different approach, carefully balancing the subtle attitudes of the EU member states with respect to increased regulation from Brussels. More surprisingly, the member states were overwhelmingly in favor of the Report. The issues at stake had obviously gained so much importance that it would have been difficult not to agree.

The Lamfalussy Report proposes a new procedure with four steps to speed up the legislative process. In the first step, the EU political bodies would adopt principles on an issue, which provide a framework for later detailed regulatory proposals. In the second step, the Commission develops detailed rules to implement the principles, with the assistance of a technical committee. The rules are decided upon by a political committee, which is the core of the comitology procedure. The European Council and the European Parliament, though, can vote down the proposal. The third step consists of member states implementing the rules in a cooperative and mutually consistent way, again assisted by committees on the European level. Finally, the fourth step calls for strengthened oversight by the European Commission to enforce the rules. If legislation by the EU is needed, the Lamfalussy Report also suggests that the EU use the instrument of a regulation, as regulations, unlike directives, take effect directly without the need for transposition into national legislation. These proposals represent a wide-ranging shift of power not only from member states to the EU bodies, but also from the European Parliament to the Commission. To safeguard the Parliament's rights, the von Wogau Report includes information rights and procedures in case of disagreement among the EU bodies.

The Lamfalussy Report also proposes priorities for equity markets, including a single prospectus for issuers across the EU; the modernization of admission requirements for listing; a generalization of the home country principle (that is, mutual recognition); the modernization and expansion of investment rules for investment and pension funds; the adoption of IFRS; and a single "European Passport" for recognized stock markets, which means that a prospectus, once approved in a member state, is accepted also in other member states. There were critical comments, too. In the responses to the EU proposals, concerns were raised as to overregulation, because the proposals are oriented toward the needs of cross-listed and large corporations.[34]

Some of the suggestions for change had already been taken up by the European Commission in proposals for directives or amendments dealing with listing admission, prospectuses, investment services, and market abuse. They follow the principles-based regulation approach suggested in the Lamfalussy Report. There were drawbacks, though. For example, to improve transparency in capital markets, the EU originally proposed quarterly reporting by listed corporations. A majority of the respondents opposed this requirement, mainly because of the short-termism it induces. They also opposed a limited auditor's review of quarterly reports, because of its cost. In fact, the draft transparency directive found a striking approach to interim reporting: it required detailed half-yearly report (according to IAS 34) and quarterly interim management statements, including a narrative description of the financial position and material events, but no quantitative information whatsoever (earlier proposals required at least net sales and an income figure) where a company does not issue a full quarterly report. The final directive, published in December 2004, reduced the requirement even further. Quarterly reports are not required at all, but there is a mild requirement for qualitative information in between the half years. Obviously, it was not possible to gain member states' acceptance for quarterly reporting, even though 8 of the then 15 member states already required that by national legislation.[35] This solution is illustrative of the difficulties of disclosure regulation even in the new regime.

In mid-2001, the EU created two committees to develop detailed rules for the regulation of financial markets and react quickly and flexibly to future challenges. The European Securities Committee (ESC) comprises high-level representatives of member states. It has both advisory and regulatory capacities. It advises the European Commission on securities policy issues in draft legislation based on the framework principles. Later on it will act as a regulatory committee under the comitology procedures. The Committee of European Securities Regulators (CESR) grew out of the Forum of European Securities Commissions (FESCO), founded in 1997. It serves as an independent advisory group to the Commission for technical implementation issues. Composed of representatives of national public authorities overseeing financial markets, it also is expected to be important in the implementation of EU law in the member states via guidelines, recommendations, and standards. CESR already issued standards on enforcement of financial reporting (see below) and a recommendation on the transition to IFRS.

Corporate Governance

Many of the efforts of the European Commission focused on the capital market institutional environment; however, the Commission was also active in overhauling company law. In 2001 it set up the High Level Group of Company Law Experts to work out a proposal. The Group presented its report a year later in the Winter Report. The Commission was quick in proposing an action plan based on the report,[36] because company law should be compatible with capital markets law by 2005, and perhaps also because the Commission felt it had to react to the recent measures the United States introduced with the Sarbanes-Oxley Act of 2002.

A major objective of the plan is strengthening shareholder rights and third-party (particularly creditors) protection. The plan includes the proposal to differentiate rules between listed and private companies rather than using limited liability as the major criterion for a legal distinction. The plan considered the need to introduce a European corporate governance code but concluded otherwise because of the well-known difficulties of developing a unified code. The European Commission plans to coordinate the national corporate governance codes instead, because they appear to be more flexible and adapted to the respective national requirements. In late 2004, it set up a European Corporate Governance Forum and proposed that it take an active role in coordinating and converging national codes. The Commission is not willing to rely fully on voluntary adoption of the codes but proposes that listed corporations be required to include in their annual reports a statement on corporate governance. In particular, the statement should describe shareholder rights, the operation of shareholder meetings, board and committee members, major shareholders and their relationship and transactions with the corporation, and the risk management system. Moreover, the statement should refer to the national corporate governance code and the compliance (or noncompliance) with the code via a comply-or-explain requirement.

The Commission also plans to regulate the management structure. Following the Winter Report, it proposes that listed corporations should be able to choose between a one-tiered and a two-tiered board structure. It addresses the board composition, particularly the independence of committee members, and proposes shareholder approval, recognition, and disclosure of the individual directors' remuneration. Another issue considered is capital maintenance, which has had high priority in the directives as part of creditor protection. The Winter Report made some suggestions for an alternative regime, but the European Commission has not yet decided if it wanted to (or could) change the present rules.

The modernization of the rules governing company information is less controversial, and the European Commission has made good progress with a proposal to change the First Directive, which regulates the filing and disclosure by limited liability companies. The relevant amendment was adopted in June 2003. The changes, which are a response to the recent developments in information technology, require member states to make possible an electronic filing of company documents by 2007 and make documents available electronically. In its recent transparency directive, the EU announced plans to create an electronic network of financial disclosures of all European listed corporations. It should allow users easy access via the Internet to all relevant financial information they seek from a single source. The objective is similar to what is achieved in the United States by the SEC's EDGAR system and efforts undertaken in the United Kingdom with creating regulatory news services. The directive does not include details of how this should be done, leaving this to the national securities regulators.

While it appears that the European Commission is the major player in the current changes, another player is the European High Court, which has held a very liberal view with respect to the fundamental objectives of the EU, including freedom of trade and capital, in recent decisions. It values mobility across borders higher than national law and opens up competition of national regulatory environments within European countries. An example is the freedom of incorporation independent of where the major business is undertaken.

The Adoption of IFRS

With respect to financial disclosure regulation, the adoption of IFRS is the most significant change from the present legislation. In a strategy statement in 2000,[37] the European Commission announced its plan to propose that listed corporations domiciled in a member state should be required to prepare consolidated financial statements in compliance with IFRS. The proposal immediately followed the endorsement of IFRS by IOSCO, even though the endorsement contained some clauses allowing regulators to require supplemental treatment where necessary to address, as it is called, "outstanding substantive issues at a national or regional level."[38]

The proposal, enacted in June 2002 by the so-called IAS Regulation, requires a mandatory application of EU-endorsed (see below) IFRS for listed corporations as of 2005, thus ending the era of voluntarily improved financial disclosures on a national basis. The IAS Regulation refuses to introduce market competition among globally accepted standards by not allowing corporations to use U.S. GAAP. Lobbying by global players, particularly by German corporations, to allow their continued use of U.S. GAAP had only limited success. In a concession, the IAS Regulation includes the option for member states to postpone the requirement to adopt IFRS to 2007 for corporations whose shares are listed in a non-member state and who use internationally accepted standards other than IFRS for this reason. This directly speaks to the SEC's requirement that all corporations listed on U.S. exchanges still must either use or reconcile to U.S. GAAP. Urged mainly by French corporations, the Regulation includes a similar option for corporations who have only listed debt securities. Curiously, a postponement of the IFRS adoption would seem to imply that the EU considers it easier to change from the GAAP of member states to IFRS than from U.S. GAAP. Therefore, there is still successful lobbying going on under the ambitious work program of the EU.

From a regulatory point of view, the EU used a regulation for the requirement to report under IFRS, which takes immediate effect as a direct obligation of listed corporations domiciled in an EU member state, allowing quicker enactment of the rule. The member states, which in the past were often reluctant to transfer more power to the European Commission, were willing to submit to this process, following the recommendations in the Lamfalussy Report, and reacted very positively to the new strategy. The IAS Regulation was even adopted in a fast-track legislative process by the EU.

The IAS Regulation requires more than 7,000 listed corporations to prepare IFRS financial statements by 2005. The Commission encouraged member states to accept IFRS even earlier. Before the 2005 deadline, there were only few hundred corporations already reporting under IFRS. The distribution of early adopters varied across member states. For example, Germany and Austria had very high voluntary usage of IFRS, whereas adoption was very low in the United Kingdom and Ireland. A reason may be that there are several EU member states that did not allow corporations to report solely under IFRS, but had to prepare financial statements under national GAAP. Support among the listed corporations is high: a PricewaterhouseCoopers survey undertaken in early 2002 showed that more than 60 percent of the CFOs of listed corporations agreed that IFRS will help establish a pan-European capital market, and 71 percent of current IFRS users among them said that IFRS are beneficial to their companies.[39]

In the light of the experience with the difficulties of accounting harmonization in the EU, the unanimity with which IFRS were adopted by the member states is amazing. A reason may be that adoption of IFRS is restricted to the limited number of listed corporations. It is too early to judge the quality of the implementation of the IFRS by corporations in the various states, particularly in the now enlarged EU. It is no coincidence that the EU is working hard on ensuring efficient enforcement mechanisms in the member states (see below), which are necessary to assure the quality of financial disclosures.

The IAS Regulation also provides an option for member states to permit or require companies that prepare consolidated statements, or even all companies, to use IFRS instead of national GAAP. Essentially, it would mean that international standards set by a private body, the IASB, would replace national GAAP. According to a survey of the European Commission, the member states take different routes toward the use of these options.[40] Most states permit, but do not require, non-listed companies to use IFRS for their consolidated statements, and some half of the states (e.g., Denmark, Finland, Greece, Netherlands, Sweden, and the United Kingdom) plan to extend the option to individual statements.

A side effect of the IAS regulation is that non-EU corporations whose securities are listed in a regulated European securities market must also follow IFRS starting in 2007 unless their "third-country GAAP" are qualified as being equivalent to IFRS as endorsed by the EU.[41] If third-country GAAP are not considered equivalent, issuers from such countries that want to list on a European capital market will have to restate (or perhaps reconcile) their financial statements under (endorsed) IFRS as of 2007.

The European Commission set up a mechanism for assessing equivalence under the comitology framework and has already asked its Committee of European Securities Regulators (CESR) for technical advice in assessing Canadian, Japanese, and U.S. GAAP.[42] This equivalence need not be shown by a line-by-line comparison of specific standards. Rather, the intention is to assess whether use of other GAAP would enable investors to make decisions that are similar to those that would be made using IFRS, as indicated by the views of market participants and others involved with the market, such as standard setters and regulators. This procedure provides the EU with some bargaining power against the United States, which, to the displeasure of the EU, has not accepted IFRS without reconciliation to U.S. GAAP for foreign listed companies. While it is probably difficult to argue that U.S. GAAP are not equivalent to IFRS, particularly in the light of the recent convergence, some major differences persist and may be used to motivate the SEC to forego its requirement for a reconciliation on a mutual recognition basis. Indeed, the SEC has indicated that the reconciliation requirement may be eliminated by 2009.

With the adoption of IFRS for (at least) all listed corporations, the EU, in substance, delegates the development of accounting standards to an international private standard setter over which it has no direct control. This is a remarkable move because it contrasts with the usual pattern of accounting standard setting, whose domain is that of political interest groups that do not want to lose influence. However, a loss of control of accounting standard setting seems unavoidable if internationally developed standards are desired. Nevertheless, many critics fear either the loss of power of setting accounting standards or doubt that the delegation of standard setting to the IASB is lawful under the EU's constitution.[43] To address these concerns, the IAS Regulation contains an endorsement mechanism that would guarantee that IFRS are adopted only if they conform with the "true and fair view" that is dominant in the accounting directives, if they are conducive to the European public good (which is not elaborated on), and if they meet the criteria of understandability, relevance, reliability, and comparability.[44] All existing and future IFRS should be evaluated along these lines before they are endorsed. Consistency with the directives is not an explicit criterion.

Two new committees were established in 2001 at the EU level to help the Commission make the endorsement decisions. The European Financial Reporting Advisory Group (EFRAG) is a technical expert committee meant to provide a quick technical assessment of IFRS in the European context and contribute to the work of the IASB on a proactive basis. The EFRAG replaces the Accounting Advisory Forum. The other committee is the Accounting Regulatory Committee (ARC), which represents the political level. In addition, a subcommittee of the Committee of European Securities Regulators, CESRFin, is involved in supporting the Commission on technical issues relating to endorsing and enforcing IFRS.

The idea behind the creation of the endorsement mechanism was to recognize that while rejection of an IFRS would be a rare exception, the possibility should nevertheless be a credible threat. To avoid undesirable rejection of a standard, the EFRAG is expected to proactively articulate any potential difficulty and thereby influence rather than attempt to reject the development of final standards.[45] The IAS Regulation stipulates that the current IFRS should be endorsed by the end of 2002. In fact, in a draft letter to the Commission from May 14, 2002, the EFRAG recommended the endorsement of all existing IFRS at that time, en bloc. However, several constituents, mainly banks and insurance companies, and member states, notably France, opposed the accounting treatment of financial instruments prescribed by IAS 39. At issue were the measurement of many financial instruments at fair value and the narrow definition of hedged items, which many believe induces volatility in the financial statements even if the economic transactions do not exhibit volatility. As a result, in September 2003 the European Commission endorsed all existing IFRS and interpretations, with the exception of IAS 32 on presentation and disclosure and IAS 39 on recognition and measurement of financial instruments (including the related interpretations), with a view of reconsidering these standards after revision.

The decision appears strange because the issues had been on the table for quite some time, and the Commission did not suggest an alternative accounting approach to financial instruments. It rather seems politically motivated, so as to prove that the endorsement mechanism can be a serious instrument to discipline the IASB. In fact, the IASB reacted quickly and promulgated a limited amendment of the financial instruments standards to settle the concerns about the narrow hedge accounting requirements that were at the heart of the opposition. However, this obviously was not sufficient. Just 2 months after having published a major revision of the financial instruments standard, the IASB exposed a revision of the revision after the European Central Bank voiced late concerns about a broad fair value option that was included in the revised standard. The European Commission backed the European Central Bank by indicating it would not endorse the standard as it was. Indeed, in December 2004 the Commission endorsed IAS 39 with two so-called carve-outs: one is that the (optional) fair value measurement of liabilities is not permitted (thus restricting an IAS 39 option), and the second is to broaden the applicability of hedge accounting to core deposits (thus enlarging an IAS 39 rule). The understanding was that this partial endorsement is exceptional and only temporary. However, this is not the case. The IASB had backed down to the European Commission's lobbying and published a draft that restricts the fair value option drastically, with a view that this would resolve the partial endorsement threat. However, there was strong disagreement of respondents in the comment period with the exposure draft, leading the IASB to develop another solution, which would restrict the fair value option. The amendment was enacted in June 2005, and endorsed in late 2005. Nevertheless, the differences on hedge accounting of core deposit remain.

The continuing controversy around IAS 39 could well to be the starting point for the development of "official" European IFRS (or, analogously, of other country-specific IFRS), with the EFRAG as the companion or associated standard setter. (Uniform interpretation across member states is another issue.) There were two further instances that the Commission controversially discussed: the endorsement of other statements, including IFRS 2 (Share-Based Payments) and an interpretation on accounting for emission rights. While IFRS 2 was endorsed in February 2005, EFRAG recommended that the emission rights interpretation not be endorsed. The IASB reacted boldly to the pending adverse endorsement decision and withdrew the interpretation.

Amending the Accounting Directives

In its 2000 strategy statement, the Commission announced that apart from the IAS Regulation, it would also propose a modernization of the accounting directives by the end of 2001. A proposal was finally published in mid-2002, and a directive encompassing changes of several directives, including the Fourth and the Seventh Directive, was enacted in June 2003. Its main objectives are (a) to remove inconsistencies between the accounting directives and the IFRS and (b) to provide a level playing field between companies that use national GAAP with those that adopt IFRS.

The directive includes an option to member states to deviate from the rigid formats of the balance sheet and the income statement to achieve a presentation consistent with IFRS. This is notable because the formats are considered a major building block of the Fourth and the Seventh Directive. Other changes include the option for extending fair value measurements to categories of assets besides financial instruments, a change of the definition of provisions, and a change of the definition of subsidiaries. The directive contains also changes for the auditor's report and audit opinion.

In the view of the history of accounting standard setting by the EU, it is not surprising to observe that the amendment basically consists of providing a large set of options for member states to allow or require all or any classes of companies to apply accounting methods that are in line with current IFRS, without eliminating the original provisions in the accounting directives. To us, this appears to be the easy way to achieve unanimous agreement among all member states and get a "fast-track" approval for the amendment. Otherwise, some member states would perhaps have been reluctant to accept a move toward IFRS for all firms, particularly when there is a link between financial statements and tax assessment. However, there are disadvantages in inserting additional options in the directives, as they will actually lead to a reduction of the level of harmonization and comparability across EU member states or across companies within member states, provided the member states allow the options to the companies.

A major change brought about by the new directive is the requirement of a more comprehensive annual report that should include a "fair review of the development and performance of the company's business and of its position." This review should require reporting of both financial and nonfinancial key performance indicators, including environmental and employee information to the extent that this information is necessary for understanding the company's performance.[46] We see this requirement as an attempt by the EU to be more innovative, appealing to best practice in financial disclosure, although it is difficult to assess when such disclosures would be "necessary" from the companies' perspective. The requirement to consider the disclosure of environmental issues is in line with the Commission's recommendation from 2001 and may give it more influence.

In October 2004, the European Commission published another proposal for a revision of the accounting directives, mainly to increase disclosure requirements on related parties and on off-balance-sheet items.

Auditing

In 1996, the Commission published a "Green Paper on the Role, the Position and the Liability of the Statutory Auditor within the EU," which raised concerns about the diversity of rules relating to statutory audits and made proposals for their harmonization. It acknowledged that the regulation of auditing was incomplete, because the 1984 Eighth Directive deals only with a subset of issues, and even these were partly outdated or created barriers to the freedom movement of auditing services.

In 1998 the Commission created the Committee on Auditing (CoA), whose members come from audit regulators and the audit profession and which reports to the Contact Committee. Its objective is to develop a common view of auditing at the EU level. Major tasks are the development of minimum requirements for quality assurance, principles for independence and audit objectivity, and a review of International Standards on Auditing (ISA) as a basis for EU audit requirements. The CoA has close ties to the FEE, which provides technical input to the Committee, and with the International Auditing and Assurance Standards Board (IAASB)[47] of the International Federation of Accountants (IFAC), which issues the ISA.

The underlying premise of EU activity in this area is that "monitored self-regulation" of and by the audit profession is preferable to government fiat or explicit direction. Based on the work of the CoA, the EU issued two recommendations that are directed to member states, but it was hesitant to directly regulate auditing at that time. The merits of using recommendations are that they are much faster to promulgate. On the other hand, they are not binding, and it is unclear what to do if a member state does not follow a recommendation. The underlying "threat" is that if member states do not follow the recommendations, the Commission would propose replacing the recommendations with binding legislation.

In 2000, the Commission issued a recommendation on minimum standards for quality assurance in the statutory audit in the EU.[48] Member states should install quality assurance systems for statutory auditors; they can be either peer review systems or monitoring systems operated by a professional body or regulator in the respective country, and they should also include a public oversight structure on top of that. In 2002, the Commission published a recommendation on fundamental principles of statutory auditor independence.[49] It recommends the public disclosure of audit fees, restrictions for audit partners on joining the management of a client company, the provision of certain non-audit services to the client company, and the establishment of an internal control system within the audit firm to overview independence issues.

Both recommendations are in the process of being implemented by the member states. Despite this, the European Commission has recently moved back to regulation via directives. This suggests that the "soft" way of harmonization by recommendations does not achieve what was intended. In March 2004 the Commission proposed a new directive on the statutory audit to replace the Eighth Directive. The introduction states: "This proposal is not a knee-jerk reaction to recent corporate scandals. It is the logical consequence of a reorientation of the EU policy on statutory audit started back in 1996."[50] However, it is clear that the proposal was a reaction to the recent provisions by the Sarbanes-Oxley Act in the United States, which establishes the Public Company Accounting Oversight Board (PCAOB) that would affect European audit firms besides U.S. firms. The EU opposes the registration of European audit firms and aims to have an institutional setting in place that is comparable to that in the United States, which could be the basis of mutual recognition of auditors.[51] Public oversight of the audit profession was already the theme of the recommendation on quality assurance from 2000. Its implementation led to diversity across the member states, and the Commission now wants to harmonize public oversight to a greater extent.

The proposed directive requires member states to establish an independent public oversight mechanism for audit firms and includes general principles that should be followed. It favors a "home country control" approach and does not propose a public oversight body on the European level, but requires mutual recognition of the national bodies and sets out rules for effective cooperation among them. Auditors from countries outside the EU should be registered by an authority in a member state to guarantee high-quality audits, except if they are subject to equivalent quality and oversight systems.

The proposed directive further includes professional ethics and independence rules, and it introduces a public electronic register for audit firms eligible for statutory audits. It also liberalizes the audit market to allow audit firms to serve clients within Europe. Moreover, it states that all statutory audits should follow the International Standards on Auditing (ISA) promulgated by the IAASB. This idea had already been suggested by the FEE in 2001.[52] Studying national auditing standards, the Committee on Auditing has already found a high degree of similarity with the ISA. The Commission proposes an endorsement mechanism similar to that for the endorsement of IFRS, and a new committee, the audit regulatory committee, assisting the Commission to make such decisions and to detail and implement the principles via the comitology approach. It is therefore interesting to observe how effectively the endorsement mechanism for IFRS works. The existing, relatively young Committee on Auditing will be renamed the Audit Advisory Committee and will serve as an advisory and preparatory body between regulators and the audit profession. The Commission fears that individual member states could amend the ISA with idiosyncratic requirements based on traditional auditing standards in their respective countries, thus reducing the desired mutual recognition approach. Hence, it restricts such amendments.

The proposed directive includes additional rules for audits of "public-interest entities," which are defined as entities of significant public relevance due to the nature of their business, their size, or their number of employees, including listed companies, financial institutions, and insurance companies. It requires the internal or external rotation of the auditor, a transparency report of the audit firm (including a governance statement and a description of its internal quality control system), and rules for dealing with the audit committee of the auditee.

The proposed directive is still principles-based; however, it is more prescriptive than the Eighth Directive and statutory audit requirements that are included elsewhere. The European Commission expected the proposed directive to be adopted in a "fast-track" way by mid-2005, due to the urgency of the issues, and a transformation into the national laws of the member states by 2006. This ambitious goal has not been achieved.

Enforcement

As we have noted, there is currently no legislation on the EU level for enforcement, and actual enforcement measures differ widely across the member states. The Lamfalussy Report sees strengthened enforcement as the fourth level of the proposed path to integrated capital markets but remains relatively vague in its recommendations. While a European securities oversight body was discussed as a potential way to ensure enforcement, this is not what the European Commission proposes. The Commission seems to want to rely on national enforcement with a committee on the European level to coordinate enforcement practices in a consistent way across countries. This is consistent with the opinion of the FEE as laid out in a discussion paper on enforcement.[53]

IAS Regulation 2002 states that the European Commission will take a first step to develop a common approach to enforcement in liaison with the Committee of European Securities Regulators (CESR). CESR issued its first Standard "Enforcement of Standards on Financial Information in Europe" in March 2003. It includes a total of 21 principles that are intended to provide a basis for the harmonization of enforcement in the EU. The Standard confirms that enforcement should remain in the hands of the member states; an independent administrative authority should be responsible for enforcement. Although the authority may delegate enforcement to another body, typically a self-regulating organization, it will supervise it. Enforcement should be based on a selection of companies and documents, which should consider the risk of deviations. Purely reactive enforcement is not allowed. Pre-clearance of prospectuses by an enforcement agency is considered a standard enforcement method. Enforcement actions are not defined in detail; they can include reconciliations, corrections, restatements, and a suspension from trading or even delisting, depending on their appropriateness. A disadvantage of decentralized enforcement is that enforcement may diverge over time; CESR, therefore, is working to ensure coordination and convergence of the national enforcement agencies.

The Standard does not define sanctions but maintains these are in the domain of national legislation. Member states do have different approaches to enforcement, and the extent to which the Standard can produce convergence cannot yet be assessed. For example, corporations with securities cross-listed across Europe will still have to comply (only) with the enforcement laws of the country in which the company is headquartered. A market-based regulatory approach (e.g., a choice of enforcement mechanisms by cross-listed corporations) is currently not supported. This suggests that enforcement probably remains an obstacle to a truly integrated European capital market.

The Standard addresses enforcement only for listed corporations and those that applied for a listing, which is in line with the current efforts to create an efficient capital market across the EU. It does not capture enforcement for the many other companies that are regulated by the accounting rules of their countries.

A second standard from April 2004 provides principles on the coordination of enforcement activities across Europe, including a formal information system on enforcement experiences in different countries.

CONCLUSION

The pace of the developments and changes of the EU regulation of capital markets is amazing. The driving force has been the vision to establish an efficient European capital market that can compete with international, in particular U.S., capital markets. The EU currently is modernizing capital market regulation, including accounting and disclosure, auditing, and corporate governance, and tightening the standards significantly. A major decision was to adopt the IFRS (at least) for listed corporations, rather than to develop its own European standards. However, the endorsement mechanism that showed its teeth in dealing with the accounting for financial instruments and hedges is likely to lead to "European IFRS." It reminds us also of the potential disadvantages of a single set of accounting standards, which we explore in more detail in Chapter 10. In the European context, it is not obvious that the requirement to apply IFRS improves capital market efficiency over and above a self-selection of the accounting standards.

Auditing, corporate governance, and enforcement rely on the member states' efforts because they are more deeply embedded in the national institutional settings. Consequently, harmonization progresses slowly. While many important changes have been achieved, much remains to be done. The EU has many outstanding proposals with more or less detailed regulation. Most of the changes have only recently become effective in practice, which makes even an intermediate assessment difficult.

The orientation toward satisfying the demands of international capital markets participants created a strong force to separate listed corporations from the general company law in which accounting is regulated in the EU and provide for a tailor-made disclosure regulation for these corporations. However, there is a concern in many member states that the EU strategy is oriented too much toward the needs of large cross-listed corporations and ignores different needs by small locally listed corporations, for which the newly adopted rules would be very costly to implement. Alternatives to such a "one size fits all" approach may be a differentiation of the rules according to the risk the corporation poses on investors (e.g., measured by market capitalization or volatility) or including options that would allow corporations to select the rules that promise the highest benefit over the cost of compliance. Another concern is that the European Commission seems to follow a piecemeal approach to adopting a more transparent financial disclosure environment. There are many proposals, recommendations, and revisions related to the same set of rules that seem to miss a grand plan but appear to be the result of individual and specific issues.

The European Commission usually cites internationally competitive solutions and points out that it seeks European solutions, which means solutions that respect the different traditions, cultures, and needs of the member states. This is not obvious for the IAS Regulation, which does exactly the opposite, namely imposing a single set of (international) accounting standards on all member states. Many of the proposals are triggered by U.S. developments, which seem to serve as the benchmark.[54] It is difficult to discern a unique European approach that would qualify as innovative or pushing the frontier other than using IFRS. Minor attempts at innovations, such as environmental reporting and nonfinancial reporting, have not yet proved effective. A benefit may be that overregulation at the EU level is less likely to occur.

History has taught that the EU legislation was usually slow, sometimes ineffective, and not easily enforced. The new regulatory approach based on principles and the increasing trust in technical committees seems to improve on this but is still too new to convincingly show its efficiency. The legislative procedure proposed in the Lamfalussy Report may result in quicker standard setting, but it is inherently complex and obscure because of the establishment of many new committees whose tasks are often not well distinguished. We also observe that many of the proposals of the European Commission were delayed relative to their announced time schedule.[55] The delays on various levels are a result of the ambitious program that strains many participants in the process, or is used by them to link their acceptance with other issues.

The success of EU regulatory efforts depends to a great extent on the political support by a few large member states, and their support is conditional on the support by leading persons, institutions, and other idiosyncratic political circumstances. Political agreements have sometimes changed within a few years. A notable illustration is the political difficulty of adapting the European Treaty to the expansion of members in 2004, which has been postponed after rejection in two member states. The Treaty includes procedures for developing legislation and may thus have an impact on the Lamfalussy process that is at the heart of the current legislative changes. In autumn 2004, the European Commission has been newly staffed, and it is not clear how the new Commissioner for the Internal Market will pursue the strategy developed by the former Commission. We also cannot assess what effect the integration of the new member states will have on the progress of accounting and disclosure regulation and its application. Accounting scandals, even if they mostly appear in other nations, notably the United States, and the recent measures the United States took to prevent them in the future, have triggered major changes, as evidenced, for instance, by the audit proposals.

Studying the EU efforts to harmonize financial accounting and disclosure, particularly in the light of the globalization of capital markets, is instructive. It highlights many of the issues that are likely to also arise in a global effort toward harmonization. In fact, the difficulties could be just the tip of the iceberg of difficulties and challenges that may arise in an effort to standardize financial disclosure on a global scale. One essential difference with respect to global standardization is that the EU is, at least formally, in a position to enforce the implementation of standards due to the duties of its member states, while a market solution to more standardization has to rely on clear and individually calculable benefits relative to their costs to the participating countries, stock exchanges, auditors, or corporations. It would also require agreement among many countries that have no obligation to agree on a common or harmonized standard of financial accounting or auditing.

8

Corporate Financial Reporting and Regulation in Japan

Both financial markets and the accounting architecture in Japan have been undergoing radical change for several years, a process that continues. At this writing, despite its modest economic growth in 2003 and 2004, Japan's economy is still likely to struggle in the future, especially as its population continues to age. Some of Japan's economic problems have roots in the structure of the country's financial markets. However successful the government may be in its attempts to overcome the nation's economic problems, the outcome should have an impact on the financial system, the regulatory regime, and public accounting.

Much of our study of Japanese financial markets and accounting offers comparisons with other commercially developed countries. As a convenient shorthand or "straw man," we characterize these countries as "the West."[1] Japan provides a very interesting case study of a government's ability to make radical changes and, more recently, seeking to harmonize internationally both financial markets and accounting. This is because Japan has been subject to most types of regulation, from laissez-faire to very strong central government control. Some elements of all these regimes survive to this day.

As we discuss in detail, there have been efforts in recent years to harmonize Japanese accounting with international standards. This experience illustrates the difficulties of importing foreign regimes into Japan.

BACKGROUND ON THE JAPANESE ECONOMY AND FINANCIAL SYSTEM

To provide a context for our review, it is useful to begin with a brief overview of the Japanese financial and economic system.

Until the buildup to war from the mid-1930s, the Japanese financial system was very similar to that in the United Kingdom and the United States. Equity finance dominated, and bond financing and bank finance were of approximately equal importance. The Tokyo Stock Exchange traded the shares of more than 1,200 firms, and the total value of all shares exceeded the Japanese gross domestic product (GDP) by the mid-1930s.[2] Shareholders seemed to monitor enterprise conduct actively and require a stream of dividends.

From the mid-1930s to the Second World War, the government began to control long-term fund flows, direct lending by banks, and consolidate banks so that they could meet the increased requirements placed upon them to fund the war. The government sought to have only one bank for each prefecture and to enhance the role of these big banks. The importance of shareholding was symmetrically decreased, and all securities markets were suppressed.

After the Second World War, the Japanese government (at the behest of the United States) introduced a financial markets regime similar to the U.S. model. In particular, the post-war securities and banking laws mimicked those in the United States. The Securities and Exchange Law (SEL) copied the U.S. Securities Act of 1933 and the Securities Exchange Act of 1934. A Securities and Exchange Commission (SEC) was established in 1948. Although Japan copied the Glass-Steagall Act in the United States—prohibiting banks from being directly involved in securities underwriting—the Japanese act was less strict in at least one key respect: banks could hold 10 percent of security firms' shares, and this amount could be increased by share cross-holdings. The Act also strictly partitioned banks into a number of specialist categories; for example, only specific types of banks could make long-term loans. The SEC was abolished in 1952 because it did not fit with the centralized model of financial market regulation that Japan eventually adopted. It was replaced with oversight by the Ministry of Finance.

During the post-war period, it wasn't just the financial system that the Japanese government managed centrally: the government took the same approach to the entire economy, and for much of the time this seemed to work remarkably well. From the Korean War until the early 1990s, Japan's GDP grew at an annual average of 10 percent until the 1973 oil shock. But even after that traumatic event, economic growth resumed, varying between 2.5 and 5 percent between 1978 and 1987.

Japanese financial and real estate markets also expanded in scale and complexity throughout the post-war period. However, from the mid-1980s until the early 1990s, Japan experienced an "asset bubble": both equity and real estate prices soared beyond any reasonable level justified by the underlying economic fundamentals.

Bubbles never last forever, and the Japanese asset bubble was no exception: it "popped" in 1991. Though the economy suffered anemic growth for over a decade later, land prices continued to fall throughout the 1990s. As of early 2005, Japanese equities prices are still only about half of their pre-bubble peak.

The collapse of stock and real estate prices devastated many Japanese companies, and in turn the Japanese banks that loaned money to them, backed by stock or real estate as collateral. Yet Japanese banks were not forced by their regulators to make significant loan loss provisions for their large volume of nonperforming loans until 1997. By one estimate [Beason and James, 1999, p. 84], nonperforming bank loans in September 1995 represented 8 percent of GDP, even after very substantial write-offs. In early 2005, the economy is expected to return to respectable levels of growth (3 percent or higher, although the forecast for 2005 is around 1 percent), largely in response to heavy and sustained doses of monetary stimulus. Later parts of this chapter chart how government policy to overcome these problems has caused alterations in the financial market system and the accounting architecture in Japan.

Generally, over the post-war period, companies have not been highly focused on shareholders, nor have securities issues on the equity markets been an important source of corporate finance. Reflecting this lack of interest in shareholders, earnings have been less important as a source of finance (at around 35 percent) than in other commercially developed countries. Since the Second World War, bank debt has been the major way of financing companies; even now this source is very important for smaller companies. For large companies, bank debt averaged 30 percent of total liabilities and equity in 1980, falling to 20 percent in 1998 (the U.S. equivalent was 10 percent in that year). For smaller companies, the comparable figures were 47 and 35 percent in 1980 and 1998, respectively (compared to 19 percent in the United States in 1998).[3] Because large companies have been so dependent on banks for financing, Japanese regulators have been unusually interested in maintaining the banking system's viability. Understandably, depositors and investors therefore have perceived that the government stands behind large financial institutions.

The dominance of Japanese banks in funding Japanese corporations has also given banks a large role in corporate governance (as we discuss later). Japanese corporations have very high holdings of cash and cash equivalents, including bank deposits (52 percent of the total financial assets owned by the household sector at end of 1994). Comparable figures for the United Kingdom and United States were 24 and 19 percent, respectively.[4]

The corporate governance system in Japan has unusual characteristics. Members of the one-tier boards of directors are executives of the company, managers of closely associated companies (reflecting substantial share cross-holdings), and bank representatives (reflecting banks' substantial direct and indirect shareholdings). This configuration of executive power has made hostile takeover bids almost impossible.

In 1995, 41 percent of shareholders in Japan were financial institutions, 25 percent were other nonfinancial firms, and 23 percent were private individuals. In contrast, in the United States, individuals and pension funds dominated, constituting 70 percent of all shareholders.[5]

The main aims of Japanese accounting over the post-war period were stewardship, creditor protection, and satisfaction of tax requirements. These characteristics are reflected in Japanese legal codes.

LEGAL CHARACTERISTICS OF CURRENT FINANCIAL MARKETS

Just as the Japanese government centralized its regulation of financial markets after the Second World War, it took the same approach to the financial system itself. The reconstruction after the Second World War involved government directly in the allocation of funds to industry and commerce through banks, which also played a crucial role in the development of the post-war economy. This formed one of the roots of what is called the "main bank" system, which associated a bank with a firm or corporate group in a long-term relationship. Government intervention culminated in the allocation of funds to perceived winning (sunrise) industries, to restructuring declining (sunset) industries, and to the provision of detailed information about what were seen as important industries.

The central pillars of both the existing and past financial market systems are a strongly codified legal system where codes (laws) must be obeyed literally, but where otherwise firms are free to do what they wish, including finding ways around the codes. The essence of this system is what is called the triangular, three-code legal system. These statutory codes form a self-supporting nexus controlling the financial system. The codes are closely integrated and interact with each other.

The three codes are the Commercial Code (CC, enacted in 1890), the Securities and Exchange Law (SEL, enacted in 1948), and the Corporate Income Tax Law (CIT, enacted in 1947). The CC regulates financial reporting, mainly in the disclosure area, and strongly emphasizes the protection of creditors and to a lesser degree shareholders. The CC applies to all limited liability companies but places different requirements on different-sized companies and is administered by the Ministry of Justice. All companies must provide single-entity, or individual, accounts to company meetings in accordance with the Code's requirements. Only the balance sheet must be officially published. Listed companies must also publish an income statement in a newspaper or the Official Gazette. These statements must be audited, but only large companies are required to have external (CPA) audits. Following the German model from which the Code was derived, the focus is on the protection of creditors and the legal determination of dividends.

The SEL, in additional to the CC, applies to publicly traded corporations and requires additional disclosures beyond the CC. The Ministry of Finance is responsible for administering and enforcing the SEL. This code seeks to provide information for investment decision-making and for measuring managerial performance, although it maintains a strong stewardship perspective. Accounting reports must be filed with the Prime Minister's Office and the Stock Exchange on which the firm is listed semiannually and annually, and when new securities are issued. Consolidated accounts were required under the SEL in 1976 after a long debate, which started in 1965. These statements do not have to be disseminated to shareholders, although they are available at the general meeting and for public inspection. Following many discussions between ministries and advisory bodies, the amounts of net assets and net income under the SEL are now consistent with those declared under the CC, because the accounting treatments are taken from the CC. Balance sheets and income statements reflect a degree of conservatism based on the SEL's focus on protecting creditors.

Japanese corporate income tax laws, CIT, also play an important role in corporate accounting. These laws generally follow the practices of some continental European countries by allowing companies to deduct only those expenses that are shown in CC accounts of companies. At the same time, the CIT also requires companies to file a separate set of financial statements that are consistent with the rules of the CC. Companies often follow tax guidelines where treatments for accounting items are not specified in either the SEL or the CC.

After earlier difficulties, the three codes seem to operate relatively smoothly together. Thus, listed companies have to provide three sets of accounts (based on the requirements of the CC, SEL, and CIT), while other companies do not have to follow the SEL requirements.

Some authoritative Japanese commentators suggest that with regard to accounting, the CIT is "first among equals" with regard to the other two laws. In contrast, the Japanese Institute of Certified Public Accountants (JICPA) gives primacy to the CC because of its conservatism. The JICPA says that the SEL seeks to protect investors and to aid investors in decision-making and suggests that where there are differences, the very low activity of private investors in Japanese stock markets (until recently) makes this law less relevant than the CC. Auditors are generally satisfied to allow companies to follow accounting treatments required by the CIT and to choose alternatives that serve to minimize their tax burden. Japanese commentators suggest that these codes reduce flexibility in the markets, enforce traditional accounting, and are difficult and time-consuming to change, as this requires much discussion and ultimately legislation. This combination of factors reduces the ability to reform accounting so that it follows current international standards.

THE REGULATION OF FINANCIAL MARKETS

Over time, the Ministry of Finance has come to dominate the regulation of the financial and tax systems. Until the 1970s, the Ministry of Finance and the Bank of Japan made it difficult for Japanese firms to raise funds, whether domestically or from abroad, by requiring licenses and government approval before the firms could issue equity or debt. For example, the Bank of Japan required substantial collateral on issues of bonds. The Ministry of Finance licensed financial institutions in all market sectors and provided very strong informal guidance to them, usually behind closed doors in a process of bargaining and power relationships.

The Ministry of Finance's (then) Securities Bureau specifically enforced the SEL during this period. Investor protection was very weak, as private investors were relatively rare and other participants in the market had very close relations with corporations, which were believed to allow them access to any information required. The main bank system ensured that banks maintained very close relations with firms, often through share cross-holdings and interlocking directorates. Banks therefore had access to private information not available to investors generally. This is still the case, although share cross-holdings have become less important. All the while, however, banks continue to have direct access to the internal information of companies. Because financial institutions also were the dominant players in securities markets during most of the post-war period, any published information was directed more to their needs than to other shareholders.[6]

The Ministry of Finance supervised all financial institutions, implicitly guaranteeing their viability (to avoid financial disruption). In its regulation of banks, the Ministry maintained what came to be known as the "convoy system," which ensured the survival of the weakest banks by requiring stronger banks to help them. This informal system impeded the growth of the larger banks. The Ministry of Finance also regulated securities firms, which were allowed to engage in brokerage dealing (trading on own account, and underwriting and selling securities) and retail trading.

Banks and securities markets met the shorter-term funding needs of borrowers. Life insurance companies underwrote pensions and were a source of longer-term funds. The Postal Saving System was also instrumental in channeling much of the nation's savings (in the form of deposits in the Postal System) toward longer-term projects. This was accomplished often through the placement of funds in the Fiscal Investment and Loans Program, which directed resources toward officially approved industries through much of the 1950s and 1960s.

Japanese finance was biased against equity issues in several ways. As in the United States, issuers could deduct for tax purposes their interest payments but not their dividends. The government required firms to issue shares at par value, which strongly discouraged firms from issuing additional equity when market prices were higher than par value. The government also sought to protect existing shareholders from dilution by heavily restricting the underwriting of equity and requiring firms to meet stringent conditions before issuing additional stock. Even the securities exchanges were restrictive in their listing requirements (relating to minimum amounts of equity, earnings per share, and dividends). Many of these restrictions were not relaxed until 1998.

The Ministry of Finance also seems to have been very slow to recognize and do something about financial crises. For example, in the 1990s the Ministry allowed financial institutions to maintain bank loans at par, without special write-offs, and to continue to use accounting techniques that disguised loan problems. Later on, in 1997, listed firms were allowed to value holdings in other companies and land at either cost or market value, where cost did not have to take account of lower market values. Corporate holdings, therefore, were often valued at historical cost, thereby maintaining higher-than-market values in the face of declining markets. This had the effect of bolstering through overstatement the supposed strength of company balance sheets. The policy also allowed banks to use the "extra" reserves created by the revaluations to absorb write-offs of nonperforming loans.

HISTORY OF JAPANESE ACCOUNTING AND ITS REGULATION

The JICPA was established under the Certified Accountants Law in 1949. The JICPA was closely related to the Ministry of Finance, which, as a practical matter, really controlled, and to a degree still does (see below), the profession. Since 1966, all CPAs were required to be members of the JICPA. Audits by CPAs for companies covered by the SEL were not required until 1951, and this requirement was not expanded to nonlisted companies until 1971.

In principle, the Ministry of Finance oversaw the accounting profession. In practice, however, the Ministry was not especially proactive with regard to standard setting for reporting or auditing.

The three codes (laws), CC, SEL, and CIT (described earlier), form a fairly detailed statutory foundation for disclosure under Japanese generally accepted accounting principles (GAAP). All other parts of what might be called Japanese GAAP, including accounting standards, must be consistent with these codes and cannot override them. Each element of these codes must be followed. The JICPA issues implementation guidance to the codes and for auditing. This body also issues informal advice on accounting.

Until recently, the nearest equivalent to a standard setter was the Business Accounting Deliberation Council (BADC, set up in 1948), which, although an advisory committee to the Ministry of Finance, really is a creature of the Ministry, with the Ministry determining the membership of the BADC. The BADC also issues auditing rules, which have legal status. The SEL makes clear that companies should follow GAAP, while the Ministry of Finance requires BADC statements to be considered as part of GAAP. The BADC sets out a number of basic principles (which we review later). Until the financial markets were reorganized by the 1996 Japanese "Big Bang" (also discussed below), the BADC was not active in producing standards, guidance, and interpretations, although it spent much time reconciling various accounting requirements of the Codes. The BADC issued pronouncements infrequently, sometimes with a gap of several years: for example, in the period from 1980 through 1990, it issued only five statements.

The SEL required external auditing of listed companies in 1951. In 1974, the CC also required auditing for all large companies (capital greater than ¥500 million or liabilities greater than ¥20 billion), following a number of major reporting crises. Prior to this audit requirement, the CC required "parent only" audits by the company's internal auditors (or "statutory auditors," whom we discuss later). In addition to the audit requirements of the SEL for large companies, insurance companies and banks have also been subject to external audit since 1975.

Consolidated accounting statements faced a great deal of opposition, and it was not until 1977 that consolidation was required under the SEL, but not the other codes. The requirements were not as rigorous as in some countries. Consolidation applied only for subsidiaries in which the parent company owns more than 50 percent of the voting stock or where the parent directly or indirectly controls more than 50 percent of the voting. There was no "influence" test (i.e., no qualitative standard in addition to or in lieu of a quantitative standard). A modern standard for consolidation was introduced in 2003. The financial statements required under the SEL are an income statement, a balance sheet, a cash-flow statement, an auditors' report, and a variety of business reports. The Ministry of Finance has issued detailed guidance on how financial statements should be presented.

The general principles originally pronounced by the BADC, which are still in force today, are a set of concepts not substantially different from those adopted by developed countries in the late 1940s, but with a strong earlier German influence. For example, a shared concern with the safety of dividend distribution is exemplified by the Japanese requirement that prior to paying a dividend, firms must set aside an amount that maintains statutory earnings and capital reserves at 25 percent of the stated capital.[7] Similar German regulations require a reserve of 10 percent.

The principles issued by the BADC flow from those of the CC. These include orderly and accurate bookkeeping, distinctions between capital and earnings in presentation, continuity, conservatism, consistency, and a "true and fair view." These CC principles generally reign today. However, the BADC principles differed from usual practice in a number of ways. There was no "going concern" concept (made mandatory for listed companies only in 2002) and no requirements to make prior period adjustments (the CC still does not allow restatements). "True and fair" is said to be the primary principle incorporated in the first BADC statement in 1949, reflecting Western influences, but is interpreted as being satisfied if firms comply with all other sets of subordinate principles (as is the case in Germany). Substance over form is not included as a principle. However, there are some nonconservative surprises: for example, for some time, setup costs and expenditures on research and development could be capitalized and amortized over 5 years.

These accounting principles generally contained many items that are usually found in financial reports in the West, such as a strong reliance on historical cost accounting, although there were many gaps. As noted earlier, the CC did not require consolidated accounts until 1977. The CC did not allow revaluation of stocks or financial instruments. It did not require firms to recognize a liability for vested pension obligations or for the benefits of prior employee service. The CC rules offered company managers many opportunities to hide very large amounts of profits during the bubble economy, when asset values exceeded their historical values by large amounts.

These and other weaknesses in accounting supported an international view that Japanese accounting was of relatively low quality. This state of affairs helps explain why U.S. regulators required Japanese firms seeking funds in the United States to provide accounts consistent with U.S. GAAP.[8]

Applications of seemingly conventional accounting principles must allow for Japanese interpretations. Professor Hiroshi Tanaka has observed that the "true and fair" principle has no clear meaning in Japan (personal communication). He suggests that in much of Asia truth is interpreted as stating just the good news and that meaning of "fair" is not clear in Japan. He also suggests that the essence of Japanese accounting practice is to follow the relevant laws literally and exactly. Japanese accounting therefore does not seek to follow the spirit of any regulation. Full freedom of conduct is allowed in unregulated areas. Given this freedom, Japanese companies often sought to exploit any loopholes in GAAP and frequently changed accounting principles. Companies (especially banks) did not recognize bad loans for many years. Similarly, auditors acceded to "window dressing" in accounts.[9]

It can be argued that the rather weak accounting principles enshrined in Japanese GAAP at this time were not too important. The close relationship between companies and fund providers meant that information required for decision-making was obtained from sources other than the published accounts. Similarly, the monitoring of management was undertaken without the need for information in the accounts. Published accounting reports were important, though, for determining taxes on companies. In circumscribing corporations' ability to pay out dividends, the published reports also provided some protection for creditors. However, managers of Japanese corporations generally did not assign much importance to the payment of dividends. During the boom years there generally was little need to "window dress" accounts or to take advantage of the scope for manipulation allowed by the then Japanese GAAP, except in crises in specific industries. The very large unrecognized profits accumulated by firms provided a cushion both to firms and investors in downturns.

The weaknesses of Japanese GAAP became more important after the bubble economy of the 1980s turned into the stagnation of the 1990s. Previously, unrealized profits were declared as profits, and a lot of "window dressing" was used so that accounting reports portrayed the story management wished to give. However, at the same time, pressure for change began to build from a number of sources. Foreign investors and financial institutions scrutinized Japanese accounts in more detail and found them wanting. Overseas investors put more emphasis on the profitability of Japanese companies and on dividends and wanted to understand the accounts from a consolidated perspective. When translated into U.S. GAAP, the financial statements of Japanese companies seeking finance abroad highlighted the difference between Japanese and U.S. accounting practices, which, at least in the United States at that time, were regarded as of higher quality. Companies seeking funds abroad also became more concerned with measuring profitability in a more meaningful way. The desire to have internationally acceptable accounting also highlighted the need for changes in reporting, which we discuss below.

The laxity of Japanese accounting also highlights a number of problems inherent in any effort to harmonize international accounting standards. The existence of a number of accounting codes for different purposes, which may not be fully consistent, makes it difficult for both firms and their auditors to decide whether any one code, any combination of codes, or all of the codes should be followed and for what purposes. In particular, the existence of the three Japanese accounting codes has been seen as an obstacle to harmonization just within Japan. More generally, a code-oriented system implemented through a strong central government can be slow to respond and inflexible in a changing environment. Government control over accounting practices allows government officials to use accounting for political purposes, as they did to forestall recognition of banks' actual financial condition during the bad-loans crisis of the 1990s.

The Japanese experience illustrates that even if reporting standards eventually were harmonized, they may be used in different ways, especially if firms and auditors in some countries respect only the letter of accounting standards and see them as representing maximum requirements. Harmonization is also likely to be of little use if firms can easily exploit loopholes in standards (as we discuss in Chapter 3).

Accounting issues should not be considered apart from the broader changes in Japanese financial markets, dating from the late 1970s.[10] The relaxation of earlier regulations substantially expanded opportunities for large firms to raise finance in the equity and bond markets. Some firms went overseas for finance (especially bond funding). Over the period 1970 to 1990, the aggregate share of bank loans declined, especially to larger firms. For example, the percentage of bank debts to total assets of large manufacturing firms declined by from around 30 percent in 1980 to nearly 13 percent in 1990. The range of options available to savers also increased, but at a much slower rate.[11]

Regulations governing bond issues were relaxed significantly during the 1970s. Rationing was substantially abandoned in 1975, while collateral security requirements were reduced. The walls segmenting banks from other financial activities also began to come down. Banks replaced the business they lost from high-quality businesses, which turned to the bonds markets, by instead extending loans backed by land and property. Hoshi and Kashyap [2001, p. 312] implicitly suggest this was one of the seeds of the 1990s financial crisis, a view shared by other commentators.

CHANGES IN THE REGULATORY STRUCTURE DATING FROM THE "BIG BANG" IN 1996

Japanese policymakers have long wanted Japan to become a world leader in finance and for the yen to become a fully international currency. For this to happen, however, reforms were required. As the Ministry of Finance stated in 1997[12]

> The major challenge for Japan in the 21st Century is to maintain its economic vitality against the rapid ageing of the population.... [I]t is necessary for Japan to undertake a structural reform of its social and economic system. *In particular, financial systems, the artery of the economy, must be reformed so that it should effectively support the economic activity of the coming century.* [emphasis added].

More specifically, the Ministry sought to:

1. Expand the choices of investors and borrowers
2. Improve the quality of financial intermediaries and promote competition in financial services
3. Establish a reliable market framework and ensure fair and transparent transactions
4. Ensure market stability by speedy disposal of bad loans and increasing disclosure requirements.

Specific actions, including accounting reforms, were scheduled to be completed by 2001. Much was to be done much earlier. Although not highlighted in the plan, major changes in corporate governance also were planned. Thus, what is called the Japanese Big Bang actually represents more of a "slow burn" that is still ongoing.

Among the most important changes was the transfer of financial services regulation from the Ministry of Finance to a new independent Japanese Financial Services Agency (JFSA). The JFSA, which seems modelled on the U.K. Financial Services Authority, was established in July 2000 and is charged with making the financial system reliable, vigorous, fair, and efficient. The JFSA is responsible for designing financial systems and the inspection and supervision of financial activities covering banks, securities businesses, and insurance. It has a number of other objectives, including the promotion of competition; ensuring the supply of funds to small and medium-sized enterprises (which currently obtain their finance mainly from the banks); and generating a market of sufficient quality to attract international capital. The JFSA must also protect the buyers of financial products via regulation and education.

A major objective of the JFSA is to ensure transparency and fairness in the market. As is usual across the world (except for the U.S. SEC), it does not have responsibility for financial accounting reports, but reforms are proceeding in this area, which we discuss shortly. The JFSA also views harmonization of reporting rules with other countries to be an important objective.

One important section of the JFSA is the Securities and Exchange Surveillance Commission (SESC), which also was transferred from the Ministry of Finance in 1992. The SESC is responsible for compliance inspections with regard to securities and requires securities firms and exchanges to provide trading information. It monitors the markets daily. The SESC has strong enforcement powers carried out through the JFSA, which can take disciplinary action. It also can refer criminal cases to official prosecutors, although financially related prosecutions have been minimal. In 2002, 10 cases involving 22 people were referred for prosecution, some 30 requests for administrative disciplinary actions in the securities industry were made, 135 inspections were completed, and offenses were found only in 50 companies (SESC Annual Report 2002/2003).

The Law on the Sales of Financial Products, enacted in 2001, was another important innovation. This law requires retailers of financial services to provide investors with information on risk to the principal of an investment, including the effects of changes in, for example, interest rates, security market prices, currency exchange rates, and the business of the securities retailer. The retailer is liable for damages equal to the amount of loss to the investor of investments where the required information is not provided. The law is written in a way so as to avoid the general Japanese legal principle that puts the burden of the proof of loss flowing from the lack of information on the plaintiff.

Collectively, these reforms amount to a complete revolution in the Japanese financial system, with consequential effects on accounting. Most of the specific Japanese characteristics of the system discussed earlier are being deliberately dismantled and replaced by a market much like that in other market-oriented economies. With respect to accounting, priority has been given to a new, more international, approach to consolidation, which was issued in 2003.

FINANCIAL DISCLOSURE BY PUBLICLY LISTED CORPORATIONS

Prior to the Big Bang in 1996, accounting weaknesses were welcomed and exploited by at least some companies in Japan, especially as the other methods of monitoring bad performance, such as the main-bank system, had broken down in a large number of instances. The focus on parent-only accounting reports meant that many accounting problems could be hidden in a complexity of subsidiaries or maneuvered off the balance sheet. The historical cost principles used in Japanese accounting allowed very large hidden gains on assets to be accumulated and then used to cover up losses incurred later.[13]

In February 2001, the JICPA and nine other bodies, with government support, announced the launch of a new private-sector standard-setting body, the Accounting Standards Board of Japan (ASBJ). This Board was formed to respond to the rapidly changing economic environment and changes in the international standard-setting process. The underlying objective at the time of its creation was to move Japanese accounting standards toward international norms.

Indeed, even before the creation of the ASBJ, Japanese standards were heading in this direction in what is called the "Accounting Big Bang" of the late 1990s and the early 2000s. This process sought to produce accounting standards of international quality and of similar coverage to the International Financial Reporting Standards (IFRS) issued by the International Accounting Standards Board (IASB) and those issued by the U.S. Financial Accounting Standards Board (FASB) and to aid the international convergence of accounting standards. Thus, for example, the accounting standards for financial instruments issued in 1998 radically departed from past practices, especially Japanese GAAP, and required substantial changes to the SEL and the CC. Moreover, in the 7-month period from March to September 2001, the JIPCA issued more than a dozen important accounting pronouncements, the BADC (then the accounting standard setter) issued seven others, and the government issued five new laws or proposals dealing with or affecting accounting.

The BADC, which previously had operated behind closed doors, also had already enhanced the transparency of its procedures by publishing exposure drafts of its proposed rules. The organization also placed its deliberations on a website. Since 1998 major gaps in Japanese standards have been addressed seeking to cover areas similar to those of the IASB and the FASB.[14] Recent Japanese accounting standards follow the logic of other international standards; sometimes they follow IFRS but seem more influenced by U.S. standards. Generally they seem to opt for the most conservative option. They also contain some substantial deviations from the output of international standard setters. For example, the business combination standard still allows pooling of interests under strict conditions and requires the amortization of goodwill, whereas both the FASB and the IASB prohibit pooling and systematic amortization and favor the use of amortizing goodwill with impairment tests. The financial instruments standard does not allow the fair value option permitted by the IASB but not the FASB.

In May 2002, the Diet (Japanese Parliament) made major changes to the CC, effective April 1, 2003. The CC was amended to require consolidated accounts for large joint stock companies with issued capital of more than ¥500 million and total liabilities exceeding ¥20 billion (the SEL previously required consolidated accounts only for listed companies). The CC also was changed to allow a "fair value" approach to the recognition and measurement of financial instruments similar to that of the IASB (in the face of strong objections to the use of fair values). Around this time, the necessity for all accounting requirements to be enacted as part of the CC was removed and authority for issuing accounting requirements as regulations rather than by legislation was given to the Ministry of Justice, thereby allowing implementation with less delay and argument.

This package of accounting reforms has moved Japanese GAAP much nearer to Western practices in many areas. The JFSA has claimed that taken together, these changes have produced a dramatic improvement in the quality of accounting standards, declaring that "Accounting, auditing and disclosure systems in Japan are essentially equivalent to and consistent with internationally recognised systems" [JFSA, 2004, p. 4]. In reply to a 2002 report on GAAP convergence by the International Forum on Accountancy Development (an organization of international accountancy firms) that stated that Japan did not intend to converge its own accounting standards with IFRS, the ASBJ stated that it "will continuously make maximum efforts to contribute to convergence of accounting standards and to enhance harmonisation of our standards with IFRS." (Indeed, on Oct. 12, 2004, the ASBJ and the IASB agreed to launch a joint project to minimize differences between their outputs with final goal of convergence.) However, the ASBJ qualified this commitment by also stating that convergence should be based on sufficient discussion and consensus building in the domestic market. This pronouncement reflects the continuing importance of consensus in Japanese society.

Still, Japanese GAAP historically have allowed the recognition of many more so-called special items than those treated in the West as extraordinary items. As we have noted, prior-year adjustments are not allowed under Japanese law and the going concern assumption, at least until recently, has been of lesser importance in Japan than in some other countries (so that significant uncertainties about the going concern status of a company do not need to be reported). Since July 2002, though, the use of the going concern concept has been mandatory. Similarly, there is no requirement to show information about discontinued operations and impairment of assets. Revaluations of fixed assets (including property investments) are prohibited, as are reversals of impairment as per U.S. GAAP. Writing down inventory to market value is optional unless acquisition cost is substantially above market value and the decrease in market value is permanent. The creation of provisions does not require the showing of a legal or constructive obligation as do IFRS. The treatment of leases in Japan is more flexible than under the IASB and also under suggestions by an international group of national standard setters for the reform of the IASB leasing standard. The pooling method has been generally used for business combinations, even where they should be considered acquisitions under U.S. GAAP and under IFRS, in order to maintain the status of the managers involved, who otherwise would be seen as "losers" in a takeover. As has been said, the new Japanese standard on business combinations still allows pooling under strict conditions.[15]

Overall, the changes enacted so far move much of Japanese accounting much nearer to IFRS and U.S. GAAP, although our cursory study identifies several major differences between Japanese accounting standards and IFRS. Nonetheless, the broad sentiment in Japan is that Japanese accounting standards are now equal in quality to those of the IASB and the FASB.[16] For example, the Japanese Business Federation, whose members include over 1,500 major Japanese corporations, has stated that Japan's accounting and auditing standards have been raised "to a level that compares favorably with international levels. It is important that this should be fully understood by people involved in the market both within Japan and overseas" [Nippon Keidanren, 2003]. The JFSA has stated that "*Japanese GAAP has been rapidly developing and we believe it has become consistent and equivalent with international accounting standards*"[17] [emphasis in the original]. This is written in the context that European regulated securities markets currently accept Japanese GAAP for Japanese companies that want to offer securities or are listed on these markets. However, beginning in 2007, companies located in non-European Union countries will have to use IFRS unless their home accounting standards are deemed equivalent to IFRS by the European Commission with the help of the Committee of European Security Regulators (CESR). As we are in favor of competing international standards (see Chapter 10), we support such an attempt to assess equivalency. However, we suspect that it is very difficult to do or demonstrate and, perforce, involves judgments and the ability to interpret and apply standards with different explicit or implicit objectives.

There are some items that are being considered by international standard setters with which the Japanese accounting community disagrees. Treatments of business combinations have already been mentioned. Additionally, there is disagreement with the IASB's proposal for a new approach to reporting financial performance. In particular, there are strong objections to the superiority given to comprehensive income over the traditional net income measure and to taking all gains to comprehensive income rather than allowing some of these to be treated as just part of shareholders' equity. The latter approach is current Japanese practice for a number of items, including gains on the fair value of financial instruments and foreign exchange adjustments. There are equally strong objections to the possibility of allowing fair-value accounting for financial assets and liabilities regardless of the purpose for which they are held—a practice critics argue will mislead investors. Similar objections are made to the suggestions that fair value should be used in accounting for postemployment benefits (see, for example, Nippon Keidanren, 2004).

In short, Japanese accounting standards continue to differ in substantial ways from U.S. GAAP and IFRS, and Japanese standards setters place different weights on some concepts and international suggestions for changing these standards.

Reporting Under Other Accounting Systems

Surprisingly, for nearly 30 years the Ministry of Finance by special regulation has allowed a few companies that were registered with the U.S. SEC to submit U.S. GAAP consolidated statements to the Ministry rather than statements based on Japanese GAAP. In April 2002, this special regulation was replaced by a new one that allowed this substitution for all companies submitting Forms 20-F to the U.S. SEC. This does not seem to be a back-door way of introducing U.S. GAAP into Japan, as only around 30 multinational companies are eligible, although these corporations are important in the Japanese economy. Some multinationals also present reconciliations with either U.S. GAAP or IFRS. Others simply translate Japanese GAAP financial reports into other currencies with a rearranged layout for the "convenience" of foreign readers.

A New Accounting Standard Setter

The new accounting standard-setting process set up in 2001 consists of the Financial Accounting Standards Foundation (FASF), the ASBJ, and an agenda committee. The FASF has an oversight role in promoting accounting disclosure and thus helping to ensure the soundness of Japanese financial markets. The FASF has 16 trustees reflecting the founding bodies, who are responsible for the selection of 13 directors and who also advise on business matters. The 13 directors of the FASF have responsibility for funding the standard-setting system via membership fees from a wide range of parties, not including government. Structured as an advisory council, the FASF appoints the members of the ASBJ in a transparent and presumably fair way. The 13 members of the ASBJ, of whom 3 are full time, develop accounting standards and guidance on implementation of accounting standards reflecting the business environment of Japanese companies. Both these bodies have full-time staffs. A technical committee is set for each major project. The ASBJ seeks to contribute to the development of a high-quality set of IFRS. The Board's makeup differs from those of other national standard setters. Not all the members are accountants. Several have close connections with the sponsoring organizations, and three are academics. This wide range of interests on the Board may facilitate consensus regarding accounting standards in the financial system.

The formal authority of the new standard-setting process is not yet clear. The standards are deemed to be part of Japanese GAAP and therefore have the same legal status as those issued by the BADC in its previous accounting standard-setting role. But whether or not the government will attempt to influence or control the Board remains to be seen.

What is clear, though, is that the standards will be constrained by the three legal codes and by regulations issued by the Ministry of Justice. The standards must be accepted in the accounting and business communities. If a standard follows IFRS, this will lead to its acceptance, though it will need to be "Japanized" for the home economic environment. It is not yet clear to what extent recently promulgated standards and those likely to be adopted in the future will be consistent with the contents of the existing tax code, or indeed with those of other codes, which often must be amended to allow new standards to fit with them. The likely solution to this problem is unresolved. The previous standard-setting body, the BADC, still survives, but without its standard-setting role. It is now an advisory committee to the JFSA and issues opinions on accounting and issues audit standards and is governed by Cabinet Office orders and regulations. Thus, it seems that the BADC is not intended to disappear, but its influence in the new system and how it will integrate with the new private-sector standard setter is unclear. There could be rivalry between it and the standard setters.

In short, in Japan, a very large number of government organizations have some role in accounting regulation. There is a large web of advisory bodies to the Ministry of Finance and other ministries. Whether these bodies will have influence in future standard setting is not yet determined. In any event, the standards issued by the IASB will have to fit the Japanese context or be amended.[18]

A major gap in the structure of the new standard-setting body is in enforcement. There do not seem to be any plans to have a body similar to the U.K. Financial Reporting Review Panel (FRRP) or the U.S. SEC to review financial statements. We suggest in Chapter 5 that the FRRP has done a good job in the U.K. environment but may turn out to be a weak agency for enforcement, even with its recent proactive role. We also have doubts about the SEC's ability to monitor financial statements.

INVESTOR PROTECTION

For most of the period covered by our review, the private investor did not figure strongly in government policy and share cross-holdings by firms were not held for investment returns as such. The government's main contribution toward protecting investors was to ensure that the economy continued to grow, while financial markets remained stable and firms remained viable.

Formally, at least, shareholders have substantial rights. The annual general meeting is the ultimate decision-making body. Shareholders have a substantial say in the nomination and pay of directors. In practice, however, management generally has exercised all these powers. Shareholders could and still can sue errant directors, but this is expensive and onerous for plaintiffs.

Similarly, although by law the Ministry of Finance has been responsible for investor protection, in practice it has been more interested in protecting the organizations it regulates (especially banks).[19] Even today there is little evidence that banks will be allowed to fail, as Japan's then fifth largest bank (Resona) was bailed out in 2002 with public funds. Additional investor protection only seems to follow these crises.[20] Nonetheless, investors seem not to have demanded protection, in part because, at least in the boom years, they may have believed that the government would somehow ensure that share prices would bounce back after any periods of decline.[21]

The history of investment trusts, which are similar to mutual funds in the United States and unit trusts in the United Kingdom, provides a case study of how Japanese regulation has evolved toward protecting investors. Scandals in the securities markets in the 1990s weakened the appeal of investment trusts, when both ordinary investors and some larger securities clients suffered losses that were not compensated by the industry or the government. This was a shock, because at the time investment trusts were marketed on the promise of security of their principal. At the same time, however, many investors also believed that investment trusts had not provided good value in the past because of excessive "churning" of shareholdings (which generated commissions that benefited the securities houses sponsoring the trusts). The obvious solutions to the problems in this segment of the financial industry would have been to allow greater competition, especially by foreign firms, and encourage fund sponsors to provide more information about performance and how the sponsors were compensated.

But reforms took time. Competition was not really encouraged until 1992, when the Ministry of Finance allowed bank affiliates into the market, and again in 1995, when the Ministry allowed new trust management companies, including those of foreign sponsors, to be established. Yet despite the opening to foreign entrants (who had pushed for the change since the 1980s), foreign sellers of investment trusts still have difficulties distributing their products.

The Ministry of Finance's handling of the investment trust industry shows that the Ministry eventually does respond to problems, but only after crises. Another example of crisis-driven change occurred in the 1990s after various scandals had rocked the securities industry. The Ministry responded by establishing the Securities and Exchange Surveillance Commission to improve inspection and monitoring. This body now belongs to the JFSA.

Since the Big Bang, the JFSA has become the single authority responsible for a comprehensive program of investor protection. Its oversight is still a work in progress. Some in Japan believe that when it is complete, the Japanese investor protection program will match the best practice in the West. However, in our view, such a judgment is premature. Japanese authorities have a history of being too slow to recognize failure. The Ministry of Finance, in particular, has hesitated in the past to take quick action in order to preserve financial stability. It is too early to know whether this attitude will persist or whether the JFSA will truly mark a different course and accomplish what the optimists hope it will in terms of protecting investors.

The Audit Process

The arrangements for auditing in Japan have been and still are quite different from those in Western countries. Each major company in Japan has two types of auditors: statutory (or corporate) and external. Corporate audits by statutory auditors were required by the CC in 1950, but the CC did not require these audits to be carried out by CPAs because there was a shortage of such individuals. Public audits by CPAs for listed companies, however, were required under the SEL in 1951 and were applied to all large joint stock companies in 1974 by the CC.

Statutory Auditors

The nearest equivalent Western term for the statutory auditor is "internal auditor," but the three statutory auditors that are typical for each Japanese listed corporation differ from what most in the West would understand to be typical of an auditor. For one thing, Japanese law does not require any of the statutory auditors to be qualified accountants, although one must be full time and 50 percent must be "outsiders" (from 2005), having never been employed by the company. They are elected by the shareholders at the annual general meeting.

Since it was required by the CC in 1993, the statutory auditors now form a board of auditors, although each member is supposed to be independent and must arrive at his or her own personal judgment of the company's affairs and its reports. The board's main task is to audit the executive functions of company directors and report on this in an audit report. The audit board also must consent to the appointment of the external auditor, evaluate the external auditor's work and the financial statements, and set out the principles used in the company's audit. The board of corporate auditors may dismiss the external auditor for violating auditing duties or committing misconduct. The board also may make recommendations concerning internal controls and any instance of possible appreciable damage to the corporation. In related fashion, the board must report to the directors any breaches of statutes and articles and make recommendations. The board also must report on any illegal act by a named director.

The general view is that such statutory audits are not very strict. Perhaps the most important reason is that the statutory auditors are either company employees or "outsiders" appointed on the nomination of the board of directors, often in practice by the president of the company. It is thus unlikely that these auditors would accuse directors of illegal actions or of obtaining benefits without appropriate payment. This is especially so since, upon learning of illegalities, the overall board must then bring legal proceedings against other directors who have allegedly violated the law. This is not likely, especially among Japanese boards, where consensus is very much the rule.

External Auditors

External audits (the CPA audit) for listed companies are conducted by independent, qualified accountants, CPAs, who legally must be members of the JICPA. Japanese CPAs must be partners or employees of a CPA firm (an audit corporation that is difficult to form in Japan) and must resign from the JICPA if they take other employment. Individual auditors have personal responsibility for audits carried out by them.

The external audit focuses on several major issues: whether the financial statements and books of account state matters correctly and are in accordance with the law, Japanese GAAP, and the company's articles of incorporation and bylaws. The external auditors thus essentially monitor the financial legitimacy of the actions of the directors of the company.

Auditing standards are set by the BADC; together with guidance by JICPA, they provide generally accepted auditing standards (GAAS). The audit profession is controlled by the Ministry of Finance. In particular, the Ministry authorizes and has responsibility for conducting CPA examinations. The JICPA has responsibility for training. The pass ratio for those taking the CPA examination is very low by international standards (some 7 percent).

The audit requirement is that the financial statements report fairly in accordance with GAAP. The aim is that the quality of the external audit should be similar to that of an audit in the United Kingdom or the United States. In practice, however, the quality of external audits in the past has been weak. There was no audit committee in Japanese companies. A company's board of corporate or statutory auditors is not equivalent to an audit committee, because only half of its members must be even nominally independent. As we note earlier, in practice these boards are really part of management. Moreover, generally there are insufficient independent directors on traditional Japanese boards to form an independent audit committee.

In fact, in the past auditors have cooperated with management in providing "window dressing" of company accounts. In the mid- to late 1990s, for example, a substantial number of securities firms were declared bankrupt after understating the extent of nonperforming loans, engaging in fraud, and using accounting manipulation as allowed under the loose disclosure requirements of the time.[22] When Japan's fourth largest security company at the time, Yamaichi Securities, went bankrupt, it was discovered that its managers hid very significant debts for many years by shifting losses temporarily to other companies. These and similar gross financial statement misstatements were not discovered or reported by the corporations' external auditors.

To foreign investors, the bankruptcy of Yamaichi Securities and certain of its competitors signaled weakness in the audit process. This view was reinforced when in the 1990s companies such as Nissan Motors included in their financial statements a caveat to the usual statement that still appears today that "the consolidated statements have been prepared in accordance with Japanese principles and practices." That caveat warns by adding, "which may differ in certain material respects from the accounting principles and practices generally accepted in countries and jurisdictions other than Japan."

Recent Audit Reforms

As with every other area of Japanese accounting, auditing in Japan recently has changed substantially, at least formally. This has not been easy process, since (as we have noted) the highlighting of problems is not welcomed in Japanese society, corporate ethics policies are often unclear and flexible, and external auditors historically have had a close, strongly loyal, and long-term relationship with companies. Furthermore, until the past few years, auditors effectively were immune from the threat of legal action by shareholders because, under Japanese law, the burden of proof falls generally on plaintiffs.

Significant changes have gradually been made over the past decade. In 1993, the CC enhanced shareholders' rights, which led to an increase in the numbers of shareholder actions, even though the burden of proof was not changed. Perhaps for that reason, none of these actions had been successful as of the year 2000.

Several ministries have since offered suggestions for reforms, and many were enacted into law in 2002. The more general reform, which allows corporations to opt for a more Western style of corporate governance (see below), now allows companies to set up an audit committee to replace the existing board of auditors. Whether there are sufficient outside and independent directors available to justify confidence in the audit committee, however, remains doubtful. The general principle in Japanese commercial law, which places the burden of proof on shareholders to show that a deficient audit report led to damage, was converted into a duty on the audit firm to prove that no such relation existed between the report and any damage. Japanese law also was changed to allow the filing of class-action lawsuits against CPAs.

The JICPA, meanwhile, has introduced reforms relating to the audit profession, including a revision of the code of ethics and the introduction of a rotation of individual external auditors for large companies and peer review. It has also started a consideration of a limited liability system for audit corporations. Training innovations include the improvement of continuing professional education courses.

In May 2003, major changes to CPA auditing were contained in an amendment to the Certified Public Accountants Law that was strongly influenced by the U.S. Sarbanes-Oxley Act. Nonaudit services that may be offered to audit clients were severely restricted.[23] The internal rotation of engagement partners over a 7-year period (rather long compared to other countries' requirements) was made mandatory and a "cooling off" period of 1 year (comparatively rather short) was introduced before an engagement partner may join a past client. The CPA examinations were simplified. A modest amount of limited liability was introduced.[24]

The most important changes to the CPA law made statutorily mandatory the JICPA's audit quality control review system for audits and established a Certified Public Accountants and Auditing Oversight Board (CPAAOB). The JICPA's review system requires a review by JICPA professional staff of all auditors engaged in listed company audit every 3 years. The CPAAOB does not review auditors but rather monitors the JICPA review system and its outcomes. It may inspect the JICPA, audit firms, and audit clients to discover the state of audits from a public interest perspective. As distinct from the U.S. Public Company Accounting Oversight Board, it does not set audit standards, which remains the responsibility of the BADC. The Board can make recommendations to the JFSA to issue orders to improve audit operations and for disciplinary actions.[25]

Efforts have also been made to strengthen the audits performed by corporate or statutory auditors by recruiting auditors independent of corporate management and increasing the number of statutory auditors employed by a company. Even with these changes, though, it is difficult to believe that the Japanese audit profession can yet be regarded as providing a world-class service. The global audit firms, through their associated firms, can do much to import global auditing standards, but their ability to innovate is limited, as audit reports still must be prepared under Japanese law and GAAP.

CORPORATE GOVERNANCE

The usual definition of corporate governance in the United States and Europe refers to arrangements that address the "agency problem"—namely, that management may not act in the best interests of shareholders but instead further their own interests. Yet in Japan, through most of the post-war era, corporate governance has not been left to private law, but instead to the government, which has heavily influenced corporate behavior to achieve certain national objectives: growth in revenue and employment. In addition, Japanese banks exert significant influence on Japanese companies. As we have discussed, Japanese corporations tend to be funded by a lead or "main" bank, which also typically owns shares in its borrowers. Japanese companies have used this secure source of funding to provide lifetime employment for their workers, with promotions based on seniority.

The formal system of corporate governance in Japan is that the shareholders are the ultimate authority. The board of directors is generally very large, often over 40 persons, and therefore is an ineffective decision-making body that rubber-stamps the consensus decisions of corporate executives. There are generally a very substantial number of company executives on the board and very few, or no, outside and independent directors in the Western sense, although there are bank and cross-shareholding representatives. The board combines both top policy and executive functions and would have difficulty in distinguishing between these functions. The "greater" (one larger than) majority of the board have executive or operating responsibilities.

Thus, the traditional Western practice of the board acting as a monitor on senior executives cannot be effective, even though the CC places this duty on the board. The CC also requires the board to act against directors who do not obey legal requirements or respect the articles of incorporation of the company, thereby expecting the management of a corporation to monitor and discipline itself. The board of statutory auditors also has this responsibility. Given the makeup of the board and its size, the actual power in Japanese companies rests with management and especially the president (chairman), who can make the most important decisions, including nominating directors and corporate auditors.

In short, although formally shareholders may have ultimate authority over the operations of Japanese companies, in reality these companies put the welfare of their workers and the desires of government officials and bankers first.

Through the 1980s, the Japanese system of "corporate governance"—if it can be called that—was widely viewed in Japan as a success. After all, the Japanese economy had grown rapidly since the end of the war; why question that success? Of particular pride was the "main bank" system. Many scholars, inside and outside Japan, believed this system provided a secure, long-term funding source for companies, which in turn allowed Japanese managers to take a longer view than was the case in the West, where capital markets seemed to reward and punish much shorter-term results.

The main bank also was seen as the principal method of overseeing the company and monitoring management. This role follows from the perceived need for the bank to safeguard its investment by monitoring managerial actions, although the bank perspective may differ from that of shareholders. Banks had most power when companies became financially distressed, and banks typically intervened to provide direction.

Corporate financing in Japan is changing, however, diluting the role of banks in monitoring corporations. As we noted earlier, Japanese authorities first allowed corporations to raise funds by issuing bonds in the 1980s. The bull market in the 1990s, in turn, made equity financing easier as well. Both of these developments cost banks some market share in finance, and thus some influence.

In principle, the external audit also has provided some means of "corporate governance." After all, external auditors have been required to state whether the financial statements present the financial affairs of the company correctly according to the law and the articles of incorporation. However, as we have noted, the external auditors report to the board of statutory auditors, who in turn are controlled largely by management.

In recent years, a number of larger Japanese companies, especially those seeking funds from overseas, have restructured their boards and have introduced elements of Western corporate governance. Mergers and acquisitions have become a more important influence. Litigation by shareholders has increased and, as mentioned earlier, become less expensive, and class actions are now allowed.

From the late 1990s, the Japanese government and even the private sector have considered many plans for reforming corporate governance, including some from government. Although the Ministry of International Trade and Industry adopted some reforms in 2000 (see below), it was preceded by Sony, which restructured its board in 1997 and introduced elements of Western corporate governance, including a Western-type board of directors and an audit committee.

The push for further change comes from a reaction to the bursting of the Japanese stock market bubble and the desire of Japanese companies to gain access to foreign capital markets. Global auditing firms and financial institutions doing business in Japan also have supported reform. To be sure, skeptics may wonder whether Japanese corporations really will adopt change or will adopt the changes for the wrong reasons. For example, Ahmadjian [2001] suggests that some top managers may support governance reforms as a way of curbing the influence of other powerful managers in the corporation. It is too early to tell whether the skeptics will be proven right.

The changes to the CC are significant, however, in that they allow corporations to choose between the traditional Japanese model of corporate governance and an alternative model based substantially on the U.S. system. This new optional system requires corporations to separate executive functions from those of a much smaller board, with at least one outside director, providing that they adopt the system of having remuneration, nominating, and audit committees, with the audit committee having independent members. Companies adopting this approach can dispense with the board of auditors. There is no requirement to split the role of the president (chairman) and the chief executive officer, as is familiar in Europe (but not in the United States).

A survey by the Japanese Corporate Auditors Association in 2003 of over 1,000, mainly large, companies suggests that only some 20 percent of the companies were considering or planning to adopt the committee system. Such a relatively poor showing is most likely due to feelings among corporate officers that the present system accords with the cultural climate in Japan and that transparency and efficiency can be achieved by reforms within the existing system. Most Japanese managers also believe that the overwhelming objective of their companies is to improve the wealth of the Japanese nation and aid a considerable range of stakeholders. Some 50 percent of those surveyed wished to retain the corporate audit system, although with substantial reforms. Other surveys have produced similar views, and these are shared by some leading companies, such as Canon and Toyota. If Western corporate governance is truly to take root in Japan, it will somehow have to be "Japanized."

The strong desire of Japanese managers to maintain their traditional boards of auditors (with refinements) who are charged directly with monitoring management has caused strong resistance to the U.S. Sarbanes-Oxley Act (which does not recognize a role for a board of auditors). For this reason, it was expected that many Japanese firms might choose to de-list from American stock exchanges.[26] However, the U.S. SEC has since ruled that a board of auditors is equivalent to an audit committee for purposes of the act.

Traditionally, the board of directors in Japan is seen as the final, but only formal, authority for the results of corporate consensual decisions. To delegate this power could cause confusion. Currently, the president in reality nominates his or her successor, directors, and members of the board of auditors.[27] Given that corporate leaders rise through the ranks internally, it is difficult for them to see how outside directors can have a sufficiently detailed knowledge of the company and its environment to be helpful in running the company. Some in Japan argue that any weaknesses in corporate governance are mitigated by the fact that top corporate officers in Japan are not paid the extraordinarily high multiples of the wages of average workers nor generally are rewarded with stock options, as is the case in the United States. Consequently, it is argued that there is less of an incentive for these managers to act contrary to shareholders' interests in seeking to maximize their rewards.

CONCLUDING REMARKS

The Japanese experience illustrates that change is possible and indeed is well underway. The most progress is apparent in financial markets, where Japan has moved away from a bank-centric system toward relying more heavily on capital markets, which are open to foreign participants. Meanwhile, market regulation has become more coordinated under a single independent regulator. With respect to accounting, at least for listed firms, Japan is rapidly moving to international norms, with standard setting by an independent private sector body rather than the government. Changes in auditing and corporate governance are moving more slowly. On the surface there have been radical changes, and the dynamic for further changes is clear. However, it is too early to assess the results of these changes and to know whether they will be enforced.

Many Japanese commentators believe nonetheless that the Japanese financial system, after the Big Bang, compares well with the best in the rest of the world. Coupled with the cultural resistance to change, this belief also complicates efforts at further reform, such as the Japanese desire to harmonize their accounting and auditing standards with global standards. Nonetheless, reform indeed has occurred, and now both Japanese financial markets and accounting systems are seen in Japan as comparable to the West.

The process has taken and will continue to take time, however. Consensus needs to be achieved in Japan, which inevitably results in delay. Moreover, although Japanese rules and standards on the surface may look like their Western counterparts, in practice the reality can and does differ. There is a history in Japan of honoring the formal substance of regulations, while in practice doing something else. For example, one informed critic, writing from the United Kingdom, sums up the accounting situation in 1999: "Despite the rhetoric from the Japanese government and BADC on the virtues of transparent, creditable financial reporting, the attitudes of company leaders seem not to have changed much" [Gordon, 1999, p. 53]. Only time will tell whether these attitudes will change.

There are reasons for caution. Shiba [2001] studied a group of 372 public companies listed on Japanese stock exchanges over the period December 1999 to July 2000. He asked executives to compare the importance of Japanese-style management practices in 1999/2000 and 10 years earlier. He found that a very substantial majority of executives believed that little had changed in the areas of lifetime employment; the main bank system, even in face of evidence to the contrary; promotion from inside the company; a good welfare system; and good retirement benefits. Only promotion based on years of service was regarded as no longer applying. Fifty percent of the respondents said that there had been no change in cross-shareholding, while 34 percent said this phenomenon no longer applied. Some of these answers are surprising, especially in the light of evidence to the contrary. Nevertheless, they do reflect a belief that in these areas, at least, the traditional system still applies or is perceived still to reign. This survey evidence suggests that there are still many difficulties ahead for accounting and financial market harmonization in Japan.

Acknowledgments We do not pretend to be authorities on the Japanese financial markets, the market regulatory regime, and the accounting system. We have gained substantially from the help of Japanese academic colleagues, especially Professor Kenji Shiba (Kansai University) and Hiroshi Tanaka (Kanagawa University), and Japanese practitioners. We have relied heavily on original sources (in English translation) but have also used a wide variety of other sources. Some of the most recent of these are included in the references to this chapter. Especially useful were, in the financial markets area, Allen and Gale [2000], and Hoshi and Kashyap [2001], and in the accounting area, materials from the JICPA, Professor Y. Kawamura [website], and Gordon [1999]. All these sources are in English and therefore do not capture fully the underlying Japanese nature of the system being discussed, as the institutions and changes to them should be seen through a Japanese rather than Western lens. For example, it is generally agreed that all innovations imported into Japanese have to be "Japanized." Such subtleties are missed in our discussion.

9

Corporate Disclosure Diversity: A Comparative Assessment

In this chapter we pull together observations and conclusions from the chapters on the financial disclosure regimes in the United States, United Kingdom, Germany, and Japan and, where relevant, in the European Union (EU). While there are substantial differences in many characteristics, such as the regulatory regime and culture, economic, government, and legal contexts, it appears that responses in all the countries we study to current developments in capital markets have much in common and share many of the same problems. In this chapter we provide a comparative assessment of how differences in some of these factors have affected accounting, auditing, and corporate governance, concentrating on differences in the environmental setting, particularly with respect to government systems, the legal setting, corporate taxation, and financial markets. These differences are widened when the view is extended to cover even more countries.

We believe that diversity in financial reports prevails worldwide, and we discuss how companies react to and with changing information demands and regulatory requirements and constraints. Although diversity may not matter that much on average, it can make a noticeable difference to the key financial figures of individual companies. Diversity in accounting regimes can be confusing and hence costly for companies that must meet different reporting requirements and for investors seeking to compare the results of companies in countries that have adopted different accounting regimes. This is the driving reason behind the effort of the Financial Accounting Standards Board (FASB) in the United States to achieve convergence between U.S. generally accepted accounting principles (U.S. GAAP) and International Financial Reporting Standards (IFRS). The

Appendix to this chapter illustrates accounting diversity by describing crucial differences among international financial rules and standards (IFRS) and national standards, in particular U.S. GAAP.

THE ENVIRONMENTAL SETTING

A large literature seeks to classify together those accounting systems explained by the same set of environmental factors.[1] Such exercises involve a very broad set of factors and have reached little overall consensus, although it is generally agreed that the legal regime and the character of financial markets are important differentiating characteristics for accounting systems. Empirical work has suggested some important groupings of accounting systems, although even these groups incorporate substantial differences and overlaps. Important groups are centered in the United Kingdom, the United States, and Western/Northern Europe. Another favored classification is pairing the United Kingdom and United States (representing a British origin) on the one hand and Germany and Japan (representing a continental origin) on the other.[2] Here we briefly review how differences in state governance systems, legal and tax systems, and financial markets have affected accounting, audit, and corporate governance regimes in our four countries, and what has changed recently.

Government Systems

The purposes of government in the United Kingdom and the United States can be summarized crudely along four dimensions: to ensure that individuals have the freedom to pursue their own preferences and firms have the ability to achieve their objectives by using markets; to provide public goods (e.g., defense and other goods) where government is believed to be more efficient; to promote a socially acceptable degree of redistribution of income and provide a safety net for individuals who are hurt or substantially inadequately served by market forces, in some fashion; and to protect society from anticompetitive behavior and the unfair use of asymmetric information. With such a governance regime, regulation should be used only where necessary to ensure that markets work well and are fair to all participants, or at least are not biased. Self-regulation or independent regulation is preferred where markets are believed to be effective, efficient, and fair. In the arena of corporate governance, governments in both the United States and the United Kingdom rely on market contracts and the shareholder, as the residual risk bearer and the predominant stakeholder, to monitor behavior by corporate officials.

Government intervention is much stronger in Japan and has considerable strength in Germany. In Japan generally, the government is really seen as the head of the Japanese family and is charged with developing the country, especially its economic growth and international status. Historically the Japanese government has been the principal initiator and problem solver. Statute law is the predominant source of authority.

In Germany the state is less interventionist than Japan and works in cooperation with other elements of the economy, including local authorities that are interventionist in their areas. The state is charged with facilitating the economic growth of the country, ensuring the smooth running of the economy, and protecting society from anticompetitive behavior while maintaining a fair standard of living for all. Generally, in both Germany and Japan government acts when consensus is achieved with the major social groups. Regulation of financial markets and accounting has been strongly influenced by government in these two countries, and corporate governance covers a wide range of stakeholders. This was fully the case in both countries until recently. Both countries have now introduced independent accounting standard setters (Germany in 1998 and Japan in 2001), variants of a financial services authority (Germany in 1994 and Japan in 2000), and shareholder-oriented corporate governance (Germany in 2002 and Japan in 2003). These innovations are part of a move to reorganize (in Japan, revolutionize) financial markets along Anglo-Saxon lines.

The Legal Setting

Germany and Japan are both Roman- or code-law countries where the law is promulgated in the form of detailed and extensive legal codes, with the courts presumably only applying the law and not developing it. Additional regulation must be consistent with the codes. This framework allows people and firms to pursue their own interests in areas not covered by law and regulation. La Porta et al. [1998, 2000] argue that the contents of national laws, including the degree of investor protection in a country, flow from the legal "families" developing from English (common law), French and German (both derived from Roman law), and Scandinavian origins. They conclude that common law provides the strongest investor protection.[3] The United Kingdom and the United States are representative of common law countries, where a statutory framework is supplemented and developed by the courts, with superior courts laying down precedents for lower courts. Settlement following the threat of litigation, and occasional actual litigation, is the traditional way of settling disputes between parties. Behavior is meant to respect the spirit of the law and to anticipate the likely views of the courts. However, this dichotomy of legal systems is not precise. For example, the introduction of the EU's accounting directives (Fourth and Seventh Directives) into U.K. law imposed very detailed statutory requirements on accounting for the first time.

The law in Germany, Japan, and the United Kingdom makes commercial litigation more difficult than in the United States, where class actions and contingent fees are allowed and the losing party does not have to pay the winning party's costs as the loser does in the United Kingdom. Consequently, those who believe that litigation is important for regulating financial markets see the systems in countries other than the United States as weak.

Corporate Taxation

The governments in all four countries strongly regulate the information required to determine the amount of corporate taxation. In the United Kingdom and United States tax computations, although based on accounting profits, are subject to many adjustments that need not be followed in published financial reports. In both Germany and Japan tax computations are based on entity (individual firm) published accounting reports (although separate tax accounts are provided) that must follow the accounting treatments set forth in the tax regulations for companies to deduct the relevant tax allowances. This approach has a long history in Germany. However, in both Germany and Japan, adjustments are made to accounting figures in the tax accounts, some of which reflect government policies to encourage specific corporate behavior. The wish to maintain this general approach to accounting for taxation is one reason why entity accounts in Germany continue to follow German GAAP, even though the government could allow IFRS to be used for entity accounts now that IFRS must be used in the EU for the consolidated accounts of listed companies as of 2005. The need for listed companies to maintain two sets of accounting reports (entity and consolidated) suggests difficulties for the global acceptance of IFRS or U.S. GAAP. Similar problems will arise in Japan as Japanese accounting standards come to be based on IFRS decision-oriented accounting standards.

Financial Markets

Financial markets are relatively similar in their characteristics in all the countries surveyed and in the EU, but with some divergences and considerable size differences. Equity capitalization of domestic companies on the New York Stock Exchange (NYSE) (at US$11.3 trillion) at the end of 2003 was almost 4 times that of the Tokyo market (US$3.0 trillion), 5 times that of the London Stock Exchange (LSE) (US$2.3 trillion), and approximately 7 times that of the Deutsche Börse (US$1.6 trillion).[4] The capitalization of non-U.S. companies listed on the NYSE at the end of July 2003 of US$5.9 trillion is itself larger than the capitalization of any other stock exchange in the world. However, the proportion of international companies quoted on the LSE (around 50 percent) is greater than that on the NYSE (approximately 30 percent), although the number of international companies on the LSE has been declining.[5] Of the 500 largest global companies in 2004, 227 were listed in the United States, 18 in Germany, 58 in Japan, and 136 in the EU (including Germany).[6]

All national governments and major stock exchanges want to sustain and grow their securities markets and are becoming highly competitive in seeking to remain or become global players in providing finance, especially to international firms, and in attracting international investors. However, there is little evidence that this competition has driven standards downward. Rather, competition has led to increased transparency in terms of trading mechanisms and information on new share issues and more detailed self-regulation, including a demand for high-quality accounting reports and greater concern for corporate governance. Against this, governments and stock exchanges also seek to maintain many of the traditional characteristics of their markets that give them advantages, at least domestically, thereby taking advantage of firms' and investors' "home country bias." The desire to increase transparency by listed companies traded on global markets has led to efforts to harmonize accounting standards across countries. The trick is to achieve harmonization of accounting reports while allowing for legitimate differences in national accounting regimes.

Financial markets in the United States and the United Kingdom are strongly equity oriented, while Japanese and German financing is still substantially more focused on debt (mainly supplied by banks rather than markets). Japan has the second largest stock market globally in terms of capitalization but is less active in terms of transactions than markets in either the United States or the United Kingdom. Germany and Japan still impose substantial limitations on takeovers, while there are few inhibitions in the United States and the United Kingdom, and takeovers are frequent. Markets in Germany are concentrated due to domination by financial institutions, shareholdings by other companies, and continuing family ownership of businesses they originally fully owned. In Japan ownership concentration is dominated by financial institutions and by nonfinancial companies, even though the cross-holding of shares has declined substantially. In contrast, in the United States and United Kingdom concentration of ownership is much lower, and there is a greater representation of individual and independent institutions among the shareholders.

With these differences, it might be expected that more attention would be focused on ensuring an adequate flow of public information to investors in the United Kingdom and the United States than in Germany and Japan, but this is not the case, at least for large companies. However, in the United States and the United Kingdom company-reported information is geared more to facilitating decision-making, whereas German and Japanese individual financial reports have been and still are more focused on protecting investors (primarily banks) and, especially, creditors. One question is how the latter two countries will adapt to using the more decision-oriented IFRS (required of German companies for consolidated accounts in 2005 and increasingly adopted by Japanese accounting).

The financial markets in all our countries have been and are heavily regulated—formally by law in Germany and by law and centralized government presence in Japan until recently, when in 2000 a financial services authority was introduced and made compatible with the law (which still dominates). Regulation by independent bodies and self-regulation by financial institutions dominates in the United Kingdom, which has only a light statutory framework. The United States has strong federal laws regulating securities markets and a government agency, the Securities and Exchange Commission (SEC), that regulates stock exchanges and financial service firms in great detail, but with a strong element of self-regulation. Generally, the regulations imposed are not dissimilar in all the countries we examine, although the rules are more comprehensively defined and de-tailed and anti-insider trading restrictions are greater in the United Kingdom and the United States.

The general similarity of the scope and depth of regulation in the United Kingdom and Germany is due not so much to any explicit effort by the two countries with two substantially different regimes in the past to harmonize their regimes, but more to efforts by the EU. The EU had opted for harmonization of capital market regulation at a relatively low but in-creasing level rather than standardization; in contrast, it imposes stringent capital adequacy rules on financial service firms to protect investors. When the regulations in the home country of a financial service firm meet the EU minimum rules, the firm is given a license or "passport" to trade in other countries of the EU under the rules and enforcement powers of its home country.

U.S. regulation arose independent of other countries (other than some early reliance on the contemporary U.K. law) and imposes more detailed and comprehensive rules issued by the SEC. Recent moves in Japan toward regulatory structures and regulations that are similar to other countries seem to be the result of a conscious attempt to "internationalize" the Ja-panese market regulatory mechanism by selecting the "best" from other countries. For example, the Japanese Financial Services Agency (JFSA) is strongly modeled on that of the United Kingdom. That harmonization is possible in some areas is suggested by Germany's opting in 2002 for a corporate governance regime similar to that of the United Kingdom, and attempting to take the best from the U.K. and U.S. approaches for an enforcement agency. Although those market regulatory regimes do seem to generate a similar set of current rules, the processes generating these rules are substantially different. The emphases of the regimes also often differ in terms of contemporary interests and focus. This raises a general problem for achieving accounting standardization or harmonization, which must be pursued in environments of national market regulatory regimes.

In all the countries we examine there is a strong assumption that the managements of firms will exploit asymmetric information in dealing with investors and others, such as creditors. In retail investment markets espe-cially, legislators and regulators fear that firms will attempt to take ad-vantage of less sophisticated investors. Many regulations seek to prohibit past practices perceived to be misleading or fraudulent. Other regulations seek to avoid problems that are thought by regulators and professionals as likely to arise. In none of the countries has any explicit attempt really been made to counter these problems by giving incentives to firms to avoid generating these problems or allowing competition among regulators.

Enforcing transparency of the markets and of the activities of firms and individuals is a major means of achieving investor protection. Regulators in all of the countries put great weight on financial statements providing accurate information to investors, thereby emphasizing the importance of disclosure and transparency. In all of the countries other than the United Kingdom, the various authorities (which, at times, have included stock exchanges, professional accountancy bodies, and accounting standards committees whose pronouncements are accepted by government regulators) and/or the government or government agencies have regulated reporting and auditing practices. Although auditing has been the province of professional accountancy organizations, accounting standards have increasingly been determined by governments or government-recognized boards. In Germany and Japan, though, only government has determined accounting rules. However, both of these countries have recently introduced a standard-setting body (for consolidated accounts in Germany) formally free of government control, possibly as a reaction to international pressures for countries to have clear and explicit structures for setting standards, including an independent and due-process standard setter. Currently, it is not clear what authority these standard-setting bodies will obtain and, in Japan especially, whether the standard setter will be free of government influence.

In the United States, the SEC is by law the ultimate authority in the accounting area for listed companies, although it delegates accounting standard setting to the Financial Accounting Standards Board (FASB). Before enactment of the Sarbanes-Oxley Act (2002), the SEC delegated auditing regulation to the American Institute of Certified Public Accountants (AICPA). However, that act established the Public Companies Accounting Oversight Board (PCAOB), which oversees both auditing and public accounting firms and reports to the SEC. The SEC provides inputs into standard setting, issues statements on important accounting issues, and influences the agenda of the FASB with regard to what it sees as controversial matters of concern to the wider business and investment community. The SEC also is subject to strong lobbying by business and some politicians, as it oversees the FASB.

Over time it is likely that national regulators will become more involved in accounting and related matters, in changing reporting standards, and requiring additional information over and above that contained in the financial statements. These activities are inconsistent with and likely to inhibit the development of a single international reporting convention, since different national regulators may require different information.

MARKET AND REGULATORY INFLUENCES ON ACCOUNTING

As we have discussed, while the United Kingdom and the United States have similar market and regulatory regimes that have similar effects on their accounting, there are important differences in the two regimes. Accounting standards in the United States are rules-based and seek to cover most perceived eventualities in dealing with an accounting issue, the number of issues dealt with is very large, and many issues are of relatively special interest. The richness and complexity of the rules and the wide coverage of standards is increased by the additional outputs of the Emerging Issues Task Force (EITF), Interpretations issued by FASB, additional guidance offered by Technical Bulletins, and Staff Opinions.

In contrast, accounting standards in the United Kingdom promulgated by the Accounting Standards Board (ASB) are much more principles-based, as are those of the International Accounting Standards Board (IASB). These standards set forth the general method of dealing with an accounting problem but do not seek to deal with all ramifications of the issue, leaving the details to the exercise of professional judgment within the principles established by the standard (see Chapter 3 for a discussion of principles- vs. rules-based accounting standards). Thus, U.K. standard setters do not issue interpretations. Although the U.K. Urgent Issues Task Force (UITF) issues interpretations, they tend to be narrow in scope, generally address detailed items, and do not seek to be comprehensive. Consequently, U.K. standard setters and also the IASB have not dealt with as many accounting issues or with as many specialized issues as is the case in the United States.

The usual reason suggested for the use of the rules-based approach in the United States is its litigious climate. Precise and detailed guidelines are presumed to provide protection to auditors and the business. The United States may rely on rules because it lacks a dominant requirement for accounting reports to show a "true and fair view," which requires that any gap in or potentially misleading application of accounting standards be filled by the exercise of professional judgment. Without a strong attachment to the true and fair doctrine, principles-based standards would give greater opportunities for managerial manipulation of accounting information. However, the exploitation of gaps in and letter-of-the-law application of general accounting standards, as occurred at Enron and other companies in the United States, shows that even comprehensive and very detailed GAAP cannot provide full protection against such activities. Thus, it is unlikely that just one factor, such as the propensity to litigation, provides a complete understanding of differences between national accounting regimes.

Just as the accounting regimes in the United States and United Kingdom can be expected to have some similarities, so can those of Germany and Japan. Until recently, these latter countries' systems produced strongly conservative financial reports that allowed income smoothing by management. Both countries were slow to adopt changes to financial reports, such as introducing a requirement for consolidated accounts and market values for financial assets and liabilities. Both countries have lagged behind U.S. GAAP and IFRS approaches to "modern" accounting "challenges." Japan has not yet incorporated into its accounting a number of international standards, even though it seeks convergence with IFRS, in part because it disagrees with several of them, as does Germany. For example, both countries currently disagree with the increasing use of fair value measurement in the financial statements.

Another area of commonality is the political nature of standard setting. Imposition of accounting standards requiring specific accounting treatments may benefit some firms and people but harm others. Those who are harmed may be expected to lobby for their alternative preferred option when they perceive that the cost to them of a standard is high. This politicization is hidden in the traditional German and Japanese systems because accounting regulation is part of the normal process of achieving consensus, both formally and informally, about new laws, with government and ministry views dominating. In the United Kingdom, the private sector standard body, the ASB, and its predecessor (the Accounting Standards Committee) have been relatively free of concentrated lobbying, although they have been perceived as acceding to industry pressure in a few cases. There have not been any explicit threats of government or parliamentary intervention. This is not the case in the United States, where the SEC and the Congress have intervened in several controversial cases. For example, expensing stock options was abandoned in 1993 on the threat of Congressional action. When in 2004 the FASB issued a draft standard that would require expensing stock option, strong lobbying against this procedure, including Congressional interference, began again—although this time it failed, as the revised standard now requires expensing. The IASB has also been subject to pressure on stock options and a number of governments and institutions that lobbied the EU not to endorse IAS 32 and 39 on financial instruments, both of which lobbying attempts also failed.

In summary, it is useful to crudely partition the accounting regimes of our four countries into two pairs, Germany and Japan on the one hand and the United Kingdom and the United States on the other. This partition is based on roughly common government systems, legal settings, methods of corporate financing, and past methods of market regulation in the two sets of countries, though our classification admittedly still is somewhat simplistic and may have to change as factors affecting accounting regimes in these countries also continue to change.

COMMONALITIES IN ACCOUNTING

The EU has introduced considerable commonality into accounting in the United Kingdom and Germany (as well as other EU countries) via the quite detailed frameworks and processes introduced by various accounting directives. However, these directives were and are fairly flexible and contain a number of options, and their transformation into local legislation allows the incorporation of some local concerns and interests. For example, the need to show a true and fair view is still the ultimate objective for financial reports in the United Kingdom, thereby allowing additional flexibility of accounting treatments for British companies. Following generally accepted rules for accounting is thought in Germany (and many other countries) to be sufficient to provide the "true and fair" view that is required by the EU.

Individual company accounts are more important in Germany and Japan than consolidated accounts, because of their legal effects on taxation and dividends, than in the other two countries, which suggests that the objective of financial disclosure differs from that of providing only a true and fair view or that an accounting-determined true and fair view is the best basis for taxation. Both sets of accounts are accorded equal parity in the United Kingdom.

Most of the accounting issues and the ways they are being addressed in the four countries are similar, although the emphasis on particular outcomes differs. The scope and comprehensiveness of accounting principles are greater in the United Kingdom and the United States, although both Germany and Japan would argue that their selected principles produce higher-quality accounting. Standard setters in the United Kingdom have attempted to lead accounting developments and believe their standards, measured by international norms, are perceived to be of high quality. The United States has always prided itself on the quality of its accounting standards and on its regulatory system for financial markets and has seen its GAAP as the standard that others should meet. Indeed, the SEC has long insisted that corporations that want to have their stock traded on U.S. stock exchanges must reconcile their accounting reports based on national standards or IFRS with U.S. GAAP. Following the Enron scandal and others, the possibility of moving to principles-based standards is being considered, as are some treatments used by other accounting standard setters for some problematic accounting items. Nonetheless, neither the SEC nor the FASB seems inclined to abandon their movement to require use of fair values for a wider range of financial assets and liabilities and perhaps also for all assets and liabilities. This attitude is shared by the IASB.

The principles on which accounting standards are based, though, differ between the two sets of countries. Germany and Japan emphasize stewardship and creditor protection and constraining the payment of dividends while allowing management scope to smooth income. Although historically U.K. and U.S. accounting principles have reflected similar values, there is movement in both countries to increase the presumed investor-decision relevance and transparency of accounting reports, a view adopted by the IASB and, presumably, by EU policymakers. Prudence, realization, and matching are held to reduce decision relevance and to produce less economically meaningful balance sheets. (As we explain in Chapter 2 and also discuss in Chapter 11, we disagree with these assessments; rather, we conclude that fair value accounting that is not based on reliable and relevant market prices allows managerial manipulation that reduces decision-relevancy and transparency and that the matching concept tends to produce a useful and trustworthy measure of net income and its components.)

There are currently dozens of differences between FASB standards and IFRS.[7] Most of these are insignificant. The IASB and FASB have agreed to seek convergence both in the short and longer term. In a short-term convergence project, both standard setters compare existing standards that are very similar in content to seek to eliminate immaterial differences. Both standard setters have made amendments to several standards to conform with the allegedly higher-quality standard. More recently, the IASB and FASB are coordinating their work on more fundamental issues, such as business combinations, the conceptual framework, performance reporting, and revenue recognition. It remains to be seen whether these projects will be more successful in achieving convergence than earlier efforts to develop standards jointly, which often ended with substantially different standards (as, for instance, for segment reporting).[8]

Against this striving for more conformity, the IASB issued in 2003–04 several IFRS that generate new, keep, or increase existing differences with U.S. GAAP. These rules relate to financial instruments, inventory, investment property, joint ventures, and income statement presentation. Much more important to obtaining future convergence between FASB and IASB standards is U.S. participation in a number of joint working parties of standard setters who are tackling important controversial accounting problems, including some fundamental differences for which there are no current convergence plans, such as revaluation of fixed assets. In the Appendix to this chapter, we describe significant differences in more detail. For some of these there are no present plans for convergence.

In all the countries we review, accounting standards differ, some even within the same country. Differences in standards relate to criteria such as listing status, size, legal form (in particular limited liability and corporate governance), and industry. Furthermore, accounting standards for non-corporate entities, charities, government bodies, and the like also vary.

Both Germany and the United Kingdom have difficulties in imposing accounting requirements on smaller companies, as is required by EU directives for all companies with limited liability. These problems will increase when large firms are allowed to use IFRS for their financial reports. In both countries it will be possible for most companies to continue using their national GAAP. Thus, in both countries there may be two accounting regimes (GAAP and IFRS). In the past, both countries have allowed concessions (some different) to smaller companies while seeking to ensure that all limited liability companies are driven by the substance of the same accounting regime in return for the benefits of limited liability. The IASB has launched a project to develop standards for small and medium-sized entities (SMEs) and has drawn a line between entities with "public accountability" for which the full set of IFRS would apply and others that could opt for less demanding SME standards. The IASB's intention is to reduce presentation and disclosure requirements for SMEs, whereas modifications of recognition and measurement rules are still under debate.[9] Perhaps such standards will make it easier for countries to accept IFRS for other than listed companies.

In contrast, Japan and the United States distinguish only between listed and nonlisted companies. Japan requires nonlisted companies to report according to the Commercial Code, while listed companies also have to report under the Securities and Exchange Law. The United States has no reporting requirements for corporations that are not subject to the jurisdiction of the SEC (generally companies with less than US$5 million in equities, and for securities sold entirely to accredited investors, such as institutions and wealthy individuals and securities that are not traded or not sold interstate).

CORPORATE GOVERNANCE

In both the United States and the United Kingdom, the market for shares has been the principal means of "corporate governance." Investors buy shares in firms that perform or are expected to perform well; conversely, investors sell the shares of poorly performing companies. Market pressure increases the possibility of takeovers that either displace the managers of poorly performing firms or give them strong incentives to correct their mismanagement. Litigation and the fear of litigation are also assumed to promote good governance. Independent audits are required in both countries, which also serve to improve managerial performance (as we explain in Chapter 2).

The law also "governs" corporate behavior by vesting ultimate responsibility in a single board of directors who have a fiduciary duty to enhance and protect investor welfare. In both countries the law also sets out the roles of directors, officers, and shareholders. The basic rights of shareholders include the right to vote on a number of items (e.g., the election of directors) at the corporate annual general meeting and on major corporate changes (e.g., takeovers), receive necessary information in share prospectuses, and receive annual financial reports.

In Germany and Japan shareholders have similar rights to be involved in the corporation as in the other countries, although litigation is not very important in either country. In both Germany and Japan corporate accountability is more widely defined, and less reliance is placed on the market to discipline companies. Until recently, both countries have viewed shareholder welfare as only one of several corporate objectives. Indeed, the doctrine in Germany was that management should serve the company's interest, seen as a mix of stakeholders' interests. Until about the late 1980s, Japanese managers considered shareholders to be of relatively minor importance.

Both Germany and Japan rely heavily on banks, which typically own shares in as well as extend credit to companies, to provide corporate governance. In Japan, boards of directors are usually large. Many of the members are company executives, with all, or a great majority, connected to the company in some way and few or no outside directors. This means that management dominates the company and the board. Banks compensate, or try to compensate, for this weakness.

Japanese-government influence, both formal and informal, is also an important element of corporate governance, as is the corporate workforce. The formal inhibitions on management are small. The board of directors is supposed to act against directors who break the law or fail to respect corporate articles of association (charter). In this responsibility, it is aided by a board of statutory auditors (in other countries the nearest equivalent is internal auditors). Japanese business has argued that the board-of-auditors approach to corporate governance is both legitimate and no weaker than other approaches, because only those who have worked their way up the company can have the company- and industry-specific knowledge necessary to run the firm. This corporate governance approach was strengthened by an amendment to the Commercial Code in 2002.

In Germany, a listed company must have a two-tiered board system: an executive and a supervisory board. The supervisory board is composed solely of outside directors who represent a variety of stakeholders, including a large representation of the firm's workforce. This is intended to ensure the separation of supervision and management that many commentators believe is a major element of corporate governance. There is no requirement, but a "comply or explain" rule, to set up an audit committee.

All the countries we examine, except for Japan, have put great efforts recently into developing extensive and generally similar systems of corporate governance. However, Germany and the United Kingdom have opted for a very different approach to the United States. The emphasis in Germany and the United Kingdom is on voluntary codes of behavior and relatively little legal authority ("soft law"). Boards need not follow requirements that they feel are not appropriate for the company, providing they explain why they have not complied. Both countries' codes are generally similar and are still new. A major distinction is that the German system pays more regard to non-equity stakeholders than does the U.K. system. The take-up rate by listed companies in the United Kingdom of at least the major requirements of the (combined) governance code is high (as it is with the largest companies in Germany). However, in a "comply or explain" system, compliance may be formal and limited to window dressing. In practice, management still dominates and the codes may not have much effect on company management, unless non-executive directors take a strong role in defending shareholder interests. Because the legal authority backing the codes is weak, in time legislation may be needed to strengthen them.

The recent reforms to corporate governance in the United States stem from the corporate "scandals"—fraudulent or seriously misstated financial statements that had to be restated and instances of senior executives apparently looting their companies—in 2001–02, although concerns about managerial power and its misuse predated these events. Additional "scandals" have since been uncovered both inside and outside the United States, prominent examples being the failure of Parmalat (2003) in Italy and the overstatement of oil reserves by Royal Dutch/Shell (2004). The Sarbanes-Oxley Act (2002) was the main instrument of reform in the United States. Among its many features, the CEO and CFO are made responsible for their companies' internal controls to prevent improper or inadequate accounting and must document their compliance systems and certify, at the cost of personal liability, that they have reviewed the financial statements and attest that these statements do not contain any untrue statements of material fact or material omission. Some business opinion in the United States has questioned the need for such extensive, detailed, and reportedly costly reviews. The Act also requires that the audit committee comprise independent directors with the authority to hire, monitor, and dismiss the external auditors. The major stock exchange in the United States, the NYSE, also acted with its own set of reforms. Among the most important are that boards must consist of a majority of independent directors. It is too early to assess the impact of these changes.

The U.K. view is that many of the Sarbanes-Oxley requirements should be voluntary. Another major difference with the United States is separating the board chair and CEO roles, which is increasingly the practice in the United Kingdom but is opposed in the United States, where boards tend to believe that such a split will reduce entrepreneurial drive and confuse the lines of authority.

Recent efforts to enhance the effectiveness of corporate governance in Germany have substantially increased the importance of the Supervisory Board, which appears to be fairly independent of management because it comprises outside directors. However, a number of members are often retired managers of the company, and usually half of the members represent the labor force.

The Japanese government recently (2002) allowed listed firms to opt for an alternative method of corporate governance, following the U.S. approach and incorporating similar regulations. The take-up so far has been very low and very slow in happening.

To summarize, corporate governance in the four countries reviewed here exhibit similar trends that increase regulatory coverage and detail, generally stemming from reactions to the U.S. corporate scandals. Mandatory regulation is the approach in Japan and the United States. In Germany and the United Kingdom the emphasis is on voluntary compliance with full explanation of noncompliance, thus providing at least transparency. Some observers doubt, though, that voluntary compliance is sufficient to ensure adequate information on some important items. Indeed, the EU and the German government seem prone to regulate by law some of the rules currently contained in corporate governance codices. In general, there is little theory or empirical evidence indicating that firms using more sophisticated corporate governance methods are more profitable over the long run or are managed in a way that makes management more accountable to shareholders.[10] Nonetheless, it is likely that in all four countries there will be additional demands on accountants and auditors, as discussed next.

AUDITING

In all four countries for many years the law has required external and independent audits of corporations and has specified who may qualify as an auditor. In all the countries the audit of listed corporations is carried out by private sector independent public accountants (IPAs), usually organized in firms, and the auditor may be sued for lack of care, but generally only by shareholders. In Japan the individual IPA is personally responsible for the audit and affixes his or her name on the attestation, whereas in the three other countries the responsibility is that of the audit firm. Even then, the individual IPA signs his or her name to the attestation statement in Germany, but not in the United Kingdom or the United States. We believe that personal responsibility and identification of the auditor in charge of the engagement and the confirming partner give them an incentive to avoid the loss of their personal reputations.

In three of the four countries (not Japan), until recently the setting of auditing standards and the regulation of the profession were matters for private organizations in a self-regulating regime. In Japan audits have been governed by law and government agencies, particularly the Ministry of Finance. Although differing in detail, the role and the scope of the audit and codified auditing standards have been similar in all four countries. However, the quality of the audit differs among countries. In particular, there is a general view, at least outside Japan, that audits in that country are not up to international standards, but this view may reflect the quality of earlier Japanese accounting and auditing standards; certainly this is not now the Japanese view.

At bottom, the auditors in all four countries do the same things. They give an opinion on the accounting statements and on the consistency of any other reports included with the financial statements and (except in the United Kingdom) report on the company's internal controls. In addition, auditors may have to report on compliance with a corporate governance code. In none of the countries is the audit expected to detect all frauds and misstatements.

The audit opinion differs among the four countries. In the United Kingdom, Germany, and the EU a true and fair view must be attested, usually interpreted as being consistent with the national law and GAAP. In contrast, in Japan and the United States the audit opinion certifies that the financial reports report fairly in accordance with national GAAP.

The characteristics of auditors are similar in the four countries. They must be independent, must be members of a professional body recognized by the state, must not offer accounting (bookkeeping) services to audit clients, are variously restricted in the ancillary services they can offer audit clients, and must generally practice rotation of audit lead partners. Additionally, large audit firms have been subject to peer review. Apart from the United States, the other countries are seeking to converge their auditing standards with the International Standards on Auditing (ISA) issued by the International Auditing and Assurance Standards Board (IAASB), which is a subsidiary of the International Federation of Accountants (IFAC), an organization of national professional accounting bodies. IPAs in the United States must at least follow U.S. GAAS or risk being liable in legal actions for failure to conduct an adequate audit. However, there is some way to go before all the national audit standards converge with ISA. Prior to the recent U.S. financial "scandals," the relevant professional bodies had introduced a strong self-regulatory process for auditing. (For example, in the United States since 1977 the AICPA required all auditors of SEC-registered corporations to be members of an SEC practice section and be subject to peer reviews.)

Following Enron's bankruptcy, governments in the four countries restructured the regulation of their audit professions. The United States enacted the Sarbanes-Oxley Act of 2002 without much discussion or evidence on the extent and magnitude or even identification of the actual causes of the auditing problems with which the act sought to deal. That the SEC already had the power to regulate and discipline auditors was ignored. Instead, the Act created a new agency, the PCAOB, which is charged with registering, monitoring, and disciplining auditors of corporations subject to the SEC's jurisdiction. The PCAOB in turn is overseen by the SEC.

The Sarbanes-Oxley Act also now requires auditors to keep records for 7 years, to have a second review partner, and to rotate the lead partner on an audit every 5 years and specifies nine services that auditors cannot provide to their audit clients. Section 404 of the Act requires listed corporations to show that they have an effective system of internal controls; both the external auditor and the CEO and CFO must attest to this. This requirement has resulted in corporations having to incur considerable expense, including engagement of another set of auditors to assist the CEO and CFO. This controversial requirement is undergoing review with the goal of reducing the cost.

The Act continues and extends the SEC's practice of common regulatory oversight for both domestic and foreign participants on U.S. markets. This means that the worldwide staffs of firms that audit companies listed in the United States are covered by the PCAOB's audit oversight requirements. These requirements, though, may conflict with those of the "home" countries in which national branches of the firm are located. Thus, U.S. domestic regulations now extend to other countries and for a time seemed to be infringing on the sovereignty of other countries.[11] The

PCAOB has addressed this perception by announcing that it will consider national audit regulatory regimes and rely on those it deems of sufficient quality for the Act's purposes. Where this is not the case, there will be a hierarchy of PCAOB inspections.

The U.K. government has implemented a system very similar to that in the United States, except that the oversight agency is independent. In Germany, many of the regulatory mechanisms that are consistent with the Sarbanes-Oxley Act were established prior to the passage of the Act, although the number of ancillary services that the auditor cannot offer was increased.

The EU has also proposed a replacement to its Eighth Directive, which will require all EU countries to have an accounting oversight board compatible with each country's approach to regulating auditors. Mutual recognition will apply throughout the community. The European Commission is also proposing that ISA, after endorsement, should apply to all European statutory audits. An EU-wide committee will be established to oversee that ISA are applied consistently throughout Europe and not changed to allow for special features of each country's audit regimes.

Japan has been rapidly introducing an audit and oversight system that is very similar to that used in our other countries, following changes in the Certified Public Accountants Law 2003, which governs who may be a IPA and what their functions are. Japan also has changed its enforcement arrangements for audits and auditors. Currently, the Japanese Financial Services Agency (JFSA) receives reports on all audits. An amendment to the law permits it to undertake on-site inspection of audit firms, as can the Japanese Institute of Certified Public Accountants (JICPA) and the audit oversight board (see below), and allows the JFSA to issue conduct directions to audit firms.

ENFORCEMENT: ACCOUNTING AND AUDIT

All four countries have basic legal requirements for companies to keep proper accounting records and prepare financial accounting statements, at least annually, that report "fairly" under the relevant GAAP. Similarly, all these countries have complicated regulatory regimes for financial markets aimed at ensuring fairness and transparency, with emphasis on dealing with fraud and anti-insider trading, and the power to inspect for violations and to impose severe disciplinary penalties. Deficient accounting reports and auditing often figure in market regulatory actions. Professional associations also play a role in enforcing accounting and particularly auditing standards. Litigation, actual or potential, is especially important in the common-law countries: the United States and to a lesser extent the United Kingdom.

Apart from stock market laws and regulations, accounting and auditing regulations can be enforced in a number of ways. The most important are enforcement by an accounting regulator, enforcement by the profession, and enforcement by the courts via litigation.

Accounting Regulation

The United States has the strongest and most comprehensive government-run enforcement regime for accounting and auditing. For many years, the SEC has had the power to refuse to register financial statements not in conformance with U.S. GAAP and to require restatement of deficient accounting reports. However, the number of such restatements has been in the hundreds, compared to the some 12,000 companies that file financial statements with the SEC. Either there were few reasons for restatements or the SEC was not aware of the need, because it has rarely reviewed the periodic financial statements filed with it. This lapse in oversight was brought to public attention when the SEC revealed that it had not reviewed the statements filed by Enron and most of the other scandal-ridden corporations; hence, the SEC failed to uncover their accounting problems. However, the U.S. Congress must shoulder some of the blame, since it had consistently failed to provide funding that the SEC had requested, while requiring the agency to transfer the considerably greater amount of fees it collected to the Treasury. Since passage of the Sarbanes-Oxley Act, Congress has reversed course and substantially increased funding for SEC enforcement.

None of the market regulators in the other three countries monitor or require at the time of filing that financial statements should be consistent with the country's GAAP. Rather, their concern is only that the filings are complete and are filed on time. The United Kingdom, though, has a well-established system for investigating allegations of deficient accounts and for remedying them via the Financial Reporting and Review Panel (FRRP), which currently reports to the U.K. accounting oversight body, the Financial Reporting Council. The FRRP has statutory power to apply to the courts for an order to restate accounting reports that do not give a true and fair view, with directors personally liable for the costs. Since 2003, proactive investigations were introduced, with the Financial Services Authority (FSA) publicizing firms whose accounting statements are especially at risk. The FRRP intends to review 300 to 400 companies a year out of a population of over 2,000. So far, the FRRP has been able to obtain accounting restatements from all companies without recourse to its formal powers. Over half the allegations made to the FRRP have been found to be unsubstantiated.

Japan does not have a formal system for remedying deficient financial reports, although the relevant ministries may carry out investigations.[12] This basically was the situation in Germany until 2005, when a mechanism similar to the United Kingdom's FRRP was installed that is empowered to act proactively. If consultation with a company fails, the German Federal Supervisory Authority can be asked to intervene. It has the power to require companies to correct any errors, and it may apply to the courts for prosecution of individuals.

The Law

Relative to the other countries in our study, the United States relies more heavily on litigation for preventing (and obtaining compensation for damages growing out of) misleading financial reports. The Securities Act of 1933 and the Securities and Exchange Act of 1934 allow investors to sue accountants for gross negligence, even when the investors did not contract with the accountants and may not even have seen, much less relied upon, the financial statements. Germany, Japan, and the United Kingdom have legal systems that make litigation difficult to mount and to prosecute successfully. In 1993 Japanese shareholders were given some rights to sue auditors. This process was continued in 2002 and relaxed the general principle of Japanese law that the burden of proof lies with the plaintiff. Defendant IPAs now have to show that no relation existed between a deficient audit report and any damage alleged. Class actions were also allowed. It is too early to say how this new legal regime will work; up to 2001, no such legal actions had succeeded. Germany is about to facilitate litigation, but here, too, it is too early to assess the effect. Thus, it is reasonable to conclude that legal enforcement is an important instrument only in the United States.

Enforcement of Compliance With Auditing Standards

The current mechanisms for enforcing audit requirements (GAAS) were reviewed earlier in this chapter. Generally, these show considerable convergence across the four countries. All our countries have some type of public company accounting oversight board with non-accounting members, but it is fully independent of government only in the United Kingdom. All have some type of disciplinary board for auditors with strong powers or access to other bodies that have such powers. All have some type of method of reviewing the audit process, split between peer review in Germany and a variety of monitoring boards in the other countries. In all countries the professional bodies also have power to discipline their members. Although this strong convergence is relatively new, it does not appear to be entirely or even largely the result of the Sarbanes-Oxley Act in the United States. Rather, the current developments build on and extend previous enforcement efforts.

Given that all of the enforcement regimes are relatively new, it is not possible to evaluate how effective they will be. It is conceivable that they will degenerate into simply "box ticking" compliance. The past evidence is not too hopeful. In the United States the SEC has been reluctant or unable to discipline many auditors and audit firms, despite their having "signed off" on clearly egregiously incompetent audits or fraudulently prepared financial statements [Benston, 2003A, 2003B].

Generally, the picture is similar in the other countries. The professional disciplinary process in the United Kingdom has been very slow and time-consuming, with light penalties in the few serious cases dealt with. In Germany, in 2002 one of the professional bodies reviewed some 17,000 audit opinions and barred just 10 auditors, referred 9 to the courts, and penalized 7 auditors. In Japan, the JICPA examines how well IPAs have performed their audit tasks and whether their audit opinions can be substantiated. In the period April 2001 to March 2002 it concluded only 26 cases; of these, 10 comments were issued to the involved IPAs and 8 cases were forwarded to a disciplinary body [JICPA, 2004].

From the data on audit enforcement internationally, one cannot determine whether there are very few grossly incompetent or dishonest auditors or whether the enforcement mechanism is so poor that only a few have been caught and punished. But even among those who were chastised for incompetence, it difficult to avoid the impression of lax sentencing.

DOES DIVERSITY MATTER, AND HOW CAN IT BE DEALT WITH?

So far, we observe that accounting standards differ across countries for various reasons, although recently there has been a move toward more convergence. It is by no means obvious if these differences are important and detrimental in the capital markets. There is no systematic way to predict the impact of the differences in the financial statements of particular companies prepared under different countries' GAAP. Some differences are one-time effects that result from the application of earlier standards, such as business combinations recorded as pooling-of-interests under previously acceptable U.S. GAAP but as purchases under IFRS. The initial differences, in turn, are likely to give rise to future differences. Other differences are recurring ones, such as accounting for R&D and other intangibles. Large differences can be the result of just one item that is accounted for differently, or they can be due to a number of items. Differences can have countervailing effects (e.g., deferred taxes and the differences giving rise to them). A major difference between the accounting treatments under two sets of GAAP may have a negligible effect on one company but a large effect on another. Such differences may induce either a positive or a negative earnings effect, depending on the particular structure of the business transactions that are accounted for differently. Additionally, differences arise as apparently similar standards are applied in different ways.

Barth and Clinch [1996] analyzed the extent to which ostensibly similar income statements and balance sheets vary when different sets of GAAP are applied. They compared the financial statements of corporations domiciled in the United Kingdom, Australia, and Canada that reported their numbers according both to domestic and U.S. GAAP in 1992. They found differences of the means of domestic and U.S. GAAP net income and stockholders' equity over 1985 to 1991 of between 6 and 13 percent.[13] Harris and Muller [1999] found even lower impacts arising out of differences between U.S. GAAP and IFRS: a mean difference of earnings scaled by IFRS book value of equity of just 0.28 percent (in absolute terms)

Table 9-1 Daimler-Benz Restatement of German to U.S. GAAP
Net Income and Shareholder Equity

	German GAAP	U.S. GAAP
Net income 1993	615	(1,839)
Net income 1994	895	1,052
Shareholders' equity 1993	18,145	26,281
Shareholders' equity 1994	20,251	29,435

In millions Deutsche Mark.

and a mean book-value-of-equity difference of 4.25 percent. Thus, it appears that while there are differences and the numbers determined by different sets of GAAP, they do not appear to be overwhelmingly great.

The case of Daimler-Benz (now DaimlerChrysler), an automotive manufacturer headquartered in Germany that commenced listing on the NYSE in 1993, is often cited as a notoriously contrary example.[14] The reconciliation between German GAAP and U.S. GAAP net income yielded a huge difference in magnitude, as shown in Table 9-1.

The major differences are due to the different treatments of business combinations and goodwill, minority interests, pension provisions, hedge accounting, and deferred taxes. These large differences have been cited as proof of how flexible German GAAP are relative to U.S. GAAP and how much better, therefore, are U.S. GAAP. But in the years after 1994, the differences in the net income numbers were generally within 10 percent. The earlier significant differences appear to be transitory.

Why Companies Should Be Concerned About Diversity

The benefit to investors of purchasing the stock or debt of companies is reduced to the extent that they find it necessary to expend resources to understand and interpret those companies' financial statements. Hence, company managers can reduce their costs of capital and benefit their shareholders by reducing the costs incurred by financial statement users. This cost is likely to be high for companies that seek capital in foreign countries, because investors in those countries may not be familiar with the GAAP under which the companies report.

The extent to which companies and investors seek funds and investments in other countries is discussed in Chapter 1. Additional insights can be gleaned from a questionnaire-based study of European institutional investors by Choi and Levich [1996]. Some 85 percent of their respondents said they make cross-country comparisons to look for investment opportunities, and 42 percent believe (but 34 percent do not believe) that a common set of financial reporting standards would encourage investment into foreign firms.[15] Their preferences for financial statements that conform to U.S. GAAP or IFRS are similar: 58 percent would be more likely to consider investing in foreign corporations if IFRS were used, 44 percent if

U.S. GAAP were. However, other factors, such as country-specific risks, size and liquidity of markets, regulatory barriers, and the like, are important, too. Investors were also asked about their reaction to a lack of specific financial disclosures. One group of responses was that investors actively try to acquire more information; the other group was that investors demand a higher return, which would increase the cost of capital. Both types of responses are costly, the first to the investors (and eventually to the companies) and the second directly to the companies.

Some empirical studies of the stock market find that firms that produce financial statements that are (or appear to be) more useful to investors have lower costs of capital. For example, Leuz and Verrecchia [2000] compared German listed corporations that switched from reporting under German GAAP to international accounting standards (either IFRS or U.S. GAAP). They found that these companies had significantly lower bid–ask spreads and higher trading volume but no significant differences in share price volatility (after controlling for other factors that influence these variables). The results are consistent with the hypothesis that increased (and continuing) disclosure in the form of internationally accepted accounting standards reduces the cost of capital. However, it is difficult to attribute the cost of capital decrease to the change in financial disclosure alone, as it may be that corporations that switch to IFRS or U.S. GAAP simultaneously change management strategy to emphasize shareholder value maximization and improve corporate governance.

Hail and Leuz [2003] studied the cost of equity capital across 40 countries using a cost of capital measure that equals the interest rate implied by the market price of equity when it is recalculated by a discounted cash flow valuation using analyst forecasts. They found that the average country cost of capital is systematically lower in countries with strong disclosure rules and legal enforcement of compliance, after controlling for other factors that contribute to differences in the cost of capital. Therefore, companies on average have an interest in better rules.

How Companies Can Deal With Diversity

Corporations that want to reduce investors' costs of analyzing their statements could provide selected disclosures to supplement their financial statements prepared under national GAAP. Although this step is less costly than a complete restatement of its financial statements into GAAP recognized by interested investors, it suffers from some important shortcomings.

First, the corporation may not select the specific items in which investors are interested, and the bulk of the statements are still prepared under national GAAP. Second, investors have reason to fear that some corporations will disclose only favorable information, particularly because there is no disclosure standard that directs the contents of the "enhanced disclosures." Third, there is no consistency requirement for voluntary information. This makes financial analysis more costly.

One example of an adaptation of national GAAP to meet demands of particular groups of investors is "convenience translations." A translation of financial statements into different languages and converting figures into different currencies is an inexpensive way to make translated statements look more familiar to foreign investors. However, convenience currency translation is far from providing the same quality of information that would result from a full translation of the financial statements to another reporting currency, because it usually just uses the exchange rate as of the balance-sheet date to convert the currencies.[16]

Alternatively, companies can go "all the way" and recast financial statements into whatever GAAP they believe interested investors want. This procedure, though, would appear to be costly; we are not aware of systematic evidence on the costs of preparing financial information under a second set of GAAP or, indeed, under national GAAP. If corporations collect such costs, they probably consider them proprietary and do not make them available.[17] Anecdotal evidence indicates that one-time costs particularly can be substantial. For instance, the initial cost for a major Japanese company of converting Japanese to U.S. GAAP was said to be at least US$1 million [Biddle and Saudagaran, 1991, p. 72]. Bay and Bruns [1998, p. 345] reported that the cost of an initial listing on the NYSE cost a major company (apparently based on the Daimler-Benz experience) several million U.S. dollars.[18] Considering these costs and that EU-listed companies are or soon will be preparing their statements in accordance with IFRS, there is no reason to believe that IFRS are inferior to or more misleading than U.S. GAAP, and that company managers have strong incentives to meet potential investors' demands for information, the SEC should permit any company to substitute IFRS- for U.S.-GAAP-prepared statements.

There are two ways to present financial statements produced with two or more sets of GAAP. One is a reconciliation of net income and owners' equity under the different sets of GAAP, including a description of the differences (see the Appendix for examples of such differences). Such a reconciliation from domestic GAAP to U.S. GAAP is required by the SEC in its Form 20-F for foreign listings. Usually, there is no requirement to make additional disclosure requirements over and above those required by domestic GAAP. The other way is to present parallel financial statements under different sets of GAAP. These reports contain all the disclosures required by the GAAP followed, but reconciling net income or owners' equity is difficult, if not impossible, for an investor.

How Investors Might Cope With Diversity

What investors might do when companies use different sets of GAAP depends on their investment strategies. If an investor follows a passive or index-tracking investment strategy, then financial accounting issues do not play an important role. Such strategies do not involve picking individual stocks. Investors might use macroeconomic variables to determine the proportion of the portfolio that should be in the stocks in different countries and in equities or bonds, but this exercise does not involve evaluating individual corporations. Other investors who, once having decided the proportion of their portfolios that should include investments in different countries, might then choose among individual companies. In this situation, it is comparability of corporations *within* a country that matters. Other investors might want to allocate funds within a particular industry on a global level to utilize industry-specific knowledge. Such a stock-picking strategy requires a high level of comparability of financial information *across* countries.

In any case, investors who find it useful to analyze an individual company's financial statements should be aware that taking reported financial figures at face value is potentially dangerous (not only among countries using different sets of GAAP but also for companies that are subject to the same GAAP). Their exact contents may differ even if the items look similar, such as provisions or non-current assets, and many of these differences are not visible from reading the notes to the statements. Trustworthiness is likely to differ, depending on the GAAP under which they were prepared and the extent to which compliance with the auditing and accounting standards is monitored and enforced. In fact, a case-by-case analysis finds that compliance levels differ across companies and countries.[19] Therefore, similar accounting methods across countries need not ensure comparability of the resulting figures.

CONCLUSIONS

In this chapter we survey the findings of the country chapters. The authorities in the countries we survey emphasize protecting investors, primarily with laws and regulations that govern how information about individual listed corporations is produced and disseminated. Investors also benefit from competition among corporations and institutions for their funds. Consequently, if requirements designed to protect investors are so costly that they discourage companies from listing on securities markets and make retail trading onerous and costly, consumers will be hurt rather than helped.

All our countries and the EU seek to provide investors with open, well-functioning, deep, and liquid markets while maintaining the quite distinct characteristics of national financial markets. The different financial market systems and different types of finance requirements in those countries suggest that agreed standardized requirements for markets across countries would seem difficult, if not impossible, to implement.

The difficulties inherent in international standardization of accounting reports are illustrated by the quite different approaches to corporate governance of some of our countries. Auditing and the enforcement of the accounting standards differ among our countries. Auditing systems are converging, at least on the surface, to satisfy U.S. requirements for global companies. The factors that shape the use of any international accounting standards in a given country imperil comparability across countries, where for any standard there is implicit diversity of practice internationally. The international accounting standards setter's reaction to these problems may mirror those of domestic standard setters and tax authorities: seeking to close loopholes by drafting more detailed standards or providing detailed guidelines, thereby creating more loopholes that can be exploited by bright accountants, finance practitioners, and lawyers.

A major weakness in all countries is the lack of enforcement across the financial regulation systems, especially in the accounting and audit areas. In all countries the statute law is resorted to only in cases with major public visibility, and even here cases are highly complex and time-consuming and outcomes are uncertain. It is too early to say how successful the various new approaches in our countries will be, but it is unlikely that they can enforce compliance with their accounting and auditing standards in any comprehensive way. Across the regimes, a major weakness is a lack of the power to and resources for scanning the economy to detect the need for enforcement relevant to accounting and auditing. More specifically, in the accounting area enforcement is still weak. Accounting regulators seem to be able to address only a small subset of likely problems. All these problems and a large number of others raised in this section and in our country chapters suggest major difficulties for seeking international accounting standards, the subject we address in the next chapter.

However, the paucity and general ineffectiveness of government and professional enforcement should not be taken to imply that accounting and auditing standards are routinely or even more than occasionally violated by IPAs. IPA firms and individual IPAs have strong incentives to protect their professional reputations. The demise of the major accounting firm Arthur Andersen as a result of its loss of reputation provides an example of what could occur. Although some accounting and auditing failures or scandals have been well publicized, in large measure because they involved some well-known companies, our review of the evidence does not support the casual belief that such acts have been widespread or have even affected more than a small proportion of listed corporations.

However, market forces alone are likely to be insufficient to reduce deficient reporting to a politically and perhaps economically acceptable level. This is a role that government agencies should and could play. In fulfilling this role, though, government agencies should attempt to balance the costs imposed on corporations and IPAs with the benefits from more pervasive and stronger reviews and enforcement.

Financial disclosure in a country emerges as one of a number of interacting factors that together make up the national financial markets and corporate governance regime. Changing just one of the factors in this complex nexus, say financial reporting standards, may destroy an extant subtle balance and result in a reduction of the efficiency of capital markets. There is a special danger of this outcome with regard to changes in accounting, as accounting requires the most interpretation and judgment and directly affects contractual relationships. We do not conclude, though, that there have not been some serious problems that could be dealt with more effectively.

APPENDIX: INTERNATIONAL FINANCIAL REPORTING STANDARDS COMPARED TO U.S. GAAP STANDARDS

It is impossible to do full justice to the complicated question of what differences exist between current International Financial Reporting Standards (IFRS, which include International Accounting Standards [IAS]) and the generally accepted accounting principles (GAAP) of each of the many countries that are participating in the effort to develop and refine the international standards.[1] The standards differ in scope and complexity and they evolve over time. What we do in this Appendix, therefore, is to give a flavor of key differences between IFRS and the GAAP of the United States and a few other countries. We focus on U.S. GAAP as the country benchmark because these standards compete with IFRS on global capital markets, and the United States is the prime barrier to IFRS not being more universally accepted. While subtle differences exist between IFRS and other sets of GAAP in almost every area, we do believe that many of them are not based on insurmountable conceptual differences. In fact, convergence has been achieved over the past couple of years, although of relatively minor issues.

Comparing standards literally does not fully capture their actual application in the business community. Controversial discussion on some interpretations by the International Financial Reporting Interpretations Committee (IFRIC), such as emission and concession rights, provide evidence that it is far from simple to arrive at an acceptable accounting method for certain types of transactions. Moreover, as we noted earlier, accounting standards and practices are part of a complex web of legal, economic, and cultural environments of the respective countries. The national influence surfaces if a standard's application to a certain event is not entirely clear at the outset. With respect to national standards, there exist rules, methods, and traditions of how to handle such situations. However, IFRS have not been developed in a specific national context; thus, there is no guidance for their interpretation outside of that provided by the IFRS themselves. It is not surprising, therefore, that preparers, auditors, and enforcement agencies, even if they wish to apply IFRS faithfully to the best of their knowledge, end up with results that have a country-specific flavor. The same difficulty would apply to U.S. or any other country's GAAP if it were exported to other countries.

BACKGROUND OF THE IFRS

In the years after its foundation in 1973, the (then) IASC promulgated standards that more or less described existing acceptable practice in various countries around the world. As practices differ, the first such standards contained many options to capture the preferred practices. The objective then was to narrow the existing differences by harmonizing national regulations, which should also help developing nations by providing a benchmark or template for setting their own accounting standards, or by providing them with a set of standards that they could adopt.

Looking for cooperating partners to promote IAS worldwide, the IASC forged an agreement with the International Organization of Securities Commissions (IOSCO) to develop standards that would be useful to corporations seeking access to international capital markets. The IASC acknowledged that the then existing standards allowed for too much flexibility and thus did not provide a sound basis for (at least apparent) "apples to apples" comparisons on a global scale. It began to develop standards that were much more demanding, particularly on the disclosure side, and that included significantly fewer options. Major revisions of standards went into effect in 1995 and 1999, with the consequence that corporations reporting under IAS had to make many accounting adjustments, thus reducing comparability over time. In 2000, the IOSCO recommended that its members permit multinational issuers to use financial statements prepared under IAS for cross-border offerings and listings (subject to reconciliation, supplemental disclosure and interpretation, or even—in exceptional circumstances—waivers). In the same year, the IASC began reorganizing its own structure analogous to that of the U.S. standard setter, the FASB, and in April 2001 the new IASB was formed. A principal change was to liberate itself from the International Federation of Accountants (IFAC) and rather establish close liaisons with leading national standard setters around the world to pursue the convergence of national standards. With the decision by the European Union (EU) and a number of other countries to adopt IFRS by 2005 and the self-doubts of the United States with regard to its own standards, the IASB has received significant recognition as a global standard setter.

The first activities of the IASB, besides renaming its standards (from IAS to IFRS) and the body that issues interpretations (from Standing Interpretations Committee [SIC] to IFRIC), included an "Improvements Project" that aimed to reduce the number of options in the IAS, to clarify standards, and to include more guidance. The revised standards became operative in 2005. In 2003, the IASB also started a convergence project, together with the FASB, that sought to eliminate differences between IFRS and U.S. GAAP.

The following comparison of major accounting and disclosure issues should be judged against this background of the IFRS and GAAP in other countries. It is a snapshot at a specific time within long-term developments. In Table 9A-1, we provide a brief overview of key differences between IFRS and U.S. GAAP that are explained below.

GENERAL DIFFERENCES

A characteristic feature of IFRS is their style. IFRS are more principles-based standards, whereas U.S. GAAP are more rules-based. The most obvious consequence is that U.S. GAAP are much more voluminous

Table 9A-1 Key Differences Between IFRS and U.S. GAAP

Subject	IFRS	U.S. GAAP
Style of standards	Mostly principles-based, restricted overriding	Mostly rules-based, no overriding principle
Intangibles	Recognition of R&D if certain criteria are met	Recognition of R&D not allowed (except software development)
Financial instruments	Option to measure any assets and liabilities at fair value through income	Measurement at fair value through income restricted to trading assets and derivatives
Leases	General principles to distinguish between finance and operating leases	Bright line rules to distinguish between capital and operating leases
Revaluation of noncurrent assets (excluding financial assets)	Optional	Prohibited
Investment property	Option between cost and fair value measurement	Measurement at cost
Impairment of assets	Value in use (entity-specific) as relevant measure if indicators for impairment exist; reversal of impairment required	Fair value as relevant measure if indicators for impairment exist and impairment loss exceeds a certain amount; reversal of impairment prohibited
Inventory	LIFO prohibited	LIFO allowed
Provisions	Recognition if liability is more likely than not, measurement at expected value	Recognition if probable, measurement at best estimate
Employee stock options	Recognized in income	Recognized in income*
Business combinations	Purchase method required, minorities included in group equity	Purchase method required, minorities outside group equity
Joint ventures	Option between proportionate consolidation and equity method	Equity method required
Format of financial statements	Options for layout of balance sheet, income statement, and changes in equity	Prescriptive layout of balance sheet and income statement (SEC rules), and comprehensive income
Segment reporting	Segmentation according to risk-and-rewards approach	Segmentation according to management approach
Interim financial reporting	Discrete approach	Mix of discrete and integral approach

*For public companies according to the revised SFAS 123 (2004).

than the IFRS. The principles-based approach is somewhat similar to the law-based accounting systems, such as those of many EU member states. There had been some discussion about the approach when the IASB took over in 2001, and the outgoing IASC Board and the (new) Standards Advisory Council (SAC) urged the IASB to continue with the principles-based approach, while acknowledging the need for more interpretative guidelines.[2] In the aftermath of the failure of Enron, there is now discussion in the United States that appears to be leading to a more principles-based approach. When literally comparing IFRS with U.S. GAAP, the different styles and levels of detail produce long lists of minor differences.[3]

A question related to the predominance of principles or rules governing the standards is how a potential conflict between individual rules and basic principles should be treated. An overriding principle was introduced into IFRS (by amendment in 1997) that requires departure from a rule if compliance with it would result in a misleading presentation of the company's financial position. Such a circumstance is considered to be extremely rare. A similar, though not as restrictive, "true and fair override" is present in U.K. GAAP and in the EU directives. In contrast, other countries, such as the United States and Germany (although a member of the EU), do not allow departures from standards.[4] In the 2003 revision of IAS 1, the IASB included a qualification that the overriding principle, in order to be effective, must be allowed in "the relevant regulatory framework." Thus, countries can prohibit it, and companies in that country can still produce full IFRS financial statements without following the override. This seems to be a first example of the IASB explicitly allowing for country-specific IFRS—a process that, if continued, could eventually lead to the fragmentation of rules across countries (precisely the situation that the IFRS were designed to avoid, and the outcome with which we are more comfortable, as we outline in the conclusions to this book presented in Chapter 11).

SPECIFIC DIFFERENCES

Differences between various sets of GAAP can arise as a result of differences in the following factors:

- The criteria used by the different systems for recognizing particular items in the financial statements
- How certain items might be measured
- How financial statements are presented
- What disclosures are required.

Some differences necessarily arise if the respective standards mandate differing rules; other differences may arise if one standard permits options in reporting methods and others do not. Some accounting differences just change the timing of the allocation of revenues and expenses over periods, thus resulting in differences that are reversed in later periods, while others lead to permanent differences.

In what follows, we discuss the differences and their conceptual roots.[5] We draw on examples of U.S. GAAP reconciliations to identify key differences among international standards and those of some of the leading countries that are or should be of most interest to market participants, particularly equity investors. They offer an indication of how regulators and market participants (as judged by an outside observer) vary in their views as to what elements of corporate disclosure are or should be most important in the marketplace.

Intangibles

The recognition and measurement rules for intangibles vary significantly across countries. IFRS until recently required that initially recognized (capitalized) intangibles must be amortized linearly over a maximum of 20 years (though this threshold was rebuttable). This was generally in line with many other countries' GAAP; U.S. GAAP allowed up to 40 years. In 2001 the FASB adopted a new goodwill treatment, and with that the general requirement for annual amortization of intangibles was abandoned and two categories were introduced, intangibles with finite and those with indefinite useful life. The latter are not systematically amortized but are annually tested for impairment. In 2004 IFRS followed that distinction and thereby also eliminated the 20-year useful life threshold for intangibles.

IFRS requires the recognition of development costs if and when certain criteria are met, while under U.S. and German GAAP all internally generated research and development costs must be expensed as they are incurred. Inconsistent with that, software development costs are treated under U.S. GAAP similarly to IFRS.

Accounting for intangibles has become more and more the focus of debate as intangibles are one of the key value drivers in "new" economy companies, but are not—or are only to a small extent—included in the financial statements. Rather than changing the accounting for intangibles, many favor supplemental nonfinancial disclosures. We consider this issue in Chapter 11.

Financial Instruments

Effective in 2001, IFRS adopted an approach similar to U.S. GAAP under which held-to-maturity instruments are recorded at cost and trading instruments and derivatives at fair value, with gains and losses included in net income. Available-for-sale financial instruments are also valued at fair value, but gains and losses are included directly in equity and thus in a supplementary income statement (comprehensive income) under U.S. GAAP, whereas IFRS provided an option to include them either in net income or only in equity. Financial liabilities, except for trading liabilities, are measured at amortized cost under both U.S. GAAP and IFRS. Similarly, the EU accounting directives were amended in 2001 to allow for fair-value measurement of certain categories of financial assets to avoid divergence with IFRS.

In late 2003 the IASB adopted a revised standard, IAS 39, for the measurement of financial instruments. As before, IAS 39 includes four categories of financial assets (held-to-maturity, loans and receivables, available-for-sale, and trading, a category that has been extended and renamed "fair value through profit and loss") and prescribes different subsequent measurement rules for the categories (cost for the first two categories, fair value with changes directly in equity, and fair value through income). Had the standard been fully adopted, it would have given companies enormous discretion in the valuation of financial instruments towards fair value; in particular, it would have allowed companies to voluntarily follow a full fair value approach with gains and losses included in net income. As such, it would have been different from most other countries' GAAP. Following concerns voiced by the EU, the IASB issued an amendment that restricts the fair value option to cases where an accounting mismatch is reduced, to financial instruments that are managed and which performance is evaluated based on fair values, and to hybrid contracts that include embedded derivatives.

Leases

IFRS follows the lease accounting concept that distinguishes between finance (capital) and operating leases based on the economic substance of ownership rights they provide rather than on legal ownership. Lease payments of an operating lease are recognized as an expense. Under a finance lease, the lessee recognizes the leased asset and a lease liability on its balance sheet; the lease payment includes a portion reflecting the financial charge and a portion that reduces the outstanding liability. IFRS states this principle and gives guidance on factors and covenants that indicate who substantially bears the risks and rewards incident to ownership in the leased asset and, hence, whether a lease should be treated as "finance" or "operating." This rule requires professional judgment. On the other hand, U.S. GAAP provide detailed rules or "bright line guidance," including quantitative criteria, under what circumstances recognition of a leased item as an asset is required. Consequently, in the United States there is a propensity to structure lease contracts so as to achieve a desired accounting treatment.

Due to the considerable discretion both in structuring contracts and in judgment, lease accounting is under scrutiny internationally. An alternative method that is being discussed is to avoid the categorization and recognize the fair value of the rights and obligations that are conveyed by the lease.

Revaluation

Under IFRS, companies can choose between historical cost (less accumulated depreciation and impairment losses) and revaluation to fair value for groups of fixed assets (property, plant, and equipment, and, under restrictive circumstances, intangibles). Conceptually, revaluation is a form of physical capital maintenance. Revaluation must be made regularly, and fair value is usually determined by appraisal. Revaluation gains are credited directly to equity under a separate revaluation reserve and circumvent the income statement totally; they are not recycled upon disposal of the asset. The revaluation leads to assets measured at fair value in the balance sheet, but the revaluation gains are never recorded as profit in the income statement, although they would appear as other comprehensive income. Revaluation is popular in the United Kingdom and in Australia, and several other EU member states permit it. In contrast, U.S. and German GAAP require a strictly historical cost approach for other-than financial assets and do not permit revaluation accounting.

Investment Property

IFRS grants an option to measure investment property either at (amortized) cost or at fair value. Investment property includes land and buildings held to earn rentals and/or for capital appreciation. If a company opts for the fair value model, it measures all investment property at fair value; gains and losses are included in net income. Under the cost model, investment property is measured under the same rules that apply for other tangible assets, but its fair value must be disclosed in the notes.[6] The fair value model is not allowed under U.S. and many other countries' GAAP.

Impairment

Most GAAP require some kind of impairment test of long-lived assets (an exception is Japanese GAAP). The standards differ with respect to the trigger for an impairment test and measurement of the lower value. According to IFRS an impairment test is made if there is an indication that an asset may be impaired. An impairment loss is measured as the difference between the book value of an asset and its (lower) recoverable amount, which is the higher of its fair value less costs to sell and its value in use. The value in use is an entity-specific value—that is, it includes company-specific synergies. Under U.S. GAAP, an impairment loss is the difference between the book value and the (lower) fair value, which is an arms-length market (exchange) value rather than the value in use. An impairment is required when the sum of undiscounted cash flows is below the carrying (book value) amount, which serves to limit the recognition of "small" impairments. IFRS and similarly the EU accounting directives require reversal of an impairment loss if the reasons no longer exist. U.S. GAAP prohibit reversal of impairment losses.

Inventory

Inventory is generally measured at the lower of cost or market. Standards differ with respect to the cost formulas used. IFRS prohibit LIFO as of 2005, whereas LIFO is allowed under U.S. GAAP. LIFO is a peculiarity in the United States in that it must be used for financial reports if it is used for income tax assessment. Reversal of a write-down is required under IFRS but prohibited under U.S. GAAP because U.S. GAAP consider a written-down amount the new cost for subsequent accounting procedures.

Provisions and Contingencies

Present obligations of uncertain timing or amount are recognized under IFRS if they are "more likely than not" to occur and the amounts can be reasonably estimated. They are measured using the statistical concept of expected value. Long-term provisions must be discounted. Under U.S. GAAP an expense is recognized if it is probable (likely to occur, which requires a greater likelihood than "more likely than not") that a liability has been incurred and the amount of the loss can be reasonably estimated. The liability is measured at its best estimate, which is generally the most likely amount. If there is a range of estimates with no amount more likely than the others, the best estimate should be used. Discounting of expected losses is not explicitly mentioned but is implied since the amount of the loss is as of the balance-sheet date.

In many EU member states, especially Germany, provisions are governed by conservatism, which leads to a more likely recognition, a measurement above the expected value of the provision for provisions that are highly uncertain, and the prohibition of discounting. As a tendency, therefore, provisions are higher in Germany than under IFRS, which are again higher than those under U.S. GAAP. A particular area in which such differences are substantial are corporate restructurings, and both IFRS and U.S. GAAP impose highly restrictive recognition and measurement requirements.

In June 2005, the IASB published an exposure draft that seeks convergence of its recognition rules with U.S. GAAP. In particular, the IASB proposed avoiding the term "provisions" and using "non-financial liabilities" instead. However, differences remain.

Post-Employment Benefits

Pension, health care, and insurance systems for retired employees vary widely across the world and reach substantial magnitudes. According to IFRS and U.S. GAAP, post-employment benefits are measured under the projected unit credit method that allocates the expenses to set up the future liability to the periods in which the employees provide services using specific actuarial assumptions (including current market interest rates and expected future salary increases), and they are presented in the balance sheet net of plan assets held for funding the obligations. Pension assets are supposed to be stated at fair value. Earnings or losses on those assets are netted against increases in pension liabilities to determine the periodic pension expense. These earnings or losses are not amounts actually experienced but are calculated with an average expected rate of return. The difference between the actual and expected returns is smoothed under a "corridor" approach that keeps differences less than 10 percent of the liability (or the pension asset if it is greater) off the balance sheet and requires an amount over and above the 10 percent to be amortized systematically. Changes in the pension liability due to changes in the actuarial assumptions are also subject to smoothing via the corridor approach. FAS 87 started the corridor approach as a compromise for recognition of pensions, and the IASB adopted it. However, the IASB also allows recognizing all actuarial increases and decreases in pension liabilities directly against equity rather than in pension expense, an approach that follows U.K. GAAP.

Stock Options

In early 2004, the IASB issued a standard for share-based payments. As a general rule, it requires recognition of such payments whether settled in equity instruments of the company, in cash, or other assets. In particular, employee stock options are measured at their fair value at grant date and recognized as expenses. The FASB struggled unsuccessfully for a long time in the 1990s to come up with a similar standard and allowed but did not require expensing the fair value of the options. In December 2004, the FASB revised the standard to require expensing the fair value of options for public companies.

Business Combinations

A central issue in accounting for business combinations is under what circumstances the assets, liabilities, revenues, and expenses of another company should be consolidated with those of the reporting company. The usual criterion for consolidation is control, which is the power of the reporting company (the parent) to govern the financial and operating policies of another firm (a subsidiary). Assessment of control is difficult for special-purpose entities (SPEs), which are established and constructed to avoid explicit control by the sponsor company. According to IFRS a company must consider a range of qualitative criteria, including the risk and returns it retains. U.S. GAAP generally rely more on majority ownership but, in response to the practices of Enron, require consolidation of variable interest entities if the company absorbs the majority of returns or losses. Previously, the U.S. Securities and Exchange Commission had ruled that an SPE created for the benefit of a company, but not owned by the company, nevertheless had to be consolidated with its financial statements if independent equity holdings were less than 3 percent of total assets. The rebuttable "rule of thumb" now is 10 percent.

Both IFRS and U.S. GAAP require the use of the purchase method for an acquired company. According to that method, the reporting company recognizes in its consolidated statements the amount paid for the acquisition (the market value of shares of the reporting company's stock exchanged for shares in the acquired corporation or ownership interest of an unincorporated entity at the time of the acquisition). The individual assets and liabilities of an acquired company are recorded at their estimated fair values at the date of acquisition, and the difference between the sum of those values and the amount paid is recorded as "goodwill" (which can be negative if the sum exceeds the amount paid). In a joint exposure draft on business combinations from June 2005, the IASB and FASB propose requiring recording goodwill at its full fair value, independent of the actual percentage held by the parent. Minority interests are stated at the minority's share in the fair values under IFRS, whereas under U.S. GAAP they currently are stated at their share in the carrying amounts.

Some sets of GAAP require (e.g., Canadian), favor (e.g., Japan), or allow (e.g., German) the pooling-of-interests method for a merger of equals, under which the book values of assets and liabilities are simply combined, and any excess of the purchase price over the book values is simply adjusted against equity, so that no fair value revaluations and goodwill arise. Until 2001 this method was allowed by the FASB and until 2004 by the IASB.

Other differences can arise for joint ventures that are controlled by more than one company. Under U.S. GAAP, they are accounted for the equity method, wherein a company that owns at least 20 percent of the equity of another company (but less than a majority interest) must record its share of that company's net income as income or expense, with an adjustment to its investment. IFRS and the EU directives permit the equity method or proportionate consolidation. Under proportionate consolidation, the parent's share of all assets and liabilities is included in its statements (e.g., half the land, buildings, and so on), which is odd because a company does not have control over a portion of any of those assets and liabilities by itself.

Goodwill

Together with abandoning the pooling-of-interests method, the FASB fundamentally changed the accounting method of goodwill arising from a business combination. In contrast to the treatment before 2001, goodwill is now considered a non-wasting asset and consequently is not amortized on a regular basis. Rather, it is at least annually tested for impairment, and revaluation upward is not allowed. In 2004, the IASB followed this approach. Convergence in this issue seems to result from firms' favoring the non-amortization of goodwill, which systematically increases their net income, a pressure the IASB apparently could not resist. However, the impairment tests under IFRS and U.S. GAAP differ significantly, so that the carrying amounts of goodwill are likely to differ under the two regimes.

Under U.K. GAAP, it was common to charge goodwill directly against equity reserves, thus avoiding charging amortization against income in the future and also reducing the equity base without a negative income effect. Although the United Kingdom abandoned this approach, it is still allowable under the EU directives. Consequently, many European countries permit charging goodwill directly against equity.

Deferred Taxes

Deferred taxes are a complex subject that arises because the accounting rules for calculating income taxes in most countries typically differ from the rules governing financial reporting. Accordingly, the tax liability on net income reported in a particular year often differs from a company's actual tax liability. For example, a company that uses accelerated depreciation for tax purposes and the straight-line method on its books would generate larger deductions in periods following acquisition of the depreciated asset and smaller deductions in later years. The company thus defers paying an income tax until periods when book depreciation is greater than tax-deductible depreciation.

Both IFRS and U.S. GAAP take what is called a "comprehensive approach" to tax questions, requiring companies to recognize the tax effect of all reversing differences between accounting for tax and financial reporting purposes as deferred tax assets and liabilities. Many continental European countries recognize only the tax effects that result in differences affecting the income statement. They also permit a "partial approach" whereby only differences in tax payments expected to "crystallize" and be paid or that are deductible in the next few years are recognized as a liability or asset (deferred taxes). While under this approach perhaps "too little" deferred tax is recognized, perhaps "too much" deferred tax is recognized under the IFRS and U.S. GAAP approach, because neither allows for discounting deferred taxes.

Presentation of Financial Statements

Differences among sets of GAAP are highly visible in the formats and layouts of the financial statements. For example, under SEC rules items on the balance sheet are presented in the order of declining liquidity, while under IFRS the common format begins with non-current assets and with equity, respectively. Minority shares are not considered to be a component of equity under U.S. GAAP, whereas they are included in equity under IFRS as of 2005.

The income statement under SEC rules is based on the total cost of sales method, while IFRS also allow the nature of expense method, which shows material, personnel cost, and depreciation as separate line items. Most GAAP require separate disclosure of unusual and extraordinary items. Although they have no bearing on the bottom line, net income, different classifications affect subtotals, such as earnings before interest and tax. As of 2005, the IASB abandoned the category "extraordinary items" altogether.

The way that changes in equity are reported differs widely. U.S. GAAP require the presentation of net income and other comprehensive income (due to events recognized in equity), totaling comprehensive income. IFRS allow various layouts of the reporting of changes in equity. There is no equivalent disclosure requirement in the EU directives and in several other countries. Both the IASB (joint with the U.K. ASB) and the FASB have considered changing the way firm performance is reported. After negative reactions to a proposal that includes a matrix layout, with an operating profit and a remeasurement column, the enthusiasm over fundamental changes has vanished and the project has been slowed down.

Although less prominent, cash flow statements differ, too, because of slightly differing definitions of cash and cash equivalents and differing classification of interest, dividends, and income taxes under IFRS and other sets of GAAP.

Segment Reporting

Segmentation of a company's operations follows different criteria depending on the information that is considered most useful to users. IFRS, similar to the previous U.S. GAAP standards, follow a risks-and-rewards approach, which leads to a segmentation according to business and geographic characteristics. U.S. GAAP adopted a management approach that goes back to the form and content of a company's internal reporting system. While segment reporting under IFRS tends to allow a better comparison of segments across companies, U.S. GAAP is preferable to users who wish to get an understanding of how management sees its operations. Required disclosures for each reportable segment differ, too. However, the IASB announced plans to adopt the U.S. GAAP standard.

Interim Financial Reporting

IFRS follow a discrete approach under which each interim period is considered a "normal" financial reporting period. Consequently, it does not alter accounting methods that apply to annual reporting. U.S. GAAP has more of the flavor of an integral approach under which interim periods are considered part of the full financial year. Hence, it modifies some accounting methods for interim periods so that they might be better predictors of the annual results. For example, inventory losses from market declines need not be recognized if they are expected to be restored by the end of the fiscal year, and some costs affecting more than one interim period can be smoothed even if this were not allowed across financial years. Thus, U.S. GAAP interim reporting potentially provides a better indicator for the annual performance but also provides additional earnings management opportunities, which question its trustworthiness.

10

Global Financial Reporting Standards: Their Establishment and Enforcement

In previous chapters we documented a strong disjunction between increasingly global capital markets and the continued supremacy of national rules governing markets and disclosure. In this chapter, we ask the question: "What, if anything, should be done to improve international financial reporting?" Many commentators favor a single set of global accounting standards. We consider this potential solution in the light of the diversity we find across countries, but given the costs and benefits, we conclude that this is unlikely to be a viable solution for various reasons. We further consider auditing standards and auditor oversight, which are important for ensuring trustworthy financial reports, and corporate governance and enforcement issues. Although there is considerable variation across countries, there has been an increase in convergence over the last few years, mainly to the U.S. model, which has forced other countries to establish very similar institutions.

THE CONTEXT FOR GLOBAL FINANCIAL REPORTING STANDARDS

The U.S. finance markets still dominate the supply of finance to domestic and international firms. The capitalization of the 467 foreign companies on the New York Stock Exchange (NYSE) at mid-2003 was $5.9 trillion.[1] The number of foreign companies on the Deutsche Börse, the London Stock Exchange (LSE), and the Tokyo Stock Exchange at the end of 2003 were 182, 391, and 32, respectively.[2] The nearest rival to the NYSE in listing international companies is the LSE, with a capitalization of some $3.3 trillion at the end of 2003.[3] The number of new international companies listed on the NYSE is slowly increasing, but that of the LSE has recently declined very rapidly. It may be doubted whether the competition for the listing of international companies is entirely sensible, insofar as markets are reorganizing to attract global companies seemingly without concern about whether this also helps domestic-listed companies. There is an element of "wasted" competition seeking to attract firms from a relatively fixed set of international companies that favor cross-listing (but not necessarily multiple cross-listing).

Nonetheless, the fact remains that product, services, capital, and managerial markets are increasingly global in character. Firms are therefore looking for a global standard of efficiency in all their operations. Product market pressures are argued to be causing convergence to the most efficient way of organizing global organizations, such as the reorganization of elements of national infrastructure, including markets, regulatory regimes, accounting and auditing, and corporate governance. Offsetting this pressure is the desire of governments to ensure the public accountability of global companies. In parallel are those pressures from financial markets seeking to meet global requirements for finance and to encourage cross-border investment, which also have an impact on accounting, auditing, and corporate governance.

Developed stock exchanges across the world are investing in the provision of deep, liquid, and transparent markets with a high-standard regulatory regime. Corporations may cross-list not just to gain access to efficient finance markets, but also to be able to adopt a system of corporate governance more responsive to shareholder concerns, and therefore one that is more driven by stockholder wealth-maximization. Associated with this trend is a growing interest in having financial disclosures that provide adequate transparency, which in turn creates a demand for independent auditing to give validity to that information. Similarly, a strong corporate governance regime may be seen as part of high-quality regulation of financial markets. While seeking to respond to all these pressures, national governments want to maintain their sovereignty and the intrinsic national characteristics of their financial markets, as do domestic stock exchanges and regulators, because these characteristics appear to attract the most market participants—companies and investors with a national bias.

Financial markets in the United States and the United Kingdom have had the above characteristics for some time, whereas those in Germany and Japan have recently been transformed (revolutionalized in Japan) to compete. The U.S. Securities and Exchange Commission (SEC) has very strong powers to regulate security markets, including the retail trade and accounting and auditing.[4] It investigates possible offenses across its domain and has strong disciplinary powers, including requiring specific conduct and fines. Relative to other regulators, it is very hands-on and its views have strong force, even when not backed by law or regulations. The U.K. Financial Services Authority (FSA) covers all financial markets, including banking, insurance, and home loans. Some commentators view this holistic stance as an advantage over the SEC. The U.K.-style system of comprehensive or consolidated regulation is still relatively new (previously there were a number of regulators), and the FSA is not yet as active as the SEC. It has strong investigatory and disciplinary powers focused so far mainly on the retail trade.

Both Germany and Japan now have independent agencies similar to the U.K. FSA (in Japan, the Financial Services Authority; in Germany, the Federal Supervisory Authority). Both have a close relationship with their respective ministries of finance and with government. An explicit requirement imposed on the Japanese regulator is to attract international capital. Given the history of government market regulation in these two countries, it may be doubted whether these regulators are fully independent agencies. It is too early to know whether the changes in both countries represent a true transformation in market regulation or just "window dressing" to signal to market participants the existence of modern markets. It is not yet clear whether U.S.-type market regulation will win out against the U.K.-type variant, but this competition in approaches is to be welcomed and contrasts with the desire on the part of some in the accounting world to have one set of international accounting standards.

What is clear is that global competition in product markets, with its focus on global companies, and in financial markets (in cross-listing and in cross-border investment) is driving a requirement for transparent, internationally comparable, and high-quality accounting and auditing.

CONVERGENCE OF ACCOUNTING STANDARDS

Three of our four countries are either going to use International Financial Reporting Standards (IFRS), at least for consolidated reporting (Germany and the United Kingdom), or seek convergence with them (Japan). The United States, while retaining its own generally accepted accounting principles (GAAP) and implicitly regarding its system as superior (by insisting on reconciliation of other sets of GAAP with U.S. GAAP for firms that want to be listed on U.S. stock exchanges), is slowly seeking convergence between existing U.S. accounting standards and IFRS. The United States also is working with other standard setters on common future standards, which it has been relatively successful in "Americanizing." For example, in June 2005 the FASB and IASB jointly issued an exposure draft on business combinations.

The general willingness to leave standard setting to the FASB and IASB is surprising. Many countries question the superiority of these bodies but nevertheless submit to them. In Chapter 2 we indicated our concern about their asset/liability (rather than revenue/expense) approach and their use of mark-to-fair-values when these are not based on actual market prices, as well as the flexibility still allowed to firms by contemporary global accounting standards.[5] We further discuss these and related issues in Chapter 11.

The impetus behind global accounting standards is illustrated by those stock exchanges that in the past accepted financial reports of foreign countries for registration but will soon accept only IFRS (for example, the United Kingdom) and in some cases U.S. GAAP. The current approach is one where concern for the accounting used by a relatively small number of global firms is driving accounting requirements not just for all listed companies but is influencing accounting for all limited liability companies. In many countries, including Germany, Japan to a degree, and the United Kingdom, accounting standards for global companies rob accounting of the ability to reflect long-established national approaches and objectives and inhibit the growth of different national approaches to accounting.

In Germany and Japan, single company accounts are still accorded primacy and serve a number of roles unlikely to be satisfied by global standards, including tax determination and the protection of creditors and shareholders. Germany has attempted to solve this problem by requiring "entity" or "single company" accounting reports to follow German GAAP.[6] In Japan the law that governs nonlisted companies is being slowly adapted to be consistent with IFRS, but entity accounts are still prepared following mainly traditional Japanese GAAP. In the United Kingdom firms may choose to use either IFRS or U.K. accounting standards (while they still exist, as convergence with IFRS is the aim). The European Union (EU) also aims at converging the accounting principles in its directives with the IFRS. In the United States the SEC has dominion only over companies with publicly owned shares. However, the rules established by the FASB must be followed by all certified public accountants (CPAs); hence, the SEC and FASB ideally determine the accounting standards on which statements attested to by all CPAs are based.

The existence of two or more sets of accounting approaches in any country, of course, can be confusing. Dual accounting systems may evolve in at least three ways. First, global standards may come to dominate national GAAP, even though they generally are believed to be too costly and too complex for many companies. Only a few, mostly smaller, companies would then stick to national GAAP. Second, the domestic accounting system may dominate, while cross-listed national companies follow global standards. Third, the domestic system dominates, and in recognition stock exchanges revert to a "passport system" where domestic financial reports of suitable quality are accepted by stock exchanges internationally. This third approach is favored by the EU to overcome problems arising out of the insistence by U.S. authorities (so far) on reconciliation of financial reports prepared under IFRS with U.S. GAAP. As we discuss in Chapter 9, such a result is unavoidable. Many countries already use different accounting standards for different purposes—for financial reporting, for tax purposes, and for different-sized firms—and many countries will maintain national GAAP for smaller firms. Companies can cope with this, although at a cost. Countries are reluctant to pass over too much power to a global standard setter and almost certainly will retain authority to set country-specific rules for tax accounting.

COSTS AND BENEFITS OF GLOBAL FINANCIAL REPORTING STANDARDS

The globalization of capital markets in recent years has led to a call for developing and implementing a single set of worldwide reporting standards.[7,8] In principle, there should be several benefits from having a single global standard. A single standard, in principle, would make it easier for investors to compare financial statements of firms in different countries and should reduce the risks investors face and thus lower the cost of capital.[9] Having one standard should improve the allocation of capital across national boundaries by helping investors allocate their funds to their most profitable uses, adjusted for risk. A single set of standards also should reduce existing home country bias in investing. As PricewaterhouseCoopers [2003, ¶17, p. 1003] summarized: "the case for harmonisation is compelling. Global businesses and international investors need to have accounting information that they can understand when running businesses and making investment decisions."

Investors seem to recognize these virtues. In a survey conducted by McKinsey and Company, reported in the summer of 2002, 90 percent of large institutional investors worldwide wanted companies to report their results under a single world standard, although European and American investors had very different preferences: 78 percent of Western Europeans favored IFRS, while 76 percent of the Americans preferred U.S. GAAP.[10]

So far, there has been much interest in and work devoted to the development and implementation of uniform global standards for financial reporting, mainly by the profession and standard setters. In 1973 the International Accounting Standards Committee (IASC) was established as an international body of private-sector national accounting standard setters, which sought to develop a single set of global accounting standards of high quality. It is often the case that a new organization is formed in response to a pressing short-term demand that may differ from the ostensible objective. The United Kingdom, in particular, was highly interested in the IASC because, as a new member of the EU, it faced difficulty in influencing the already advanced stage of harmonization within the EU financial system, with its focus on codification and financial stewardship. Standard setters in the United Kingdom wanted to gain influence over this process by participating in an international body that developed financial reporting standards. As we discuss in Chapter 7, the United Kingdom was successful in bringing substantial parts of its national accounting standards into the EU accounting directives, and so a major motivation to support the IASC's work faded away soon after the organization was established.

Nevertheless, in the long run, the then IASC successfully developed standards that received some recognition in international capital markets.

In 2000, the International Organization of Securities Commissions (IOSCO) recommended that national regulators permit multinational issuers to use financial statements prepared under IFRS for cross-border offerings and listings, subject to reconciliation, supplemental disclosure, and interpretation, or even waivers where thought necessary. These addenda allowed the SEC (as a member of IOSCO) to accept international recommendations without having to change its requirement that foreign companies listed on U.S. stock exchanges report under U.S. GAAP or provide a reconciliation of equity and net income from IFRS or national standards to U.S. GAAP. The SEC imposed the reconciliation requirement ostensibly in order to allow investors transacting on exchanges in the United States to better able make "apples to apples" comparisons of financial statements of companies from different countries based on the yardstick of U.S. reporting conventions. The SEC's policy also was consistent with its view of "national treatment": that there be no distinction in regulation between home and foreign companies listed in the United States. However, the SEC's chief accountant has predicted that the reconciliation requirement could be dropped in this decade, providing that foreign filings based on IFRSs are found of acceptable quality and that the developments surrounding IFRSs continue in the "right way" (Nicolaisen, 2005).

To increase the likelihood of being accepted in the United States, the IASC was restructured in 2001 along the lines of the FASB in the United States. The IASC is now organized as the International Accounting Standards Board (IASB) under the International Accounting Standards Committee Foundation (IASCF), which generates funding. The restructuring was deemed necessary to appoint members on the basis of knowledge and experience independent of their national origins and to professionalize the standard-setting work and the funding of the IASB. National representation had been an overriding principle in the IASC's composition. The objectives of the IASB were amended so that it was "to work actively with national standard-setters to bring about convergence of national accounting standards and IFRSs to high quality solutions." Previously, half of the IASB members were liaison partners of national standard setters and were in close contact with them on IASB projects; now all members have this responsibility.

In late 2002, the IASB met with the U.S. FASB and agreed to attempt to converge IFRS and U.S. GAAP in the short term as well as to coordinate their future projects under the Norwalk Agreement.[11] The joint efforts to analyze the respective standards and identify the best have already had some effect on standards. For example, the IASB has incorporated U.S. GAAP rules into some of the international standards, such as accounting for assets held for sale and discontinued operations. The IASB also is working with other standard setters to change the rules on contingent assets, restructurings, government grants, deferred taxes, and a number of other projects. It is working with the FASB on a "revenue recognition" project, with the expectation that new standards issued by each body will be similar, if not identical. The first example is the draft statement referred to in the Appendix to Chapter 9. The FASB, on the other hand, is about to revise rules concerning changes in accounting policies, exchange of assets, cost of inventories, and earnings per share to the comparable IFRS.

As we noted in the previous chapter, IASB and the FASB have achieved convergence so far only with respect to minor issues. Currently, over 100 differences between IFRS and FASB Standards remain.[12] It is arguable as to which standard is the "better" one to which to converge.

In contrast to the observed convergence on minor items, the IASB recently issued standards that create new and much more significant differences between IFRS and U.S. GAAP as of 2005 (we discuss major differences in Chapter 9 and its Appendix). Examples are rules for accounting for financial instruments (the IASB added a relatively broad option for designating financial instruments as to be valued at fair value), inventory (the IASB eliminated LIFO), extraordinary items (the IASB eliminated this category), and minority interests (the IASB now considers them as equity). The agenda of IASB also includes a controversial standard on pensions. There have also been a few instances in which the predecessor IASC began work on a joint project with a national standard setter only to end up with standards that differ even in their basic concept. For example, in the mid-1990s the IASC worked with the FASB on new standards on segment reporting. Eventually they ended up with different standards: the IASC followed the risks and rewards approach to business segmentation, while the FASB adopted the management approach. However, the IASB recently indicated that it would adopt the U.S. approach.

Given the efforts put into harmonization, especially by the EU, and into convergence, and the experience gained from many countries, we find it hard to believe that a single set of global standards can eventually evolve and more importantly be sustained in the face of often substantially different national accounting regimes. The potential solutions to specific accounting problems are too different, as are the economic effects that result from applying accounting standards to countries that differ with respect to their fundamental economies. While the desires for convergence of market regulators and preparers and users of the financial reports of international companies appear to be similar worldwide, their relative powers differ widely, as does the political pressure on the national standard setters in the countries who themselves must agree on each worldwide standard.

Sheer political considerations suggest that the same domestic political interests that were successful in the past in influencing the direction taken by a national standard setter would resist any shift of decision-making to an international body that could not be as easily swayed by the local interests of some national constituencies. There have been instances of heavy lobbying of the IASC and now of the IASB, with mixed success. The IASC had been careful in dealing with the accounting standard for employee stock options in the wake of the highly visible political reactions the FASB triggered in the early 1990s when it attempted to require expensing the fair value of employee stock options. Facing heavy opposition and even U.S. Senate involvement, the FASB backed down and allowed but did not require expensing, although details about the options granted and the amount not expensed had to be disclosed in notes to the financial statement. When the IASB commenced its deliberations on an options standard, the chairman of the Committee on Financial Services of the U.S. House of Representatives, Michael Oxley (co-sponsor of the Sarbanes-Oxley Act of 2002), wrote to the IASC Foundation saying that the development of a standard that required expensing would undermine the acceptability of the IFRS. To its credit, the IASB did not give in and eventually adopted a standard in 2004 that requires expensing employee stock options, together with other share-based payments. The FASB recently followed with a similar standard.

In another instance lobbying turned out to be successful. After 1.5 years of public deliberation, the IASB adopted a revision of IAS 39, its financial instruments standard. The revised standard included a fair value option that permits companies to designate upon initial recognition any financial asset or liability "at fair value through profit or loss," which requires revaluation to fair value at each balance-sheet date with the increase or decrease reported in current-period income. The IASB justified providing such a broad individual option by claiming simplification—namely, that the option would avoid separate accounting for embedded derivatives while allowing hedge accounting for a hedge with a non-derivative hedging instrument. The IASB could have provided exemptions for such cases but chose to extend the fair value measurement option to all financial instruments.[13] Several European financial institutions and even the French president voiced their concerns about allowing an extensive fair value option for all financial instruments, culminating in intervention at the IASB by the European Central Bank—after the standard already had been issued.[14] The Central Bank's approach was backed by the European Commission, which indicated it would not endorse the IASB's standard if differences were not resolved (see Chapter 7). To the surprise of many observers, the IASB in February 2004 voted to reopen the revised IAS 39 issued in December 2003 to significantly limit the option to measure financial instruments at fair value and published an exposure draft in April 2004. The draft generally excluded loans, receivables, and liabilities from the fair value measurement option. However, even though the large majority of responses in the comment period were negative, the IASB issued the requisite amendment in June 2005, which the EU recently accepted. In short, the IASB caved to political pressure.

The experience with IAS 39 demonstrates that it is not just the FASB that can be swayed by interest group lobbying. To the contrary, it turns out that lobbying the IASB also can be successful, particularly if it comes from a powerful party such as the European Commission.[15] As we discuss in Chapter 7, there are additional instances where the EU lobbied the IASB, and this could be only the beginning.

There are two other lessons from the IAS 39 episode. First, the IASB did not enforce its own rules of due process when it reopened a standard it had adopted only 2 months before, after an unusually long official comment period. Second, the new proposal has all the ingredients of a typical rules-based standard; relative to the original principle of the fair value option, it now has three explicit exceptions from the rule, most of which require professional judgment.

These concerns, if they are repeated in the future with another standard, could undermine the IASB's reputation as a (or, *the*) global standard setter in the long run, especially as IASB standards themselves have no political authority backing them. Instead, IASB standards have only as much legitimacy in any country (or in the EU) as they are given by a national government, which could withdraw support for specific standards or for all of them. Indeed, the fact that some in the EU already believe the IASB to be strongly Anglo-Saxon and dominated by developed countries does not augur well for the future.[16] Nor does the fact that so far IFRS have been used only on a voluntary basis in commercially developed countries, and it has been shown that often IFRS had not been applied fully or always correctly. The fact is that international standards are still widely untested as national compulsory accounting standards.[17]

There are countries that have, or believe they have, financial accounting standards that are superior to any potential global standard. Many in the United States, the United Kingdom, and Australia, to mention a few, would claim that their standards are superior to the IFRS. Accepting the global standard would then decrease the quality of their financial reporting systems, a cost that they and others believe would outweigh the benefit of easier international comparability. For example, the SEC's refusal so far to accept IFRS without reconciliation may be a result of its concern that accepting IFRS for foreign listed companies would mislead and misinform investors in U.S. capital markets. Perhaps most importantly, the SEC believes that U.S. accounting standards would be weakened. The SEC also may fear a loss of power, particularly if U.S. investors prefer IFRS or at least do not avoid investments in corporations that use IFRS.

Nevertheless, debate continues about how important the differences really are between U.S. GAAP (and those of other countries) and IFRS, and whether the SEC is right in its claim that the international standards actually are weaker. The SEC noted that while some studies "have concluded that IASC standards are too broad and general to ensure that similar accounting methods are applied in similar circumstances or that results are consistently achieved," it was also the case that "IASC standards may be more rigorous than national standards of some countries and, in some circumstances, may be equally or more effective than U.S.

GAAP [citing differences in the accounting treatment of inventories]."[18] This latter acknowledgment seems prescient in the wake of the questions surrounding the adequacy of U.S. GAAP after the Enron affair, and specifically the allegedly lax treatment of off-balance-sheet entities under U.S. GAAP. Indeed, while the SEC appeared to become more sympathetic to accepting IFRS given all the convergence efforts undertaken,[19] the EU's requirement that IFRS must be endorsed by the EU before they must be used by EU countries may provide the SEC with a new excuse for not embracing IFRS.

It is not clear what would happen to national accounting standard-setting bodies if the IASB were to take over standard setting. Of course, the countries could pass the resources they now provide to their national standard setters over to the IASB, but they would thereby lose their influence and potentially expert accounting knowledge in their own countries. The national standard setters in the EU are very much aware that moving to IFRS calls into question their very existence. The IASB wants them to provide input into its projects, to be a mentor of IFRS in their countries, to monitor application of IFRS, and to deal with national peculiarities not captured by IFRS and deal with any national GAAP that remain. However, this list of tasks is not so exciting as to ensure sufficient funding for maintaining national standard setters. Hence, it should not come as a surprise to observe that they are reluctant to give up too much power to the IASB or another global standard setter.

But even if a global standard could be developed and globally accepted, there is skepticism about the sustainability of worldwide accounting standards in the long term. Any worldwide standard must be applied in many different countries with all their peculiarities, and with their different national enforcement bodies that are expected to ensure its uniform application. These differences are indicated in detail in our country chapters, including the EU chapter and in Chapter 9 on diversity. A need for ongoing interpretation occurs particularly in new and unanticipated situations. Which body or bodies would discharge this function? The situation worsens if the standards are translated into different languages and then applied.[20] The SEC already accepts IFRS when it overviews reconciliations. Clearly, if national accounting authorities remain in charge, for the purpose of making national interpretations of international accounting standards and for governing reporting by nonlisted companies, any initial set of standards would fragment, at least to some extent, along country lines. Different institutional environments, such as litigation proneness, may induce a demand for more and more detailed rules in one country than in another. Over time, the world could return to where it started, with different standards in different countries, although to be sure the intercountry differences could be smaller than they are now.

The IASB could reduce (although not prevent) fragmentation arising out of national differences, if it, and it alone, was responsible for all interpretations of the standards and their subsequent clarifications.[21]

However, this solution would mean that nations would have to surrender *permanently* a further part of their "financial sovereignty" to an international organization. In adopting IFRS, the EU was particularly aware of this problem, and with the Committee of European Securities Regulators (CESR) it has a body that should coordinate enforcement across European countries. But coordination outside the EU faces substantial difficulties. Ultimately, it is unavoidable that national courts will have to interpret IFRS in cases that involve accounting numbers.

Beyond politics, vesting one international body with the sole power to interpret and update financial reporting standards runs a major danger of chilling experimentation that can freeze standards in the wrong place. This outcome could be avoided if firms were permitted to choose whether to use U.S. GAAP or IFRS for listed companies, without reconciliation, an option we explore shortly.

Another threat to a global standard is if countries adopt that standard with qualifications. The EU and some other countries adopted IFRS outright, at least for listed European companies, although with an endorsement mechanism (see Chapter 7) designed to prevent undesirable developments by the IASB that would be incompatible with EU directives (including ensuring and maintaining EU sovereignty). What looked like just a formal mechanism required for legal reasons may turn out to be the basis for the development of European IFRS if certain IFRS were not endorsed and substituted by some other standards. This possibility may also arise with Australia's endorsement mechanism. Other countries attempt to converge their own standards with those of the IASB or publish exposure drafts of the IASB in their countries. This can easily lead to a "cherry picking" of standards (Japan provides an example with regard to some IFRS) and a situation where it is not clear at all how similar the applied standards are to the global base standard.

To be sure, a global accounting standard would be useful for companies that use the increasingly international capital markets. The IFRS, like U.S. GAAP and other standards, are strongly geared toward satisfying the information demands of investors in capital markets. They are not necessarily optimal for smaller or privately owned firms. As we discuss in the country chapters, the EU member states currently have accounting systems in place that are applicable for all limited liability companies, including listed companies. Introducing a global standard for listed companies creates a tension as it is not obvious how far it should extend to other limited liability companies. Some countries allow or require other companies to also use IFRS; others do not. Each option has its problems. They range from legal issues (if taxes or dividend distribution depends on financial reports) to comparability across companies located in the same country. Interestingly, the United States seems to live with such differences in financial reporting within the country for listed companies and unlisted firms not subject to the SEC's oversight. (However, any statement attested to by CPAs who are members of the American Institute of

Certified Public Accountants [AICPA] must conform to U.S. GAAP as determined by the FASB and the SEC.) Moving to a global standard may thus incur very different costs and benefits to countries. It remains to be seen if the IASB succeeds in developing standards acceptable for companies that are not in the domain of public interest, which includes most small and medium-sized companies.

THE ADVANTAGES OF COMPETITION AMONG STANDARDS

An alternative way of bringing greater harmony to reporting standards would rely on some degree of competition in standard setting. As we explain in Chapter 3, even within a single set of accounting standards, comparisons among companies are limited by several factors, including differences in amortization schedules, the effects on accounts of unadjusted changes in price level that affect companies differently, alternative organizations of accounts, and so forth. These differences probably are exacerbated by different sets of accounting standards. Therefore, why allow any competition at all?

One reason is that harmonization is a utopian goal that probably cannot be achieved for a lasting period, for reasons we have already laid out. A second reason is that there are problems with any monopoly standard setter—whether it be the FASB, the IASB, or any other similar body—in that it has no incentive to respond quickly to market forces or necessarily search for the highest-quality accounting standards, let alone keep its actions free from political influence. An international rule-making body, where consensus must be reached across standard setters from different countries, may be even slower in issuing new rules, especially as it would have to cope with a wide set of political regimes.

As in private markets, the solution to monopoly is competition.[22] Although there are differences between competition among standard setters and competition among private firms, there is also a key similarity. In both contexts the presence of more than one provider helps to keep all more responsive to the interests of users than is the case under monopoly. Although standard setters do not have to satisfy the test of profitability, the standards they set do have to be sufficiently widely adopted by companies to be taken seriously; otherwise they lose funding and political support. So, even though standard-setting organizations do not sell a product for a direct price or seek to maximize the wealth of their owners, they have a similar interest in satisfying users of their product (accounting standards). As in business competition, which benefits consumers, investors benefit from competition among product providers.

Competition in standards is fundamentally at odds with the notion that the benefits of total uniformity—which presumably makes it easier for investors to attempt to make "apples to apples" comparisons across firms and countries—are worth the cost. In our view, fear that comparability is significantly hampered with more than one set of accounting standards is overstated. As we have noted, even under a single set of standards, firms have discretion and must use judgment in reporting their results, which means that investors do not now have the ability to make full "apples to apples" comparisons. Furthermore, as we describe in Chapter 9, the financial community has found ways to deal with diversity, and as long as diversity is reduced to a few, qualitatively similar standards, the benefits of uniformity of a standard are overstated. Moreover, under a regime of competitive standards, private sector analysts would have strong commercial incentives to translate or reconcile reports prepared under different standards. The availability of a few sets of accounting standards is likely to reduce the potential fragmentation from monopoly standards, as countries may choose that set of standards that best meet their objectives and that would result in its wide application and enforcement.

Another problem with a global standard, to which we have already alluded, is that the single standard setter would become a major focus for political lobbying, perhaps even more so than that which already plagues national standard setters. Competition is the only system capable of offsetting political and commercial influences on standard setting. Under competition, standard setters would have to satisfy their clients (investors and reporting firms and their auditors) in order for their standards to have relevance in the marketplace. Where there is choice, firms can opt for that system of accounting standards least subject to political influences.

Just as innovations change the nature of business and markets, they also constantly raise new issues relating to disclosure. For example, the more extensive use of stock options has intensified interest in the issue of how to account for them. Similarly, the rising importance of intangible assets has generated a debate over how to report these assets in financial statements. One of the virtues of having different standard setters is that this allows for different approaches to answering these questions. In fact, to reap benefits from competition among standards, the standards that compete against each other must be significantly different in some respects. This view raises doubt about the convergence program the FASB and the IASB have been following. As we discuss in Chapter 2, the FASB's and the IASB's support of the asset/liability and the fair value approaches to financial accounting is not unanimously believed to be the best of all solutions. Why, then, should all companies have to follow it if this becomes the global standard? Why not allow companies to choose an alternative set of standards that emphasizes reliability?

We also envision that a certain set of accounting standards could perform well for certain industries but badly for other industries. For example, the *Neuer Markt* in Germany allowed listed companies to freely choose between IFRS and U.S. GAAP. Over the years, use of the two standards was almost equal, but there were industry preferences: film and media companies preferred IFRS, biotechnology companies favored U.S. GAAP, while software companies showed almost equal preferences.[23]

We are not aware of unanimously agreed-on measures of the quality of accounting standards, or of a particular solution to an accounting theme. There is empirical evidence that high-quality standards tend to reduce the cost of capital, but comparing two high-quality standards, such as IFRS and U.S. GAAP, typically yields inconclusive results.[24] This finding implies that investors are well served by different standards. Indeed, considering that no one standard is likely to be best for all companies, given that their operations and circumstances differ, it would be remarkable if one set of standards would fit them all best. For example, changes in the purchasing power of the monetary unit considerably affect some companies (e.g., those with relative high levels of long-lived assets) more than others. Changes in market conditions and technology similarly affect some companies differently. Hence, a standard that permits price-level adjustments or appraisal-based changes in asset valuations is likely to be more useful to investors in some but not all companies. As we discuss in Chapter 2, equity holders could benefit if companies could choose the standards that best communicate information to investors.

Furthermore, accountants, companies, and standard setters might develop new and preferable means for communicating financial information to investors, make improvements to existing procedures, or abstain from using procedures that communicate ineffectually or even dysfunctionally. In a monopoly standard-setting environment, these alternatives may not get a chance to be implemented and prove their efficiency, since a well-known characteristic of monopoly is slow adaptation to technical change. Empirical studies could then not get data to compare the proposed (nonexistent) financial reporting regime with incumbent standards. We believe that it is best to let the market determine which standard is the most cost-effective in general, or more likely for certain industries or even for individual companies.

An objection to competition is that the "market" for accounting standards is truly a natural monopoly. To the extent there are network benefits associated with one or perhaps two sets of accounting standards, multiple sets of standards may be inefficient. This can be especially true for smaller investors, who are not likely to have the expertise or the time to sift through differences in various standards. Therefore, even if one started off with multiple standards, as did computer operating systems and videocassette formats, the market might eventually settle for a single standard, although there is no guarantee that the standard so chosen by the market necessarily would be what academic researchers and scholars or the accounting authorities might choose.

We do not believe, however, that a single set of standards is the likely outcome of a market-choice process, for several reasons. First, history provides ample evidence of different developments existing simultaneously and changing over time. Second, as we discuss earlier, the accounting authorities in all or even most countries have experienced great difficulties in agreeing to and then accepting a single set of standards.

And third, there are examples of competition in regulation that have not resulted in a monopoly, even in cases where the competing standards contain very different requirements. For example, U.S. companies can choose the state in which to legally incorporate, independently of the place they conduct their business. It has turned out that about half of all public U.S. companies have chosen to incorporate in Delaware, which has relatively flexible corporate legal standards. Nevertheless, it is only half of the firms that choose to incorporate there.

Nor do we believe that a market among standards necessarily would lead to a "race to the bottom," also for several reasons. There will always be corporations that choose to comply with what the market deems to be the highest-quality standard. As we explain in Chapter 2, companies benefit their owners when they present to them and potential investors (including creditors) financial statements that meet their demands for creditable and useful information, because this reduces investors' cost of investing in those companies and thus reduces the companies' cost of capital. Indeed, in Germany large listed companies voluntarily adopted IFRS before the EU considered requiring IFRS for all listed companies. After the Enron affair in the United States, one of the leading U.S. companies announced plans to substantially enhance disclosures about the details of one of its more opaque businesses, GE Capital. How many other companies choose to follow suit will depend on the cost of capital differential the market demands for adherence to the different standards. And, again, Delaware provides useful insights. Its corporate legal standards are flexible—too flexible in the view of some, who believe that Delaware law provides too little protection to stockholders, thus validating what seems like a "race to the bottom." Yet, according to a recent study, incorporation in Delaware is associated statistically with higher firm value, controlling for other influences.[25] A major reason for this finding is that Delaware law facilitates takeover bids, which motivates corporate officers to maximize shareholder value rather than to act in their own personal interests.

Nonetheless, some fear that competing standard setters simply would copy rules from each other if there were pressure from some constituencies to provide a similar treatment or lose their support. This fear, even if valid, does not invalidate the case for competition, however.

A good example was provided in 2001, when the FASB changed its business combinations standards significantly by eliminating the pooling-of-interest method and adopting the impairment-only approach for goodwill under the purchase method. The draft standard had proposed amortization of goodwill similar to the then IFRS treatment over (generally) a maximum of 20 years. Industry, supported by some empirical studies that showed that the relevance of goodwill amortization was low or insignificant to investors as indicated by "value-relevance" studies that correlate stock-market values and accounting numbers, pushed for the impairment-only approach that eliminated systematic amortization of goodwill.

The result was that U.S. companies reported significantly better earnings per share numbers as of the year they applied the new standard. Companies that used IFRS complained that this gave a competitive advantage to U.S. firms in international capital markets and suggested the IASB would have to level the playing field, which it did in 2004. In any case, the result of such a convergence is not a disadvantage of competition among standards, because it would probably be obtained from a monopoly standard setter, too. Indeed, some observers might argue that competition between the two standard setters resulted in adoption of the best alternative procedure.

COMPETITIVE STANDARDS: THE ALTERNATIVES

There are at least three levels on which competition in standards might take place: among countries, among stock exchanges, and among individual companies.

The *among-countries model* includes competition between countries or groups of countries. It is close to our current situation. The evolution of accounting standards has always been very nation-oriented; it is only recently that countries have allowed or required the use of standards that come from outside their country. At the other end of the competition spectrum, all countries opt for the same standard; in effect, this would be the global standards scenario we discuss above. If groups of countries, such as the EU, decide to adopt a single standard, the result falls between the extreme cases, as do the benefits and the costs of doing so.

A more ambitious approach is competition on the stock exchange level, which we call the *exchange-competition model*. Competition among exchanges, each with different listing requirements, would bring about competition in disclosure systems, including accounting standards. For stock exchanges, the required financial reporting standards permitted or required by their listing requirements can be a key criterion for differentiation in ever-increasing globalizing capital markets. Indeed, stock exchange competition already is well under way. The LSE recently established a market segment for Dutch companies, in direct competition with Euronext (the combination of the Paris, Brussels, and Amsterdam stock exchanges) for these firms, while both a Swiss and a Swedish stock exchange have subsidiaries in London. Exchanges in some European countries, such as Germany, required IFRS or U.S. GAAP rather than national GAAP for a listing in premium market segments years before the EU's move to IFRS.

There is a commonsense rationale for an exchange-competition model. If all exchanges had the same listing requirements, it would be difficult for any to gain a competitive advantage over other exchanges. After all, it is the stock exchanges that are (and, in the United States before creation of the SEC, were) keen monitors of enforcement of standards, and they can build up expertise in those standards. The exchange-competition model coincides with the among-countries model if there is only one stock exchange in a country. Sometimes there is more than one stock exchange in a country, and then the exchange-competition model would require countries to accept the possibly different accounting standards that the different stock exchanges might require.

Companies can and do decide on which stock exchange they want to list their shares or debt instruments. Stock exchanges with the most attractive reporting standards, measured by their impact on the cost of capital, should be able to attract sufficient clientele.[26] Of course, listing requirements include many more rules than accounting standards, so exchanges actually compete on many dimensions other than accounting standards. For example, to the extent exchanges have different corporate governance rules they compete on that particular dimension as well.

Accordingly, under one variation of the competition model, corporations are allowed to list their shares on multiple exchanges, which may not be as burdensome as it once was—after all, as we have noted, the number of firms whose shares are cross-listed has been rising over time. Of course, multiple listing entails some additional cost. In contrast, if firms listed on a single exchange are allowed to choose among reporting standards (as we next describe), they need not pay the additional expense associated with listing on another exchange simply to take advantage of its different disclosure system.

Exchange competition can work only if investors in participating countries are permitted to access foreign stocks directly within their home-country borders (e.g., through computer screens based there) rather than having to engage a foreign broker to execute trades abroad. A U.S. Council on Foreign Relations study recommends this option not just for reporting standards but also for the entire system of disclosure and corporate governance rules.[27] In particular, the study suggests a system of mutual recognition under which host countries, such as the United States, would allow exchanges from other countries with acceptable disclosure regimes to impose their own rules on corporations whose shares are initially listed on those exchanges, but that are also traded on exchanges in the host country, as long as those countries afford U.S. exchanges reciprocal rights.

The *firm-choice model* is the most ambitious approach to setting standards competitively. Under this model, individual companies would be allowed to select among a given set of competing financial accounting standards. Companies could choose to report under the standard that they believe does the best job of lowering their (net) cost of capital and which best fits the individual and environmental setting in which they operate. Governments, stock exchanges, or enforcement bodies would have to be involved in ensuring that firms select the standards that they deem of sufficiently high quality. However, there would be a global understanding of what standards are eligible.

Of course, the firm-choice model would sacrifice some degree of comparability relative to global or monopoly standard setting. At the same time, however, the amount of that sacrifice is least among all the standards competition models. It is likely that firms would have an interest in selecting the standard with the best cost/benefit tradeoff. Firms that are economically similar are likely to choose similar, if not identical, standards. In practice, this probably would lead to common standards by industry.[28] This result is especially likely for newly public firms, which have a strong incentive to compare their operations with firms already in their industry, thereby reducing potential investors' costs of evaluating the new entrants' operations.

In short, under the firm-competition model, investors would be comparing firms with their self-selected peer groups, without concern with where they are located or on which exchange they are listed. Such a model is in line with recent forms of a "management approach" in financial reporting, which tends to prefer more detailed firm- or industry-specific information relative to cross-industry comparability.

Although we would prefer to allow individual companies to choose among accounting standards, we expect that this alternative is not politically feasible. The accounting regulatory authorities and elected officials are unlikely to allow firms to do as they please—a seemingly anarchic result—notwithstanding the lack of empirical evidence to support their belief that investors have been better served by financial accounting since standard setting became a government-directed and -enforced enterprise. In particular, accounting scandals in the United States have been just as frequent, if not more so, since the SEC was created and standard setting was expanded under the FASB. When such scandals have occurred, the financial press and legislators (including those who profess to believe, almost religiously, in freely competitive markets) typically have called for more regulation, and at least thus far have shown little interest in a competition-based alternative to setting accounting standards.

On balance, therefore, we believe that "constrained competition" within a small set of high-quality standards offers the most feasible and flexible setting to cope with increasingly global capital markets. This option would achieve some of the benefits of both competition and standardization. In addition, it promises the most harmonization without losing most of the benefits from competition. Under this approach, companies would be allowed to choose among two or possibly more financial accounting standards that are widely recognized to be of high quality by investors in international capital markets. IFRS and U.S. GAAP are natural candidates that currently compete in some areas already. The "constrained competition" option would not preclude some convergence of the eligible standards, a course on which international standard setters are now intent. However, the importance of such efforts would be much reduced if the constrained competition model were in force.

However, allowing multinational companies to choose among these international standards will not achieve all the rich set of objectives for accounting reports in the variety of national contexts indicated in Chapter 9 and the first section of this chapter. Thus, other accounting standards may be desirable for tax purposes, for the reporting of smaller listed companies, and for nonlisted companies. In many countries, this already is the situation, but allowing companies to choose among international standards will increase the number of different standards. There may be a need for domestic firms to account in a way that reflects national legal characteristics, especially in countries where entity accounting reports are regarded as highly valuable. In countries that require the same accounting principles for all limited liability companies, there will be a need to ensure that global standards encompass their national accounting requirements.

Several countries are experimenting with a number of approaches to these problems. In the United Kingdom, firms will be able to choose to use IFRS or national standards, whereas in Germany firms must still use national GAAP for individual accounts. In Japan listed companies have to provide accounting reports under the Securities and Exchange Act, and all limited liability companies must provide somewhat different accounting reports under the Commercial Code. Thus, we expect that even if the choice of global standards is restricted, as we suggest, many countries will still entertain more than one set of standards for financial reporting in order to reflect national requirements and characteristics.

One obvious concern is that global and national standards do not deviate from each other too much (i.e., do not fragment too much). But fragmentation may suit the needs of the government and citizens of a particular country, and experience shows that it is difficult for government to agree to adopt a single standard for all companies. However, companies that seek foreign investors would benefit from adopting an internationally recognized standard. Therefore, we conclude that this choice should be available to them, without requiring that all companies conform to that standard or standards.

AUDITING OF FINANCIAL REPORTING STANDARDS

The information provided to investors in financial statements, whether in hard copy or via the Internet, is only as useful as the numbers reported are trustworthy. Investors can analyze the numbers, compare them with those reported by other companies, examine them for trends and relationships, and if Extensible Business Reporting Language (XBRL) is available, reformat and restructure them. Analyses of this type often can reveal shortcomings and misleading aspects of the numbers. However, only a well-done audit by an independent public accountant (IPA) can reveal and often prevent fraud and misapplication of accounting standards. Hence, effective auditing procedures are a vital input to accounting standards, and enforcement of the correct application of auditing standards is necessary for the enforcement of accounting standards.

Many, if not most, of the accounting scandals that have rocked the accounting profession, both recently and in the past, appear to be due to audit failures that resulted from poor or incompetent audits rather than failure to follow either GAAS or GAAP.[29] Although an audit that fails to uncover a massive fraud necessarily yields misleading financial statements, an inadequate audit often is at fault rather than deliberate violation of GAAP (as distinct from using adherence to the letter of GAAP to produce statements that violate the intent of GAAP). Hence, the extent to which auditing procedures have been inadequate and/or the failure of IPAs to apply existing auditing standards should be examined.

One important auditing shortcoming appears to have been the increased reliance of IPAs on analytical auditing rather than on examination of individual accounting items, at least in the United States and many European countries. Analytical auditing involves calculating and evaluating relationships among accounts to determine if some are "out of whack"—possibly in error. Analytical auditing is a valuable tool. Indeed, U.S. GAAS (Statement on Auditing Standard, SAS, 56) requires the use of analytical procedures in planning the nature, timing, and extent of audit procedures and in conducting an overall review of financial information. But while analytical procedures are helpful for substantive testing, there has been a tendency within the auditing profession to make these procedures a *substitute* for the much more costly detailed examination of transactions and accounts. Furthermore, the firm's accountants can readily subvert analytical tests by arranging or falsifying the accounts to produce ratios that look satisfactory. This type of fraud is more likely to be successful when the CFO or chief accountant of a company was an auditor with the IPA firm that audits the company's accounts, as is often the situation. They know what the auditors look for and how they work, and thus are well equipped to fool them.

Statistical auditing is only *suggested* by current auditing standards, possibly for three reasons. One is that this form of verification tends to be more costly than judgmental samples, which are often smaller and easier to acquire. Second, auditors fear that a plaintiff's lawyer could argue that, in accepting a reasonable error rate of, say, 10 percent, the auditor deliberately allowed the client to get away with what may be viewed as a large fraud in money, if not proportional, terms. Third, many IPAs are ignorant or insufficiently aware of the advantages and method of statistical sampling. Although their audit manual and auditing standards describe statistical sampling and the procedure has been successfully used for over a half-century, there is reason to believe that it is not often used.[30]

Section 404 of the Sarbanes-Oxley Act calls for a specific assessment by management of listed corporations' internal control over financial reporting. This requirement is being interpreted as requiring a specific extensive, well-documented evaluation and written assessment by management to be submitted to the external auditors. Although management's hiring another audit firm to prepare the report is not required, many find this necessary.[31] Because the report covers a corporation's consolidated statements, it includes an assessment of financial reporting by foreign subsidiaries and the auditors of those subsidiaries. The primary audit firm then reports its assessment of management's report first to the company's audit committee and then (to the extent its assessment is modified) in its attestation of the corporation's annual report. The cost of this additional activity is believed to be substantial.[32] To our knowledge, however, no study exists documenting that inadequacies in internal control systems have been a cause of, or even played a minor role in, recent or past audit or reporting failures. Nor is there any evidence or analysis of which we are aware that a second audit is cost-effective. Hence, we question the benefit to investors of this additional "404" audit procedure.

We discuss in Chapter 3 that auditing standards can be efficiently set by auditor organizations themselves. This is what happens in most countries. GAAS have been less controversial than GAAP because they are mostly oriented toward procedures governing effective auditing work and as such have no directly observable effect on the amount of financial information in capital markets. They also tend to be technical with respect to accounting procedures, which the public and politicians seem to believe are best left to professional accountants. Hence, there is much less politics involved in agreeing on auditing standards. Nevertheless, auditing standards in most developed countries are different mainly because of their historical development and the occurrence of specific events. For example, the United States requires the physical examination of inventories and confirmation of accounts receivable (although the use of negative confirmations, wherein the receivables firms are asked only to notify the auditors if the account balances sent to them are incorrect, is of little probative value).[33] Other countries do not.

The major global player for convergence of auditing standards is the International Federation of Accountants (IFAC). A subcommittee that is now called the International Auditing and Assurance Standards Board (IAASB)[34] develops International Standards on Auditing (ISA). Its objectives are to develop high-quality auditing, assurance, and quality-control standards and to facilitate convergence of national standards. These goals are similar to the IASB's objectives for financial accounting standards. Indeed, the IAASB reports in its Annual Report 2003 that 70 countries have either adopted ISA or noted that there are no significant differences between them and their national standards. We report in Chapter 7 that the EU is considering adopting ISA for their statutory audits, but that no major consequent changes in auditing practice are expected to occur in most EU countries. In the United States, enactment of the Sarbanes-Oxley Act has vested in a new agency, the Public Company Accounting Oversight Board (PCAOB), the responsibility and authority to oversee the operations of IPAs who audit publicly traded corporations. The agency, therefore, may become actively involved in setting and enforcing auditing standards. Although the SEC, to which the PCAOB reports, has had this authority, previously it largely delegated it to the American Institute of Certified Public Accountants (AICPA), as we describe in Chapter 4.

The developments in the United States have given impetus to the IAASB to improve its own standards. In particular, the IFAC [2003, p. 39] reported that the IAASB is in the process of several upgrades, including a requirement that auditors perform specified procedures to identify the existence of fraud, even when the company does not appear to have a high risk of fraud. We join with the IFAC in recommending the upgrade, but we see a demand rather for uniform minimum auditing standards, not necessarily the global GAAS that the IAASB is aiming to provide. Just as we are skeptical about the desirability or permanence of a single set of accounting standards, we similarly believe it is unlikely that all countries will agree on a single complete set of global auditing standards. Agreement on *minimum* auditing standards is more feasible. Such standards would lower the burden for globally acting companies and make it less costly to guarantee the same level of audit quality of domestic and foreign operations. Due to their focus on auditing processes, GAAS are upwardly compatible in that more stringent standards add to the body of standards that are applied but do not usually contradict them. This is in contrast to financial accounting standards that result in different numbers when more or less demanding standards are applied.

We support the development of different-quality GAAS, which is in line with our arguments for constrained competition in GAAP. We envision the existence of a small set of differently stringent GAAS, but all satisfying the same minimum requirements. Higher-quality GAAS lead to more expensive audits but to more trustworthy financial statements, and there should be a differentiation between firms for whom the benefits outweigh the costs, as well as others for which this is not the case.

There are different levels of choice or competition among GAAS. One is that countries can require more or less stringent standards. For example, the United States, with its penchant for regulation, might very well add to the list, much as Sarbanes-Oxley has added a costly and, relative to potential benefits, probably unneeded attestation of internal controls. Second, stock exchanges can require more stringent standards to differentiate themselves from other exchanges. And third, companies can self-select their audit quality level, which is the model we favor, since it offers the most efficient cost/benefit tradeoff for companies. Audit firms could either offer all levels of service or differentiate and specialize to a certain level.

AUDITOR OVERSIGHT

The reliability of accounting reports depends to a significant degree on effective audits. We urge the accounting authorities in various countries to examine the reasons for past audit failures and revise their auditing standards accordingly. Although we argue in Chapter 3 that these standards are best set by private organizations of IPAs, recent experience has indicated that some badly done audits may cause investors to lose confidence in the trustworthiness of audited financial statements generally. Of equal, if not greater, importance is that fact that governments tend to step in after highly visible audit failures with legislation that often is much more costly than beneficial (e.g., Section 404 of the Sarbanes-Oxley Act). Hence, it is very desirable for audit firms jointly to establish and monitor compliance with effective auditing procedures. However, associations of audit firms have neither the inclination nor the power to discipline incompetent and dishonest auditors. Consequently, we prefer to have government take responsibility to enforce this important aspect of auditor oversight.

In the area of audit and audit regulation the U.S. model dominates, at least post-Enron, but with some differences between countries and with some anticipation of extant U.S. requirements. The U.S. PCAOB should have much more bite than its predecessor, the Public Oversight Board (POB, a self-regulatory body). In the United Kingdom, the Financial Reporting Council (FRC) hosts the Professional Oversight Board, the Audit Practices Board, and the Investigation and Discipline Board. All our other countries now have similar oversight arrangements. Moreover, the EU has proposed that all its members should make a public oversight arrangement for their audit systems.

In Japan and the United States, regulators review auditors and audits. Both Germany and the United Kingdom in the past used a peer-review system for both of these functions. Both countries have revised their approach, however, to satisfy the U.S. PCAOB's worldwide inspection requirements concerning firms that audit U.S.-listed companies. Under the PCAOB's rules, national audit regulatory systems must be of equivalent quality to those of the United States. In mid-2004, the PCAOB agreed to accept national audit systems that fully satisfied this requirement in lieu of detailed direct regulation and inspection. This amounts to a "passport system" but also illustrates the reach and importance of U.S. requirements in particular.

The Sarbanes-Oxley Act has attempted to limit auditors' potential conflicts of interest by prohibiting them from performing a large amount of specified nonaudit services for their audit clients. As we describe in Chapter 4, this prohibition is not grounded in evidence that the now-prohibited practices resulted in or contributed to audit failures. To the contrary, there is some suggestion that having the same audit firm providing nonaudit services both enhanced the effectiveness of the audit and resulted in lower costs to shareholders.[35]

The Sarbanes-Oxley Act also requires audit firms to rotate their auditors in charge of audits of specific clients at least every 5 years. This might keep individual auditors from becoming too close to their clients, which carries the risk of losing the skepticism necessary for an effective audit. Corporations, though, are not required to change audit firms periodically. There are only few countries worldwide, such as Italy, that require such an external rotation (which did not prevent accounting scandals such as that of Parmalat).[36] A 2004 proposal for an EU audit directive includes an option for member states to require internal or external rotation, which is already required in our countries.

Another option for enhancing the enforcement of disclosure standards across national boundaries is to harness the expertise of existing professional accounting and/or auditing organizations. Until the Enron failure, this looked like a more politically and substantively desirable option than it now appears. In January 2001, approximately 30 member firms belonging to the International Federation of Accountants (IFAC), an international professional organization of accountants, launched a major self-regulatory initiative on a global level that, at the time, appeared to offer some promise and may still do so in the long run with sufficient mechanisms to ensure independence. The participating members of this "Forum of Firms" envisioned a new process for ensuring the quality of audits of transnational companies (essentially all those listed on more than one exchange) that would be open to other auditing firms of all sizes that have or are interested in having multinational auditing assignments and agree to be bound by the policies and procedures of the Forum. In addition, to ensure compliance, the IFAC created a Transnational Auditors Committee (TAC) to act as the executive arm of the Forum and to oversee a set of regular reviews of each firm's auditing methods and procedures, as well as individual audit engagements.

In the aftermath of the Sarbanes-Oxley Act and the creation of the PCAOB, however, the prospects for this self-regulatory initiative have evaporated, at least for now. But we urge that it remain an option for the future, especially if the new highly regulated audit regime falls short of expectations.

ENFORCEMENT OF FINANCIAL REPORTING STANDARDS

There are two basic approaches for improving the reliability of the financial disclosure system: improvements in monitoring those charged with producing and verifying the information, and changes in the incentives of those responsible for producing the numbers and for their verification. These approaches are not mutually inconsistent and ideally should reinforce each other.

Monitoring essentially builds on improving the functioning of audit committees within firms[37] and on other corporate governance methods, including the use of external "independent" directors, and on public oversight of the auditing profession.

Harnessing incentives for all groups involved in the financial disclosure system is just as important as monitoring, if not more so, because it may be less expensive and more effective. Management's incentives to "cook the books" would be reduced, for example, if firms did not grant excessive stock-option plans to their executives. The new stock option expensing rules of the IASB and FASB should help in this regard. In addition, the Sarbanes-Oxley Act requires CEOs and CFOs of corporations subject to SEC regulations (generally those with publicly traded securities, whether domestic or foreign) to repay any earnings-based bonuses if the company has to restate its earnings. Unless this feature of the Act is changed, it appears that corporate executives who are citizens and residents of other countries might have to make payments to the United States. If enforced, this might lead to some interesting reciprocal legislation.

The Sarbanes-Oxley Act also ameliorates conflicts of interest between management and auditors (to the extent that they exist) by vesting the power to hire, fire, and monitor the auditors in the board of directors' audit committee, supplemented with a requirement that all members of audit committees be independent. A number of other countries have made similar arrangements. Alternatively, this conflict might be dealt with by having the auditors engaged and responsible to an agency outside the firm, such as the stock exchange or another enforcement body. We do not recommend this alternative, though, because it would be costly and perhaps impossible to administer. For example, who would determine the extent and depth of an audit and the amount of audit fees? Would there be competition among audit firms? If so, who would determine which firm would be awarded a contract for specific companies? How could potential collusion be prevented between audit firms and the employees of the stock market or government agencies who employed them?

Litigation also can be a strong force in corporate governance, as demonstrated by the experience in the United States. However, litigation against accountants, in particular, simply because a company's stock price has dropped significantly, may not be as effective as a deterrent to auditing and reporting abuses as some of its advocates claim. Accounting firms often have substantial incentives, in terms of both their reputation and their financial standing, to settle cases rather than incur the costs of trial, whether or not the firms have done anything wrong. The frequency of out-of-court settlements means that little information about the reasons for audit failures or the need for changes in accounting principles emerges from the litigation process. In the other countries we cover in this book, litigation may still be very costly and uncertain of success.

Whether or not litigation is an effective goad for improving corporate governance, transparency at least can make capital-market participants aware of poor corporate governance practices and possibly prevent or reduce conflicts of interest that put shareholders at a disadvantage. Among the items worthy of disclosure are full details of the compensation arrangements for individual managers, nonaudit fees, and the nature and degree of investment analysts' involvement in the companies they monitor.

The prospect of public disclosure of such information may constrain bad behavior or make a takeover and displacement of poorly performing managers more likely.

No major international pressure has arisen as yet in favor of one particular form of corporate governance, although the Organisation for Economic Co-Operation and Development (OECD) has set out basic principles,[38] which in reality are more like minimum requirements than a comprehensive set of corporate governance standards. This is not surprising, given the difference in corporate governance approaches we have identified just among the countries surveyed in this book: the shareholder orientation in the United States and the United Kingdom, and broader stakeholder perspective in Germany and Japan.[39]

The EU attempted to overcome national corporate governance requirements by establishing a separate legal form for public limited liability companies doing cross-border businesses in the EU, the Societas Europaea. Firms undertaking cross-border business can choose their corporate governance structure from among those available in several European countries and are not bound to those of the country in which they are located. This move has been only partly successful, however, because although it gives some leeway to companies (e.g., with respect to the board structure), national peculiarities prevail.

UPGRADING OF OVERSIGHT AND ENFORCEMENT

However accounting standards are set—by a single global organization, or through some form of competition—the information reported under them still will not be equally, or even roughly, comparable across or within countries without equally effective systems of enforcing those standards. Our view of enforcement approaches in the different countries suggests that enforcement generally has been sparing and often implemented in a cumbersome way, and then only when major crises have occurred. For example, the collapse of Enron and other major companies in the United States demonstrated that the combination of market forces and a supposedly strong enforcement regime were not sufficient to prevent those financial and reporting failures. Yet the response to this state of affairs was an even more intense effort at regulatory oversight, not just in the United States but in other countries we survey here.[40]

Therefore, the key issue with enforcement is upgrading rather than convergence. To the extent that market forces that drive companies to publish trustworthy financial reports, monitoring by boards of directors (corporate governance), and the self-interest of audit firms are insufficient, government monitoring and intervention may be necessary. All our countries have significantly upgraded their government-agency enforcement systems and now have similar complex methods of enforcement for financial markets and to a lesser degree for accounting standards and auditing.

The responses differ, though. The United States has relied more on government and the United Kingdom on privately organized agencies, and Japan and Germany have turned to some combination of the two. Generally, effective enforcement requires an ability to obtain tips and follow up on them and a healthy dose of proactive inspection. Until recently, the SEC in the United States, supposedly the most aggressive enforcement body in the countries surveyed here, had failed on both counts. The Commission only sporadically examined financial statements, and only then if a company failed, was sued, or was alleged to have engaged in some kind of wrongdoing. Even then, the SEC staff criticized few financial statements; most restatements were generated by companies or their auditors. With the SEC allowed to keep more of the fees it collects following the enactment of the Sarbanes-Oxley Act of 2002, it is widely believed, or at least expected, that the agency will become a more aggressive enforcer.

In more litigious environments, in particular the United States, it is common that the enforcement agency is willing to settle on an agreed penalty without an admission of guilt by the company. While this obviously reduces the threat of being sued by the plaintiffs' attorneys, it also reduces the ability to learn from past cases and means that precedents for the future are not available. Without considerably more comprehensive inspection and wider and successful enforcement, much of the recent revolution in all countries in the organization and control of the accounting and auditing profession will degenerate into box-ticking and "wither on the vine."

Both as a supplement and an alternative to government enforcement, the costs of misconduct to individuals can be increased. Officers and directors of corporations could be charged with legal fiduciary duties to govern firms in the shareholders' interest.[41] Regulatory bodies, including self-regulatory bodies and prosecutors who have authority to assess penalties (incarceration in egregious cases), can go after auditors, directors, and managers for failure to adhere to prevailing standards. In particular, we believe that enforcement officials should be able to work with a rebuttable assumption that the IPAs who were in charge of audits of listed companies that materially misstated their financial statements are, at the very least, guilty of professional incompetence. Unless these accountants can demonstrate that their failure to detect and correct the misstatements was reasonable (i.e., the frauds and errors were such that any well-regarded senior auditor would not have caught and dealt with them), these auditors and perhaps their firms should be barred from auditing listed companies. In extreme cases, legal action for fraud also might be taken against the auditors.

Although, as we discuss in Chapter 3, there is reason to expect audit firms to monitor and prevent their auditors from allowing clients to present materially misleading financial statements, recent U.S. experience indicates that this expectation has not always been observed. As we describe in Chapter 4, the auditors in charge of audits of very important clients have incentives to do whatever is necessary not to lose the client, and U.S. audit firms, at least, have strong incentives not to discipline these auditors after they have come under fire. Hence, there is a strong case for enabling accounting enforcement bodies to impose severe, perhaps draconian, costs on individual IPAs who are deficient in their professional responsibilities. This requires a major change from past practice, where there has been a strong disinclination to pursue accountants and to impose severe penalties.

Meanwhile, the threat of private lawsuits remains—against companies and their directors and officers as well as against those who audit and attest to financial information. This threat makes it even more important for the authorities to make it clear that they will take strong actions against individual auditors. Otherwise, the firms to which they belong are likely to protect individual partners or employees in order to avoid firm liability when these persons' misdeeds are exposed.

Effective enforcement depends not only on the penalties for failing to adhere to standards, but on the financial accounting standards themselves. As we discuss in Chapter 2, standards that are based on reliable measures, such as historical cost, are much easier to enforce effectively than standards that emphasize measurement that may be deemed more relevant but less reliable, such as fair values when there are no market values.

HARMONIZATION OF ENFORCEMENT

Gaining international agreement on measures for enforcing accounting and auditing standards is likely to be difficult because nations maintain sovereignty over financial regulation and accounting regulation and use different combinations of enforcement measures. The legal institutional setting in countries is much more important for enforcement than for the establishment of accounting standards, as eventually it is the power of the state that is needed to impose sanctions and fines on individual persons living and companies located in its territory. Currently, it is almost impossible for one state to enforce sanctions against citizens of another country. Although the Sarbanes-Oxley Act implies that non-U.S. residents may be subject to its penalties, for example with regard to repaying bonuses following restatements, we do not expect that the United States actually will be able to punish nonresident professionals.

Nevertheless, there are ongoing attempts toward convergence of certain enforcement methods, prodded by the Sarbanes-Oxley Act. Although other countries may not agree that the Sarbanes-Oxley reforms are necessarily the right ones, the importance of U.S. capital markets makes compliance with U.S. rules important. For example, foreign companies with shares listed in the United States must implement the internal control systems required by the Sarbanes-Oxley Act, and their CEOs and CFOs must take an oath on the truthfulness of the reported financial statements. Their (foreign) auditors must register with the PCAOB. As we discuss in Chapter 7, the EU objects to many of these measures but has acceded and has begun to build up similar enforcement institutions that the United States would accept on a mutual recognition basis.

Because the post-Sarbanes-Oxley reforms have been in place for a short time, it is too early to tell how much convergence toward common enforcement measures actually will take place. Nonetheless, it is useful to consider several possible ways this result may be brought about. When the preoccupation in the United States and elsewhere with the flaws in enforcement exposed by Enron and the accounting problems of other well-known corporations eventually fades, attention may finally turn to some of the ideas we now describe.

One obvious approach is for other countries simply to "follow the leader"—in this case, the United States. A second approach is the one adopted by the EU, which seeks the coordination of national enforcement among EU countries through a common set of enforcement principles and minimum requirements. These principles are issued by the CESR, which we describe in Chapter 7, and are inspired to a significant degree by the U.S. enforcement system. What the EU has not yet taken up is harmonization of sanctions dealing with wrongdoing across countries. If developed and implemented, common sanctions within the EU, if adopted elsewhere, could contribute to an effective global enforcement system using national enforcers.

The global equivalent of the CESR is the IOSCO. IOSCO has been involved in harmonizing accounting standards and admission rules of stock exchanges. As a minimum, IOSCO could be a means for improving the coordination of national investigations of audits involving multinational enterprises. More ambitious would be to have IOSCO investigate audit failures involving multinational firms, while leaving penalties to be determined and enforced at the national level. More ambitious yet, IOSCO could be given the authority both to investigate and to impose sanctions for violations of auditing standards, much as the PCAOB in the United States is authorized to do.

The main complication associated with any international effort, except perhaps one that relies only on enhanced cooperation, is that national governments are likely to be very reluctant to cede much authority to a supranational body. The experience of the EU is indicative of such difficulties; even though the member states have many legal principles in common, it has not been possible to forge a European enforcement agency. There is similar experience with the Basel Committee, which for the last decade has set minimum bank capital standards. It is the most intensive cooperative effort to date among national financial supervisors, which provides a caution to those who would rush to embrace an official multinational regulatory response as the solution to variations in enforcement effectiveness across countries. Although central banks have used the Basel Committee to coordinate their regulatory activities, they have *not* ceded their authority to discipline weakly capitalized or insolvent banks to the Committee.

A different approach, in a global markets context, is to delegate the authority for enforcing disclosure standards for publicly held companies to the equities exchanges themselves. After all, the exchanges are the locus of activity where the listing and trading of equities take place, so why shouldn't they govern the conditions under which listing takes place? As it is, some exchanges already monitor the quality of information disclosed in prospectuses and the prevalence of insider trading. The task this option would impose on the exchanges is to actually enforce whatever reporting and auditing standards are in place, as well as other corporate governance measures relating to disclosure that they may prescribe (over and above those that may be required by regulatory agencies). To the extent that high-quality disclosure is viewed as an asset of the exchange, competition among different exchanges along the dimension of disclosure enforcement that could help in interesting investors and firms in doing business on the exchange could provide a powerful market-driven incentive for improving disclosure. Governments could help ensure that outcome by holding exchanges liable for the disclosure of any failings of the companies that list with them.

The exchanges would have the authority to impose penalties for the failure of firms and their auditors to adhere to the relevant standards. In the case of failure by listed companies, the penalties could range from fines imposed on their officers, directors, and the companies themselves, to delisting of the companies for either serious violations or a pattern of lesser violations. Although the exchanges would have no direct authority over auditors if they did not also select them, they could exert their influence indirectly by disciplining listed firms for continuing to use the services of auditors found by others to have breached their professional duties.

The exchanges are not likely to adopt this approach, however, for several reasons. First, many would shy away from imposing fines on individuals and companies, in particular if they are foreign firms. Some or even most exchanges may fear liability for *failing* to enforce adequately, which would raise their costs and put them in a potentially far more adversarial position vis-à-vis the companies that list with them than is now the case. Furthermore, governments are likely to have concerns about delegating such wide powers to exchanges, most of which are private entities. Finally, it is also far from clear that delegating such duties to exchanges would make disclosure more consistent across exchanges and countries. To the contrary, delegating disclosure enforcement to exchanges could lead to more fragmentation of enforcement results across countries (and exchanges), or at the very least, not produce any more harmonization than exists now.

CONCLUDING ASSESSMENT

In principle, a single set of global accounting standards would seem to be the obvious answer to improving the efficiency of capital markets worldwide and attracting global firms and major foreign investment. Indeed, the IASB is seeing itself in the role of the standard setter to provide such standards. Yet, as our review of the various options should make amply clear, there is no single, compelling answer to the challenge to corporate disclosure posed by the increasing globalization of capital markets. There are pluses and minuses to each of the options.

However, we believe that a single global standard is not desirable for reasons of efficient standard setting—nor is it likely to come about, considering the strong belief of individual countries that their standards are the best. In fact, although the IASB and the FASB have been pursuing convergence of their standards, there are several recent examples of new standards issued by one of the bodies that intentionally depart from the standards of the other, evidence that full convergence is not achievable.

We imagine instead the coexistence of a few private standard setters worldwide, including the IASB and the FASB, that would develop globally acceptable financial reporting standards. We call this model "constrained competition." A convergence of IFRS and U.S. GAAP is not desirable, though, because it would limit the alternatives that could compete in the market for standards.

Even if convergence of the two major standards were desirable and could be achieved, we strongly doubt that a single global standard could be universally enforced. The survey of our four countries and the EU strongly suggests that national differences will persist even though there are considerable efforts under way to converge national systems of financial reporting and their institutional environment, including audit standards, the audit function, oversight, corporate governance, and other enforcement regulations. Paradoxically, the stronger and more effective enforcement becomes, the lower is the chance that a single set of accounting standards can survive, because more and more institutions will have to interpret the same standards. It is most unlikely that they will be able to coordinate to such an extent that different applications and interpretations can be avoided.

Global standards will not be able to achieve all of the rich set of objectives for accounting reports that exist in the variety of national contexts. Any unmet requirements will emerge in some way and distort harmonization of international standards and cause more than one set of accounting standards to be used in some countries that may vary in their content among countries. Ideally, national standard setters would allow choice between sets of competing accounting standards, even if not all of them have global reach.

Potentially more important for investors than a single global accounting standard, whether for comparing financial data of companies within their countries or across countries, is how whatever standards are in place are actually enforced. We are mindful that this issue will have to be resolved first at the national level, but eventually it should reach the international stage. When it does, the most likely course is for some type of official, supranational action—beginning with more coordination of national enforcement efforts, and perhaps one day culminating in limited supranational jurisdiction over the investigation and perhaps sanctions of the auditors of multinational firms. This is essentially the type of process the EU has begun through the CESR. Other nations would be advised ultimately to join the effort.

11

Summing Up and Charting a Future for Standard Setters

In this, our concluding chapter, we outline the challenges that accounting standard setters will face in the future and offer our suggestions as to how those challenges should be met. But first, it is helpful to review our argument up to this point.

SUMMING UP

One of the major themes of this book is that capital markets have become more "global" in nature over time, and that this process will continue. By this we mean that investors, both individually and institutionally, have increasingly become interested in purchasing and transacting in the equity shares of companies worldwide. Similarly, firms have increasingly sought funds in the most advantageous markets globally. Consequently, interest in the meaning, usefulness, and limitations of the financial statements produced by corporations has increased.

But as we have painstakingly documented in different chapters of this book, as yet there are no (and perhaps never will be) universally generally accepted accounting principles (GAAP) on which these statements are based. This makes investor research into the financial performance and condition of foreign corporations more difficult and probably contributes to the "home-country bias"—the tendency of investors to overweight the securities issued by domestic corporations in their portfolios. Individual-country GAAP also make it difficult for foreign corporations to offer securities to investors in foreign markets, as these corporations often must translate their domestic standards into those of the foreign countries or reconcile the numbers to those that the foreign standard would have produced. Independent public accountants (IPAs), who audit the financial statements of corporations that have branches or subsidiaries in several countries, are similarly confronted with having to follow the dictates of different countries' standards.

Nevertheless, as we document in Chapter 1, finance has become increasingly global. In part this is due to the increasing globalization of production and trade. Advances in technology also have played an important role, as investors now can purchase and sell shares worldwide from almost any location and at almost any time of day. It may be that financial statements based on a single universally accepted and used GAAP would have accelerated the globalization of finance. But, as we argue further here, it is not clear that it is desirable or even possible to have "universal GAAP" for all time.

In Chapter 2 we consider and analyze the nature of the financial information that investors might use. We point out that the founders of the corporation and its shareholders benefit from providing investors (including creditors) with financial information that they might want in order to evaluate potential investments in the company, because this lowers the investors' costs, which reduces the company's cost of capital. Companies also are likely to know what sort of information potential investors want. A company's basic problem is convincing potential investors that the information provided to them is trustworthy. To the extent that these investors distrust the numbers, prudence dictates that they will tend to discount severely the value they place on investments in the company to compensate them for possible undisclosed negatives and false positives. To assure investors that the financial statements present an unbiased and not materially misleading representation of a corporation's financial condition and past performance, corporate founders and managers have employed IPAs, even when not legally required, to examine (audit) the accounts and attest that the accounts are presented in accordance with GAAP, with exceptions (if any) noted.

We outline the extent to which accounting data can serve the information needs of investors and creditors. The data reported in financial statements are necessary (but not sufficient) for investors to evaluate the performance of corporate managers and motivate those managers to perform in the interests of shareholders, as well as to decide whether to purchase or sell shares in corporations. We argue that the traditional accounting model that emphasizes the income statement and that is grounded on trustworthy amounts serves investors better than an approach that attempts to measure economic income, an approach that necessarily is based on subjectively determined amounts that often cannot be reliably verified by IPAs. International accounting standard setters nonetheless are moving toward the latter approach, specifically toward revaluing assets and liabilities at their "fair" values. We criticize this tendency in the next section of this chapter.

In Chapter 3 we examine the structures and regimes of accounting and auditing standards for meeting the demands of investors and other users and of financial statements. IPAs have played a very important role by helping to assure investors that the numbers presented by managers in financial statements are trustworthy. They conduct an audit of those numbers to determine that they are what they purport to be, and they so attest in a letter to the directors and separately to other users of the financial statements. Auditing and accounting standards provide an efficient means for investors to understand what they can expect and not expect from the numbers presented in accounting statements. In the past, these standards developed from professional practice. Government was involved in setting standards in a general way in both the United Kingdom and Germany since the middle of the 19th century, and the United States in a substantial way during the Great Depression of the 1930s. We analyze the benefits and costs to consumers, IPAs, and investors of standards set by professional accountancy bodies, stock exchanges, and government agencies (and combinations thereof). Although there is much to be said for having the standards set by professional accountancy bodies (as they were in the past), perceived weaknesses in their procedures have led to government involvement in the process. We conclude that nongovernmental standard setters to which governments have delegated their power, such as the Financial Accounting Standards Board (FASB) and International Accounting Standards Board (IASB), are preferable to direct action by government.

These three initial chapters provide a basis for examining the accounting and auditing standards in four major countries (the United States, the United Kingdom, Germany, and Japan) and in the European Union (EU). For each of the four countries we first provide brief descriptions of the financial markets to which corporations report their financial condition and performance. We then present brief histories of each country's regulatory structure, because these experiences have affected the evolution of those structures and resulted in differences that, we later find, are often difficult to reconcile.

The United States enacted the most extensive laws governing the presentation of financial statements by corporations with publicly traded shares with the passage of the Securities Acts in 1933 and 1934, aimed at protecting investors and stock markets. Previously, stock exchanges and professional accountancy bodies and professional practice determined the way and extent to which company accounts were presented in financial statements. The United Kingdom, though, enacted the earliest laws governing financial disclosure in the mid-19th century. These laws dealt primarily with the interests of shareholders in conjunction with statutes that established limited liability for corporations. Germany's laws, enacted in the late 19th century, were concerned primarily with the interests of creditors, largely in reaction to scandals involving overstatements of assets and earnings. Japan was similar to the United States in having stock markets rather than legal statutes governing disclosure, until the 1930s.

The Japanese government intervened primarily to control the economy. After the Second World War, the U.S. securities laws were the model for Japan. However, unlike the situation in the United States, where the development of accounting and auditing standards was delegated to the accounting profession, Japanese government agencies played an active controlling role. The EU's experience in developing standards for its member states with different domestic standards and, following that, endorsing International Financial Reporting Standards (IFRS), described in Chapter 7, illustrates the problems, failures, and successes involved in structuring and gaining acceptance for a universal standard.

We describe the present regulatory regime in each of the country chapters. This description includes regulations and regulatory bodies, both governmental and government-sanctioned, the GAAP governing the contents and presentation of financial statements, and the entities to which the disclosure requirements apply. Investor protection generally and corporate governance particularly are described and discussed. Generally accepted auditing standards (GAAS) to which IPAs must conform are described, as are the means of enforcing the application of those standards and GAAP. Finally, each country chapter (and the EU chapter) concludes with an outline and discussion of the shortcomings of the present regulatory regime. We show that the accounting architectures of countries are affected by all these factors, and therefore changes to accounting systems should not be looked at in isolation.

Chapter 9 summarizes and contrasts the key financial disclosure and auditing regimes in the four countries and the EU. This chapter makes clear that the GAAP in the countries are similar but have important differences. An appendix to that chapter contrasts the key differences between U.S. GAAP and the IFRS that are mandatory for corporations with publicly traded securities as of 2005 in the EU and some other countries.

Given the differences among the key countries we analyze, in Chapter 10 we consider whether and to what extent a universal set of GAAP and GAAS might be and should be established. Although there are advantages to universally accepted standards, the analyses of our four countries and the EU leads us to believe that the wish to seek convergence of standards between the FASB and IASB is unlikely to come to a successful end; even if it did, it would not be sustainable. In addition, there is reason to believe that any agreed-upon global standards are likely to be differently interpreted and applied, such that in many instances the same label for an accounting item will actually have different meanings in different countries and standard-setting regimes. More importantly, we believe that a global standard is not even desirable, because there are considerable benefits from allowing companies to choose among alternative standards, so that market forces rather than the decisions of governments, regulators, and standard setters play a basic role in the development of GAAP and their application by individual corporations, as they have strong incentives to provide investors with information that is useful to them.

In this final chapter we consider the ways in which GAAP and financial accounting statements are currently being, or might be, extended to include information that investors would find useful. First, we examine (and reject) the movement of the FASB and IASB toward increasing use of fair values when these are not based on trustworthy numbers derived from relevant market transactions and the related "asset/liability" rather than the traditional "revenue/expense" approach. Second, we suggest that supplementing financial statements with additional disclosures may be a solution to some difficulties of recognition and measurement because it does not compromise a traditional strength of financial statements—providing trustworthy numbers. We consider the benefits of voluntary disclosure and then discuss management's discussion of the operations and financial condition of the company that interprets and goes beyond the information provided in the audited financial statements and how information on intangible assets, risk, and nonfinancial measurements of a company's position and performance is or can be presented.

THE ASSET/LIABILITY APPROACH

In the 1980s or thereabout, the FASB and the (then) International Accounting Standards Committee (IASC) began shifting their emphasis from the income statement to the balance sheet. Most recently, this balance-sheet, or asset/liability, approach has become the major driver of changes in the standards issued by both bodies. Both have suggested that current economic values, as shown on the balance sheet, rather than assets and liabilities stated at historical cost, are what investors really require to make informed decisions.[1] Both bodies have also expressed dissatisfaction with the traditional "matching concept," which, as we outline in Chapter 2, computes net income as the total of actual or expected cash flows from transactions minus the costs expended to produce that revenue (costs associated with unrealized revenue are deferred and carried in the asset section of the balance sheet).[2] Instead, the standard setters now emphasize that balance-sheet values provide a more conceptually valid basis for determining the revenue and expense that should be reported in the income statement.[3] If assets and liabilities were recorded at their economic values at the end of a period, the amounts reported as revenue and expense would be obvious: the difference between the economic values at the beginning and end of the period less additional investments by and plus distribution to shareholders.

We agree that in markets in which all assets (including internally created goodwill) and liabilities can be traded at the same prices for all traders, income defined as the difference between the current (market or fair) values of net assets at the end and beginning of a period (adjusted for additional investments by and disbursements to shareholders), which has come to be called the economic or Hicksian definition of income, is conceptually correct.[4] However, as we describe in Chapter 2, the required values for all items on the balance sheet—notably those items for which there are no timely arms-length prices—cannot be objectively (trustworthily) measured. Only the market value of the *entire firm* can be objectively ascertained, if the firm has shares that are publicly traded, but these values provide no help for assigning values to particular assets and liabilities.[5] The Hicksian definition of income surely is not the sum of changes in the fair values of financial assets and only some other assets and liabilities and the realized gains and losses from dispositions and expensing of other assets (e.g., buildings, equipment, intangible assets) whose fair values are not estimated under some or all GAAP. Although the fair values of buildings and equipment may be estimated under IFRS, not all assets are revalued periodically, and long-term liabilities are not revalued. And although the assets and liabilities of acquired firms are recorded at their fair values (such that they sum to the purchase price), these fair values are added to the historical costs of the acquiring firm. Thus, even when fair values are used, the net amount is not equal to the economic value of net assets at the end of an accounting period. Hence we conclude that the "fair-value, asset/liability" approach to measuring income (or economic values as of a point in time) as a consistent conceptual approach is not now achievable and, we believe, cannot be achieved in practice.

Indeed, most fair values (even for many financial instruments) would seem to be derived from estimates that are not based on objectively determined and verifiable amounts, including those based on managerial judgments that, perforce, allow managerial manipulation. Such fair value estimates cannot be used in a trustworthy accounting system, as they cannot be audited. We follow up on this theme in the next section.

FAIR VALUES

The vigorous move of FASB and IASB to the asset/liability approach goes hand in hand with an increasing use of fair values. In Chapter 2 we briefly examine the introduction of "fair values" and "mark to market" in financial accounting statements by the FASB and the IASB. "Mark to market" refers to valuing assets and liabilities at their market values, based on actual and verifiable market prices, at the end of the accounting period and taking any gains or losses over book values directly to income. When there are no transaction-based market prices, fair values are used instead. Fair value is defined as "the amount at which an asset (liability) could be bought (incurred) or sold (settled) in a current transaction between willing parties, that is, other than in a forced or liquidation sale [SFAS 133, paragraph 540], where settled means paid off or relieved of the burden of the liability."[6] The objective of fair value measurement is to estimate the market prices of assets and liabilities in the absence of actual market transactions by the firm, simulating as much as possible the characteristics and workings of a relevant market, including the absence of duress on the market participants.

At present, fair values are used in some accounting standards, including those concerning financial instruments (IFRS and U.S. GAAP), and to a degree for other financial assets and liabilities, for agricultural assets (IFRS) and energy contracts (FASB), optionally for investment property and revaluation of fixed assets (IFRS), for revaluing impaired assets (FASB),[7] for both financial and nonfinancial assets and liabilities acquired in business combinations (IFRS and U.S. GAAP), and for subsidiaries designated as "investment companies" (U.S. GAAP). So far, beside contractual assets and liabilities discussed later, we know of no plan to extend the use of fair values to nonfinancial assets in other circumstances.

We discuss the advantages of the revenue/expense approach relative to the asset/liability approach combined with fair values in Chapter 2. Here we look in more detail at the theory underlying the use of fair values in accounting reports, assuming that these can be measured in a trustworthy way.[8]

Arguments for Fair Value

It is easy to see the appeal to standard setters of measuring assets and liabilities at their fair values. If these values could be measured adequately and if there were no intrafirm externalities and transaction costs, they would represent the market's view of the future cash flows that individual assets and liabilities are expected to generate or require, adjusted for their believed timing and risk. Under these conditions, the use of fair values would seem to solve many of the problems of standard setters, especially those of trading off decision-relevance against information reliability. Fair values would ensure that current values are reported in accounting reports and these are used to determine income, thereby allowing more realistic performance measurement. Fair value increases the transparency of accounting information, portrays the market's view of the firm's prospects (as embedded in the value of its net assets), and demonstrates the volatility of markets. This increased information should allow investors to make their decisions in the best-informed way.

However, in markets where not all "supranormal profits" (those above what should be expected given a firm's risk-adjusted cost of capital) have been competed away and internal goodwill is not included in financial reports, the accounting net asset value (carrying value) will always understate the firm's equity value. This reiterates the point made in Chapter 2 and above that accounting figures cannot be expected to capture all of the elements affecting the stock market value of the firm. The use of market values and their fair value proxies, though, if they could be trusted, would reduce the gap between the firm's stock market value and its accounting value.

In markets with additional market imperfections, the "bridge" between the security market value of the firm and the net value of its assets will be wider than just the value of supranormal profits and will include the differential values used by the market and by accounting valuation systems. Thus, all accounting systems are second-best methods, with their own comparative advantages and disadvantages. Even if a fair value accounting system both accurately and reliably reflected current prices and market estimates of future cash flows, it cannot capture all information that is needed by investors and other users of financial statements.

The standard setters' major argument for fair value is that accounting valuations should provide current information on five elements as seen by the market: the amount of expected cash flows, expectations of changes in the amount or timing of cash flows, the time value of money, the price of the risk inherent in assets and liabilities, and other, sometimes unidentifiable, factors, including illiquidity and market imperfections [SFAC No. 7, ¶23; similar to the Proposed Statement, FASB 2004, ¶A2]. The standard setters argue that fair values capture all five and that other valuation systems do not.

For example, fair values could be based on managerial information rather than on that of the market [SFAC No. 7, ¶24]. This use of managerial estimates in accounting would mean that different companies would value identical accounting items differently. Although this is often the case in traditional accounting (e.g., different companies may use different depreciation patterns for identical assets), one of the presumed important advantages of fair value accounting is that financial statements of different companies would be comparable, because economic market values would be used instead of historical-cost-based figures.

Another presumed advantage of fair values is that managers could be judged on how well they have taken advantage of or foregone past and current opportunities reflected in the market as measured by fair values in financial reports. However, there are many other opportunities that would not be reported in accounting statements that often are more useful to investors, for example the possible benefits from alternative products and different sales plans.

In the oft-quoted words of David Tweedie, Chairman of IASB, the wish is to get management to "tell it as it is" in accounting reports and avoid managerial manipulation. Using market prices does reduce somewhat the scope for "storytelling," but at the cost of denying investors access to private managerial information at least in the accounts; for example, managerial information could be reflected in provisions in accounts, although their use is now substantially restricted by many standard setters. The downside is that allowing the use of fair values based on estimates would allow management to "tell it like they want."

Measurement Problems With Fair Values

The fair value exercise poses several essential conceptual problems. We identify four problems next and consider whether entry (purchase) or exit (sale) prices should be used later.

First, the value of assets to a firm (or, indeed, to any purchaser) is almost always greater than their market values. If these values in use did not exceed market prices (even if transactions costs were zero), the assets should be, and, with this knowledge, would be sold. Thus, market prices will understate the value of corporate assets to investors in corporate stock (even though the understatement usually is less than with amortized historical cost).

Second, the present value of the net cash flows to a firm expected from assets that are used jointly or in common and in combination with liabilities should be greater than that of the expected net cash flow from the individual assets. This intrafirm externality (or rent) is the *raison d'être* for the existence of firms. Because markets are not complete, market prices for such bundles of assets can rarely, if ever, be found.

Third, in incomplete markets, the market prices of many assets, particularly intangible assets, do not exist. In these situations, unverifiable estimates of the present value of net cash flows would have to be used, which raises important questions about the trustworthiness of the reported amounts.

Fourth, observable prices often are imperfectly and poorly representative of the prices at which the assets held by a firm could be sold or purchased in arm's-length transactions. These prices may be "noisy," in that they reflect transient events that affect the demand for and supply of the goods in question. They may not be representative of the amounts of assets held, in that they reflect the market clearing prices of larger or smaller quantities. They may include or exclude transportation, commission, special handling, and other costs. Market prices may under- or over-shoot rational bounds on prices (i.e., they may transiently fail to reflect the "fundamentals" of asset values, expected future cash flows) and be affected by "herd" instincts. Strictly, an accounting system based only on market prices of assets and liabilities contains no new information for investors, assuming they knew the type and quantities of the assets and liabilities, because they usually could access such market prices elsewhere, though it would be less expensive for firms to do this.

Use of Entry Versus Exit Prices

Markets are not perfect; hence, transactions costs are positive and often large. This situation presents the problem of whether entry (purchase) or exit (sales) prices should be used—the amounts a corporation must pay to obtain an asset or discharge a liability or the amount it would get or pay if it sold an asset or purchased a liability.

Transaction costs are affected primarily by information, marketing, and distribution costs, which often are substantial (compare the amount one might pay for a car and the amount one might get if the car were sold a few moments after it was purchased). The amount at which an asset (liability) could be bought (incurred) or sold (settled) in a current transaction between willing parties—the standard setters' definition of "fair value"—depends on whether the transaction is a retail purchase from a supplier (in which event the amount includes most of these costs) or a sale by a party who does not sell regularly (in which event the amount is smaller, as the buyer would discount for these costs). The calculated amount of fair value also depends on whether the asset has a special or general use. The entry price of a special-use asset usually is substantially greater than its exit price. For example, a company would have to pay significantly more for a specially designed machine that only the company could use than it would get for the machine's scrap value.

The standard setters have not clearly resolved or been consistent in applying the exit versus entry price alternatives because they generally have limited fair values to financial assets, for which transactions costs tend to be low when the assets are bought and sold in an organized trading exchange. SFAS 115 mentions bid and ask prices in dealer markets but does not indicate which should be used. The *Proposed SFAS: Fair Value Measurements* [FASB 2004, pp. 5–6] states: "the price used to estimate fair value, that is, the price in the most advantageous market, shall not be adjusted for these [transactions] costs. . . . [F]air value shall be estimated using bid prices for long positions (assets) and asked prices for short positions (liabilities)." If the exposure draft were adopted, exit prices as seen by nondealers would be required. Bid prices are dealers' buying prices and ask prices are dealers' selling prices. Thus, assets are to be valued at exit prices. However, the FASB appears to contemplate only the use of ask price for liabilities. This price is the amount the firm would have to sacrifice if it settled a liability—that is, the dealer's selling price, the price at which the market would be willing to hold the firm's debt as part of their assets [Horton and Macve, 2000, p. 28]. This value would be even smaller than an "average" fair value, which again is smaller than value in use, as was discussed earlier.

The Joint Working Group (JWG, 2000),[9] whose proposals are more radical than current practice, favors exit values. The Group's proposal concludes that derivatives and other financial instruments should be carried at their exit market prices and that losses and gains on these prices should be taken to the income statement (so-called "mark-to-market" accounting, but actually requiring much "mark-to-model" and "mark-to-estimates"). The Group also suggests that exit prices of financial items are consistent with the usual definitions of assets and liabilities used by most standard setters, although standard setters also use entry prices. However, we know of no fundamental logic that favors exit values, except for the important role of indicating firm liquidation value as some sort of lower bound on the firm's value of its net assets.[10] In principle, firms should regularly compare their exit values with continuing as a going concern in whole or in part. If the exit price were greater than the present value that might be obtained from the firm or any of its assets (its value in use), liquidation and distribution of the proceeds to the shareholders would be the preferable act, for the shareholders at least.

However, highlighting the short-term performance from managing financial items may divert managerial efforts from possibly more profitable endeavors. Thus, both banks and insurance companies have argued that fair value performance measurement emphasizes short-term results, whereas their businesses are long term and provide intertemporal smoothing to the economy that fair value accounting may inhibit (European Central Bank,

2004; Geneva Association, 2004; JWGBA, 1999; Clark et al., 2003). More importantly, banks and insurance company executives have argued that while fair value accounting may portray better the real volatility of the market for financial assets, it tends to generate artificial volatility for the company as a whole, because the intended use of the assets generates cash flows that generally do not fluctuate. The volatility in the books comes from opportunities not taken. Long-term liabilities matched to the financial assets are usually not revalued, which also results in artificial volatility.

Even financial markets often are far from perfect. Standard setters implicitly admit this by accepting that estimates of market prices often have to be used in this area. Selling (secondary) markets are absent for bank loan contracts and are limited for insurance and reinsurance. Under fair value accounting, financial institutions (and, indeed, other firms where financial assets and liabilities are an important part of their resources) would have an incentive to hedge, securitize, and smooth results where such structuring of real transactions is available, to forego certain transactions, and to search for new methods to reduce the variance in their reported net profits. Fair value accounting may thus generate decisions involving real resources simply in order to avoid "bad" accounting results. Many contracts, moreover, involve limited bargaining between only two or a few parties, one of which may be at a substantial disadvantage (e.g., a firm with a reduced credit rating seeking additional funding). Hence, the prices achieved may not resemble active market prices. Again, fair values move away from prices in a well-organized market. The possible effects of fair value accounting discussed in this and the previous paragraph can be evaluated only by looking at the empirical evidence when it becomes available. Standard setters have no special access to such evidence, although they do have the results of a limited number of case studies in some situations.[11]

Fair Values for Nonfinancial Assets

One major challenge that standard setters have yet to take up is the general application of fair value accounting to nonfinancial assets. Currently, many nonfinancial assets (company-produced intangibles in particular) are excluded from the balance sheet, and revaluation of recognized nonfinancial assets is not allowed under some accounting regimes (e.g., U.S. GAAP and German GAAP). Without this extension of fair value accounting, financial reports will continue to be unbalanced by their different treatments of the items in the financial reports.

It can be argued that improving the accounting of some elements in financial reports would improve accounting overall only if the elements so treated have no effect on other elements and the factors reflected by their accounting provide no information about other untreated elements in the accounting reports—but this is generally unlikely. For example, changes in the values of financial assets or liabilities caused by a change in market yields give signals about the value of a company's nonfinancial assets that currently go unrecorded. Thus, the lack of the use of market prices for valuing nonfinancial assets in U.S. GAAP and many other standards produces "lopsided" accounting because the carrying values of nonfinancial assets do not reflect changes in the market that affect their cash flows. For example, when interest rates increase, companies would record a gain on their existing fixed-interest liabilities if they were marked to market. The possible offsetting losses in the value of nonfinancial assets (assuming their cash flows cannot be increased to cover the increased interest charges) will not be reported contemporaneously in financial reports (unless the changes are sufficient to cause asset impairment). Not revaluing nonfinancial assets, therefore, means that the effects of the "drivers" of the changes in their values go unrecorded in financial reports. Moreover, it may not be possible to deduce the correlated effects of changes in the value of financial items on the values of nonfinancial assets. The direction of correlation may differ among companies and may be nonexistent in some cases.

Economic reasoning supports the valuation of nonfinancial assets at their market values using entry prices (assuming that the assets will not shortly be sold), providing that these prices are taken from well-organized markets and can thus be audited. Long practice in some accounting regimes, such as Australia and the United Kingdom, allows market prices estimated by professional appraisers working in well-organized markets to be used for specific assets not themselves actually traded in such markets.

The Joint Revenue Recognition Project of the FASB and the IASB

In this chapter and in Chapter 2, we have discussed the difficulties of abandoning the matching concept for determining net income, which seems to be the direction in which both the FASB and the IASB are headed. We now provide another, more complex, example of the limits of moving in the direction that both standard setters appear to advocate.

In 2002, the IASB and the FASB set up a joint project to develop a general revenue recognition rule and provide particular guidance for complex sales and service contracts. This project is a further challenge to the traditional definition of revenue that is based on the allocation of cash inflows to current or future periods from the company's operations. The focus is on contracts that include multiple components being delivered or rendered at different dates, such as construction contracts, service contracts, and contracts that include guarantees, extended warranties, updates, and other promises. The project extends the asset/liability approach to such contracts in that it proposes to recognize preperformance obligations (as a liability) and the corresponding rights (as an asset) to receive a consideration.

The key issue we discuss here is the measurement of preperformance assets and liabilities. Both standard setters discuss using fair values if at all possible. This would add another category of assets and liabilities that are measured at fair value. Both standard setters recognize the fact that such determinations can be difficult and discuss two alternative approaches: "legal layoff" (or wholesale) and "retail."

Under the legal layoff approach, the fair value of the contractual obligation (liability) is determined by the amount that would have to be paid to a third party to take over the obligation from a company. Under the retail approach, that fair value is based on that company's other transactions with customers, which usually is the amount the customer would pay (in traditional revenue/expense accounting, "sales revenue"). This also is presumed to be equal to the fair value of the consideration promised. Consequently, it includes all the profits expected to flow from the company's acceptance of the obligation. The legal layoff approach, though, usually yields a lower value of the liability than will the retail approach. This is because it includes only the (fictitious) third party's profit margin from servicing the obligation. Because the liability determined by the legal lay off approach is less than the fair value of the asset received, when the contract is recognized there is a "day-one" gain equal to the profit over the amount accruing from servicing the contract. Both standard setters seem to favor the legal layoff approach. If adopted, managers would be given an additional opportunity to use estimates that directly affect net income, as it is unlikely that many actual business-to-business prices are available for contractual obligations such as services and warranties.

For example, consider the application of the proposed approach to a long-term construction contract. At present, companies may use the "percentage-of-completion" or "completed contract" methods to allocate revenue and expense to an accounting period intermediate to the life of the contract. Under the percentage-of-completion method, engineers or other professionals estimate the degree to which the contract has been fulfilled as of the end of the period, often using the money amounts of resources expended. Revenue then is recorded equal to the expenses plus the expected net profit, with the asset or liability recorded to reflect under- or over-payments made by the customer. Or, based on the percentage of completion determined, the revenue called for in the contract is recorded and expenses are matched to and charged against that revenue, with excess (wasted or unexpectedly greater) expenditures charged additionally as a current expense. Thus, the numbers reported are based on the opinions of construction professionals. Under the proposed legal layoff approach, management would have to estimate how much someone might pay for the incomplete project or have to be paid to finish the project. Since such assets rarely (if ever) are sold, it is not clear how they could determine or auditors might validate these estimates.

Another example is a service warranty. At present, past experience with the cost of such warranties is used to determine a company's liability and the amounts that are charged as an expense are matched to the revenue that includes a service-or-replacement guarantee. Under the legal layoff approach, this amount would be that which another firm might charge to take over the contract. If the warranty service obligation could be sold to another firm, the amount that would be paid could provide a trustworthy measure of the cost of the warranty that should be charged against revenue. The following period(s), then, would report the gains or expense of fulfilling the warranty obligation, including the profit that a firm taking over the obligation might have made. However, if there are no such firms or layoff possibilities, the amounts must be based on managers' determinations of the amounts that the firm might have had to pay.

Under both current practice and the proposed approach, estimates are necessary. Currently, the estimates usually are based on professional or actual experience. Under the proposed approach, managers' estimates of the amounts that nonexistent firms might charge to take over obligations would be used. The use of such estimates, in our view, is precisely why the fair value approach is misguided: it affords too much leeway to firms and their auditors without having well-accepted methods for verification.

Conclusion

If the fair value approach were adopted, the balance sheet could not be a statement that gives readers the economic market values (or reasonable approximations thereof) of individual assets and liabilities. For a going concern, exit values are useful only for assets and liabilities with very low transaction cost, and internal goodwill (supranormal profits) would have to be measured and recorded. As we discuss later in this chapter, most intangible assets cannot be estimated with much precision (if at all), and the values in use (or even the entry or exit values) of many usually important identifiable individual assets, such as special-purpose equipment, are either very costly or not possible to measure. Consequently, the balance sheet cannot provide investors with a listing and sum of the economic values of assets and liabilities, the difference of which is the economic value of their enterprises. Investors in corporations with shares traded in efficient markets, though, can obtain this number from share prices simply by consulting a newspaper, the Internet, or a stockbroker. For these reasons, we prefer financial statements based on traditional amortized historical cost based on actual market transactions, with revaluations grounded on reliable prices that can be audited and verified. We consider next in how these numbers could be presented to shareholders without distorting the trustworthiness of financial statements.

AN ALTERNATIVE APPROACH TO VALUATION

From our analysis of investors' information requirements in Chapter 2, we conclude that a key attribute of the information items presented in financial statements is that they are trustworthy. Traditionally, for the most part accounting has recognized changes in the values of assets and liabilities (and, hence, in changes in the claims of shareholders as reflected by reported income and expense) when evidenced by actual market transactions. In recent years, revaluations of traded financial assets (but not liabilities) have been recognized when these are based on prices in markets characterized by low transaction costs.

Financial accounting could and we believe should be extended to encompass all trustworthy numbers. We argue in Chapter 2 that current market prices and professionally validated estimates of them (mainly for land and property) should be incorporated into financial accounting reports where they reflect the economic values of the firm's resources and are objectively measured and verified (i.e., are trustworthy). In particular, inventories that a company expects to replace could be stated at opportunity cost—the amount that will be expended to replace the inventory. By the time financial statements are presented, these numbers usually would be known, as the inventory would have been replaced or ordered. The change in inventory values (replacement cost less original acquisition cost) then would be reported as a holding gain or loss. Manufactured inventories (finished goods and work-in-process) also could be reported at their opportunity costs. When the production process is not operating at full capacity, this is approximated by variable costs. At full capacity, the relevant number would be the net realizable value. Considering that inventories are a much more important asset for many enterprises than are financial assets, this represents a meaningful extension of the present movement toward more relevant numbers without sacrificing the benefit of trustworthiness.

The values of other assets and liabilities could also be reported when these are trustworthy. For example, debt securities for which reliable market prices are available should be revalued with changes in values reported as current income or expense, whether or not they are held to maturity. Given low transactions cost, a managerial decision to hold such securities is, for investors, equivalent to the decision to sell the securities and then repurchase them, except that taxable income is not affected. Changes in the values of interest-bearing assets and liabilities as a result of changes in applicable market rates of interest also can and should be reported as current-period holding gains and losses.

However, the matching concept should be maintained. Changes in the values of assets and corresponding liabilities that can be reliably measured should be reported as income or expense only to the extent that the values of economically related assets and liabilities can be reliably measured as having changed by at least those amounts. For example, a firm may have sold a future designed to offset (hedge) changes in the value of contracts to deliver oil at fixed prices should the market price of oil change. Assume that the contracts are not traded and, hence, have no reliable market price. If the price of oil increased, the firm would have to pay the futures holders, but its contracts would be worth more. The firm would then report a loss on the option and the same amount as a gain on the contracts, if it is determined that its contracts had increased in value by at least that amount. If the contract increased in value by less, there would be a net loss; if the contract value increased more, no net gain would be reported until the contract was realized. If the price of oil decreased, the futures holders would pay the firm, which would report a gain and also a loss in value of its contracts. How assets and liabilities designed to be hedges are determined would be explicitly stated in advance by management and be audited by its IPAs.

SUPPLEMENTARY DISCLOSURES

Trustworthiness as a key characteristic of the information in financial statements has its own shortcomings. It substantially constrains what information is included in financial statements. Investors may find other information useful, even if they must discount it for its lower degree of reliability. Moreover, companies may want to provide supplementary disclosures outside the financial statements; indeed, many companies do so. Supplementary disclosure is also more flexible than that in financial statements, as it is less restricted by the formal financial bookkeeping system and by accounting standards.

In this section we consider first whether supplementary disclosures should be required or voluntary. We then examine four kinds of supplementary disclosures: management's or directors' report to shareholders that interprets and puts the information presented in the financial statements into context, and those relating to intangibles, risk, and non-financial (innovative) measures of performance.

Voluntary Versus Mandatory Disclosure

The almost universal existence of standard setters and accounting regulators suggests that they, at least, think reliance on voluntary disclosures is generally insufficient to produce a level of financial transparency in capital markets (and that they could determine a "better" level of disclosure by regulation). The basis is their belief that managers will disclose information only if it is in their own best interest to do so.

There are two reasons, though, to favor voluntary over mandatory disclosure. One is that the costs and benefits of providing information vary substantially among firms. Hence, almost any mandatory rule is likely to affect firms differently, forcing those for which the costs exceed the benefits to subsidize other firms' information. Moreover, some rules will negatively affect many firms, such that the sum of their costs may exceed the total benefits to the economy. The other reason is that there is not yet sufficient experience with innovative fields of disclosures, so that firms should be encouraged to experiment with diverse disclosure approaches.[12] This is particularly true with current issues, such as intangibles and risk disclosures.

Compulsory disclosure would be reasonable only if there were a major market failure arising from inadequate voluntary disclosure of information that investors would find essential if available at reasonable cost and that is not otherwise generated by financial institutions and analysts.[13]

Whether these sources of information are sufficient to overcome possible managerial reluctance to report information useful to investors is an empirical question. Evidence from the 1930s in the United States, before the passage of the Securities Acts (see Chapter 5), suggests that voluntary disclosure was a popular means of decreasing information asymmetry. Although there is anecdotal evidence that managements are loathe to provide forward-looking information, there are sensible reasons for this unwillingness, including the risk to their reputations if results deviate from announced plans or from what was achieved in the past (as they will) and the avoidance of litigation. Managers also might be concerned that proprietary information would be made public, eventually to the detriment of shareholders. As far as we know, there is no general empirical evidence of a market failure that is sufficient to justify major governmental or other regulatory intervention to require companies to disclose "supplementary information."

However, the decision between mandatory and voluntary disclosures need not be black and white. There are alternatives with elements from both mandatory and voluntary disclosure. One approach is that a standard setter or regulator requires that companies make disclosures on particular themes but does not specify the contents or form. Such disclosures may even include the statement that the company has nothing to report on a theme, which is also informative to the market. We discuss below such an approach next with the new U.K. regulation on the Operating and Financial Review (OFR) and (later) with risk reporting. Another approach is to provide standards that companies can choose not to follow, but they must explain their reasons for this choice ("comply or explain"). This approach provides a focal point for disclosure and has been adopted for disclosures on corporate governance in many European countries. A related approach has been taken by the IASB with interim reporting: IAS 34 contains rules for interim reporting that come into place if the respective country's regulator charges companies to provide interim reports without dictating their detailed contents. This approach offers the benefits from a common standard for disclosures without actually mandating the specific information that must be disclosed.

MANAGEMENT'S OR DIRECTORS' REPORT TO SHAREHOLDERS: THE U.K. MODEL

In looking at what types of supplementary information are required by regulators and to evaluate whether such information should be mandated by governments or regulators, we consider the U.K. government's original intention in 2003 to make mandatory and expand the existing voluntary OFR in the United Kingdom. But, as mentioned in Chapter 5, on November 28, 2005, the government in a surprise about-turn abandoned the introduction of a mandatory OFR, requiring only that companies meet the lesser compulsory prescriptions of the EU Modernisation Directive [2003] in this area. This change in policy was part of a new government program to abolish "red tape," including the "gold plating" of EU directives, by adding U.K. requirements. Nevertheless, we will still consider the story of the development of a mandatory OFR, as it illustrates the difficulties associated with mandating substantial and detailed supplementary disclosures.

Following Enron and other financial crises, the U.K. government in 2003 enthusiastically accepted the recommendations of a government-established Company Law Review Group [CLRG, 2001] that the OFR should be mandatory, and used its detailed recommendations for the contents as the basis for revision. The government had put in place requirements, effective in 2005 [Department of Trade and Industry, 2005]. These requirements are similar to rules in other countries, such as the U.S. Management Discussion and Analysis (MD&A) and the EU's Accounting Modernisation Directive [EU, 2003], that require an enhanced review in the directors' report.

The OFR was required only of listed companies. Its objective was to give the directors' view of the business by providing "a discussion and analysis of performance and the main trends and factors underlying the results and financial position and likely to affect performance in the future, so as to enable users to assess the strategies adopted by the business and the potential for successfully achieving them" [CLRG, 2001, ¶8.32].[14] As with other U.K. company reports, the OFR is addressed to shareholders.

The mandatory topics in the OFR were those deemed to be material for assessing a company. Defined in rather general terms, these are the company's business and business objective, strategy and principal drivers of performance, the dynamics of the business, known economic events, trends, uncertainties, and other factors that may substantially affect performance, including investment programs [dti, 2004, ¶3.40]. The review of the business must include descriptions of the company's resources and the principal risks and uncertainties of its capital structure, treasury policies and objectives, and liquidity [dti, 2004, ¶2].[15]

A large number of other items were to be included to the extent management thinks it necessary, including information concerning social and community issues, using key indicators for financial, environmental, and employee matters, essential relationships with the company, receipts and returns to shareholders, and, where appropriate, additional explanations of amounts in the annual accounts, thereby also providing information for stakeholders other than shareholders [dti, 2004, ¶4–7].[16] Relying here on "good faith" judgments by managers may provide a loophole for those who wish to restrict information. Directors had to state when information about any of the above items was not disclosed. Forecasts were not required, and U.K. past practice suggests they will not be provided voluntarily.

More detailed disclosures for each of the items were to be set forth in standards, similar to accounting standards, issued by the U.K. Accounting

Standards Board (ASB). This requirement for highly detailed information for each major area to be reported seems to follow the approach adopted by SEC for the MD&A since its introduction in 1980. However, the MD&A has a much stronger requirement for supplemental financial information and less for business plans.

OFR standards would have the same force that the law is believed to give to accounting standards—that is, compliance with OFR standards will give rise to the presumption of compliance with the legal requirements concerning the law requiring a mandatory OFR. As with accounting standards, directors would have to state whether they have complied with the OFR standards and explain any departures. The CLRG advocated granting "safe harbors" for certain forward-looking statements to encourage "candid and experimental reports." However, the government decided that such a provision would be impractical and inappropriate, even though there are similar provisions in the Listing Rules for Securities and for the U.S. MD&A. Similarly, no exclusion on the grounds of confidentiality would be allowed, as this could lead to abuse and would be difficult to police. One general standard had been issued setting out general content requirements and specifying what information should be given about key performance indicators and their method of calculation, but no detailed standards had been issued, and their likely contents were not clear. However, a very baroque structure for their promulgation would have had to have been erected if these were as detailed in approach and in quantitative disclosure as are existing accounting standards. Such detailed standards were likely to have encouraged boilerplate presentation and box ticking and discouraged experimental disclosures, as seems to have happened with the U.S. MD&A [SEC, 2003B and 2003C].

The OFR mandatory requirement for a wide range of information represents a departure both from previous practice and, to a degree, from the recommendations of the CLRG, which required less mandatory information and relied more on guidelines as to appropriate voluntary information. The government was well aware that this whole exercise could degenerate into box ticking and encourage firms to minimize the voluntary content of the OFR. The formal enforcement structure was therefore complex and could have been very demanding if all the available powers were used (although this itself might encourage boilerplate compliance) and was similar to the process for remedying defective accounts, which, as noted in Chapter 5, overall was not that strong. Directors who knowingly or recklessly were party to approving a deficient OFR would face an unlimited fine. The Financial Reporting Review Panel (FRRP), which has similar responsibilities with regard to financial statements, would have reviewed a sample of OFRs annually (starting in 2006) and required OFRs found to be defective to be remedied, and if necessary asked courts to order the rewriting of the defective reports. These penalties and powers now apply to enforcing the requirements of the Modernisation Directive. It is not yet known whether the FRRP will still sample reports.

Originally the implied duty of care placed on directors was very strong, as was that placed on auditors. The auditors were to report both on whether the directors had prepared the OFR only after "due and careful enquiry"[17] and on the adequacy of the processes used in making the directors' judgments. They also had to give a positive opinion that the OFR presents a balanced and comprehensive analysis of the development and performance of the company, and that due care was taken over each statement in the OFR and that the information presented in the OFR is not inconsistent with either the accounts or knowledge gathered in the process of the audit. Following complaints about the severe rigor of these requirements and consultation, the government relaxed these requirements in 2005.[18] With regard to the directors' report, which incorporates the requirements of the Modernisation Directive, directors are now required to apply due care, skill, and diligence, which are the same requirements as for the compilation of financial statements. Similarly, auditors will now be required only to state in their reports that the directors' report is consistent with a company's financial statements and indicate any matters coming to their attention that were inconsistent with information in the directors' report. With regard to forward-looking statements included in the directors' report, the government said that directors should clearly distinguish statements based on good-faith judgments from those based on objective verifiable information and may warn users to treat with caution the former. A minor confidentiality protection was introduced, allowing the withholding of information concerning matters in the course of negotiation. The government has provided no reasons for these relaxations.

This story conflicts with the government's view that the OFR was an example of "gold plating" EU requirements, as the suggestion of a detailed and mandatory report seems to be a U.K. initiative. It is moot whether the abandonment of the compulsory OFR will generate many savings, as these would accrue only to quoted companies that will still be under pressure from the market to provide or continue to provide a similar voluntary OFR. Moreover, quoted companies along with all large and (with certain exemptions) medium-sized companies will have to satisfy the EU Modernisation Directive in their directors' reports. This requires a review of the development and performance of the business and its position, including its principal risks and uncertainties and appropriate financial key performance indicators that provide information on environmental and employee matters. Considerably more flexibility in meeting these requirements is allowed to companies and detailed standards will not apply. Of all the essential information previously required in the OFR, that relating directly to business objectives, trends, strategies, and capital structure no longer need to be provided.

We see major difficulty with mandatory approaches to management reports, especially of the OFR and the MD&A type. Our country studies suggest that much of the information investors require concerning a company is likely to be specific to the company, business, and location. Such information is unlikely to be fully captured by universally requiring detailed information about a very large range of issues.

Although we favor voluntary disclosure, we also support some general and legal requirements to provide information along the lines of the previously stated objectives of the OFR and similar to the level of disclosure required for financial reports in the U.K. Companies Acts. Such a requirement would alert investors to those companies that are strongly derelict in this area, though the absence of voluntary reporting might also provide a signal to this effect. We also favor authoritative but voluntary guidelines based on perceived best practice. This approach would not inhibit firms from experimenting with innovative approaches to information provision, which, however, may be the result of the U.K. government's and the SEC approaches in this area.

INTANGIBLES

The management or directors' report to shareholders usually includes some information relating to the difference between the stock market value of the firm and the balance-sheet value of its net assets. This difference is called by a variety of names, including internal goodwill, organizational efficiency, intellectual capital, and intangibles. It is the present value of expected return on enterprise net assets that is greater than the normal expected return on the book value of those assets (supranormal profits). This discounted value of supranormal profits is generated by independent projects that have positive net present values, the benefits from assets (such as intangibles) not recognized in financial statements, and profits flowing from interrelationships (synergies) between the firm's assets and liabilities and its networks of activities.

Much of the difference between the market value and the book value of net assets is attributable to intangible assets that are not included in the financial statements. Intangible assets—identifiable nonmonetary assets without physical substance—include, among others, advertising, customer goodwill, employee training, productive processes, computer programs, and trademarks. They may be purchased or created internally, either separate or embedded in another asset to which they lend value. Because they do not have significant physical form, these assets often have no market value that is independent from a company as a whole, and their value-in-use is difficult or impossible to measure. Consequently, although intangibles often generate substantial net revenue and may be vital to the enterprise, they generally are not recognized as assets in balance sheets (capitalized), with three exceptions.

When intangibles are purchased rather than created, the amounts paid are capitalized, as they are with physical assets. Patents, trademarks, and processes also might be purchased.

When an intangible is created internally, the amount expended that results in and is ascribed to a recorded asset, such as a patent, is capitalized, even though this usually greatly understates its economic value. IFRS requires capitalization of internally created intangible assets for development expenditures when the intangible asset being created has met rigorous conditions, including that its completion is technically feasible and the intention to use or sell it can be demonstrated. Recognition is restricted to expenditures incurred after the time these conditions are satisfied. This implies that even if development costs were capitalized, the amount usually is only a small part of its total development cost. U.S. GAAP allow capitalization of a (usually small) proportion of the costs of internal software development for which technical feasibility can be demonstrated. Under IFRS, capitalized intangibles can be revalued, but only if an active market for identical items exists, which rules out almost all revaluations.

The most important intangible occurs when a business is acquired, giving rise to goodwill—the difference between the fair value ascribed to the assets and liabilities purchased and the amount paid for the entire business. Purchased goodwill is recognized in the financial statements to balance the difference between the price of a corporate acquisition and the value of the net assets acquired. Purchased goodwill consists of several components, not all of which satisfy the recognition criteria for assets. Nevertheless, most standard setters state that such goodwill must be recognized as an asset. Company-originated goodwill, on the other hand, is not recognizable because it is internally generated and is not realized in a business combination.

Inclusion in Balance Sheets and Income Statements

Not reporting intangibles as balance-sheet assets has been strongly criticized because these assets can be important drivers of stock market values. Investments in successful intangibles often give rise to very large profits. For example, Lev [2001, p. 24] cites the American Airlines' Sabre reservation system, which, in return for a US$40 million investment in the 1960s and 1970s, was valued by the market as worth US$3.3 billion in the mid-1990s. Similarly, continued investment in its trademark has sustained Coca Cola's position as one of the world's highest-valued brands. Nevertheless, these very valuable intangible assets are reported on their owners' balance sheets at nominal amounts, with the amounts expended to develop them and maintain their value reported as expenses.

One way to measure the value of a company's intangibles is to compare its security market value with the present value of its net tangible assets, where these values can be obtained. Since such asset values in use are rarely known, accounting book values measured as amortized historical cost and, for some financial assets, fair values must be used to measure net tangible assets. Assuming that book values provide a valid measure of net tangible assets (a heroic assumption), the ratio of market to book value per share indicates the extent to which intangible assets are present but not reported, although not all the difference between market and book value can be ascribed to intangible assets.

Lev [2001, pp. 8–9] found that the average market-to-book ratio of the top 500 companies in the United States was around one up until the mid-1980s, then increased to a peak of just below 8.0 in 1999, falling to approximately 6.0 in 2001. Thus, in 2001 the values of net assets recorded in the accounts constituted only some 17 percent of stock market values, on average. However, this average includes some important outliers: in 1998, the ratio stood at 21.4 for the then largest Internet companies. These numbers clearly indicate the importance of intangibles for some companies.

Given the importance of intangibles, a number of authoritative commentators, particularly Lev, believe that the present practice of immediately expensing these assets leaves such a large "black hole" in the accounts that some inclusion is preferable, despite measurement problems.[19] He proposes that internally generated intangibles should be recorded as assets, but under strict conditions.[20]

Lev and Zarowin [1999] offer two suggestions for recognizing intangibles as assets, and their amortization over time as expenses. First, they would have firms capitalize intangibles that passed some technological test of feasibility, such as a clinical test for a drug. Capitalization would include all previously expensed research and development costs. This approach would require management to provide information about the progress of development projects and to satisfy a necessary, prespecified test to prove technological feasibility. No further details are given of this test. Lev and Zarowin are aware that this procedure affords managers an opportunity to manage reported earnings. However, if the capitalizations and amortizations are reported separately in the financial statements, users and analysts can reverse them easily if they wish (although there is more involved than just subtracting the respective amounts, as there are consequential effects in deferred taxes).

Second, Lev and Zarowin urge the restatement of past financial reports to reflect ex post the degree of certainty attached to past and documented changes in the factors (change drivers) affecting those intangibles that cannot satisfy their capitalization test. They have in mind items like the costs of corporate reorganization or industry deregulation, which may involve extensive employee training, plant reorganization and restructuring, and the acquisition of new know-how. The costs of restructuring or of an acquisition would be written off when incurred but would be capitalized in the future by restating past reports as the actual benefits become clear over time. With this thinking, initially it would be reasonable to write off the costs of a new research and development project that does not meet their criterion for capitalization. However, the previous accounting statements would be restated by capitalizing project research and development costs in past years as the project proceeds and it can clearly be documented that uncertainty is being resolved by, for example, the acceptance by drug regulators of a drug for commercial release. No details are given of how such restatements would be calculated, nor is it made clear what proportion, if any, of previously written-off costs should be capitalized in the light of some good but not conclusive news of commercial success. Furthermore, restatements of previous financial statements generally violate "clean surplus," because the gain on ex post capitalization is not included in the annual reported income.

We cannot support either suggestion. Despite the importance of intangibles, we do not agree that financial statements should or can provide the information investors might want about intangible values (or, indeed, all the information that investors might want about many other assets and liabilities). Reliability is an essential criterion for inclusion in balance sheets, income statements, and statements of cash flows. For some intangibles (presumably a relatively small proportion), the passing of an independent technological test is a necessary condition for them to generate future economic benefits but is not sufficient to ensure commercial success. This uncertainty can be resolved only when the products generated by intangibles are successfully marketed or the intangible is sold. Capitalization prior to this time necessarily must be based on the subjective views of management. The suggestion of capitalization as the future is resolved seems to require information far beyond existing accounting practice and would give management potentially artificial incentives to report "success." Any capitalization that did occur would be redundant, as alternative information about success would already be available.

Supplementary Intangibles Disclosures

Current accounting standards include only limited supplementary disclosures of intangibles (such as through footnotes). For example, IAS 38 (Intangible Assets) requires disclosure of the aggregate amount of research and development expenditures and encourages companies to provide a brief description of intangibles that are controlled but not recognized. Considering the ever-increasing importance of intangibles, this is generally considered not sufficient.

Many suggestions have been advanced relating to the content and form of information that should be reported to supplement financial statement numbers.[21] Most of these ideas have come from researchers and consulting firms. The proposed frameworks differ not only in their definition and the classification of intangibles, but also in the form of the report. What they do have in common is reliance on nonfinancial information to indicate the existence and importance of intangibles in a company. Many proposals draw heavily from the management and organization literature and focus more on the management of intangibles than on the provision of information addressed to investors in capital markets.[22] They usually do not prescribe specific measures, because these must be highly entity-specific but include examples of nonfinancial measures grouped in specific categories. (For a suitable fee, though, the consultants would be willing to design a procedure.) Most of the nonfinancial measures are input-oriented. Only a few are output-oriented and, because of this, they often are poor proxies for firm value creation. It is also unclear how precise, easy to manipulate, and difficult to audit many of these measures are, which casts doubt on how trustworthy they are at the end.

Lev [2001] presents a specific proposal for supplementary disclosure of intangibles. He suggests using what he calls "a voluntary quantitative score card" for an enterprise's "value chain for innovative activity." He accepts that reporting on innovation would have to be company-specific, but generally would want detailed information on nine specific areas grouped into three phases. The phase labeled "discovery and learning" requires information about (1) internal learning activities, such as R&D and training, (2) acquired innovative capability, and (3) network building. The second "implementation phase" would require information on (1) corporate intellectual property, (2) the current technological feasibility of development processes, and (3) information about the company's use of the Internet. The "final phase" provides information about the commercial development of intangibles. We see this as a well-thought-out approach to providing supplementary information useful to investors, but, we are less enthusiastic about his strong suggestion that the FASB (with oversight from the SEC) should standardize (but not require) these disclosures in some detail for all companies. We would expect such disclosures to be substantially firm-specific, and therefore we doubt that they should be mandatory. Furthermore, in contrast to Lev, we doubt whether standard setters have the necessary expertise to design the procedures that would be required, or that auditors could audit the disclosures and attest to their validity, except at substantial cost to companies.

Some standard setters have issued guidelines incorporating some of these proposals as supplementary information for financial reports. They generally say they have invested substantial resources in the issue, but, with the exception of the SEC, they have not yet come up with mandatory disclosure standards or detailed guidance. We support the development and advancement of proposals for structuring disclosures of intangibles, because it is in line with our preference for (constrained) market solutions for international accounting standards (see the arguments in Chapter 10). Given the increasing importance of intangibles, more and more companies should be interested in finding a reporting structure most suitable to their needs. A horse race among different reporting solutions could help identify useful procedures.

For example, supranormal profits (goodwill) that can clearly be attached to specific assets might be computed and reported. An example is valuation of the supranormal profits from the sale of a cellular phone service that is generated by selling cellular phones that can be used only for that service at a subsidized (less-than-marginal cost) price. If telecommunication companies can reliably estimate the additional net cash flows from cell-phone use from customers owning those phones (e.g., from a reduction in switching to another company), the present value of those net cash flows could be reported in a supplementary report.

Regulators of competition in countries where excess rate of return on investment is used as *prima facie* evidence of anticompetitive behavior, such as the United Kingdom, are already facing this problem because of the economic significance of intangibles in the asset bases of firms. The conditions for the recognition of such items in a firm's asset base, although more liberal than GAAP, are still highly restrictive. Such approaches cannot deal with the disclosures of the valuation of corporate internal goodwill, which may well be beyond the reach of accounting [see Competition Commission, 1999].

RISK

Another area where traditional accounting does not and probably cannot give adequate information is information about risk. Financial statements include values, estimated values, or risk-adjusted values of certain transactions or events. Risk is captured by contingencies and, on a general level, by conservative reporting requirements. Financial statements do not include measures of the volatility of these values, either individually or jointly, although there have been some suggestions to provide lower and/or upper bounds on individual reported values.

Many standard setters worldwide now include requirements for the disclosure of risk of financial instruments, although this is only part of the full risk situation a company faces. A major reason is that it is usually easier to quantify risk inherent in financial instruments than operational or business risks. But even then there are no generally accepted ways to measure financial risks and report about them.

An interesting approach to deal with this issue has been advanced by the IASB. It differs from the approach we discuss above for the management report in that it has a mandatory flavor but still leaves leeway to firms. IFRS7 (Financial Instruments: Disclosures), published in August 2005, deals with the disclosure of the risk inherent in financial instruments.[23] The disclosure would be given in notes to the financial statements rather than in the management's report outside of the financial statements. The new standard requires some quantitative disclosures based on the approach that management actually uses in running the business. Disclosures will, thus, follow how the management of a company manages and controls risk and how risk is measured and reported upon internally. The standard also requires quantitative disclosures to ensure that companies provide some minimal risk disclosures and to improve the comparability of such information across companies. It includes specific quantitative disclosure related to credit risk, liquidity risk, and financial market risk but not to operational risk, although such risks are part of the overall risk of the company and are related to financial risks where companies use financial instruments to hedge their operational risks.

A broader perspective for risk disclosures is taken in the German DRS 5, Risk Reporting, from 2001. It addresses operational risks and financial risks and also pursues a management approach. Similarly, the SEC requires in 10-K filings and in the MD&A the disclosure of a wide range of risks—market, operational, credit, and accounting—and requires both quantitative and qualitative disclosures. It does not allude to the management approach, though.

We suggest that with current knowledge, the best regulators can sensibly do is require that companies report on risk, but not produce long lists calling for supplementary disclosures on risk of all types. It is clear that such information is always partial in some ways, as many relevant perspectives of risk are not measurable or are dependent on other activities of the company. The risks companies confront are highly firm-specific and context-dependent. Hence, even if risk disclosures were required, they are hardly comparable across companies. However, this is a general drawback of the management approach to financial accounting.

NONFINANCIAL (INNOVATIVE) DISCLOSURES

For reasons given above, our approach is that the contents of supplementary information are not a matter for regulators and should be left to firms to provide voluntarily. For example, PwC's *ValueReporting* initiative has done much to try to persuade firms that there are advantages in providing additional information.[24] The essence of the PwC approach is to report the key information relevant to the firm's established business strategy. This information ideally might be presented on the Internet, organized along the following lines:

1. Market overview reflecting the firm's external environment
2. The firm's strategy to create value, given its competitive environment
3. The degree of achievement of the firm's financial and other targets
4. The management structure employed to obtain value and an explanation of the underlying value drivers, most of which are likely to be nonfinancial
5. A commentary on how well the firm manages its value drivers to achieve value.

Some firms do publish, either in the accounting report or in separate reports, considerable information concerning health, safety, and environmental information (HSE). Globally, up to 2,000 companies issue nonfinancial reports of a great variety of types, mainly in this area.[25] The Global Reporting Initiative (GRI), a United Nations-backed initiative, has developed detailed guidelines in this area that are used by BP among other global companies.[26] Some regulatory regimes require the reporting of information in these areas. For example, French listed corporations are required to report on ecological and social matters. Some pioneer companies, notably Scandinavian ones, have gone much further and present some measures of value drivers affecting their intellectual capital, such as staff training and employee turnover figures, employee satisfaction, computer power per staff member, amount of resources necessary to build supplier and customer relationships, customer satisfaction, new products in development, and the percentage of the product portfolio representing newly introduced products. Generally, the measures reported are chosen for the ability of the company to measure them reliably rather than their congruence with information required by a stock valuation model. Many of these figures are validated by experts in a relevant profession or the auditors and are reconciled with the financial reports where appropriate. Additionally, these companies also report targets and compare these with actual performance. Some companies recognize the importance of the balanced scorecard in management for presenting key performance objectives and indicators and showing how well these have been achieved in the past.[27] The information included may expand as the companies learn how to measure more items.

It is ironic that one of the leading companies experimenting with different levels of audit assurance, especially with regard to HSE disclosures, is the Royal Dutch/Shell Group, given that it recently paid a fine for misstating its oil reserves. This may raise some doubt about the validity of its experiments with levels of audit assurance; however, there is no doubt that it is a leader in the area of supplementary, innovative disclosures.[28]

There are a number of ways of validating the data presented. Assurance can be given that the information makes sense relative to the entity's past or is based on reasonable assumptions that have been tested against generally accepted assumptions in the area. Assurance can be given that forecasts include all relevant variables and are generated by reasonable and generally accepted procedures and systems using state-of-the-art technology. Thus, a statement indicating the degree of validity can be attached to various items of information with the appropriate assurance procedures. Although this represents only a difference of degree relating to the tasks currently facing the auditor, users of financial statements are unlikely to give the same creditability to such validations of information as to the audits of the financial statements themselves.

The verifiers of the supplementary information provided by Shell (KPMG and PwC) provide verification for a variety of items of information. For example, in the 2002 report, figures derived from the financial reports are stated to be consistent with those reports. Health and safety figures are validated as properly reflecting performance with regard to specific indicators. They employ a number of levels of verification. The lowest, aside from no verification for an information item, is a test only of the accuracy of the consolidation of the data from the countries in which Shell operates. The next higher level is checking the validity of statements based on underlying evidence possessed and presented by Shell. The highest level of assurance is that the auditors understand the systems and processes used by Shell to measure social performance and they have validated the completeness and accuracy of the data by interviewing Shell people and external experts and by reviewing documentation and confirming the use of external data. The 2003 report confined verification to those items that could be assured at the highest level. The Shell verifiers state that they follow international best practice in auditing in developing their procedures, use multidisciplinary teams, and seek reasonably reliable measures. The verifiers are not able to verify everything in the report and explicitly state that their role does not extend to verifying forecasts. In contrast, BP's auditors restrict their validation to confirming that the company's statements in its report are correct. They do not explain their assurance practices.

We favor a more general use of this type of validation on a voluntary basis, which should help the market decide what creditability to give to items in supplementary statements. This can build creditability in the market, which should be enhanced by the reputation that the verifiers have achieved in traditional auditing. Again, it is for companies to trade off the benefits and costs of such validation. IPAs, though, should be wary of lending their reputations to questionable claims by management of HSE achievements, particularly those that include monetary estimates of social benefits that are inherently difficult if not impossible to measure meaningfully.[29] Financial reports or supplementary reports contain few forecasts. Some of the Scandinavian firms referred to above have reported targets, often expressed qualitatively, for achievement in the area of intellectual capital. Geest plc, a U.K. prepared-food manufacturer and distributor, is an example of a pioneer in this area.[30] In its 2002 annual report, it estimated likely overall future growth in its markets over a period of years and forecast benefits from its plans for projects, such as cost reductions. Its 2003 annual report did not comment on these forecasts and did not make further similar forecasts. It did, however, set out its target internal rate of return on property investments, both new builds and extensions, and indicated a target return on capital employed, which can be checked by shareholders in the future.

As noted by Benston [1982], the one-time-only or watered-down claim of benefits in future reports is not unusual, because such increased disclosures were essentially public relations vehicles that were discontinued if and when the benefits wore off. For example, the 2000 Shell report set a target return on average capital employed for one year ahead and reported on its achievement. This has since disappeared and been replaced by an historical comparison of the returns in the industry. Similarly, Geest's market forecasts were less quantitative in 2003. A reduction in the level of voluntary disclosure can lead sophisticated investors, who follow the firm over a period of time, to infer bad news. Less sophisticated investors may have difficulty doing that. This is where consistency requirements for voluntary disclosures or even a mandatory note that consistency has not been followed may be useful in the capital markets.

CONCLUSIONS

The examples we have provided in this concluding chapter illustrate that there are varying benefits and costs to companies of providing supplementary information. Mandating detailed disclosure requirements at this point thus cannot be efficient. Companies should have leeway to disclose this information voluntarily. If the expected benefits of disclosure exceed their costs, companies could be quite innovative in their disclosures and the way they choose to establish the creditability of the information they provide. Experience from experimenting with disclosures and private initiatives to improve supplementary disclosures, such as the AICPA's Business Reporting and the more recent Enhanced Business Reporting initiatives, are ways to establish best practices and encourage competing approaches for such disclosures. New information technologies, such as Extensible Business Reporting Language (XBRL), further aid in reducing the costs of providing supplementary disclosures. However, we believe these additional information demands on companies should not be used to compromise one of the main characteristics of financial statement information, their trustworthiness, but rather should and can be met by developing supplementary voluntary disclosures. Disclosures useful to investors and others will survive, and the market will press other companies to provide similar information.

Notes

Chapter 1

1. In our earlier book [Benston et al., 2003] we analyzed corporate disclosure in the light of the Enron failure and other almost contemporaneous corporate reporting scandals.

2. "Table 13: Dollar Volume by Exchange." SEC Annual Report, 2002, data from SEC form R-31. Available at www.sec.gov/pdf/annrep02/ar02full.pdf.

3. On April 3, 2000, the S&P 500 opened at 1490.23, and on Dec. 31, 2003, the S&P 500 closed at 1490.23. See http://finance.yahoo.com.

4. See Deutsche Bundesbank (www.bundesbank.de/stat/zeitreihen/html/wu080u.htm).

5. See Tokyo Stock Exchange, 2004, Fact Book 2003, Tokyo: Tokyo Stock Exchange; see www.tse.or.jp/english/factbook/fact_book_2003.pdf.

6. Investment Company Institute, 2002, Equity Ownership in America 2002, Figure 1. See www.ici.org/stats/res/1rpt_02_equity_owners.pdf.

7. National Statistics, 2003, Share Ownership: A report on ownership of shares as at 31st December 2002. London: Her Majesty's Stationery Office.

8. Source: Deutsche Bundesbank statistics, September 2003, Security Deposits, Special Statistical Report 9, pp. 32. See http://www.bundesbank.de/stat/download/stat_sonder/statso9_en.pdf.

9. See TSE Fact Book, 2003.

10. TOSTNeT (Tokyo Network Trading System) was introduced in 1998 but closed in 1999.

11. For a comparison of the differences in cross-border capital movements prior to World War I and now, see Bordo, Eichengreen, and Irwin [1999], especially pp. 24–32.

12. JP Morgan ADR Group, 2004. "US Investors: Level of Investment Abroad, 3Q03." New York, January. Available at www.adr.com/pdf/3Q03Final_cap_flows.pdf.

13. www.imf.org/external/np/res/seminars/2002/global/rouwe/pdf.

14. Currency risk and transactions costs also are among the key impediments to cross-border integration of goods markets. These factors help explain why Canadians are 12 times more likely to trade with each other than with Americans, despite the physical and cultural proximity of the two countries [see Helliwell, 1998]. For a more general source on the frictions impeding cross-border integration, see Frankel [2001].

15. Tesar and Werner [1998]. For an excellent summary of the literature on "home country bias," see Lewis [1999].

16. See World Bank [1997]. For evidence of the benefits of the FDI in the financial sector in particular, see Litan et al. [2001].

Chapter 2

1. However, we are aware of unplanned claimants of the enterprise resulting from externalities (e.g., if they are involved in environmental or product liability cases). These claimants have no ex ante contractual means to protect their interests against the enterprise.

2. Under certain conditions, corporations have incentives to report truthfully even without verification. This is referred to as "cheap talk," which can be credible if the interests of the corporation and the user are relatively similar, or if diverse users (such as the capital market and a competitor) discipline the corporation's disclosure.

3. Investors probably would want to learn when they would be better off if their corporation were liquidated. However, as we just discussed, the cost of obtaining disposal values for all a firm's assets and liabilities, or even for the firm as a whole, almost always is very substantial.

4. U.S. GAAP and IFRS call for inconsistent measurements with respect to market values of securities. SFAS 115 and IAS 39 require companies that expect to keep debt securities until they mature to record these assets at their cost, less amortization, even when the securities have trustworthy market prices. While other securities are marked to market, the changes in value of "available-for-sale" securities are charged against equity and not against income.

5. For analyses, see Horton and Macve [2000]. For a discussion see Bromwich [2001].

6. U.S. experience of appraisals made by professionals for some savings and loan associations during the 1980s, prior to the collapse of the industry, was not positive. Against this, few property valuations in the United Kingdom have been questioned.

7. There is some empirical evidence of the value relevance of some fixed-asset revaluations and therefore a degree of trustworthiness (otherwise they would not be acted upon); e.g., Aboody et al. [1999] and Barth and Clinch [1998].

8. See, for example, the FASB's *Proposed Statement on Financial Accounting Standards, Fair Value Measurements,* June 2004.

9. We note that revaluation gains are reported as comprehensive income or changes to equity rather than in the income statement, but expenses are higher if the revalued assets are depreciated.

10. This section is adapted from Benston [2003B].

11. In Chapter 11 we evaluate and as a result reject the asset/liability approach now emphasized by the FASB and IASB.

12. At this writing, Ernst and Young faces a claim for £3.6 billion with regard to Equitable Life, an amount that would bring any large IPA firm down if awarded.

13. Professor Benzion Barlev (Hebrew University, Jerusalem) suggests to us that this conclusion is incorrect. He reasons that the profession has been at a crisis due to the potential cost of class-action lawsuits. This has generated mandatory peer reviews, which in turn has made auditing a common product whose production function is known to all. Consequently, IPA firms cannot earn above-normal returns. As a result, they had to cut the cost of auditing, relying on "analytical reviews" in place of substantive sampling, which has increased the potential for mistakes. This could explain why auditors moved to various management advisory services (MAS) and rely more on insurance.

Chapter 3

1. At this writing, the PCAOB in the United States is reconsidering the GAAS compiled previously by the AICPA.

2. The U.S. Sarbanes-Oxley Act of 2002 requires the senior officers of publicly traded corporations to vouch for the effectiveness of their internal control system.

3. Although it probably is politically impossible to return to having accounting standards established entirely by professional accountancy organizations and academics, the change may have been costly to investors if the benefits from reduced audit failures and better financial information disclosure have been less than the higher audit and accounting costs and restraints on information disclosure that were imposed.

4. There is some evidence that various Sarbanes-Oxley Act provisions have imposed costs that exceed benefits to investors, particularly the requirement of Section 404 that requires management assessment and an external audit of the effectiveness of a company's internal control system. A survey of 321 corporations by Financial Executives International (http://fei.org) found that the first-year costs could exceed $4.6 million per company for the largest companies, and $2 million on average for all 321 companies surveyed. The extent to which this exercise might obviate frauds and reporting misstatements is not known.

5. By mutual recognition the London Stock Exchange accepts financial statements that follow national GAAP from companies located in the EU; it also accepts IFSR-based statements.

Chapter 4

1. For a more extended description of state regulations of securities, see James S. Mofsky [1971] and *Commerce Clearing House Blue Sky Law Reporter* (current).

2. See Mofsky [1971], p. 27, note 3.

3. This narrative is based on the account given by Zeff [1972], pp. 119–126.

4. These included: (1) "Unrealized profit should not be credited to an income account of the corporation either directly or indirectly;" (2) "Capital surplus, however created, should not be used to relieve the income account of the current or future years of charges that otherwise would fall to be made there against;" (3) "Earned surplus [now called retained earnings] of a subsidiary company created

prior to acquisition does not form a part of the consolidated earned surplus of the parent;" (4) Treasury stock could be held as an asset, but "dividends on stock so held should not be treated as a credit to the income account of the company;" (5) "Notes or accounts receivable due from officers, employees, or affiliated companies must be shown separately." In 1934 a sixth was added, on "treasury stock subterfuge," wherein stock was issued to patent holder upon formation of a company, and then donated to the company to create treasury stock [Zeff, 1972, p. 125].

5. However, George Stigler [1965] showed that, per dollar of investment, the stockholders of U.S. Steel did twice as well as the stockholders of its competitors over a period of 18 years.

6. These data are taken from the 2003 NYSE Fact Book.

7. For a description of accounting and audit standards applicable to companies whose shares are not registered and traded on national exchanges, see the Appendix to Chapter 9.

8. These were the American Institute of Accountants and American Society of Certified Public Accountants until 1937, when they merged to create the American Institute of Certified Public Accountants (AICPA). Since 1973, statements issued by the Financial Accounting Standards Board (FASB) have been accepted as authoritative, with a few exceptions.

9. Reasons include timing, as many standards were promulgated before the concepts statements were developed, and reluctance to change existing standards. For example, SFAC 7 clearly states that not discounting deferred taxes, as is specified in FAS 109, is not consistent with the principles laid out in the concept statement.

10. Seven SFACs have been issued. SFAC No. 3 was replaced by SFAC No. 6. SFAC No. 4, "Objectives of Financial Reporting by Nonbusiness Organizations," is not relevant to the present study.

11. As of 2000, the SECPS had 1,285 members, 478 (37 percent) of whom had no SEC clients and 53 (4 percent) of whom had more than 10 SEC clients. About 1 percent of U.S.-based SEC registrants were audited by 50 U.S. firms that were not members of SEPC because of past violations of membership requirements. Presumably these firms were not members of the AICPA [Panel on Audit Effectiveness, 2000, pp. 181, 188]. The five largest firms audited 76 percent of SEC registrants in 1999 [ibid., p. 182].

12. AICPA web site, www.nhscpa.org/SEC%practice%section&restructuring.

13. See Appendix C of The Panel on Audit Effectiveness [2000] for a much more complete description of the audit review process and AICPA committees.

14. Much of the material that follows is derived from Thompson [2003].

15. Thompson [2003, p. 975] pointed out that this requirement can be avoided, giving as an example the merger of Time, Inc. and Warner Communications: "the managers of Time were able to fairly easily avoid the vote of their shareholders by converting the acquisition from a stock-for-stock merger to a cash-for-shares tender offer by which Time, Inc. solicited tenders for Warner shares."

16. The definition of what constitutes a "security" subject to the federal securities acts is very complex and has been made even more complex as aggrieved purchasers of investments and obligations that were not registered with the SEC sought to obtain damages based on the failure of the seller to register the investments.

17. In 1998–2000, 24 percent of the restatements were due to the SEC, compared to 16 percent in 1990–1997.

18. A follow-on study of an additional 202 of the restatements found a 3-day unadjusted market price loss of 5 percent, or $14 billion.

19. See Mulford and Comiskey [2002] and Schilit [2002], from which these examples were drawn, for many other instances.

20. Cited in Panel on Audit Effectiveness [2000], p. 205.

21. The rule also narrowed the proscription against audit-firm members who were directly or indirectly associated with an audit owning stock in that client.

22. For example, in his book *Take on the Street*, the former chairman of the SEC, Arthur Levitt, points to several such instances: Motorola paid KPMG "just $4 million for audit services but $35 million for computer consulting and another $27 million for other consulting services. General Motors Corp. paid Deloitte & Touche $17 million for auditing and another $79 million for other services. And Sprint Corp. paid Ernst & Young only $2.5 million to conduct its audit but $64 million for consulting and other services." He then continues, somewhat disingenuously: "I'm not suggesting that each of these audit firms has compromised its independence. But I have to wonder if any individual auditor, working on a $2.5 million audit contract, would have the guts to stand up to a CFO and question a dubious number in the books, thus possibly jeopardizing $64 million in business for the firm's consultants" [Levitt, 2002, p. 138].

23. The GAO [2002, p. 85] states in full: "The cases were selected based on asset size, restatement period, percentage change in earnings following the restatement, reason for the restatement, and market where stock traded."

24. Hilzenrath [2001] found that: "The state of New York, which had the most accountants sanctioned by the SEC, as of June had disciplined [only] 17 of 49 New York accountants."

25. In particular, the Act assigns joint-and-several liability only where the jury specifically finds that the defendant knowingly violated the securities laws.

26. A similar proposal is made by a committee of the American Accounting Association [Maines et al., 2003].

Chapter 5

1. The United Kingdom comprises Great Britain (England, Wales, and Scotland) and Northern Ireland. Scotland has a separate (Roman-law based) legal system.

2. LSE: Primary Market Fact Sheet, November 2004.

3. The Bank of England Act, 1998.

4. For more details on the FSA see Financial Services Authority [1997] and Financial Services Authority [2000A].

5. The FSA's statutory objectives are to sustain confidence in the U.K. financial system; promote public understanding of the financial system; secure an appropriate degree of protection for consumers by ensuring that firms are competent and financially secure, subject to consumers having responsibility for their own decisions; and aid in the reduction of financial crime.

6. See Department of Trade and Industry [2001].

7. See Financial Services Authority [2000], p. 17.

8. For similar views see International Organization of Securities Commissions (IOSCO), 1998, September, pp. 25–27, 31, 34–35.

9. As an example, see IOSCO *Technical Committee Bulletin: Investor Protection in the New Economy* [undated].

10. Here we refer to the companies acts individually. Usual practice is that when reference is made to the Companies Act, this is currently understood to be the 1985 Act as amended by the 1989 Act.

11. See Hoffman and Arden [1983, 1984].

12. Some commentators, for example Ernst and Young (UK), prefer the term "generally accepted accounting practice," reflecting a wider scope for the term and the lack of any statutory or regulatory definition of accounting principles.

13. For example, Ernst and Young issues very detailed commentaries on U.K. and international GAAP, which provides surveys of controversial items, and also gives its views, which sometimes differ from those of other firms.

14. Prior to the 1967 Companies Act, "exempt private companies" were not required to file accounts.

15. Economists also believe that the market for corporate control is important for enforcing corporate governance. Companies failing to do well by their shareholders are prone to being taken over by investors or other companies, which install management more attuned to the stockholders' wishes. Given the relative ease with which mergers and acquisitions can be mounted in the United Kingdom, this should be major influence on good corporate governance. However, generally in the United Kingdom the acquiring firm's value does not increase following an acquisition. The target company's value does on average rise, with a gain to the shareholders of the acquired company. Long-term corporate governance may therefore not be improved by take-overs, as they do not seem to yield long-term efficiency gains, although the evidence and interpretation of that evidence is mixed. The evidence from the United States is similar, except that disciplinary (hostile) takeovers based on the poor performance of extant management do create additional value to the acquirer's shareholders.

16. The three major reports are the *Report on the Financial Aspects of Corporate Governance* [Cadbury Report, 1992]; *Directors' Remuneration: Report of a Study Group Chaired by Sir Richard Greenbury* [Greenbury report, 1995], and *Committee on Corporate Governance: Final Report* [Hampel Report, 1998]. These reports were consolidated in the Combined Code by the Hampel Committee and the London Stock Exchange, published as *Committee on Corporate Governance* [1998].

17. See Smith [2003] and Higgs [2003].

18. The Secretary of State can approve suitably qualified individuals (a small number).

19. See Department of Trade and Industry [2003].

20. See the Co-ordinating Group on Audit and Accounting Issues [2003].

21. *Company Reporting*, a monthly review, regularly documents such failures, which sometimes are very serious (www.companyreporting.com).

22. Over the year 1999/2000, the FSA mounted one criminal prosecution and 11 High Court civil cases, investigated 159 cases falling within their authority, and used their powers in 110 cases. (See FSA [2000B].) The number of detailed investigations did not change substantially in 2001/2002 (FSA [2002]). However, the number (and total amount) of fines has increased from 79 (£6m) in 2001/2002 to 16 (over £10m) in 2002/2003.

Chapter 6

1. See Schneider [1995], pp. 125–128.

2. A vast number of fraudulent bankruptcies in France are considered the driving force behind that regulation. See, e.g., Walton [1995], p. 5.

3. See Schröer [1993], p. 336.

4. See Leffson [1988], pp. 3–4.

5. The original German group-accounting principles were aimed at consolidating only companies that were in fact managed by the parent company. The control concept of consolidation was introduced only as a result of transposing the Seventh Directive.

6. See, e.g., Allen and Gale [2000]. Krahnen and Schmidt [2004] provide a more detailed analysis and argue that the German financial system is currently in a transition process to a more capital market-based system.

7. Cash flow data show that German firms relied less on debt than U.K. firms over the period 1970–1989. See Edwards and Fischer [1994], pp. 264–265.

8. See Alexander and Bohl [2000], pp. 468–469.

9. See Theissen [2004], p. 141.

10. See Ordelheide and Pfaff [1994], p. 89.

11. The law includes a fall-back rule in case no such private standard setter was established. In that case the Ministry of Justice itself would establish an accounting council.

12. Interestingly, the IDW reacted to the constitution of the GASB by increasing its output of opinions and recommendations, often in areas expected to be on the future agenda of the GASB. This almost predatory move was mitigated in later years after it was recognized that the GASB was effective in setting standards, something that was not clear from the beginning when some commentators, perhaps, thought that it would be busy with internal quarrels on legal and constitutional issues.

13. This process is not dissimilar to that of other private standard setters in EU member states, notably the ASC in the United Kingdom, whose authority was at first similarly questioned by lawyers.

14. Nevertheless, many corporations adjust reserves from retained earnings so as to show a net profit in the consolidated statements equal to the distributable profit reported in the individual statements.

15. The authoritativeness principle applies to individual statements and not to the consolidated statements. However, since individual and consolidated statements are usually closely related, it carries over to the consolidated statements, although to a lesser extent, and only on a voluntary basis. There is generally no consolidated tax assessment, so each legal form is subject to tax.

16. In fact, in 2002 there were only 26 applications, of which 18 were granted permission to avoid publication.

17. The Federal Financial Supervisory Authority reported some 4,500 disclosures in 2002, compared to 5,400 in 2001, and the trend is decreasing further.

18. This move was commented on critically in the German literature. See, e.g., Küting [1993], pp. 369–372, who considered the results of negotiation between Daimler-Benz with the SEC on various items a Pyrrhic victory for the German accounting practice.

19. In the end, the stricter listing requirements neither prevented fraud in the financial statements by some of the companies listed in the Neuer Markt nor halted the strong decline in value. The Stock Exchange finally closed down the Neuer Markt as of the end of 2003.

20. The Contact Committee of the European Union published opinions asserting that there are only a few significant conflicts between the (then) IAS and the accounting directives. The GASB issued a controversial opinion (DRS 1), which

goes even further by stating that there are also few conflicts between U.S. GAAP and the directives. The motivation for these opinions seemed to be generous to companies that choose to adopt internationally accepted accounting principles.

21. See, e.g., the opinion of legal academics [Arbeitskreis Bilanzrecht der Hochschullehrer Rechtswissenschaft, 2002].

22. Share listing is possible for stock corporations (Aktiengesellschaft) and the shares issued by a certain form of partnership (Kommanditgesellschaft auf Aktien), the latter being rather rare in practice.

23. There was some argument about an extension of the option to all companies, but in the end it was not taken up. In contrast, Austria, which introduced a similar rule a year later, opened the option to all companies.

24. The thresholds for the different sizes are measured by total assets, sales, and net income and are stated in the Fourth and Seventh Directives of the European Union. They are adjusted from time to time for the value of money.

25. Leuz and Wüstemann [2004] argued that the German accounting system is efficient in its original institutional setting that serves creditors (given their privileged informational situation) rather than dispersed capital market investors.

26. The generally held belief is that the two-tiered board system is not less efficient than the one-tiered system and that in practice the two systems converge. On the EU level, there is some discussion to giving listed companies an option to choose between these two systems, even if a member state allows only for one of the two systems.

27. In companies with less than 2,000 employees, the employee representation is one third of the board members. Special rules with a tendency to more codetermination apply to companies in the coal, iron, and steel industry.

28. See, e.g., von Werder [2004].

29. See Elsas and Krahnen [2004], p. 201.

30. The Government Panel on Corporate Governance [Baums, 2001, ¶314] consciously did not issue a recommendation for audit committees, either by law or by a code of corporate governance. However, the German Corporate Governance Code recommends establishment of an audit committee to oversee accounting and risk management activities and the auditor's engagement.

31. The German Panel on Corporate Governance published the Corporate Governance Rules for Quoted German Companies aimed at listed corporations, which draws heavily from the OECD [1999] Principles for Corporate Governance. The German financial analysts association, Deutsche Vereinigung für Finanzanalyse und Asset Management (DVFA), compiled a scorecard essentially based on these rules to assess the level of corporate governance in a corporation. The other initiative, the Berliner Initiativkreis, published a German Code of Corporate Governance, which is more broadly oriented and has a general management touch.

32. See Pellens et al. [2001], pp. 1247–1249. Acceptance of the codes appears to be dependent on the actual authority of the issuing committee, while the perceived quality of the rules seems less important.

33. A study [Oser et al., 2003] shows that all DAX-30 corporations complied with the disclosure requirement. Four of them complied with all 60 recommendations, one corporation reported noncompliance with 10 of the 60 recommendations, and most of the rest did not comply with one or two recommendations. The trend is toward compliance with more of the recommendations. Smaller listed corporations show less compliance with the disclosure requirement and the recommendations.

34. The Government Panel on Corporate Governance recommended that this be changed so that audit reports of the three years preceding bankruptcy should be made available to creditors in a bankruptcy case.

35. The Wirtschaftsprüferkammer comprises auditors who are eligible for any statutory audit (Wirtschaftsprüfer) and another type of auditors with lower professional qualifications (Buchprüfer), who are restricted to audits of medium-sized limited liability companies.

36. For example, the Wirtschaftsprüferkammer conducts annual reviews of audit opinions and published financial statements. In 2002, as a result of the review of some 17,000 audit opinions, it barred 10 auditors from further performing services, brought 19 auditors to the courts, and penalized another 7 auditors.

37. In addition, the Wirtschaftsprüferkammer annually reviews published financial statements, particularly with respect to compliance with disclosure rules. In 2001, it found only 32 erroneous financial statements out of a total of 15,378 investigated statements.

38. Data from the Federal Financial Supervisory Authority Annual Report, 2002.

39. See d'Arcy [2001], p. 172.

40. This need not be the case, though; for example, tax accounting rules are often amended every year or so if the tax authority perceives misuse or if there are short-term additional tax-collection desires.

41. See Ordelheide [1998], p. 20.

42. There are only few instances in which there is documented disagreement between corporations and their auditors. In 2000, according to a review of published opinions by the Wirtschaftsprüferkammer [2001, p. 16] out of a total of 14,475, there were 58 qualified opinions and one disclaimer, as well as 331 opinions with clarifications.

43. Indeed, the standard advanced accounting textbooks include German GAAP, IFRS, and U.S. GAAP together, making teaching a mess.

Chapter 7

1. Henceforth, reference to the European Union includes the former European Economic Community (EEC) and the European Community (EC).

2. Data from European Central Bank [2001].

3. It seems even difficult to count the number of individual options, because various authors arrive at different counts. The numbers reported here are from Fédération des Experts Comptables Européens [1997].

4. Several EU member states were not used to a rigid format before the introduction of the accounting directives, most prominently the United Kingdom.

5. We note, though, that at the time the directives were adopted, the member states also had not required cash flow statements and segment reports. It would have been difficult to require these in the directives. However, financial disclosure demands have changed since, but the directives have not (at least in these important fields).

6. However, several member states subject companies with unlimited liability for their owners to the same rules, mainly to avoid differential financial reporting across legal forms of companies.

7. See Haller and Walton [1998], p. 15.

8. Moreover, the relationship between the AAF and the Contact Committee that was formed to facilitate harmonization via the accounting directives was obscure.

9. As we document in Chapter 9, the U.S. GAAP reconciliation of the original German GAAP financial statements delivered surprisingly large differences that even more undermined the position of European accounting, because many observers would take these differences to argue that U.S. GAAP must be significantly "better"—an argument that does not directly follow from the comparison of different numbers per se.

10. See Haller [2002], p. 163. Since the costly provisions introduced by the U.S. Sarbanes-Oxley Act, many foreign corporations have sought delisting in the United States, which is very difficult.

11. We note that the IAS at that time were more suggestive of the accounting directives, since they included many options. Effective 1995, a major improvement had been made by revisions of many IAS. Options have since been further cut down.

12. Even against the opposition from some member states.

13. A similar political motivation is evidenced in the work of the FASB when it compared U.S. GAAP with IAS to find an enormous amount of conflicting rules. See Financial Accounting Standards Board [1999].

14. An Insider Dealing Directive was issued in 1989.

15. In 2001, the main rules were combined and reproduced in the directive on the admission of securities to official stock exchange listing and on information to be published on those securities (2001/34/EC).

16. Small companies are nonlisted companies that do not exceed thresholds of total assets (currently €3,650,000), net sales (currently €7,300,000), and number of employees (50).

17. This holds even if member states permit corporations to prepare financial statements under IFRS or U.S. GAAP. They must be audited by an auditor who satisfies the *national* qualifications.

18. There are legal mechanisms in place that allow companies to file an appeal in case a member state failed to introduce a directive.

19. This has changed after several member states allowed companies to use IFRS or U.S. GAAP for consolidated financial statements in lieu of national GAAP in the late 1990s. A necessary condition is the compliance with the directives. This has generated a demand for interpretations of provisions in the directives and for comparisons with IFRS and U.S. GAAP.

20. Major examples include the true and fair view principle with the associated overriding of individual rules in case their application does not lead to true and fair financial statements, and an option for revaluation of long-lived assets, which follows from a physical capital maintenance principle that withholds certain holding gains from ever being shown as income.

21. European Commission [2001B].

22. In fact, all four legal families identified in La Porta et al. [1998, pp. 1117–1119]—common law, French, German, and Scandinavian—can be found in the EU.

23. See, e.g., d'Arcy and Ordelheide [2001].

24. See Schmidt et al. [2002].

25. The Fédération des Experts Comptables Européens [2000] provides a survey of the various regulatory structures for standard setting.

26. For such a classification see, e.g., La Porta et al. [1998].

27. See, e.g., Choi, Frost, and Meek [1999], pp. 34–43.

28. For a survey of the enforcement systems operative in European countries, see Fédération des Experts Comptables Européens [2001A].

29. See the comprehensive study of corporate governance codes in the member states by Weil et al. [2002].

30. Diversity in auditor liability regulation across EU member states is documented in a study on behalf of the European Union [2001].

31. See Fédération des Experts Comptables Européens [1998].

32. For details, see Fédération des Experts Comptables Européens [2000].

33. Frits Bolkestein, (then) European Commissioner in charge of the Internal Market, Taxation and Customs, in a speech on Jan. 29, 2004.

34. See European Commission [2001A] and the summary of replies received.

35. In Germany, successful companies such as Porsche were against quarterly reporting and even withdrew from the prime market segment of the Frankfurt Stock Exchange because it requires quarterly reporting.

36. European Commission: "Modernising Company Law and Enhancing Corporate Governance in the European Union: A Plan to Move Forward," COM(2003) 284 from May 2003.

37. European Commission [2000A].

38. See IOSCO [2000], p. 3.

39. PricewaterhouseCoopers [2002], p. 5.

40. The survey results are available at europa.eu.int/comm/internal_market/accounting/docs/ias/ias-use-of-options_en.pdf (January 2005).

41. The legal bases are the Transparency and the Prospectus Directives from 2004.

42. See CESR [2005].

43. A similar discussion is ongoing in other countries outside the EU that move toward IFRS. For example, the Australian government proposed in 1999 that the Australian standard-setting body should issue identical exposure drafts of standards for public comment to those issued by the (then) IASC to increase the consistency of Australian accounting standards with international standards. The proposal was met with considerable opposition from many constituents and was not adopted [see Brown and Tarca, 2001, pp. 281–284, for a discussion of reasons]. However, in mid-2002 the Australian Financial Reporting Council (FRC) announced its support to endorse the adoption of IFRS by Jan. 1, 2005, which very much conforms to the EU's accounting strategy.

44. The latter criteria are also included in the IASB's Framework.

45. The EFRAG aims at taking a more influential role in accounting standard setting, including the status as a liaison partner of the IASB. It also proposes to establish yet another committee, an Advisory Forum comprising senior-level representatives of key stakeholders to consult with EFRAG.

46. Individual financial statements of smaller companies need not meet these requirements.

47. Before 2002, the Board was known as International Auditing Practices Committee (IAPC).

48. European Commission [2000B].

49. European Commission [2002].

50. European Commission [2004].

51. Such external effects of legislation are not restricted to accounting and auditing but exist in many circumstances, most notably antitrust and export regulation.

52. See Fédération des Experts Comptables Européens [2001B].

53. See Fédération des Experts Comptables Européens [2002].

54. See also Dewing and Russell [2004].

55. For instance, in its biannual progress reports on the implementation of the Financial Services Action Plan, the European Commission usually points out several areas where progress is behind schedule.

Chapter 8

1. Countries included are Australia, all EU states, Canada, New Zealand, and the United States.

2. See Hoshi and Kashyap [2001], p. 38.

3. See Hoshi and Kashyap [2000], p. 315–316.

4. See Allen and Gale [2000], p. 50.

5. See Allen and Gale [2000], p. 92.

6. Dale [1996], pp. 106–108.

7. CC as amended in 2001; previously a reserve of at least 10 percent was required.

8. See Gordon [1999], pp. 18–24.

9. McKinnon [1986], pp. 214–215.

10. See Hoshi and Kashyap [2001], Chapter 7.

11. For a discussion of this period see Beason and James [1999].

12. This section is based on this document.

13. An example is the virtual bankruptcy of the famous Sogo Department Store Group in July 2000. This retail store network was financed with loans from a web of subsidiaries, none of which was listed on stock exchanges. The funds acquired as loans to the subsidiaries, however, were guaranteed by the parent company but not disclosed in the parent's accounts (anticipating the method to disguise liabilities used by Enron in the United States). See Hiramatsu [2001], pp. 7–9.

14. The subjects addressed include consolidation (application date March 31, 2000; a very controversial standard, given the primacy given to entity accounting reports in Japan), deferred tax (March 31, 2000), retirement benefits (March 31, 2001), financial instruments (March 31, 2001), asset impairment (Jan. 1 2005), business combinations (March 31, 2005), and earnings per share (March 31, 2006). A draft standard on stock options was published on Dec. 28, 2004.

15. Many issues are still being considered by Japanese accounting standard setters. The ASBJ, for example, has established technical committees on a number of issues, including impairment, fixed assets, leasing, stock options, and financial assets.

16. See the Study Group on the Internationalization of Business Accounting [2004], comprising mainly the representatives of business, with a 29-page appendix comparing Japanese and U.S. accounting standards and IFRS.

17. Letter to the Secretary General of the Committee of European Security Regulators (Dec. 21, 2004).

18. See, for example, the ASBJ comments on the Exposure Draft ED 3 that resulted from the IASB's business combinations project (April 4, 2003).

19. See Beason and James [1999], p. 148.

20. See Beason and James [1999, p. 147], who conclude after reviewing the government's response to a number of crises, that "Regulation of the sales of financial products in Japan has often been imperfect."

21. See Beason and James [1999], p. 142.

22. As reported from articles in Japanese by Gordon [1999], p. 31.

23. Tax advice was already prohibited. The additional prohibitions are similar to those in other commercially developed countries and include services relating to accounting, internal audit, actuarial and investment advisory services, and design of financial information systems.

24. Previously, auditors were jointly and severally liable. The amendment limited the liability for a specific audit of partners who were not engagement partners to their equity stake in the audit corporation, while retaining full liability for third-party claims.

25. See JICPA [2004].

26. See Whitten [2003].

27. See Ahmadjian [2001].

Chapter 9

1. For good reviews of this literature, see Roberts et al. [1998], Chapter 4, and Flower and Ebbers [2002], Chapter 2.

2. Comparisons of national formal accounting standards may be misleading, as the standards may be differently enforced, interpreted, and enforced [see Ball et al., 2003].

3. Their explanation of why common law provides the strongest investor protection is not compelling. It is conceivable that different legal families could provide the same level of investor protection. Therefore, the demand for equity capital may either be leading a demand for investor protection or be a result of strong investor protection.

4. Source: World Federation of Exchanges: Statistic-trends.

5. Source: Annual Reports of the LSE and NYSE, 2003.

6. F.T. 2004, Global 500 Financial Times Supplement, May 28, 2004.

7. See, e.g., PricewaterhouseCoopers [2004A].

8. In a joint exposure draft on business combinations (June 2005), the IASB and FASB for the first time even tried to converge the numbering of paragraphs. Differences in the number of paragraphs are adjusted with a "not used" paragraph.

9. The IASB's preliminary views are included in a discussion paper from June 2004. The United Nations Intergovernmental Working Group of Experts on International Standards of Accounting and Reporting (ISAR) has taken a different approach. It established an Ad Hoc Consultative Group of Experts on Accounting by SMEs that issued a proposal in 2001 for a three-level disclosure regime, one for which IFRS should apply in full, one for which only core IFRS principles should apply, and one with a simple accounting system based on cash flows with few accruals (mainly for tax purposes).

10. See Klein [1998] and Bhagat and Black [2001].

11. See Tafara [2004].

12. The JFSA does review over 50 percent of the annually filed reports, but as far as we can see nothing seems to follow from such reviews, at least in terms of publicizing or remedying deficient accounting reports.

13. However, reconciliation amounts between various foreign GAAP and U.S. GAAP are often higher. See Choi, Frost, and Meek [1999], p. 304.

14. Other examples are discussed in Wagenhofer [2005], Chapters 8 and 9.

15. Interviews with investors in the United States, United Kingdom, Germany, Switzerland, and Japan by the same authors [Choi and Levich, 1990, p. 127] revealed largely similar results. About half of the respondents said that accounting

differences do affect their capital market decisions (after adjusting their investment strategies accordingly). Results of other studies are summarized in Saudagaran and Meek [1997, pp. 133–135].

16. This is a reason why the SEC in Form 20-F requires presentation of financial statements of foreign registrants in their home currency and allows convenience translation only for the most recent financial statements.

17. See the discussion in Frost and Lang [1996], particularly pp. 101–102.

18. A questionnaire survey among German listed corporations who adopted IFRS or U.S. GAAP found the average costs (personnel, education, IT, and consulting) to be some €0.7 million and a median of €0.2 million. For the majority of the corporations the costs were less than 0.2 percent of sales. See Köhler et al. [2003].

19. For example, Street and Gray [2001] documented high levels of noncompliance with IFRS (mainly) disclosure requirements for 279 companies domiciled across the world. Generally there was no enforcement of IFRS in many of these countries at the time.

Chapter 9 Appendix

1. For more detailed comparisons of many countries' GAAP see, e.g., Nobes [2000], Ordelheide and KPMG [2001], and Deloitte [2004].

2. See the last statement of the IASC Board as of December 2000, and the first SAC meeting reported in IASB Update, July 2001, p. 1.

3. For detailed comparisons of IFRS and U.S. GAAP, see descriptions and discussions by the FASB [1999] and PricewaterhouseCoopers [2004].

4. Formally, under U.S. GAAP there would be a possibility to depart; however, this is not used in practice.

5. For the sake of brevity, we discuss only the general rules and do not mention each and every detail of standards, some of which provide specific rules.

6. Revaluation of investment property, as it is allowable for fixed assets, is not an option under IFRS, which prohibits taking the revaluation gains to equity.

Chapter 10

1. Sources: The Deutsche Börse, Fact Book 2003, and the New York Stock Exchange, Fact Book 2003.

2. Source: The Tokyo Stock Exchange, Fact Book 2003.

3. Source: The London Stock Exchange, Fact Book 2003, converted into U.S. dollars at a time when the dollar/sterling exchange rate favored sterling.

4. It delegates its power to set accounting standards to the Financial Accounting Standards Board (FASB) and its regulation of audit to the Public Company Accounting Oversight Board (PCAOB) but has retained its power to directly determine and enforce corporate governance regulations.

5. For an extensive critique of extant accounting standards, particularly with respect to Australia, see Clarke et al. [2003], Chapters 16–18.

6. However, these companies are allowed to use IFRS for their publication requirements provided they also prepare (but need not publish) parallel accounting reports based on German accounting requirements for dividend distribution and tax purposes.

7. Part of this section is based on our earlier book, "Following the Money" [Benston et al., 2003].

8. For example, the International Federation of Accountants [2003] recommends acceptance of IFRS worldwide, although they recognize (as do we) that implementation would be difficult.

9. See Barth et al. [1999].

10. See McKinsey [2002].

11. See IASB Insight, October 2002, p. 1.

12. For details, see, e.g., Deloitte [2004] and PricewaterhouseCoopers [2004].

13. This step can be regarded as a preliminary step towards a full fair value approach for financial instruments on a voluntary basis. Such an approach was suggested in a discussion paper by the (then active) IASC in 1997 and by the international Joint Working Group of Standard Setters in 2000.

14. The European Central Bank [2004] discusses the concerns of the banking sector with fair value accounting.

15. The Accounting Standards Board of Japan had expressed similar concerns to the IASB within the comment period of the exposure draft but was not successful in changing the proposed rules.

16. Reported in *Accountancy Age*, July 1, 2004, p. 1. Two thirds of the members come from countries with an Anglo-Saxon influence. The U.K. and U.S. members constitute 40 percent of the membership, and no developing country is represented. In July 2005, the International Accounting Standards Committee Foundation issued a revision of the constitutions of itself and other committees, including the IASB. This document aims to expand the geographic and professional backgrounds of the members of the Foundation to meet this criticism and broaden a criterion for the selection of IASB members from having technical competence to having professional competence and practical experience. Suggestions for strengthening the IASB's consultation process are also made.

17. See Cairns [2001].

18. SEC (Securities and Exchange Commission) [2000], under subheading "A Word About Differences" (pages not numbered).

19. See, e.g., the speech by the SEC's Chief Accountant on Sept. 28, 2004 in London (available at www.sec.gov/news/speech/spch092804dtn.htm).

20. For example, in the first German translation of the IAS in 1999, the term "financial performance" was translated into 25 different German terms in different contexts. Different translations can lead to different meanings and hence differences in the standards as they are actually applied by firms and their auditors.

21. The IASB has an institutional mechanism for doing so through its International Financial Reporting Interpretation Committee (IFRIC).

22. Others have also urged more competition among standard setters. See, e.g., Dye and Sunder [2001] and Sunder [2002].

23. See Wagenhofer [2005, p. 50] for data from various sources.

24. See, e.g., Leuz and Verrecchia [2000], Botosan and Plumlee [2002], and Leuz [2003].

25. See Daines [2001].

26. Empirical research indicates that non-U.S. corporations that cross-list in the United States are significantly different from other corporations in their countries and seem to be more similar to U.S. corporations on dimensions such as performance, risk, and aggressiveness of earnings management. See, e.g., Lang et al. [2003].

27. See Steil [2002].

28. An industry standards model is also advocated by DiPiazza and Eccles [2002].

29. We are not aware of a well-done comprehensive study of accounting scandals involving well- or lesser-known listed companies that determines the extent to which these were due to auditing or reporting failures. Our less-than-comprehensive review indicates to us that auditing failures were primarily responsible.

30. In two cases in which one of the authors, George Benston, was an expert witness (Continental Illinois and PharMor Drugs), the auditors did not correctly use statistical sampling, even though their firms' audit manuals called for its use and application of this procedure would have uncovered the frauds.

31. See, e.g., KPMG [2004], a 48-page document that outlines, in some detail, the many steps that a company should take.

32. In January 2004 the FEI (Financial Executives International) surveyed its members on their cost to implement Section 404 (available at www.fei.org/news/ 404_survey.cfm). Three hundred twenty-one companies responded, 84 percent with assets of $100 million or more (no mention is made of the universe or of possible nonresponse bias). The survey found that first-year compliance costs, both internal and external, could exceed $4.6 million for each of these companies, including an increase of 35 percent in audit fees.

33. This requirement is a result of the McKesson-Robbins accounting fraud of 1927, where the president and associates falsified the books with phantom inventory and sales, hence the physical counting of inventory and circularization of receivables.

34. Its previous name was International Auditing Practices Committee (IAPC).

35. The IFAC [2003, pp. 16–18] reviews the arguments against restricting audit firms from offering collateral services to their clients. They conclude [ibid, p. 18]: "Given this [strengthening the role of the audit committee in relation to nonaudit work] and the arguments supporting choice in the provision of services, we have concluded that a total bar on the provision of non-audit related services to audit clients would be inappropriate. However, we also conclude that there needs to be greater control ... than has generally existed in the past."

36. Indeed, the IFAC [2003, p. 33] reports: "The evidence from the only country which has had compulsory rotation of auditors long enough to be able to evaluate its effects provides no evidence that compulsory rotation of firms increases audit quality." Consequently, they do not suggest compulsory rotation, but they would limit the time an auditor might spend in a key audit role.

37. Healy and Palepu [2003] suggested the audit committee should be renamed "transparency committee" to signal its increasing tasks.

38. The original principles were published in 1999 and revised in 2004.

39. As we have discussed in earlier chapters, Germany has a supervisory board that separates the supervision of management from management itself. Japan does not distinguish between the management of the corporation and the supervision of that management, relying on the rather weak board of statutory auditors to monitor management and report deficiencies to the board of directors. Japan and the United States set out all corporate governance requirements in law or regulation. The United Kingdom has pioneered a "comply and explain" system of voluntary codes, which Germany has taken up in its new system of corporate governance, building on legal requirements built around the supervisory board. In

2002, Japan introduced an optional system very similar to that of the United States but so far with very little take-up.

40. Benston et al. [2003, pp. 66–76] discuss the provisions of the Sarbanes-Oxley Act, some of which we conclude are overreactions to the situation, as there were several self-correcting forces in the industry and audit profession. However, one could argue that these are not sufficient to prevent future problems on the scale of Enron or even much less. Given the nature of the regulatory and political process, there is a danger that anything more formal than these measures could have unintended and net counterproductive impacts. Indeed, it is not as yet clear whether, on balance, the Sarbanes-Oxley Act will be a net benefit or detriment to corporate equity investors.

41. To some extent, this already occurs in many countries. The rules differ as to who has to bear the burden of evidence. For example, in the United States the courts generally apply the "business rule," whereby what management does is assumed to be in the shareholders' interests unless there is strong evidence to the contrary. An alternative would be having judges second-guess business decisions.

Chapter 11

1. The traditional balance sheet, though, includes deferred expenses among assets and deferred income among the liabilities section, although these are not really "assets" or "liabilities." Robert T. Sprouse, perhaps the strongest and most effective advocate of the fair value-based asset/liability approach and former Director of Research and Vice-Chairman of the FASB, derisively termed these "what-you-may-call-its" [Sprouse, 1966]. Sprouse's term is repeatedly used in Storey and Storey [1998] to disparage traditional cost-based accounting that emphasizes the income statement.

2. The matching concept of income and expense recognition is explicated most clearly in Paton and Littleton [1940] and, earlier, in Schmalenbach [1919].

3. Reed Storey, a long-term technical advisor to FASB, claimed that the revenue/expense approach and the matching concept "have proven to be of minimal help in actually resolving difficult accounting issues" [Storey and Storey, 1998, p. 30]. Although he does not provide specific examples of these difficulties, they might involve questions surrounding how much of an asset amount should be depreciated or amortized and the extent to which expenditures for a long-term contract should be deferred.

4. See Hicks [1946, 1979]. Strictly, he considered only the individual computing personal income, defined as the change in the value of personal investment over a period. Other authors have extended this approach to corporations.

5. As we discuss later in this chapter, most intangible assets cannot be estimated with much precision (if at all), and the values of many usually important identifiable individual assets, such as special-purpose equipment, are either very costly or not possible to measure.

6. An alternative definition is currently being canvassed by the FASB in a recent exposure draft, without any supporting reasoning for the change: "the price at which an asset or liability could be exchanged in a current transaction between knowledgeable, unrelated willing parties" [FASB 2004, ¶4]. The IASB defines fair value with regard to financial instruments as "the amount for which an asset could be exchanged, or a liability settled, between knowledgeable, willing parties in an arm's-length transaction" [IAS 32, ¶11]. Convergence is being sought by

the FASB and the IASB to remove the now relatively small differences in these definitions—for example, whether the parties should be knowledgeable and whether the definition of unrelated parties encompasses arm's-length transactions.

7. The IASB measures impairment by comparing book value with the higher of value-in-use and fair value less disposition (selling) costs.

8. Some of this section is based on Bromwich [2004].

9. The Joint Working Group of Standard Setters [1999–2000] was a group of national standard setters that considered financial instruments and recommended that all financial assets and liabilities should be valued at fair values and be marked to market.

10. For an alternative view see Chambers [1966], who emphasized that exit prices measure the firm's financial flexibility (the ability to rearrange its resources).

11. For example, see Benston [2005], which describes and examines Enron's adoption of fair value accounting and ascribes the company's failure as due in large measure to its use and abuse.

12. This is the main recommendation of the Garten Task Force [2001], which advised the SEC.

13. Companies are generally required to disclose information to creditors as part of their debt contracts, but this information is not necessarily made available to the public.

14. In the EU similar statements are generally made in directors' reports. The U.S. MD&A is a report by management.

15. The EU's Modernisation Directive of 2003 and the U.S. MD&A include similar requirements.

16. The term "to the extent necessary" is used to be consistent with the EU's Modernisation Directive, which applies to the United Kingdom.

17. This is the same duty that the London Stock Exchange Listing Agreement places on financial institutions that act as facilitators (sponsors) for new issues and which extends to forecasts by their corporate clients.

18. See the dti (Department of Trade and Industry) statement "OFR to Boost Business and Inform Shareholders" (London: Nov. 25, 2004).

19. Empirical research suggests that the value relevance of intangibles is significant, but the coefficient of their association with equity prices is smaller than that on recognized assets. See, e.g., AAA Financial Accounting Standards Committee [2003] for a survey of such studies.

20. See Lev and Zarowin [1999] and Wallman [1996].

21. A survey is included in Zambon et al. [2003].

22. For example, the Danish Ministry of Science, Technology and Innovation [2003] includes a detailed guideline how to prepare intellectual capital statements but does not mention information to capital markets as an objective of these statements.

23. The IASB believes that risk management of financial instruments is already sufficiently settled but considers the definition and measurement of operational risks "in their infancy" (IFRS 7, ¶BC65).

24. See Eccles et al. [2001] and PwC [2004], which gives examples of best practice in 68 companies in 15 countries.

25. From the CorporateRegister (www.corporateregister.com).

26. See www.globalreporting.org.

27. See, e.g., the annual reports of the Mackenzie Financial Corporation, a Canadian financial services company that sets out progress against a number

of key objectives, such as fund performance relative to the rest of the industry, productivity performance, growth of funds, and achieving a target return on funds. See also the reports of Geest plc, a prepared-food manufacturer and distributor.

28. See the Shell Report (http://shell.com/home/Framework?siteId=shell report2003-en).

29. See Benston [1982] for a more extended discussion that concludes: "the social responsibility of accountants is to not do social responsibility accounting."

30. Geest plc annual reports 2002 and 2003 (www.geest.co.uk/gst/investors/fininfo.reports).

References

AAA (American Accounting Association) Financial Accounting Standards Committee, 2003. "Implications of Accounting Research for the FASB's Initiatives on Disclosure of Information about Intangible Assets." *Accounting Horizons* 17, 175–185.

Aboody, D., M. E. Barth, and R. Kaznik, 1999. Revaluations of fixed assets and future firm performance. *Journal of Accounting and Economics* 26, 161–191.

Accounting Standards Board, 1999. *Statement of Principles for Financial Reporting.* London.

Ahmadjian, C. L., 2001. "Changing Japanese Corporate Governance." Working Paper, Columbia Business School: Tokyo, Japan.

Alexander, Volbert, and Martin T. Bohl, 2000. "Ausprägungen von Finanzsystemen." In: Jürgen von Hagen and Johann Heinrich von Stein, eds. *Obst and Hintner: Geld-, Bank- und Börsenwesen,* 40th ed. Stuttgart: Schäffer-Poeschel, 447–470.

Allen, F., and D. Gale, 2000. *Comparing Financial Systems.* Cambridge, MA: MIT Press.

American Institute of Accountants, 1932–1934. *Audits of Corporate Accounts,* Correspondence between the Special Committee on Co-operation with Stock Exchanges of the American Institute of Accountants and the Committee on Stock List of the New York Stock Exchange.

Aoki, M., and G. Saxonhouse, eds., 2000. *Finance, Governance and Competitiveness in Japan.* Oxford: Oxford University Press.

Arbeitskreis Bilanzrecht der Hochschullehrer Rechtswissenschaft, 2002. "Zur Fortentwicklung des deutschen Bilanzrechts." *Betriebs-Berater* 57, 2372–2381.

ASBJ, 2003. *Our Stance on Convergence,* Accounting Standards Board of Japan. Tokyo, Japan, 24 April.

Baetge, Jörg, Hans-Jürgen Kirsch, and Stefan Thiele, 2003. *Bilanzen*, 7th ed. Düsseldorf: IDW-Verlag.

Ball, R., 2001. "Infrastructure Requirements in the Area of Accounting and Disclosure Policy." *4th Brookings–Wharton Conference Proceedings*. Washington: Brookings Institute.

Ball, R., A. Robin, and J. Shuang Wu, 2003. "Incentives versus Standards: Properties of Accounting Income in Four East Asian Countries." *Journal of Accounting and Economics* 36, 235–270.

Barr, Andrew, and Elmer C. Koch, 1959. "Accounting and the SEC." *George Washington Law Review* 28, 181–182.

Barth, M. E., and G. Clinch, 1996. "International Accounting Differences and Their Relation to Share Prices: Evidence from U.K., Australian, and Canadian Firms." *Contemporary Accounting Research* 13, 135–170.

Barth, M. E., and G. Clinch, 1998. "Revalued Financial, Tangible, and Intangible Assets: Associations With Share Prices and Non-Based Value Estimates." *Journal of Accounting Research* 36, 199–223.

Barth, M. E., G. Clinch, and T. Shibano, 1999. "International Accounting Harmonization and Global Equity Markets." *Journal of Accounting and Economics* 26, 201–235.

Baums, T., ed., 2001. *Bericht der Regierungskommission Corporate Governance*. Köln: Otto Schmidt-Verlag: (English summary available at http://www.shearman .com/documents/government_panel.pdf.)

Bay, W., and H.-G. Bruns, 1998. "Multinational Companies and International Capital Markets." In P. Walton, A. Haller and B. Raffournier, eds. *International Accounting*. London: International Thomson Business Press, 336–355.

Beasley, Mark S., Joseph V. Carcello, and Dana R. Hermanson, 1999. *Fraudulent Financial Reporting: 1987–1997: An Analysis of U.S. Public Companies*, Research Commissioned by the Committee of Sponsoring Organizations of the Treadway Commission, Jersey City, NJ: AICPA (American Institute of Certified Public Accountants).

Beason, D., and J. James, 1999. The *Political Economy of Japanese Financial Markets: Myths versus Reality*. Houndmills, Basingstoke, UK: Macmillan.

Benston, George J., 1969A. "The Effectiveness and Effects of the SEC's Accounting Disclosure Requirements." In Henry G. Manne, ed. *Economic Policy and the Regulation of Corporate Securities*. Washington DC: American Enterprise Institute for Public Policy Research, 23–79.

Benston, George J., 1969B. "The Value of the SEC's Accounting Disclosure Requirements." *Accounting Review* 44, 515–532.

Benston, George, J., 1975. "Accounting Standards in the U.S. and the U.K.: Their Nature, Causes and Consequences." *Vanderbilt Law Review*, 235–268.

Benston, George J., 1979/1980. "The Market for Public Accounting Services: Demand, Supply and Regulation." *The Accounting Journal*, 1–46. Republished (with small changes) in the *Journal of Accounting and Public Policy*, 1985 (Spring), 33–79.

Benston, George J., 1982. "Accounting and Corporate Accountability." *Accounting, Organizations and Society* 7, 87–105. Rejoinder, 1984, 417–419.

Benston, George J., 2003A. "The Regulation of Accountants and Public Accounting Before and After Enron." *Emory Law Journal*, 52 (Summer), 1325–1351.

Benston, George J., 2003B. "The Quality of Corporate Financial Statements and Their Auditors Before and After Enron." *Policy Analysis*, 497 (Nov. 6). Washington DC: CATO Institute.

Benston, George J., 2005. "Fair-Value Accounting: A Cautionary Tale from Enron." Working paper, Goizueta Business School, Emory University.

Benston, George J., Michael Bromwich, Robert E. Litan, and Alfred Wagenhofer, 2003. *Following the Money: TheEnron Failure and the State of Corporate Disclosure.* AEI-Brookings Joint Center for Regulatory Studies, Washington DC: Brookings Institution Press.

Benston, George J., Michael Bromwich, and Alfred Wagenhofer, 2005. "Principles-vs. Rules-based Accounting Standards: The SEC's Report and The FASB's Standard Setting Strategy." Working paper, Emory University.

Bhagat, Sanjai, and Bernard S. Black, 2001. "The Non-Correlation Between Board Independence and Long-Term Performance." *Journal of Corporation Law* 27, 231–273.

Biddle, G. C., and S.M. Saudagaran, 1991. "Foreign Stock Listings. Benefits, Costs, and the Accounting Policy Dilemma." *Accounting Horizons* 5 (September), 69–80.

Bloom, R., S. Long, and M. Collins, 1994. "Japanese and American Accounting: Explaining the Differences." *Advances in International Accounting* 6, 265–284.

Blume, Marshall E., 2002. "The Structure of the U.S. Equity Markets." *Brookings-Wharton Papers on Financial Services*, 35–59.

Board, J., C. Sutcliffe, and S. Wells, 2001. *Orderly Markets: A Report to the Financial Services Authority.* London: Financial Services Authority (FSA).

Bordo, Michael D., Barry Eichengreen, and Douglas A. Irwin, 1999. "Is Globalization Today Really Different from Globalization a Hundred Years Ago?" *Brookings Trade Forum*, 1–51.

Botosan, C. A., and M. A. Plumlee, 2002. "A Re-examination of Disclosure Level and the Expected Cost of Equity Capital." *Journal of Accounting Research* 40, 21–40.

Briault, C., 1999. *The Rationale for a Single National Financial Services Regulator.* Occasional Paper Series, no. 2. London: Financial Services Authority (FSA), May.

Bromwich, Michael, 1992. *Financial Reporting, Information and Capital Markets,* London: Pitman.

Bromwich, Michael, 2001. "Angels and Trolls: The ASB's Statement of Principles of Financial Reporting." The ACCA/BAA Distinguished Academic 1999 Lecture. *British Accounting Review*, 33, 47–72.

Bromwich, Michael, 2004. "Aspects of the Future in Accounting: The Use of Market Prices and 'Fair Values' in Financial Reports." In Christian Leuz, Dieter Pfaff, and Anthony Hopwood, eds. *The Economics and Politics of Accounting: International Perspectives on Research Trends, Policy, and Practice.* New York: Oxford University Press, 32–57.

Brown, Philip, and Ann Tarca, 2001. "Politics, Processes and the Future of Australian Accounting Standards." *Abacus* 37, 267–296.

Buckle, M., and J. Thompson, 1998. *The UK Financial System.* Manchester: Manchester University Press.

Cadbury Report, 1992. *Report on the Financial Aspects of Corporate Governance.* London: Gee Publishing, 1 December.

Cairns, D. W., 2000. *International Accounting Standards Survey 1999.* Available at www.cairns.co.uk/surveys.asp.

Cairns, D. W., 2001. *International Accounting Standards Survey 2000.* Available at www.cairns.co.uk/surveys.asp.

Cairns, D. W., and C. Nobes, 2000. *The Convergence Handbook: A Comparison Between International Accounting Standards and UK Financial Reporting Requirements,* London: The Institute of Chartered Accountants in England and Wales.

CESR, 2005. *Draft Technical Advice on Equivalence of Certain Third Country GAAP and on Description of Certain Third Countries Mechanisms of Enforcement of Financial Information.* Consultation Paper, Paris, April.

Chambers, R. J., 1966. *Accounting, Evaluation and Economic Behavior.* Englewood Cliffs, NJ: Prentice Hall.

Choi, F. D. S., and R. M. Levich, 1990. *The Capital Markets Effects of International Accounting Diversity.* Homewood, IL: Dow Jones-Irwin.

Choi, F. D. S., and R. M. Levich, 1996. "Accounting Diversity." In B. Steil, ed. *The European Equity Markets.* London: European Capital Markets Institute, 259–320.

Choi, Frederick D. S., Carol A. Frost, and Gary K. Meek, 1999. *International Accounting,* 3rd ed. Upper Saddle River, NJ: Prentice Hall.

Christensen, J. A., and Demski, Joel S., 2003. *Accounting Theory: An Information Content Perspective.* McGraw-Hill.

Claessens, Stijn, Daniela Klingebiel, and Sergio L. Schmukler, 2002. "The Future of Stock Markets in Emerging Economies." In Robert E. Litan and Richard Herring, eds. *Brookings-Wharton Papers on Financial Services.* Washington DC: The Brookings Institution, 167–212. Available at http://www1.fee.uva.nl/fm/PAPERS/Claessens/futureofstock.pdf).

Clark, P. K, P. H. Hinton, E. J. Nicholson, L. Storey, G. G. Wells, and M. G. White, 2003. *The Implications of Fair Valued Accounting For General Insurance Companies.* Sessional Meeting Paper, Institute of Actuaries and Faculty of Actuaries, March. Available at www.actuaries.org.uk/files/pdf/sessional/sm030324pdf.

Clarke, F., Dean, G., and Oliver, K., 2003. *Corporate Collapse: Accounting, Regulatory and Ethical Failures,* 2nd ed. Cambridge: Cambridge University Press.

Clews, Henry, 1908. *Fifty Years on Wall Street.* New York: Irving Publishing.

CLRG [Company Law Review Group], 2001. *Company Law Review: Final Report,* London: Department of Trade and Industry, July. Available at http://dti.gov.uk/cld/reviews.condocs.htm.

Committee of Wise Men on the Regulation of European Securities Markets, 2001. *Final Report* (Lamfalussy Report). Brussels, 15 February.

Committee on Corporate Governance, 1998. *Committee On Corporate Governance: The Combined Code.* London: Gee Publishing.

Competition Commission, 1999, British Telecommunications plc. *A report on a reference under section 13 of the Telecommunications Act 1984 on the charges made by British Telecommunications plc for calls from its subscribers to phones connected to Cellnet and Vodafone and Reports on references under section 13 of the Telecommunications Act 1984 on the charges made by Cellnet and Vodafone for terminating calls from fixed-line networks.* Available at www.competition-commission.org.uk.

Conference Board, 2003. *Commission on Public Trust and Private Enterprise, Findings and Recommendations, Part 2: Corporate Governance.* New York, January 9.

Co-ordinating Group on Audit and Accounting Issues, 2003. *Final Report to the Secretary of State for Trade and Industry and the Chancellor of the Exchequer.* London: Department of Trade and Industry, January.

d'Arcy, Anne, and Dieter Ordelheide, 2001. "A Reference Matrix." In Ordelheide, Dieter, and KPMG, eds. *Transnational Accounting*, 2nd ed., Houndmills, Basingstoke, UK, and New York: Palgrave, 1–101.

d'Arcy, Anne. 2001. "Hat sich die internationale Bilanzierung für den Neuen Markt bewährt?" In Adolf G. Coenenberg and Klaus Pohle, eds. *Internationale Rechnungslegung*. Stuttgart: Schäffer-Poeschel, 165–177.

Daines, R., 2001. "Does Delaware Law Improve Firm Value?" *Journal of Financial Economics* 62, 525–558.

Dale, R., 1996. *Risk and Regulation in Global Securities Markets*. Chichester, UK: John Wiley.

Danish Ministry of Science, Technology and Innovation, 2003. *Intellectual Statement Guidelines: The New Guideline*. Copenhagen.

Defliese, Philip L., 1958. *Influence of SEC on Accounting Principles and Procedures and the Practice of Accounting*. Accounting Papers of the 12th Annual Conference of Accountants, University of Tulsa, pp. 65–76.

Delaney, Patrick R., Barry J. Epstein, Ralph Nach, and Susan Weiss Budak, 2001. *Wiley GAAP 2002*. New York: AICPA.

Deloitte, 2004. *IAS Plus: Key Differences Between IFRSs and US GAAP*, Special Edition, June. Available at www.iasplus.com.

Department of Trade and Industry, 2001. *A World Class Competition Regime*, Cm 5233.

Department of Trade and Industry, 2003. *Review of the Regulatory Regime of the Accountancy Profession, Report to the Secretary of State for Trade and Industry*. London: Department of Trade and Industry, January.

Department of Trade and Industry, 2005. *The Companies Act, 1985 (Operating and Financial Review and Director's Report, etc.) Regulations 2005*. London: The Stationary Office.

Dewing, I. P., and P. O. Russell, 2004. "Accounting, Auditing and Corporate Governance of European Listed Countries: EU Policy Developments Before and After Enron." *Journal of Common Market Studies* 42, 289–319.

DiPiazza, S. A., and R. G. Eccles, 2002. *Building Public Trust*. New York: Wiley.

Dodd, David L., 1930. *Stock Watering*. New York: Columbia University Press.

Domowitz, Ian, and Benn Steil, 2001. "Innovation in Equity Trading Systems: The Impact on Trading Costs and the Cost of Equity Capital." In Benn Steil, David Victor, and Richard Nelson, eds. *Technological Innovation and Economic Performance*. Princeton: Princeton University Press.

dti (Department of Trade and Industry), 2001. The Company Law Review Steering Group. *Modern Company Law: For a Competitive Economy, Final Report*, two volumes. London: Department of Trade and Industry, July.

dti (Department of Trade and Industry), 2004. *Company Law: Draft Regulations on the Operating and Financial Review and Directors' Report: A Consultative Document*. London: Department of Trade and Industry, May. Available at www.dti.gov.uk/cld/condocs.htm.

Dye, R. A., and S. Sunder, 2001. "Why Not Allow FASB and IASB Standards to Compete in the U.S.?" *Accounting Horizons* 15, 257–271.

Eccles, R. G., R. H. Herz, E. M. Keegan, and D. M. W. Philips, 2001. *Value Reporting Revolution: Moving Beyond the Earnings Game*. New York: John Wiley.

Edwards, E. O., and P. W. Bell, 1961. *Theory and Measurement of Income*, Berkeley and Los Angeles: University of California Press.

Edwards, Jeremy S. S., and Klaus Fischer, 1994. "An Overview of the German Financial System." In Nicholas Dimsdale and Martha Prevezer, eds. *Capital Markets and Corporate Governance*. Oxford: Clarendon, 257–283.

Elsas, Ralf, and Jan P. Krahnen, 2004. "Banks and Relationships with Firms." In Jan P. Krahnen and Reinhard H. Schmidt, eds. *The German Financial System*. London: Oxford University Press, 197–232.

European Central Bank, 2001. *The Euro Equity Markets*. August.

European Central Bank, 2004. *Fair Value and Accounting and Financial Stability*. Occasional Paper Series No. 13, April. Available at www.ecb.int/pub/pdf/scpops/ecboccp13pdf.

European Commission, 2000A. *EU Financial Reporting Strategy: The Way Forward*. COM(2000) 359 of 13 June 2000. Brussels.

European Commission, 2000B *On Quality Assurance for the Statutory Audit in the European Union: Minimum Requirements*. Commission Recommendation 2001/256/EC of 15 November 2000. Brussels.

European Commission, 2001A. *Recognition, Measurement and Disclosure of Environmental Issues in the Annual Accounts and Annual Reports of Companies*. Commission Recommendation 2001/453/EC of 13.06.2001. Brussels.

European Commission, 2001B. "Toward an EU Regime on Transparency Obligations of Issuers Whose Securities Are Admitted to Trading on a Regulated Market," *International Market DG*, July 11.

European Commission, 2002. *Statutory Auditors' Independence in the EU: A Set of Fundamental Principles*. Commission Recommendation 2002/590/EC of 16 May 2002. Brussels.

European Commission, 2004. *Proposal for a Directive of the European Parliament and of the Council on Statutory Audit of Annual Accounts and Consolidated Accounts and Amending Council Directives 78/660/EEC and 83/349/EEC*. COM/2004/0177 final, 16 March 2004. Brussels.

European Union, 2001. *A study on systems of civil liability of statutory auditors in the context of a Single Market for auditing services in the European Union*. January. Available at http://europa.eu.int/comm/internal_market/en/company/audit/docs/auditliability.pdf.

European Union, 2003. *Accounts Modernisation Directive: Directive 2003/51/EC amending Directives on the annual and consolidated of certain types of companies, banks and other financial institutions and insurance undertakings*, 18 June. Available at http://europa.eu.int/eur-lex/pri/em/oj/dat/2003/l_178/l_17820030717en00160022.pdf.

FASB (Financial Accounting Standards Board), 1999. *The IASC–U.S. Comparison Project: A Report on the Similarities and Differences between IASC Standards and U.S. GAAP*, 2d ed., edited by Carrie Bloomer. Norwalk, CT: FASB.

FASB (Financial Accounting Standards Board), 2002. *Proposal: Principles-Based Approach to US Standard Setting*. Norwalk, CT: FASB.

FASB (Financial Accounting Standards Board), 2003. *Original Pronouncements, Accounting Standards as of June 1, 2003*, Vol. II FASB Statements of Standards, 101–150, New York: John Wiley & Sons, Inc.

FASB (Financial Accounting Standards Board), 2004. *Proposed Statement of Financial Accounting Standards, Fair Value Measurement*. Norwalk, CT: FASB.

Fearnley, S., R. Brandt, and V. Beattie, 1998. *Financial Reporting Review Panel: An Analysis of its Activities in Financial Reporting Today: Current and Emerging Issues*. London: Accountancy Books.

Fédération des Experts Comptables Européens, 1997. *Comparative Study on Conceptual Accounting Frameworks in Europe.* Brussels, May.

Fédération des Experts Comptables Européens, 1998. *Setting the Standards: Statutory Audits in Europe.* Brussels, June.

Fédération des Experts Comptables Européens, 2000. *Accounting Standard Setting in Europe.* Brussels, December.

Fédération des Experts Comptables Européens, 2001A. *Enforcement Mechanisms in Europe.* Brussels, April.

Fédération des Experts Comptables Européens, 2001B. *Proposal on International Standards on Auditing in the EU.* Brussels, November.

Fédération des Experts Comptables Européens, 2002. *Discussion Paper on Enforcement of IFRS Within Europe.* Brussels, April.

Financial Executives International, 2001. *Quantitative Measures of the Quality of Financial Reporting.* FEI Research Foundation, PowerPoint presentation. Available at www.fei.org.

Financial Reporting Council, 2003. *The Combined Code.* London: Financial Reporting Council.

Financial Services Authority (FSA), 1997. *Financial Services Authority: An Outline.* London: FSA.

Financial Services Authority (FSA), 2000A. *A New Regulator for the New Millennium.* London: FSA.

Financial Services Authority (FSA), 2000B. *Summary Annual Report, 1999/2000.* London: FSA.

Financial Services Authority (FSA), 2001. *Annual Report, 2000/2001.* London: FSA.

Financial Services Authority (FSA), 2002. *Annual Report, 2001/2002.* London: FSA.

Flower, J., with G. Ebbers, 2002. *Global Financial Reporting.* Houndsmills, Basingstoke, UK: Palgrave Macmillian.

Forum of European Securities Commissions, 2001. *Standards and Rules for Harmonizing Core Conduct of Business Rules for Investor Protection.* Paris, February.

Foster, John M., and L. Todd Johnson, 2001. "Why Does the FASB Have a Conceptual Framework?" *Understanding the Issues,* August. Norwalk, CT: FASB.

Frankel, Jeffrey A., 2001. "Assessing the Efficiency Gains from Further Liberalization." Conference volume in honor of Ray Vernon. *Efficiency, Equity and Legitimacy: The Multilateral Trading System at the Millennium.* Washington DC: Brookings Institution Press.

Frost, C. A., and M. H. Lang. 1996. "Foreign Companies and U.S. Securities Markets: Financial Reporting Policy Issues and Suggestions for Research." *Accounting Horizons* 10, March, 95–109.

GAO (General Accounting Office), 2002. *Financial Statement Restatements: Trends, Market Impacts, Regulatory Responses, and Remaining Challenges.* GAO-03–138, October.

Garten Task Force, 2001. *Strengthening Financial Markets: Do Investors Have the Information They Need?* Report of an SEC-Inspired Task Force, May.

Gebhardt, Günther, and Aaron A. Heilmann, 2004. "DRS 4 in der Bilanzierungspraxis–ein Beispiel für die Missachtung Deutscher Rechnungslegungsstandards." *Der Konzern* 2, 109–118.

Geneva Association, 2004. "Impact of a Fair Value Financial Reporting System on Insurance Companies." *Geneva Papers on Risk and Insurance: Issues and Practice* 29, 51–581.

Gordon, W., 1999. "A Critical Evaluation of Japanese Accounting Changes Since 1997." Available at http://wgordonweb.wesleyan.edu/papers/jaccount.htm.

Greenbury Report, 1995. *Directors' Remuneration: Report of a Study Group (Chaired by Sir Richard Greenbury).* London: Gee Publishing, July 17.

Griever, William L., Gary A. Lee, and Francis E. Warnock, 2001. "The U.S. System for Measuring Cross-Border Investment in Securities: A Primer with a Discussion of Recent Developments." *Federal Reserve Bulletin* October, 633–650.

Group of Ten, 2001. *Report on Consolidation in the Financial Sector* (January). Available on the websites of the Bank for International Settlements (www.bis.org), the International Monetary Fund (www.imf.org), and the Organization for Economic Cooperation and Development (www.oecd.org).

Hail, Luzi, and Christian Leuz, 2003. *International Differences in Cost of Capital: Do Legal Institutions and Securities Regulation Matter?* University of Pennsylvania, working paper, September.

Haller, Axel, and Peter Walton, 1998. "Country Differences and Harmonization." In Peter Walton, Axel Haller, and Bernard Raffournier, eds. *International Accounting.* London: International Thomson Business Press, 1–30.

Haller, Axel, 2002. "Financial Accounting Developments in the European Union: Past Events and Future Prospects." *European Accounting Review* 11(1), 153–190.

Hamada, K., 2000. "Explaining the Low Litigation Rate in Japan." In M. Aoki and G. Saxonhouse, eds. *Finance, Governance and Competitiveness in Japan.* Oxford: Oxford University Press.

Hampel Report, 1998. *Committee on Corporate Governance: Final Report.* London: Gee Publishing, July 28.

Harris, M. S., and K. A. Muller III, 1999. "The Market Valuation of IAS versus US-GAAP Accounting Measures Using Form 20–F Reconciliations." *Journal of Accounting and Economics* 26, 285–312.

Hayakawa, S., 1996. *Japanese Financial Markets.* Abington: Gresham Books.

Healy, P. M., and K. G. Palepu, 2003. "The Fall of Enron." *Journal of Economic Perspectives* 17, 3–26.

Helliwell, John, 1998. *How Much Do National Borders Matter?* Washington DC: Brookings Institution Press.

Herring, Richard J., and Robert E. Litan, 1995. *Financial Regulation in the Global Economy.* Washington DC: Brookings Institution Press.

Hicks, J. R., 1946. *Value and Capital.* Oxford: Clarendon Press.

Hicks, J. R., 1979. "The Concept of Business Income." *Greek Economic Review* (December). Reprinted in Hicks, J. R., 1983. *Classics and Moderns: Collected Essays on Economic Theory,* Vol. III. Oxford: Blackwell.

Higgs, D., 2003. *Review of the role and effectiveness of non-executive directors.* London: Department of Trade and Industry, January.

High Level Group of Company Law Experts, 2002. *A Modern Regulatory Framework for Company Law in Europe. Final Report (Winter Report).* Brussels, Nov. 4.

Hilzenrath, David S., 2001. "Auditors Face Scant Discipline; Review Process Lacks Resources, Coordination, Will." *The Washington Post* A.1 ff, Dec. 6.

Hiramatsu, K., 2000. *Changes in Accounting Systems of Japan after 1999 Financial Crisis.* Working paper, Kwansei Gakuin University.

Hiramatsu, K., 2001. *Debate on the Reform of Corporate Governance in Japan: with an Accounting Perspective.* Working paper, Kwansei Gakuin University.

Hoffman, L., and Arden, M, 1983. *Counsel's Opinion on 'true and fair'. The Accounting Standards Committee, Joint Opinion.* Sept. 13.

Hoffman, L., and Arden, M., 1984. "Supplementary Joint Opinion, 20 March." Reproduced in PricewaterhouseCooper's *Manual of Accounting: The Guide to UK Accounting Law and Practice*, 2001. London: Gee, pp. 2051–2056.

Horiuchi, A., 1995. *Financial Sector Reforms in Postwar Japan: An Overview.* Working paper, University of Tokyo.

Horton, J., and R. Macve, 2000. " 'Fair Value' for Financial Instruments: How Erasing Theory is Leading to Unworkable Global Accounting Standards for Performance Reporting." *Australian Accounting Review* 21, July 2, 26–39.

Hoshi, T., and A. Kashyap, 2001. *Corporate Financing and Governance in Japan: The Road to the Future.* Cambridge, MA: MIT Press.

IASB (International Accounting Standards Board), 2005. *International Financial Reporting Standards (IFRSs).* London.

International Accounting Standards Committee Foundation (IASCF). *Review of the Constitution: Proposals for Change.* London, November.

International Federation of Accountants (IFAC), 2003. *Rebuilding Public Confidence in Financial Reporting: An International Perspective.* New York.

International Organization of Securities Commissions (IOSCO), 1998. *Objectives and Principles of Securities Regulation.* September.

International Organization of Securities Commissions (IOSCO) [undated]. *Investor Protection in the New Economy.* Technical Bulletin.

International Organization of Securities Commissions (IOSCO), 2000. *IASC Standards: Assessment Report.* Report of the Technical Committee of the International Organization of Securities Commissions. May.

JFSA (Japanese Financial Services Authority), 2004. *Evolving Japanese GAAP: High Quality Accounting Standards.* Japanese Financial Services Agency, April 19.

Japanese Institute of Certified Public Accountants, 1999. *Corporate Disclosure in Japan: Accounting.* Tokyo: JICPA.

Japanese Institute of Certified Public Accountants, 2004, *Oversight and Independence of the CPA Auditing in Japan.* Tokyo: JICPA.

Joshua, D., and Tobias J. Moskowitz, 1999. "Home Bias at Home: Local Equity Preferences in Domestic Portfolios." *Review of Financial Studies* 7, 2045–2073.

JWG (Joint Working Group of Standard Setters), 2000. *Financial Instruments and Similar Items.* London: Accounting Standards Board.

JWGBA (Joint Working Group of Banking Association on Financial Instruments), 1999. *Accounting for Financial Instruments for Banks.* Available at www.fbe.be/pdf/accounting/pdf.

Kang, J., and A. Shivadasani, 1995. "Corporate Restructuring During Performance Declines in Japan." *Journal of Financial Economics* 38, 29–58.

Kaushik, Surenda K., and Massime Santicchia, 2002. *Capital Flows, Global Equity Market Diversification, Volatility and Policy Responses.* Unpublished manuscript (on file with the authors).

Klein, April, 1998. "Firm Performance and Board Committee Structure." *Journal of Law and Economics* 41, 137–165.

Köhler, A. G., K.-U. Marten, D. Schlereth, and A. Crampton, 2003. "Praxisbefragung: Erfahrungen von Unternehmen bei der Umstellung der Rechnungslegung von HGB auf IAS/IFRS oder US-GAAP." *Betriebs-Berater* 58, 2615–2621.

KPMG, 2004. *Sarbanes-Oxley Section 404: An Overview of the PCAOB's Requirements.* April.

Krahnen, Jan P., and Reinhard H. Schmidt, eds., 2004. *The German Financial System.* London: Oxford University Press.

Küting, Karlheinz, 1993. "US-amerikanische und deutsche Bilanzierung im Vergleich—unter besonderer Berücksichtigung der Konzernrechnungslegung und des Daimler-Benz-Listing in New York." *Betriebswirtschaftliche Forschung und Praxis* 45, 357–379.

La Porta, R., F. Lopez-de-Silanes, A. Shleifer, and R. Vishny, 2000. "Investor Protection and Corporate Governance." *Journal of Financial Economics* 58, 3–27.

La Porta, Rafael, Florencio Lopez-de-Silanes, Andrei Shleifer, and Robert Vishny, 1998. "Law and Finance." *Journal of Political Economy* 106, 1113–1155.

Lang, M., J. S. Raedy, and M. H. Yetman, 2003. "How Representative Are Firms That Are Cross-Listed in the United States? An Analysis of Accounting Quality." *Journal of Accounting Research* 41, 363–386.

Leffson, Ulrich, 1988. *Wirtschaftsprüfung*, 4th ed. Wiesbaden: Gabler.

Leuz, C., 2003. "IAS Versus U.S. GAAP: Information Asymmetry-Based Evidence from Germany's New Market." *Journal of Accounting Research* 41, 445–472.

Leuz, Christian, and Robert E. Verrecchia, 2000. "The Economic Consequences of Increased Disclosure." *Journal of Accounting Research* 38, Supplement (1), 91–124.

Leuz, Christian, and Jens Wüstemann, 2004. "The Role of Accounting in the German Financial System." In Krahnen, Jan P., and Reinhard H. Schmidt, eds. *The German Financial System*. London: Oxford University Press, 450–481.

Lev, B., and P. Zarowin, 1999. "The Boundaries of Financial Reporting and How to Extend Them." *Journal of Accounting Research* 37 (Supplement), 353–385.

Lev, Baruch, 2001. *Intangibles: Management, Measurement and Reporting*. Washington DC: Brookings Institution Press.

Levich, Richard M., 2001. *The Importance of Emerging Capital Markets*. Brookings-Wharton Papers on Financial Services, 1–45.

Levitt, Arthur, 1998. *The Numbers Game*. Remarks to New York University Center for Law and Business, September 28. Available at www.sec.gov/news/speeches/spch/220.txt.

Levitt, Arthur, 2002. *Take on the Street*. New York: Pantheon Books.

Lewis, Karen K., 1999. "Trying to Explain Home Bias in Equities and Consumption." *Journal of Economic Literature* 37, 571–608.

Litan, Robert E., Paul Masson, and Michael Pomerleano, eds., 2001. *Open Doors: Foreign Participation in Financial Systems in Developing Countries*. Washington, DC: Brookings, IMF and World Bank.

Maines, Laureen A., Eli Bartov, Patricia Fairfield, Eric D. Hirst, Teresa E. Ianoconi, Russell Mallett, Chatherine M. Schrand, Douglas J. Skinner, and Linda Vincent, 2003. "Evaluating Concept-Based vs. Rules-Based Approaches to Standard Setting." *Accounting Horizons* 17, 73–90.

McKinnon, J. L., 1986. *The Historical Development of and Operational Form of Corporate Reporting Regulation in Japan*. New York: Garland Publishing.

McKinsey, 2002. *McKinsey Global Investor Opinion Survey on Corporate Governance*. July.

Ministry of Finance (MOF), 1977. *Financial System Reform: Towards the Early Achievement of Reform*. June 13.

Mofsky, James S., 1971. *Blue Sky Restrictions on New Business Promotions*. New York: Mathew Bender.

Mulford, Charles W., and Eugene E. Comiskey, 2002. *The Financial Numbers Game: Detecting Creative Accounting Practices*. John Wiley & Sons, Inc.

Myners, Paul, 2001. *Review of Institutional Investment*. London: H.M. Treasury.

Nelson, M., J. Elliott, and R. Tarpley, 2002. "Evidence from Auditors About Managers' and Auditors' Earnings Management Decisions." *The Accounting Review* 77 (Supplement), 175–202.

Nicolaisen, D. T., 2005. "A Securities Regulator Looks at Convergence." *Northwestern University Journal of International Law and Business* 25, 661–686.

Nippon Keidanren (Japanese Business Federation), 2003. *Seeking International Collaboration on Accounting Standards, Policy Proposal.* Tokyo: Nippon Keidanren, Oct. 17. Available at www.keidanren.or.jp/english/policy/2003/096/proposal.html.

Nippon Keidanren (Japanese Business Federation), 2004. "Re: Nippon Keidanren's response to 'Review of the Listing Regime," Letter, Tokyo: Japanese Business Federation, Jan 30.

Nobes, Christopher W., ed., 2000. *GAAP 2000: A Survey of National Accounting Rules in 53 Countries.*

OECD (Organisation for Economic Co-operation and Development), 1999. *OECD Principles for Corporate Governance.* Paris: OECD.

Ordelheide, Dieter, 1998. "Wettbewerb der Rechnungslegungssysteme IAS, US-GAAP und HGB." In Clemens Börsig and Adolf G. Coenenberg, eds. *Controlling und Rechnungswesen im internationalen Wettbewerb.* Stuttgart: Schäffer-Poeschel, pp. 15–53.

Ordelheide, Dieter, and KPMG, eds., 2001. *Transnational Accounting*, 2nd ed. Houndmills, Basingstoke, UK, and New York: Palgrave.

Ordelheide, Dieter, and Dieter Pfaff, 1994. *Germany. European Financial Reporting.* London and New York: Routledge.

Oser, Peter, Christian Orth, and Dominic Wader, 2003. "Die Umsetzung des Deutschen Corporate Governance Kodex in der Praxis." *Der Betrieb* 56, 1337–1341.

Palmrose, Zoe-Vonna, and Susan Scholz, 2002. "The Circumstances and Legal Consequences of Non-GAAP Reporting: Evidence from Restatements. *Contemporary Accounting Research Conference.*

Panel on Audit Effectiveness: Report and Recommendations (Shawn F. O'Malley, Chair), 2000, The Public Oversight Board, Stamford, CT, Aug. 31. Available at www.probauditpanel.org.

Paton, W. A., and A. C. Littleton, 1940. *An Introduction to Corporate Accounting Standards.* Monograph No. 3, American Accounting Association.

Pecora, Ferdinand, 1939. *Wall Street Under Oath.* New York: Simon and Schuster.

Pellens, Bernhard, Franca Hillebrandt, and Björn Ulmer, 2001. "Umsetzung von Corporate-Governance-Richtlinien in der Praxis." *Betriebs-Berater* 56, 1243–1250.

PricewaterhouseCoopers, 2002. *2005: Ready or Not.* London, June.

PricewaterhouseCoopers, 2003. *Manual of Accounting: The Definitive Guide to GAAP in the UK, 2004. Including IFRS Comparisons,* London: Gee Publishing Limited.

PricewaterhouseCoopers, 2004. *Similarities and Differences—A Comparison of IFRS and US GAAP,* February.

Prowse, S., 1991. "Corporate Governance in an International Perspective: A Survey of Corporate Control Mechanisms Among Large Firms in the US, UK, Japan and Germany." *Financial Markets, Institutions and Instruments* 4, 1–63.

PwC (PricewaterhouseCoopers), 2004. *Trends in Corporate Reporting 2004: Towards Value Reporting.*

Rappaport, Louis H., 1963. *SEC Accounting Practice and Procedure,* 2nd ed. New York: The Ronald Press.

Ripley, William Z., 1927. *Main Street and Wall Street.* Boston: Little Brown & Co.

Roberts, C., P. Weetman, and P. Gordon, 1998. *International Financial Accounting: A Comparative Approach*, London: Financial Times/Pitman Publishing. Chapter 15, 547–580.

Saudagaran, S. M., and G.K. Meek, 1997. "A Review of Research on the Relationship between International Capital Markets and Financial Reporting by Multinational Firms." *Journal of Accounting Literature* 16, 127–159.

Schilit, Howard, 2002. *Financial Shenanigans: How To Detect Accounting Gimmicks & Fraud in Financial Reports*, 2nd ed. New York: McGraw-Hill.

Schipper, Katherine, 2003. "Principles-based Accounting Standards." *Accounting Horizons* 17, 61–73.

Schmalenbach, Eugen, 1919. *Grundlagen dynamischer Bilanzlehre*. Leipzig: Glöckner.

Schmidt, Reinhard H., Andreas Hackethal, and Marcel Tyrell, 2002. "The Convergence of Financial Systems in Europe." *Schmalenbach Business Review*, Special Issue: German Financial Markets and Institutions: Selected Studies; Günter Franke, Günther Gebhardt, and Jan Pieter Krahnen, eds. 1, 7–53.

Schneider, Dieter, 1995. "The History of Financial Reporting in Germany." In Peter Walton, ed. *European Financial Reporting*. London: Academic Press, 123–155.

Schröer, Thomas, 1993. "Company Law and Accounting in Nineteenth-Century Europe: Germany." *European Accounting Review* 2, 335–345.

SEC (Securities and Exchange Commission), 2000. *Concept Release: International Accounting Standards*. February. Available at http://www.sec.gov/rules/concept/34-42430.htm.

SEC (Securities and Exchange Commission), 2003A. *Report Pursuant to Section 704 of the Sarbanes-Oxley Act of 2002*. Washington, DC, January.

SEC (Securities and Exchange Commission), 2003B. *Interpretation: Commission Guidance Regarding Management's Discussion and Analysis of Financial Condition and the Results of Operations*. Washington: US Securities and Exchange Commission, Dec. 19. Available at www.sec.gov/rules/interp./33-8350.htm.

SEC (Securities and Exchange Commission), 2003C. *The SEC Summary by the Division of Corporate Finance of Significant Issues Addressed in the Review of the Periodic Reports of the Fortune 500 Companies*. Available at www.sec.gov/divisions/corpfin/fortune500rep.htm.

Shiba, K., 2001. *Corporate Disclosure in Japan*. Working paper, Kansai University.

Shiba, K., and L. Shiba, 1997. "Japan." In R. Ma, ed. *Financial Reporting in the Pacific Asia Region*. Singapore: World Scientific Press.

Simmonds, Andy, and Oliver Azières, 1989. *Accounting for Europe: Success by 2000 AD*. London: Touche Ross.

Smith, Sir Robert, 2003. *Audit Committees-Combined Code Guidance*. London: Financial Reporting Council, January.

Someya, K. 1989. "Accounting 'Revolutions' in Japan." *The Accounting Historians' Journal*, 16(I), 75–86.

Sprouse, Robert T., 1966. "Accounting for What-You-May-Call Its." *The Journal of Accountancy*, October, 45–53.

Stationery Office, 2002. *Modernising Company Law, Command Paper 5553*. London: Stationery Office, July.

Steil, Benn, 2002. *Building a Transnational Securities Market*, New York: Council on Foreign Relations.

Stigler, George J., 1965. "The Dominant Firm and the Inverted Umbrella." *The Journal of Law and Economics* VIII (October), 117–172.

Storey, R. K., and S. Storey, 1998. *The Framework of Financial Reporting Concepts and Standards*. Norwalk: FASB.

Street, D. L., and S. J. Gray, 2001. *Observance of International Accounting Standards: Factors Explaining Non-compliance*. ACCA Research Report No. 74. London: Certified Accountants Educational Trust.

Study Group on the Internationalization of Business Accounting, 2004. *Report on the Internationalization of Business Accounting*. Tokyo: Ministry of Economy, Trade and Industry.

Sunder, S., 2002. "Regulatory Competition Among Accounting Standards Within and Across International Boundaries." *Journal of Accounting and Public Policy* 21, 219–234.

Tarafa, E., 2004. *Testimony Concerning Global Markets, National Regulation and Cooperation*. Testimony Before the House Financial Services Committee, Washington: The US Securities and Exchange Commission, May 13. Available at www.sec.gov/news/testimony/ts051304et.htm.

Tesar, Linda, and Ingrid Werner, 1998. *The Internalization of Securities Markets since the 1987 Crash*. Brookings-Wharton Papers on Financial Services, 281–349.

Theissen, Erik, 2004. "Organized Equity Markets." In Krahnen, Jan P., and Reinhard H. Schmidt, eds. *The German Financial System*. London: Oxford University Press, 139–162.

Thompson, Robert B., 2003. "Collaborative Corporate Governance: Listing Standards, State Law and Federal Legislation." *Wake Forest Law Review* 38, 961–982.

Valdez, S., 2000. *Introduction to Global Financial Markets*. Houndsmill, Basingstoke, Hampshire, UK: Palgrave.

Veda, K., 1990. "Are Japanese Stock Prices Too High?" *Journal of Japanese and International Economics* 3, 351–370.

von Werder, Axel, 2004. "Modernisierung der Mitbestimmung." *Die Betriebswirtschaft* 64, 229–243.

Wagenhofer, Alfred, 2005. *Internationale Rechnungslegungsstandards—IAS/IFRS*, 5th ed. Frankfurt: Redline Wirtschaft.

Wallman, S. H., 1996. *The Future of Accounting and Financial Reporting: Part II, The Colorized Approach*. Remarks to The American Institute Of Certified Public Accountants' 23rd National Conference, Washington DC, Feb. 15.

Walton, Peter, 1995. "International Accounting and History." In Peter Walton, ed. *European Financial Reporting*. London: Academic Press, 1–10.

Weil, Gotshal, & Manges, 2002. *Comparative Study of Corporate Governance Codes Relevant to the European Union and Its Member States*. Brussels, January.

Weirich, Thomas, 2000. "Analysis of SEC Accounting and Auditing Enforcement Releases." In *The Panel on Audit Effectiveness Report and Recommendations*, Public Oversight Board, Shaun F. O'Malley, Chair, August 31, Appendix F, 223–228.

White, Lawrence J., 2001. *Reducing the Barriers to International Trade in Accounting Services*. AEI Studies in Services Trade Negotiations, Washington, DC: The AEI Press.

Whitten, D., 2003. "The Debate Over Corporate Governance." *Japan Inc. Magazine* April. Available at www.Japaninc.net/article/php?articleID=1067.

Wirtschaftsprüferkammer, 2001. *Bericht über die Berufsaufsicht 2000*. Berlin: Beilage zu WPK-Mitteilungen 4/2001.

World Bank Policy Research Report, 1997. *Private Capital Flows to Developing Countries: The Road to Financial Integration*. New York: Oxford University Press.

World Bank, 2001A. *Global Development Finance.*

World Bank, 2001B. *Global Economic Prospects and the Developing Countries.*

Zaloom, E. A., 2002. *Japanese Corporate Governance: Moving in the Right Direction or Dead in the Water?* Research Institute of Economy, Trade and Industry, July 12. Available at www.rieti.so.jp.

Zambon, S. (coordinator), 2003. *Study on the Measurement of Intangible Assets and Associated Reporting Practices.* Commissioned by the European Commission, University of Ferrara, Italy. April.

Zeff, Stephen A., 1972. *Forging Accounting Principles in Five Countries: A History and Analysis of Trends.* Champaign, IL: Stipes.

Zeff, Stephen A., 2002. " 'Political' Lobbying on Proposed Standards: A Challenge to the IASB." *Accounting Horizons*, 16, 43–54.

Index